Mater 2-10

HWANG SOK-YONG, born in 1943, is arguably Korea's most renowned author. In 1993, he was sentenced to seven years in prison for an unauthorised trip to the North to promote exchange between artists in the two Koreas. Five years later, he was released on a special pardon by the new president. He has been given the Mark of Respect Award, acknowledging him as a distinguished national cultural figure and leader, and is the recipient of Korea's highest literary prizes, including the Manhae Literary Prize, the Danjae Literary Prize, the Isan Literary Prize, and the Daesan Literature Prize. He has been shortlisted for the Prix Femina étranger, and for his novel *At Dusk* he was nominated for the 2019 International Booker Prize and awarded the 2018 Èmile Guimet Prize for Asian Literature. His novels and short stories have been published around the world to wide acclaim.

SORA KIM-RUSSELL has translated numerous works of Korean fiction, including Hwang Sok-yong's *Princess Bari*, *Familiar Things*, and the International Booker–nominated *At Dusk*.

YOUNGJAE JOSEPHINE BAE won the 2019 LTI Korea Award for Aspiring Translators and the 2021 *Korea Times* Modern Korean Literature Translation Award. Her translations include *Imaginary Athens* and *A Global History of Ginseng*.

Mater 2-10

Hwang Sok-yong

translated by Sora Kim-Russell
and Youngjae Josephine Bae

SCRIBE
Melbourne • London

Scribe Publications
2 John St, Clerkenwell, London, WC1N 2ES, United Kingdom
18–20 Edward St, Brunswick, Victoria 3056, Australia
3754 Pleasant Ave, Suite 100, Minneapolis, Minnesota 55409, USA

First published in Korean as 철도원 삼대 by Changbi Publishers 2020
First published in English by Scribe 2023

Copyright © Hwang Sok-yong 2020
Translation copyright © Sora Kim-Russell and Youngjae Josephine Bae 2023

All rights reserved. Without limiting the rights under copyright reserved above, no part of this publication may be reproduced, stored in or introduced into a retrieval system, or transmitted, in any form or by any means (electronic, mechanical, photocopying, recording or otherwise) without the prior written permission of the publishers of this book.

The moral rights of the author and translators have been asserted.

Typeset in Adobe Garamond Pro by the publishers

Printed and bound in the UK by CPI Group (UK) Ltd,
Croydon CR0 4YY

Scribe is committed to the sustainable use of natural resources and the use of paper products made responsibly from those resources.

This book is published with the support of the
Literature Translation Institute of Korea (LTI Korea)

978 1 913348 95 3 (UK edition)
978 1 957363 31 8 (US edition)
978 1 922310 96 5 (Australian edition)
978 1 922586 94 0 (ebook)

Catalogue records for this book are available from the
National Library of Australia and the British Library.

scribepublications.co.uk
scribepublications.com
scribepublications.com.au

Contents

Translators' Note

In *Mater 2-10*, Hwang Sok-yong depicts a Korea in flux. The novel opens in the present day but quickly carries us back to the past, to the turn of the twentieth century. Along the way, we revisit a Korea that was already nothing like the 'hermit kingdom' it was once described to be: people travelled back and forth from Korea to Japan, Manchuria, China, and beyond; they wore clothing from different nations (often in the same outfit) and not only lived in Korean hanok but also sat on Japanese tatami or heated their Manchurian houses with Russian stoves. They read works translated from German, Russian, Japanese; they used slang acquired from international socialist networks. But they also had their Korean names forcibly changed to Japanese names. Some moved to cities to live exciting new lives, while many more were forced out of their country homes to make way for the new rail lines. Some moved even further, thinking they would only be gone for a short time, only to realise too late that the border they crossed had closed behind them indefinitely.

In our first approach to translating *Mater 2-10*, we chose the usual track of making a complicated story as easy to read as possible. Family titles were translated into their English equivalents — and then mostly erased. Characters went by their personal names. We considered terms like 'front porch' and 'rice cake'. But it was somewhere around when the characters were forced to change their names and conform to Japanese ways that the hidden violence of translation became more apparent. If a story is not just about the survival of a nation but about the survival of the common people of that nation, the ones most often trod upon, then what does it mean for a translation to erase the markers of that nation's culture, of those people's identities? When a novel's characters are ordered by their Japanese bosses to change their names on the spot because Korean is too difficult to pronounce, what is the English translator's duty?

To that end, we looked for ways to decolonise our translation. We started with the easy things, such as names of foods, trusting especially that readers might be familiar with, or at least able to quickly look up, the 'rice cake' known as tteok, which features so heavily throughout the book. We also kept the activist slang used at the time — agit, org, reppo. For architecture, we took pity and asked only that our readers learn the word 'maru': in its simplest definition, it is wooden flooring; in its expanded meanings, it can be everything from a porch to a room large enough to hold a small wedding.

Our challenges did not end there. During the Japanese occupation of the Korean peninsula, education changed, too. Confucian village schools were replaced by the Japanese sohakgyo — or, roughly, 'small school' — which was later renamed 'botonghakgyo'. A direct translation of this would be 'normal school', though it would be more accurate to say 'normalisation school', as the goal of such schooling was to assimilate Koreans into the Japanese Empire. Then the name was changed back to sohakgyo before changing yet again to gungminhakgyo, or 'national citizens' school'. In our translation, however, all of these different names for what was more or less the same thing are rendered as 'primary school' — following the author's suggestion that we keep it simple — except for where the name changes are directly explained in the narration. Even the railway academy that one of the characters attends in the novel is not immune to this flux — historically, the school changed names at least nine times between 1910 and 1967.

Readers will also note that place names look different. What we think of today as 'Korea' was once known as 'Joseon', though both names would have been in use at the same time. 'Gyeongseong' was the name given to Seoul by the Japanese; the capital has gone by many names throughout its history, with 'Seoul' being made official only after World War II. The port city of Incheon was likewise simultaneously known as 'Jemulpo'. In the novel, districts of Seoul retain their colonial-era '-jeong' until nearly the end, when the post–World War II '-dong' suffix comes into use. We considered using Korean spellings for *all* place names, including cities outside of Korea, just so readers could hear how they sound in Korean. But ultimately, and to avoid confusion with well-known cities in modern-day South Korea, places over the border were given back their historical spellings as they appeared on train station signs at the time — hence, Antung, Hsinking, and Fengtian — but border rivers retain their Korean appellations, e.g. Amnokgang River for Yalu River.

Most significantly, and probably most challenging for readers, is that we endeavoured to keep not only the characters' family titles, such as Halmeoni for Grandmother, but also the syntax of the Korean. By keeping titles at the end of the person's name instead of moving them in front, a la Western naming conventions, we hoped to enable readers to hear the rhythm of Korean speech. But we did this somewhat sparingly. Korean family trees are infamously byzantine, and so we were not able to preserve every single title that appears in the book, let alone the variations on how people can be addressed. We stuck to the titles that recurred frequently (eomeoni, abeoji, gomo) and mostly dropped the ones that appeared only once or twice (jageunabeoji, jokamyeoneuri). We also tended to favour titles that were semantically linked (hyeong, hyeongnim) and dropped those that we thought might engender unnecessary confusion (jesu, dongseo).

But even this was sometimes easier said than done, as family titles change over the course of a person's life and depending upon who is speaking. Shin Geumi, for example, changes throughout the novel, being known by her family and personal name before she is married, to later Baekman's daughter-in-law (myeoneuri), Icheol's sister-in-law (hyeongsu), and Mageum's niece-in-law (jokamyeoneuri), then mother (eomeoni/eomma/eomeom/emi), and finally Jino's grandmother (halmeoni), though not strictly in that order! We did our best to strike a balance between Korean and English approaches to addressing characters; difficult choices were made at every step about which titles to preserve in the translation and where. As we did so, we noted how often the scales were tipped towards female characters being identified by their positions in the family, with some having no personal name at all, identified only by the names of their firstborn or their hometowns.

But we did not want to whitewash this aspect of Korean history and culture by simply addressing each character by their personal name, as if they were only ever atomised individuals. The novel is both a history of Korea and the story of a single, mostly ordinary family, so if there was one thing we wanted to preserve from the Korean, it was the way those family members spoke to and of each other.

If there is one regret that came with this, it's that we could not convey more of the richness behind the characters' names and titles and their meanings. We counted up our gains and losses: Ilcheol and Icheol, aka Hansoe and Dusoe — handily revealed in the source text as One Steel and Two Steel — are fitting names for men who drove locomotives and machined metal parts. Shin Geumi's name with its homonymic allusion to magic and gold is harder to convey, as is the way Mageum's name, which can also mean 'blocked', foreshadows her future. We trust that their stories will fill in any regrettable blanks. And we released, with much grieving, the word 'emi', which was one of at least four synonyms for 'mother' that appeared frequently in the book but had too many layers to unpack.

Speaking of grief, the final thing that we held on to — clung to, our editor might say — was the famously Korean exclamation '*aigo*' and as many of its iterations as we could squeeze in: *aigu, aego, aiguna, egumeoni*, and of course *aiiikuna*! Each variation offers subtle hints to the speaker and the sentiment being expressed. *Aigo*, for example, most commonly expresses sorrow and grief, but it can also be used in a happy sense, such as right before welcoming a person. *Aego* is a softer, more clipped version, handy for when you're fatigued. *Aigu* with its long *u* pairs well with trying to discourage someone from doing something foolish. There were more that didn't make the cut. But we tried to stick with the ones that looked most similar to each other, as otherwise we feared we might stretch our readers' patience too far. *Aegeu …*

Hwang Sok-yong describes his style as 'mindam realism', with mindam being something halfway between folklore and plain talk: an oral form of history-making in which ordinary folk spin their own life stories through anecdote, humour, and tall tale; realist in its depiction of how things really were experienced in everyday life. *Mater 2-10* — and its translation — is best understood in this vein. In addressing the characters by their full names and titles, the storyteller-narrator shows his respect and affection for them, as if they were his own kin. We, the translators, tasked with bringing this story out of its home language and into one almost wholly unrelated, followed suit wherever we could, extending this cast of characters our respect and affection, too.

Sora Kim-Russell &
Youngjae Josephine Bae

Author's Note

'Mater' comes from the Japanese abbreviation for 'mountain'. During Japanese colonialism, fifty Mater 1 locomotives, modelled after their Mountain-type counterparts in the United States, were built in Gyeongseong (Seoul) and at the Kisha Seizo factory in Japan. The thirty-three-carriage Mater 2, an improved version manufactured by Kawasaki Heavy Industries, was introduced and operated mainly in North Korea. *Mater 2-10* was a locomotive from this line that was captured during the Korean War by the South Korean army as they advanced north. It was originally used between Gaeseong and Pyeongyang, but ended up at Jangdan Station, south of Gaeseong, when the Allies were retreating. Then, on 31 December 1950, the US Army destroyed it to keep it out of enemy hands. For a long time, it sat abandoned and rusting like an empty tin can in the Demilitarized Zone (DMZ) between North and South, where it came to be known by the nickname Hwatong, or Smokestack. As part of the modern cultural-heritage restoration project, it was retrieved in 2004, repaired over a period of two years, and exhibited at Imjingak in Unification Park as National Registered Cultural Heritage No. 78. Behind a sign that reads 'This iron horse wants to run!', the rusted-out shell of the locomotive faces north. *Mater 2-10* is an enduring image of the Korean War that has since appeared in textbooks, newspapers, magazines, government brochures, and even its very own postage stamp. The remains of this old metal hulk have changed meaning with each change of era and government administration amid the dualities of the Cold War and anti-communism, peace and reconciliation. Like a mummy in a tomb, *Mater 2-10* has been chemically preserved and turned into a commemorative fossil of the age of division.

Hwang Sok-yong

1

Yi Jino set up his toilet on the opposite side of the catwalk, as far away from his tent as possible. On his first attempt, he tried holding onto the railing, but his upper body wouldn't stop tipping forward. He had to press hard with his big toes to not lose his balance: flexed as tight as eagle claws inside his sneakers, those toes were the only thing keeping him from falling on his face or his bum. He didn't dare miss the target.

He looked down between his legs to see if his waste was dropping into the small plastic container he'd placed on the catwalk. It had taken him a while to come up with this solution. At first, he'd used plastic bags to store his faeces, but they were useless at containing the smell, and he worried about them leaking. But then a stomach-ache one day had prompted his support team to bring him rice porridge for breakfast. After three meals of the stuff, he'd finally started to feel better, and it had occurred to him then that the porridge containers were the perfect size for a makeshift toilet. The stench was awful in the limited space of the catwalk, but once he snapped the lid back on and wrapped the container up tight in a plastic bag, the air was breathable again. As soon as he put in his request for empty containers, his support team procured a dozen and sent them up a few at a time. He used each container once before sending them all down, and his team washed and dried them carefully before sending them back up again.

This time, after sealing up his waste, Jino stood for a moment with his hands on the railing, gazing down at the unchanging view of the city. The sun was just beginning to poke its face over the horizon, and the first flush of dawn had spread through the clouds. Buildings of different heights downtown and the towering apartment complexes reminded him of a jungle. He could see a line of trees along the roadside and more trees in Yeouido Park off to the right. May was the colour of new leaves. The Omokgyo Bridge, where he'd played as a child, was now all concrete, but the stream below still flowed as true as ever into the Hangang River.

This perch that Jino had clambered up to a month earlier in the dead of night was the top of a chimney at the edge of a public power plant. It stood forty-five metres high, similar to a sixteen-storey apartment building. He was used to most apartment buildings nowadays being twenty, thirty storeys, which was maybe why the chimney hadn't looked all that tall or made him dizzy to look down from it. But the catwalk encircling it was so narrow and yet so open on all sides that, at first, he'd very nearly walked right over the railing into thin air. The chimney was six metres in diameter, and the catwalk was one metre wide and about twenty paces in circumference. No, only sixteen paces, in fact, since he couldn't count his sleeping area.

He'd learned how to survive like this from those who'd gone up tower cranes in other cities. There was Yeongsuk, an older welder and good friend of Jino's, who'd used the cabin of a tower crane as a bedroom and even grown tomatoes and flowers along the railing during her sit-in. She'd told him that the enormous steel pylons of the shipyard turned into trees every night in her dreams. Maybe those small, fragile living bodies perched atop all that towering steel felt like they'd become one with the metal itself. The cranes turned into broad-leaved trees, and she watched as other, enormous trees soared up out of the sea, here, there, everywhere. But Jino's chimney did not transform into something beautiful for him as it would have for her.

Up here, time was like a rubber band, stretching out long and taut, only to snap back the moment he let go, making it impossible to keep track of its passage. He could have estimated the time the way they did in the old days, from the height and direction of the sun and how much light was left, but he had a mobile phone that kept him informed of the exact minutes and seconds. Nevertheless, those distinctions gradually grew meaningless. Because, up here, daily life was an endless repetition in which nothing ever happened. The officially decided-upon divisions of breakfast, lunch, and dinner were the only things tying knots at regular intervals in the length of his day. Breakfast was set at 8.00 am, lunch at 1.00 pm, and dinner at 6.00 pm, and it took less than five minutes for his team to get from the main gate of the power plant to the base of his chimney with a backpack of food.

Jino was in his mid-fifties and had been a factory worker for twenty-five years. He'd started out right here in Yeongdeungpo, the district in southwestern Seoul where he had grown up, working at one place for nearly a decade, and then spent the next fifteen years working at another factory in a provincial city down south. He'd gone from being an ordinary factory employee to a supervisor, and had joined a union while still young. Yet once he'd worked his way up to division leader, he'd been fired. Well, they called it 'being fired', but what really happened was that the factory was shut down and sold off to another company and, just like that, everyone's jobs vanished and their livelihoods were wiped out. The laid-off workers had come to Seoul, to the company's headquarters in the capital, and began fighting to get their jobs back.

Now, only eleven of the twenty or so workers who had first stood with Jino and refused to back down from their demands to have their positions reinstated or transferred to the new factory were still in the fight. Five who held executive positions in the union or could afford to stay in Seoul made up the core of the chimney sit-in. They were Yi Jino and Kim Changsu, who was the same age as him, Jeong and Bak, who were in their forties, and Cha, the youngest, who was in his twenties. Jino's four colleagues took turns looking after him while holding down whatever jobs their skill sets allowed, whether that was doing odd jobs on construction sites or working as day labourers.

Teams of five officers from the local police station took turns keeping watch around the power-plant chimney where Jino stood his ground, while the guard shack at the front gate was staffed by either a police sergeant or corporal at all times. Whenever the occasional protest was held outside the power plant by people from the Metal Workers' Union or activist groups, a police bus filled with riot police would be parked at the base of the chimney on stand-by. On normal days, one member of his support team would pass through the front gate and arrive at the chimney, where the supplies they brought would be inspected for contraband and okayed for delivery. Inspections tended to be stricter in the morning than in the evening, when the mood loosened as the higher-ups got ready to leave work. Even if contraband was found, it was merely confiscated. No one got arrested or beaten, like in the old days, so they could afford to take some risks. What would happen, though, is they'd be made to write a report on the spot, detailing the items and the reasons for bringing them in, and inspections would become more difficult for at least the next ten days. They'd agreed among themselves to try to only bring new items in the evening, and anything likely to get confiscated was sent up on weekend evenings. But in the end, the police were only human, too, and there were younger ones among them as well, military conscripts who sympathised with the cause, which meant that forbidden items had a way of making it up to Jino now and then.

Before Jino started his sit-in, they did a preliminary survey of what he would need for survival, and spent several days stashing items on the chimney catwalk in the middle of the night. They bypassed the power-plant gate by propping a garden ladder against an exterior wall near the chimney, and used that to sneak in and out. A pair of pulleys and a rope were attached to the catwalk railing, for raising and lowering food and supplies. They also stashed a greenhouse tarp and some thick canvas to protect him from the wind. He bought a small tent and a sleeping bag, along with a headlamp and mountaineering supplies. He also made sure to take his mobile phone and an extra battery.

With the help of the Metal Workers' Union, his colleagues set up their headquarters under a canopy in an empty lot outside the power plant, where they took turns cooking and preparing food. They decided to send up three meals a day and figured out everything else as they went along, including how much drinking water he would need and how to dispose of his urine and faeces. Four plastic bottles of water were sent up once a day; this increased to six as the days grew warmer. Two of these bottles were for washing his face and brushing his teeth, and one was for the lettuce and other plants that were just beginning to grow. His support team had sent him seeds to help pass the time, and Jino had planted them just a few days after beginning his sit-in. The empty water bottles became urinals; he stashed them to one side as they filled. They would make for handy projectiles if the police were to try to bring him down.

The day before the sit-in, Jino climbed the chimney with Jeong and Cha to install the tarp and canvas sheeting. Their last step was to attach a placard to the outside of the catwalk. In large, capital letters, the placard read:

STOP THE SELL-OFF!

In smaller letters below that, it read:

PRESERVE THE UNION AND RESTORE OUR JOBS

Jino couldn't stop re-reading those words, visible through the backside of the placard and in reverse of how those in the world opposite of him were seeing them.

He had work to do today. A day or two earlier, his support team had sent an adjustable spanner up in the bucket with his dinner. When he saw the foil packet with two burnt fish tails sticking out of the bottom, he'd assumed that's all it was. But the moment he picked it up, he guessed from the weight what was inside. It took a long time for the spanner to stop smelling like fish, sandwiched as it had been between the two grilled saury.

First, though, his morning exercise. He had initially saved it for after breakfast, to help digest his food, but now he started his day with some stretching, to help get the kinks out after spending the night curled up. After eating, he walked for an hour back and forth along the catwalk, sixteen paces one way, and sixteen paces the other. After lunch, he took another walk and worked his muscles. Then he did the same after dinner, and stretched again before bed. He'd learned what to do from a trainer at a nearby gym, who'd coached him over the phone. His support team had connected him with the trainer by visiting the gym in person and explaining the situation. The trainer had said that the best method was to exercise in short, intense intervals throughout the day. To warm up, Jino did neck rolls, arm swings, knee bends, and other stretches, followed by sit-ups and side bends, and ending with a yoga move called 'corpse pose'. The three strength exercises that had been recommended to him were push-ups, squats, and pull-ups. But with no equipment or pull-up bars to increase resistance, he did them as a burpee instead. From a push-up, he brought his legs beneath him and pushed off into a jump with arms overhead, then landed in a squat, kicked his legs back behind him, and did another push-up to continue the round. It was a simple move, but he'd been instructed to do twenty in a row to keep himself fit. When he started, he could only do seven before he was out of breath. Now he was up to ten, but he had a long way to go before he would be able to do twenty without stopping. His phone rang. It was Cha.

'I'll be handling your meals from now on,' Cha said.

'Okay. Did Kim get a job?'

'Yes, at a construction site. He'll stop by in the evening.'

'Is everyone all right?'

'Yes. I'm on my way in now.'

Cha, the youngest of the crew, was at the front gate. Jino leaned over the railing and looked down. Cha appeared at the corner of the cement wall. A conscripted officer stationed at the base of the chimney came out to meet him. Cha opened his backpack and took out the containers of food; the officer glanced indifferently at them and stepped back. Jino lowered the rope attached to the pulley. The bucket swung from the end of it. At Cha's signal, he began slowly pulling the bucket back up.

'Thanks!' Jino shouted with a wave. Cha waved back and left.

The bucket held his breakfast of rice porridge, a fried egg, kimchi, and stir-fried dried anchovies. He'd been given six bottles of water for the day. As the weather grew hotter still, they would probably have to send his water rations up twice a day instead. He ate the egg in one gulp. The porridge was no longer piping hot, but still warm enough. And it contained plenty of vegetables for him to enjoy. It took less than ten minutes to polish off his meal. He placed the empty containers in the bucket, brushed his teeth, and poured water into a basin to wash his face with. He felt like a cat cleaning its fur in tiny licks. He was about to take one of his daily walks around the catwalk, but considering how much manual labour he had in store for him today, he decided to skip it.

He didn't know if it would happen this week or next, but he'd received word from below that a face-to-face talk with the company had been scheduled. A settlement would be okay, but he had to be prepared in case the talks fell apart. After all, a dispute that had been stewing for more than two years was unlikely to be resolved overnight. He'd come up here prepared for a tug of war. For all he knew, if negotiations did break down, the company might push for the police to end his sit-in by sending their thugs up to force him down. Since no more than one person could ascend the chimney at a time, as long as he could block that entrance, he'd be able to stand his ground until the labour union and citizens' groups had a chance to arrive. Hence the bottles of urine. But that wasn't enough to put his mind at ease, and so he'd decided to disable the ladder, which was the final stretch between the catwalk and the stairs that spiralled up the chimney. He was guessing the ladder was about ten metres high. It was covered in a clear acrylic shield. He figured that if he could remove the top screws and tilt the ladder away from the chimney, he could prevent anyone from coming all the way up.

Jino tied some leftover rope around his waist and secured the other end to the railing before making his way down the ladder. To make sure he didn't drop the spanner, he tied that to a length of rope as well and hung it around his neck. He loosened the bottom bolts, but removed the top bolts entirely and stashed them in his pocket. They were difficult to turn at first, but after he was halfway done, they started coming loose with just a twist of his bare hands. He was in the middle of removing another bolt when he heard someone shout at him from below.

'What do you think you're doing?'

He didn't respond. Why should he? As he made his way up one rung at a time, the officer ran to fetch the sergeant.

'Cease all dangerous activity right now!'

Jino looked down and grinned mischievously. The two men were climbing the spiral stairs. After a moment, they had reached the last section, right below Jino's feet. They were out of breath. But Jino was already a good three metres higher; all they could do was gaze helplessly up at him.

'You're damaging the facilities!' the sergeant barked, as if he were in charge.

The conscripted officer asked, 'Why are you removing the bolts? That's dangerous.'

Only then did Jino pause to answer.

'This? To keep you guys from coming up.'

'You think we're only standing around because we can't stop you?'

Jino removed another bolt and dropped it into his pocket.

'Come on, now,' he said, 'Isn't this better than me jumping?'

'You're a real pain in the arse, you know that? You think this is gonna go away overnight?' The sergeant turned and slowly made his way back down, muttering as he went. 'Stay up here a hundred days, for all I care. The bosses don't give a shit what you do.'

It took Jino a good hour and a half to remove both rows of bolts from ten metres of ladder. He did the final section while lying down on the catwalk. When he gave the ladder a hard shove, it swung outward and came to a rest against the acrylic shield. Now no one would be able to come up after him. Of course, he also had no way down. He had no idea when the time would come for him to leave, but he looked forward to the day when he would be able to send the bolts down to his support team so they could re-insert them one by one on their way up to him.

He ate lunch as usual, took his walk and did his workout, read a book, ate again at dinnertime, then did his workout again and ended with stretches. At this time of day, people would be getting off work and having drinks with co-workers, or going home to eat dinner and watch television. Jino called his wife and exchanged text messages with his union colleagues. It had been an ordinary day for them, the same as any other. Darkness had fallen over the city, and the night was deepening. The usual city noises gradually died down until all he heard was the occasional distant car horn. He crawled into his sleeping bag inside his tent and went to sleep. He slept well up there. With nothing to do after dark, he'd retreat to his sleeping bag just after 9.00 pm and fall easily into a deep sleep.

*

Jino woke up needing to pee. He cracked one eye open and tossed and turned, reluctant to get out of his sleeping bag. Finally, he unzipped the side and squirmed out like a caterpillar from a cocoon. A thick fog had fallen. He took a few steps away from his tent and, standing before the railing, urinated over the side. He couldn't see a thing beyond the catwalk. He shivered, turned, then paused to look back at the sea of clouds surrounding the chimney. He stuck his right foot under the railing and swept it about. The air under his foot felt solid somehow. He'd felt this urge before, during his daily walk along the catwalk, an impulse that told him to keep going, right over the edge and into the empty air. He crouched down between the bars and stuck his leg out again. It felt like stepping onto a blanket or a very soft mattress. With his hands braced on the railing, he swung both feet over this time and set them down. 'What —' he muttered in shock. 'You can walk on it!' He strode out onto the fog, his feet sinking in as he went. It felt just like walking across a snow drift. At first he sank into it up to his knees, but soon his steps grew lighter and he began to glide along. The fog still surrounded him, as if he were inside a cloud, but now he was walking on a hard, dry dirt path.

Just ahead were the railroad tracks. Then the old tavern and the shop with their low roofs and dim yellow lights seeping out from latticed windows, followed by narrow alleyways on both sides of the tracks. He followed the tracks until he saw the darkened Wounded Veterans' Hall.

As a child, he had gone there several times with his father to watch westerns. He was in the third grade or so when he learned how to sneak in. Actually, it was the barbershop kid who'd first figured it out. The Wounded Veterans' Hall was a military warehouse that had been converted into a movie theatre for wounded soldiers after the war. The warehouse itself had been thrown together from wooden planks and corrugated iron; an art workshop, where movie billboards were handpainted, had been tacked on to the side of it later. The workshop was never locked. Though it was closed at night, all they had to do was give the door a slight push to get inside. Above a pile of discarded crates and pieces of timber was a wood-slatted window that led into the warehouse-turned-movie theatre. On the inside of the window was a blackout curtain, and below that was an aisle filled with seats. Eventually, someone got caught sneaking in this way and was roundly chewed out by the usher; after that, the art workshop was locked at night, and the window was covered in chicken wire. The Wounded Veterans' Hall had three ushers, all of whom were older men — ajeoss-his — who had been injured in the war. There was Gimpy Ajeosshi with the wooden leg, who sold tickets in the booth; Goblin Ajeosshi, with the burn scar, who took tickets at the door; and One-Arm Ajeosshi, the guard who patrolled the theatre. They took turns watching the entrance, sweeping up, and keeping an eye on things, but One-Arm Ajeosshi was the scariest of the three. He used to stick a cigarette between the two hooks at the end of his prosthetic arm and coolly puff away at it while taking tickets with his good hand. But whenever he got angry, he would flash those fierce hooks and growl for the boys to go ahead and try him.

The barbershop kid had giggled as he told Jino about the next secret passageway he'd discovered. Jino followed him early one morning into the alleyway behind the theatre. Underneath some wood siding was a sheet of iron that, when lifted, released the stench of urine. The moment he saw it, Jino regretted having given the kid his ddakji collection in exchange for this. When the kid had named his price, Jino had ended up handing over his prized treasure chest along with all of his paper ddakji tiles. The chest was a metal cookie container sold in the Yankee market. But free movies or not, how could he bring himself to sneak in through a toilet? The kid explained that he'd installed footholds and had snuck in a few times already without getting caught.

That night, the two boys ripped the lids off two cardboard boxes and snuck into the theatre. There was enough light coming through the hole in the toilet for them to see the bottom. The latrine was deep and wide. They stepped across the stones that the barbershop kid had placed there in advance, avoiding the mounds of faeces, and climbed up through the hole. Before sticking their torsos through, they had to cover the ground beneath them with their scraps of cardboard. They squeezed through and found themselves inside the rest room, and made it into the theatre without getting caught.

They did this several times, and did not always manage it without getting urine on their hands or shirts, or faeces on their shoes, thanks to those clumsy adults who couldn't aim properly and pissed all over their stepping stones. Once the boys had groped their way into the darkened theatre and found empty seats, everyone around them would start sniffing at the sudden stench of urine and whispering to each other, asking where that smell was coming from. The embarrassment was more than Jino could take.

The barbershop kid lived with his older brother, who was a barber. Their parents had died young, so he had nowhere else to turn, but things were not peaceful between him and his sister-in-law. The neighbourhood kids had nicknamed him Little Clippers, which made his brother Big Clippers. At any rate, Little Clippers ran away from home and got into all sorts of scrapes. He'd lived in a junkyard with a gang of rag-pickers and learned how to catch snakes from one of the older boys, who was skilled at hunting them. Snakes were medicinal; word had it that a tonic brewed from a few of the larger ones could keep you in a healthy sweat even in the dead of winter. The snake hunter had the ability to talk to snakes. Before capturing one, he would wait for it to slither out of the grass and glare at him. Then he'd say, 'Where ya headed? Come here, Brother's got something yummy for you.' He would grab the snake by the tail with no hesitation. The snake would wriggle and squirm. But the snake hunter would simply say, 'You tryin' to bite me? There's a reason I'm only taking you and not your ma and your dad. I don't got any other choice. I got more rats than I know what to do with. That's why I'm gonna let you catch as many as you want. But if you keep fighting me like this, then I'll slam you on the ground and crush your skull!' Then he would slip the snake gently into his sack, wait for another to talk to, and slip that one into the sack, as well.

Of course, Little Clippers had made up the story of the rag-pickers and the snake hunter, but that didn't stop Jino from asking for more stories. Later, Little Clippers was sent to a reform school, where he learned to play the bugle. After he came back, a few inches taller, he kept the bugle mouthpiece with him everywhere he went. He would hold it up to his mouth, clasp his palms around the end, and play the most heartbreakingly mournful version of taps Jino ever heard. Whenever the adults asked Little Clippers what he wanted to be when he grew up, he always said a soldier or a police officer, but if his friends asked, he told them he'd rather be a cat-burglar. When his friends asked why, he said that if you were good enough at it, you could own anything in the world, and buy all the jjajangmyeon noodles you wanted to feed poor folk. But instead, Little Clippers died all too soon. Stacks of rusted girders could always be found in an empty lot near the rail works; one night, while leaping from stack to stack, Little Clippers fell. No one saw it happen, but it was easy enough to picture him losing his footing and falling between the stacks, his small body hitting each piece of metal that stuck out on the way down, and landing headfirst in the dirt. Several days passed before his body was found. According to the neighbourhood kids, a circus had come into town, and the empty lot was the only place large enough to host the big top. Never one to pass up a spectacle, Little Clippers had probably been sneaking in every night to watch the acrobats. Maybe he had been trying to imitate their high-wire acts. After all, you'd have to practise all kinds of skills, balancing and otherwise, to make it as a big-time cat-burglar. It had taken Jino all this time to realise what a wild dream it had been. Imagine — getting your hands on anything you ever wanted!

Now he was on the main street of Saetmal. The roadside was lined with shops, and new alleyways appeared on each block. A three-forked road with a large bell tree marked the start of Jino's neighbourhood. His schoolteachers had called it a 'platanus tree' while the kids all called it a 'bell tree', but the old herbal-medicine doctor called it an 'American sycamore' and explained that the evil Japanese had planted dozens of them around the same time they'd built the railroad, back before the big floods. Jino had asked his dad about it, and his dad said that he and his friends had also called it a 'bell tree' ever since they were little and so Jino and his friends should go right ahead and keep on calling it that. There was the corner house, which had once been called the 'bier house' but had since come to be known as a 'funeral parlour'. Then the barbershop where Little Clippers had lived, and across the intersection wide enough for cars to pass through was the tofu house and, next to that, the butcher. On this side was the general store, and if you passed the spot that used to be a rice mill but later became a timber mill, and ducked into that alley there, you'd find yourself in the rice-shop alley, lined with small hanok homes, at the end of which was the 'Saetmal House', where Jino was born.

Jino pushed open the front gate without hesitating. To his surprise, it swung inwards without a sound. Normally, it opened with a painful screech, as if the hinges were out of alignment. To one side was the outhouse, and past the gate was the long, narrow courtyard. The yard had originally been square, but next to the gate, Jino's Big Grandfather had built a thirteen-square-metre workshop, just as he did each time he moved. 'Big Grandfather' was what Jino's family had called Yi Baekman, Jino's great-grandfather, to distinguish him from Yi Ilcheol, Jino's grandfather. Shin Geumi Halmeoni, or Grandmother Shin Geumi, had never surrendered the main room to anyone. The house had belonged to Jino's great-great-aunt during the Japanese occupation, and though it was a small house, the beams and rafters were still as sturdy as ever. Before that, Great-Grandfather Baekman had lived in the government-owned rail workers' housing thanks to his first son, Ilcheol, but that only lasted a few years before he found the lifestyle there stifling and insisted that the family move into his sister's Saetmal House. Keeping their distance from the government housing and getting by on their own was what kept them safe, even after two of the men left for the North.

As Jino stepped through the gate and into the courtyard, Geumi Halmeoni looked up from where she was washing greens under the tap outside the kitchen and greeted him happily.

'*Aego*, my poor baby, it's so hot today! You must be exhausted from school.'

Looking down at his body, Jino was not too surprised to see that he was back in his primary-school self. His grandmother took his schoolbag, his shirt, and his singlet and pointed him towards the tap. Naked from the waist up, he bent over the basin while his grandmother poured ice-cold water over his back and neck. *Aiguna!* Shivering, Jino tucked his hands into his armpits and complained loudly about the sudden shock of cold. His grandmother responded with a sound smack on his back and told him to bend over again. His ablutions complete, his grandmother brought out a small dog-legged tray set with rice, water, dried yellow corvina torn into shreds, and a bowl of kimchi made with radish greens. Back then, there was still plenty of corvina being caught in the West Sea. People living on the outskirts of Seoul would buy the fish by the pair from Juan, a neighbourhood of Incheon, just after the start of spring. The fish were brined in salt and stored on wicker trays on the sauce terrace, or tied with straw rope and hung from the wall to dry in the sun. This was called gulbi, and every house prepared their own. Just like putting up kimchi in the early winter, salting and drying corvina every spring was a seasonal household event.

'I bet you're hungry. Mix the rice with the water first. It'll refresh you.'

His grandmother was dressed in baggy Japanese pants and a Korean summer blouse woven from hemp and fastened without a sash. Instead of a chignon, she wore her hair bobbed, without a single grey hair showing. Her modern hairstyle was the reason the neighbourhood folk used to say that she looked like a night-school teacher or one of those

New Women. She was born in Gimpo, attended primary school, which was unusual for a country girl, and took night classes while working in a textile factory. She met her husband, Ilcheol, through his younger brother, Icheol. Great-Grandfather Baekman had had trains on his mind when his son was born, and so he'd named him Hansoe, or One Steel. The next son born became Dusoe, or Two Steel. Later, when he officially added their names to the family register, he kept the meanings but gave them the more formal-sounding Ilcheol and Icheol.

While working at the textile factory, Geumi had begun reading the Bible at the urging of a missionary and found that she enjoyed it. She read the Old Testament, in particular, several times over, as it reminded her of an old storybook, and she became a skilled reader. From a young age, she'd had the ability to see ghosts hanging around certain people and would sometimes shout and try to chase them off. Once, when her brother-in-law Icheol was still a bachelor and had come to visit, she muttered that she could see two women hovering behind him, which earned her a scolding from her husband, Ilcheol. According to what she eventually told her son, Jino's father, Yi Jisan, she found out later that they were the spitting image of two women waiting to come into her brother-in-law's life. At the time, both women looked like such bad luck that she couldn't stop herself from babbling, 'Get away from him!' until finally Icheol got uncomfortable and left before he'd even finished eating. Later, it turned out that Icheol was far more of a bad luck charm to those women than they ever were to him. Geumi eventually stopped going to church, but she kept up her habit of shocking people by gazing briefly at a person she'd met for the first time and accurately stating things that had happened to them in the past and things that would happen to them in the future. She became known as the Uncanny Shin Geumi. Great-Grandfather Baekman refused to comment on his daughter-in-law's behaviour, but each time the new year rolled around, he would surreptitiously ask her if it promised to be a peaceful year for the family.

When Jino lifted his spoon, his grandmother picked up a long piece of the radish-greens kimchi with a separate pair of chopsticks, coiled it on top of the spoonful of rice that he'd mixed with the cold water, and topped that with a piece of gulbi. He ate the rest of his rice in that fashion, then lay down on the cool wooden floor inside the house and fell into a satisfying nap.

What year was that? His grandmother had told him one particular story so many times that he nearly had it memorised.

'So there was this one day I was coming down with a cold and wasn't feeling too good. I didn't have the energy to go sell clothes in the market. In fact, I barely managed to make breakfast for your great-grandfather before going back to bed and wrapping myself up in the blankets. I fell asleep at once and found myself back in the old rail workers' housing. Your grandfather wasn't supposed to be home until early the next morning, after his shift back and forth to Manchuria, but there he was, coming through the door when the sun was still high in the sky. Even in my dream, I was worried something had happened to him or that he'd been fired. And then, what do you know? With a big smile on his face, he said he'd come to drop off our son, Jisan. I was so excited, I just kept saying, "Where is he? Where on earth is my dear son, Jisan?" Then he said, "He's not all in one piece, so I can't show you just yet, but don't be shocked when you see him later because at least he made it back alive." And just like that, he vanished. I woke up, stumbled to the door, and there, standing outside the gate in a patch of shade, was this black shadow that said, "Eomeoni, I'm home." I hadn't heard from him since he'd left home at sixteen, saying he wanted to go find his dad. The war was so awful! It felt like it'd been a hundred years, or more. But there he was, all skinny and dark and — *aiguna!* — missing one leg. He was dressed in this raggedy woollen army uniform on such a hot day, with one pant leg folded in half, and wooden crutches under each arm. My boy had vanished and come back to me as an old man on one leg! You can only imagine what was going through my mind. But I did not cry. All I said, very quietly, was, "Yes, you're home. You're back. I knew you would be. Your father told me he was bringing you home."'

Yi Jisan was twenty-one at the time. Jino came along six years later, when his father was twenty-seven. Jisan had taken his certificate of release from the prisoner-of-war camp and boarded a train in Busan, and then followed the instructions he'd been given to report his arrival at his final destination and stop by the neighbourhood association where he would be living before going to the district office to receive his citizenship identification card. Alighting at Yeongdeungpo Station, he saw the ruins of the station building — which had been bombed and burned down until only the pillars were left — and the weeds pushing out of the cracks that webbed the cement. Civilian and military police were lined up at the turnstiles and examining everyone who came out. Jisan approached one of the military police officers and showed him his certificate of release.

'Uhhh, so … I'm a prisoner of war returning home?' he said.

The officer scanned the scrap of paper and exchanged a glance with one of the civilian police. Shaking the paper at Jisan, he said, 'This way.'

They went into a large army tent that had been set up in one corner of the station plaza. Several other men and women were already inside and being asked questions, so the two officers took a seat.

The military police officer gestured with his chin at a stool in front of the desk and told Jisan to sit. Then he asked, 'Were you in the volunteer army?'

'No, sir,' Jisan said. 'I was a civilian train engineer.'

'You drove trains?'

Jisan gave him the same answer he gave everyone else.

'Yes, sir, I was forced to drive for the military.'

'Where were you taken into custody?'

'Near Hwanggan, sir.'

'Hwanggan? Where's that?'

'It's right before Chupungnyeong Pass.'

The officer nodded knowingly.

'So you transported supplies to the front lines at Nakdonggang River.'

He looked up Yi Jisan's name on the list of prisoners of war, passed the certificate of release back to the civilian cop, and handed Jisan off to an older plainclothes officer. Having finished questioning the others who'd got there first, the plainclothesman looked Jisan up and down, his gaze piercing, then asked for his address. Jisan recited the address of his Saetmal home; that was one address he would never forget. The plainclothesman pulled a thick sheaf of documents out of a drawer and rifled through them, all the while stealing glances at Jisan. Suddenly he stopped and rapped on the desk with his pen.

'You're Yi Ilcheol's son. This says that traitor was mixed up with some labour-union nonsense before fleeing to the North. It also says that no one knows where *you* were before the war. You're a goddamn commie.' The plainclothesman shook his head and muttered under his breath, 'What'll our country come to if we just keep pardoning garbage like this? In the old days, they'd've shot you on sight.'

The military officer interjected. 'It's a special order from the president.'

'What happened to your leg?' the plainclothesman asked, looking down at the hem of Jisan's folded pant leg and lifting it slightly to try to steal a peek.

'I got hit during a bombing raid. They fixed it up before sending me to the POW camp.'

'You were cleared as anti-communist, right? Anyway, go home for now and report to the nearest police station within the next three days.'

On his way out of the tent, Jisan felt the plainclothesman's next words hit him in the back of the head.

'Make sure you report! Don't make things harder on everyone by getting yourself arrested over nothing.'

Jisan walked down the main street, which was still intact, in front of the train station. The alianthus trees were a deep green, and though some of the paving stones had been torn up or had pockmarks, the shops and pedestrians looked as lively as they had before Liberation, as befitting the mood of a main street. The round windows of the Japanese sweets shop where he used to stop and stare at the goods on display every day on the way home from school were still there, but the neat rows of intricate wagashi had been replaced by piles of cheap senbei crackers. He paused at the market roundabout and looked up at the old signs for the photo studio and dentist's office. There were more small shops clustered now around the Methodist church, and nearly half of the pavement was occupied by street vendors with their wares spread out on mats. The limbs of the willow tree that used to hang over the church stairs had all been lopped off. At the railroad tracks, he turned right and then left again towards Saetmal, and spotted the entrance to his village not too far away. Past the bell tree, he saw that the rice mill lay in ruins: dyed army uniforms and other used clothing hung from long posts and rods installed all over what was left of the place.

When he entered the alley near the rice shop, he saw a young woman coming towards him with a bamboo basket piled high with wet clothes balanced on her head. She wore a kerchief, a cotton jeogori blouse, and a shin-length mongdang skirt, and she was very pregnant. They were about ten steps away when they took notice of each other. Jisan paused, leaning on his crutches, for her to pass. Just as she was walking right by him, he realised who she was. She, too, looked up into his face as she went by. She'd gone about three or four steps when she stopped right at the same time that Jisan turned to look at her again.

In a quavering voice, he said, 'Aren't you … Bokrye?'

'*Omona!*'

In her shock at hearing his voice, she leaned too far forward. The basket on top of her head tipped, and the clothes spilled out. Jisan rushed forward on his crutches to keep her from falling. The woman quickly collected herself and picked up the clothes that had fallen on the ground. Neither of them could bring themselves to speak. Leaning on his crutches, Jisan gazed at her briefly then walked away.

That was how Jino's mother and father, who'd attended school together, found each other again.

Jisan returned home, reported himself to the local police station without a hitch, and let several days go by before finally telling his mother about his first day back.

'The day I came home, I ran into Bokrye …'

Shin Geumi had just filled the iron with hot charcoal and was ironing Great-Grandfather's shirt.

'Uh-huh,' she said absentmindedly, 'she must be due any day now.' She looked over at her son and added casually, 'She married well. Her husband's a lot older, but considering how difficult things are right now, she's lucky she doesn't have to worry about where her next meal will come from.'

The brother of Bak Chonggyeong, a police officer from Hwanghae Province who was famed for his meritorious deeds in routing out communist insurgents, had slipped into Yeongdeungpo along with other refugees from the North and made a great deal of money by dyeing and mending used army uniforms and other clothing that trickled out of the US military bases or Christian relief organisations and selling them in the market. At the time, cotton broadcloth was the only fabric available for making clothes, so the uniforms and donated clothing were valuable.

Geumi praised Bokrye's character and resourcefulness, saying that she had turned a tidy profit selling the clothes that Mr Bak had fixed up, and spoke at length about how kind and capable she was for someone so young.

'What awful timing for you, though,' Geumi added. 'Weren't you two close?'

With that, she stopped talking about Bokrye. Neither mother nor son had anything further to say to each other on the subject.

From where he lay, Jino could hear everything as his grandmother bustled around. At the same time, it sounded like she was whispering all their old family stories to him. The baby his mother was carrying in her belly that day in the alley became his older sister, Jeongja, born six years before him. Their names were next to each other's in the family register, except that he was Yi Jino and she was Bak Jeongja. Mr Bak of the dye shop was fifteen years older than Yun Bokrye, Jino's mother; he suffered from chronic illness, which gradually worsened with each passing year, and three years after Jeongja was born he took his last breath in a tuberculosis sanatorium. The dye shop went to his youngest brother, while Bokrye headed to the market where she arranged refurbished clothes for sale on a mat next to Geumi's shop and, as fate would have it, became Yi Jisan's wife.

2

Pale-green leaflings had budded from dry branches and grown into glossy dark-green leaves that shone in the sunlight. Meanwhile, Yi Jino's chimney-top life wore on, the same as ever. Negotiations had been promised, but early summer had come with no word from the company. Every weekend, the Metal Workers' Union gathered in front of the company's head office, cranked up the loudspeakers, unfurled their banners, and tried to make their demands heard, but their only audience were the twenty or so military-conscript police officers standing around. No response ever came from the company itself. Even the protest to commemorate the 100th day of Jino's sit-in made no waves. When word did come from the company, it was always to say that the current ownership was in a state of flux and that previous lay-offs or union matters could not be discussed until the new owners had completed the takeover and appointed a board of directors. It was an obvious trick that had been used by other owners before: to fire workers and sell off a company only to move the factory overseas and hire local workers there in order to make it appear to be a new company. But Jino and his team were determined not to change their demands regardless of who became the owner. The sit-in had only just begun.

Jino ate breakfast, stretched, did his exercises, and walked laps along the railing. The lettuce seeds that he'd planted in the seedling tray twenty days earlier had sprouted right away and were each growing three or four leaves the length of his finger. He chose the biggest and freshest-looking of these, plucked them from the tray, and transferred them to plastic water bottles that he'd cut in half to make planters. He had five of these homemade planters, each of which held three lettuce plants. Cha had purchased a small sack of soil from a nearby flower shop and sent it up. Jino watered them using his morning and evening water rations. He knelt down and studied the leaves and stems and soil very closely. There were several small white insects crawling around. Where on earth had they come from? They had to have been living in the soil somehow already. He marvelled at the busy existence of these tiny creatures that were smaller than dust and which would have been impossible to spot if they weren't in motion. How long must a day have been to them?

Around the time lunch was being sent up, the sky to the west grew dark and rain clouds gathered. The wind began to blow harder, and no sooner had Jino sent his now-empty lunch dishes back down in the basket than raindrops began to fall. He checked whether the canvas was securely lashed to the outside of the railing and readjusted the tarp as well, just to be sure. Then he tugged on each of the tent cords that were tied to the railing and chimney screws. He stashed the planters beneath the tarp and tightened the ropes around the plastic boxes that contained the pulley and his other belongings. As the rain began to beat down in earnest, he pulled on his raincoat and hat. He couldn't just sit inside his tent all day because of a little rain. There would be clear days and overcast days, rainy days and stormy days. Cold or hot, it didn't matter, it was only weather. Just as boredom, anger, sadness, and joy would pass in the turning of a day and night.

He ate his dinner with his upper body halfway inside the tent. Drops of water slid off his rain hat and into his rice and stew. After sending the dishes down again, he paced along the railing. The rain showed no sign of letting up. He walked more slowly than usual, counting his steps as he went. He imagined he was an alien. After all, was he not? This place was neither sky nor land. Not a place for human beings to live. The narrow circumference was like the cockpit of a spaceship travelling outside of everyday life and time back on earth. He was not dead; he was living, right here, and yet the world took no notice of him. He was a man on a journey who was bound to return to the rest of the world eventually. Even his wife's phone calls had begun to sound like she was relaying news of friends and relations to someone living overseas. Jino had gradually broken free of earthbound time, and his daily life on the chimney was no longer a part of reality.

*

Saetmal came to life in the evenings. The roads filled with bicycles as workers poured out of the dozens of nearby factories and people headed home from the rail works and leather and paper mills. The female textile workers threw off their work wear to reveal colourful outfits before heading home or out of the factory dorms for a night out. Wives set charcoal braziers outside their front doors and worked the bellows as the fish roasted. Husbands hung their empty lunch boxes from their bicycle handlebars and made their leisurely way down Saetmal's main street, metal chopsticks rattling cheerfully inside the tin. There were so many bicycles that at a certain hour the rattling sound would build and carry across the distance, alerting children that their fathers and big brothers were on the way home, sending them out to the street to meet them.

Nearly all of the factories had been destroyed in the war and sat dormant, but with the passage of time, the larger ones were restored to operation while new ones began to pop up in vacant lots. Children clustered inside half-demolished mills and brick factories according to their grade level to receive primary-school lessons, which continued until the schools had been rebuilt.

Yi Jino stood on the side of the road and watched the neighbourhood men return from work before heading home himself. His mother, Yun Bokrye, wasn't back from the market yet, but his grandmother Shin Geumi was due home any moment. After making breakfast every day, his mother would head to their clothing stall in the Yeongdeungpo Market to unlock the door and set out the displays. When Geumi Halmeoni came to relieve her, Bokrye would head home and make lunch for Jino's father and great-grandfather before heading back to the market again. Sometimes, Geumi Halmeoni would take that as her cue to head home; other times, when a new shipment had come in or there were a lot of customers, she would stay to help her daughter-in-law until the evening, when she would pick up some groceries and come home. Her basket never held only dinner fixings but would always include snacks for Jino. Sweet red-bean buns, striped jawbreakers, jeolpyeon rice cakes — his grandmother never failed to deliver.

The Willow Tree House was where Great-Grandfather Baekman first had himself a workshop. He wasn't able to claim any such space for himself in the rail workers' housing, of course, so the very first thing he did upon the family's move to Saetmal — indeed, as if that had been their sole reason for moving — was to build the workshop in the courtyard. As a boy, Baekman had helped out in a metal-crafts smithy. He'd set most of that aside after being hired by the Railway Bureau, where he learned how to operate a lathe, but he was still fond of making small crafts at home in his spare time. He inwardly prided himself on his abilities: while the objects didn't amount to much, making them required a level of craftsmanship that most people lacked. He made silver rings engraved with intricate patterns of ivy, and silver hairpins for his wife and for his daughter-in-law Geumi.

A lot has changed since those days, but the custom at the time was for women to take elegantly decorated wooden cabinets and chests with them when they married. Wardrobes inlaid with mother-of-pearl were only affordable for the daughters of wealthy men, but even the simplest of wooden furnishings were not considered complete for newlyweds unless it had been decorated with all sorts of metal trimmings. Anyone entering Great-Grandfather's workshop was met with a blazing-hot coke stove and the stinging smells of melting lead and burning glue. Great-Grandfather was versed in all manner of metals: white iron, black iron, tin, brass, copper, lead, gold, silver, gold leaf, silver leaf. The list went on. On top of working with every metal in the world, he also took custom orders for combs, pocketknives, and ornaments decorated with thin sheets of ox horn. He had an exclusive arrangement with a carpentry shop to supply them with these ornaments, which they attached to the wooden furniture they built before putting it on the market.

When Jino's father returned with only one leg, Great-Grandfather patiently taught him everything he knew, and after a few years of apprenticeship, Jino's father began skilfully making ornaments alongside him. Together, they crafted taegeuk symbols, deer, cranes, phoenixes, peacocks, tortoises, peonies, butterflies, and the Chinese characters *bok* for 'good fortune', *su* for 'long life', *gang* for 'peace', *nyeong* for 'wellbeing', and then some. They chatted as they worked, their mouths keeping pace with their hands.

Right now, Jino squats in the corner of his great-grandfather's workshop, eavesdropping on their conversation. He pictures his abeoji, Jisan, doing the same thing, squatting in this same spot as a little boy, back before Jino was born, listening in as Jino's harabeoji, Hansoe (who continued to be called by his childhood name Hansoe at home, instead of his grown-up name Ilcheol), helps his own father, Baekman, after work, perhaps by pumping the bellows or doing some simple gluing.

'Harabeoji, tell me about your hometown,' Jisan says to Baekman. 'How did you end up working on the railroad?'

'Well, you see, boy, I was born in Seonwon Township on Ganghwado Island, in that tiny village called Jisan-ri. It was right next to Seonwonsa Temple. We worked the fields for the monks.'

'Abeoji says that's how I got the name Jisan.'

'People there survived by farming or working on fishing boats. Ganghwa people are known for being tough. For being survivors. Some locals made their way out to places like Incheon and Mapo where they struck it rich.'

Great-Grandfather Baekman left home at the age of thirteen to look for work in Incheon, where there were many Japanese shops, inns, and taverns, Chinese restaurants and shops, and Western ships that sailed back and forth to China. It was pure luck that found Baekman working as an errand boy in a Japanese-owned rice mill just two months after arriving in Incheon. Of course, he was helped by the fact that he'd sailed to Mapo on a fishing boat with his father at the age of ten and spent a year there working in a Japanese dry-goods shop. That job, too, had been a stroke of luck: while his father and the rest of the ship's crew were busy hauling crocks of sand eels to the Mapo Dock, Baekman went up to the marketplace along the river to have a look around. Stacks of crates that looked like they'd just arrived by boat from Incheon towered in front of the Japanese dry-goods shop, and porters were scurrying to transfer all the crates inside. The shopkeeper, decked out in a yukata and geta sandals, stopped in the middle of rushing in and out of his shop to say something in Japanese to the boy. He kept pointing back and forth at the stacks and the inside of his shop, then pointed two fingers at his own face, gesturing as if to poke himself in the eyes, which the clever boy understood at once to mean that he should stand guard over the crates. When the last of the crates had been carried inside, the shopkeeper waved the boy over with a smile on his face and offered him a large round piece of candy, easily the size of an eyeball, from a glass jar. Baekman had tasted Korean yeot before, but this black-sugar jawbreaker was much sweeter and harder. Eyes a-sparkle, the young Baekman pointed at the straw and sawdust littering the ground in front of the shop and mimicked sweeping it up. The shopkeeper nodded and brought him a broom and dustpan. In a flash, Baekman had the front of the shop looking spick-and-span, just in time for his father to come looking for him. The shopkeeper summoned a young Korean man who worked in his shop to interpret for him.

'I take it he's your son? He's clever. What would you think of me hiring him to run errands? I can't pay much. All I can offer is five nyang upfront and another five nyang when I send him back to you. But I can keep him clothed, and I'll feed him three meals a day. What do you say?'

Baekman's father considered what it would mean to have one less mouth to feed, and a practically full-grown mouth at that. He had four kids at home: Cheonman, Baekman, Shipman, and their little sister, Mageum. Their names meant Ten Million, One Million, Hundred Thousand, and Done. A hundred thousand was hardly small change — he must have thought that giving his sons such high-value names would guarantee him a windfall sooner or later. Cheonman, the oldest, was already a strapping fourteen-year-old who would soon be ready to do the work of a grown man, while Shipman was only six and still just a mouth to be fed, but Baekman, the second-oldest, was ten, which seemed old enough to experience the world. That's what his father figured, anyway. And besides, look at what their world had become. The Joseon kingdom had fallen and the country had come under Japan's control. He gave his second-eldest a pat on the head, told him that since he'd been born in difficult times, he'd have to work hard to earn his food, then took the five nyang and left Mapo.

Starting that very day, Baekman wrapped a Japanese hachimaki around his head, put on a vest embroidered with the name of the shop, and began his new job as an errand boy. He opened the shop in the morning, ran deliveries, carried boxes, cleaned, and gradually learned the ins and outs of the business, while also assisting the clerk with customers. He learned to speak basic Japanese and to read Japanese script. After about a year, he found himself growing sad whenever he thought of his family back home. His father stopped by Mapo once every few months, and the following spring Baekman worked up the courage to tell him he wanted to go home. His father's response was simple:

'All right, then let's hop on a fishing boat and head back.'

Back in Jisan-ri, life was as hard as ever, and the boredom worse than before he'd experienced the hustle and bustle of Mapo. He barely made it a year before he was as itchy to leave his hometown as a hot-to-trot country girl yearning for the excitement of the city. The worst part was that every time he spotted a fishing boat in the distance as it crossed Incheon Harbour, he would stare at its lights glowing in the dark and fight the urge to dive headlong into the sea and swim over to it.

'But what really showed me just how many marvellous things there are in this newly civilised world was the train.'

'When did you first see a train?'

'While working in Mapo.'

Baekman had seen his first train while accompanying the shopkeeper from Mapo to Yongsan. He saw metal arches spanning the river in the distance. As Baekman's jaw dropped open and his eyes widened, the shopkeeper had said, 'That's the Hangang Railway Bridge. It's something, isn't it?'

The shopkeeper boasted about how Japan was as advanced as the West, and that they had built that bridge seven years ago and laid a rail line all the way from Busan up to the capital, Gyeongseong, the year before last. Baekman and the shopkeeper decided to take the ferry back to the shop; as they boarded at the Samgae Ferry Landing, a black steel locomotive let out a deafening whistle and passed over the bridge. Even from that distance, the metallic screech of the train wheels rolling over the tracks and the rattling of the steel bridge were terrifically loud.

'Look a' that! Have you ever seen such a great hunk of steel fly like the wind? Nothing can outrace it — no horse, no bicycle, certainly not a rickshaw. It's so fast that if you glance away for a second and look back, it's already gone.'

Incheon was the last stop for trains from the capital. If not for the sea, the trains might have kept on going forever. Baekman had left home again and had been working for two months in a Japanese-owned inn in Incheon, in exchange for room and board but with little in the way of entertainment; one day, weary of the boredom, he headed out to the pier. A fishing boat had come in, and amid the hubbub, a Japanese man was yelling something at the fishermen, who cursed and grumbled to themselves in turn, muttering, 'What is that fool saying to us?'

Baekman stopped to interpret for them. 'He's asking you if the fish is for sale.'

'Only by the crateful. If he's looking for one or two fish for dinner, then tell him to go buy it at the fish shop.'

Baekman explained this to the Japanese man, who responded happily that he would purchase two crates. As Baekman passed the crates over to him, he saw that they were filled with pufferfish from the Imjingang River, which abounded at that time of year. Back home, as well, when the fish were in season, Baekman used to go all the way up to Dalgoji Cape and Yudo Island to catch pufferfish. Being in season only once a year, they were so expensive that fishermen would treat themselves to only a single pufferfish, sliced and served up raw after the catch, and even that was eaten grudgingly. They knew all too well how much they could make by selling it instead. The Japanese man handed over a wad of cash on the spot, and Baekman shouldered the two crates of fish without having to be asked. He knew how crazy the Japanese were for pufferfish. The Japanese man watched thirteen-year-old Baekman stagger under the weight of all that fish, then shook his head and took one of the crates and tucked it under his arm instead.

'Follow me,' the man said. 'I'll pay you for your help.'

Baekman trailed behind him to a rice mill in an alley not far from the pier. Japanese clerks and factory workers poured out of the building at their arrival, hoisted up the boxes, and cheered.

'We'll be drinking tonight!'

'This is a rare find! They call it "pork of the sea".'

The buyer of the fish waved Baekman over and offered him a few coins. It was enough to buy five hotteok pancakes, but he shook his head and refused it. The man frowned.

'What's wrong? Not enough?'

'It's not that, sir,' Baekman said. 'I'd rather you offer me a job.'

The man looked the boy over with fresh eyes.

'Why do you want to work here?'

Baekman considered the question for a moment, then said, 'I'd like to learn a skill.'

The man smiled.

'In that case, you would have to apprentice for a few years first, which means you don't get paid until you've learned the trade.'

'That's fine, sir. Please teach me everything I need to know.'

'What's your name, boy?'

Baekman puffed out his chest and said, 'Yi Baekman, sir!'

Then he repeated his name in his best attempt at Japanese, 'Ni Hyakuman!'

The moment he introduced himself as 'Two Million', the mill employees burst into laughter. Baekman explained that he was from Ganghwado Island and that he'd apprenticed as an errand boy in a Japanese shop in Mapo. And that was how he got himself a job at the Yoshida Rice Mill. He started out by assisting several of the engineers. He kept their tools organised and did other odd jobs for them, such as oiling, tightening, or cleaning parts, as well as helping out on the line wherever the workers happened to be short of hands while processing the rice. He ate, slept, and lived inside the mill, and hardly a few months passed before everyone was coming to him for help. They complained when he wasn't available and griped at whoever was foolish enough to send him away on errands when the mill was at its busiest.

The Yoshida Rice Mill maintained a separate labour force of machinists and engineers who were responsible for machining replacements for worn-out parts and performing regular inspections and repairs of all the belts and motors. Though it was nowhere near the scale of a flour mill, the slight variations in each piece of equipment at different points in the process meant that this was a modern factory with modern equipment, a far cry from older mills that ran out of small, single-room shops. The freshly harvested rice that gathered at the Port of Incheon was polished and refined at a dozen or so rice mills clustered nearby; Yoshida Rice Mill was one of the three largest. Baekman spent three years there learning the art of lathing. With remarkable dexterity, he cut and sculpted fine, delicate metal parts.

One day, Nakamura-san, who had more or less become Baekman's teacher, invited him out to a Chinese restaurant for a bowl of udon noodles. As they sat down across from each other, Nakamura said, 'I'm starting a new job on the lathe team for the Gyeongin Line. Skills like yours are rare to find, even among Japanese boys. Why don't you come work with me there?'

Having immediately fallen in love with trains back when he'd first laid eyes on one, Baekman marched straight back to Yoshida Rice Mill that very day and told his boss that he'd found a new job. His boss in turn confessed that while he was sad to see Baekman go, he had been of a mind to send Baekman to Japan for more advanced technical training and wished him well, with a parting gift of some cash, to boot.

Though Baekman was not an official employee of the railroad, merely a special assistant-in-training, he felt as proud and elated as a young scholar of yore who'd just aced the gwageo exam. Above all, he couldn't wait to learn all there was to know about the structure of the locomotive and how the engine worked. He lingered at work long after his shifts had ended, rushing over to the trains that came in for repairs, running his eyes and hands over every inch of them as he could, and soaking it all in. Nakamura-san told him that most of the locomotive was manufactured in the United States, which meant that the maintenance and repair work carried out in the rail works was entrusted to only the most experienced and highly trained technicians, while they were to pour their energy into manufacturing and producing the rest of the train carriages.

The year Baekman turned eighteen, he married the daughter of a workman who travelled back and forth between there and the salt farms of Juan. The scent of the mudflats always seemed to hang about her. A big woman with an even bigger voice, she gave birth to Hansoe, followed by his little brother, Dusoe, two years after, and she raised them well. Baekman became an official employee of the Railway Bureau five years after starting his traineeship and settled into his position at the Yeongdeungpo Rail Works. Baekman's wife, called Juan-daek after her hometown, began to put on weight around the time their first child was born. Ever since Baekman had become a full employee, she'd begun complaining of feeling hungry no matter what she ate and would often eat two lunches or more after he had left for work in the morning. One night, when Baekman was working the late shift, she boiled an entire sack of sweet potatoes and ate several while they were still hot, then woke in the middle of the night and ate another twenty or more. She rapped on her chest, complaining that she felt like something was caught in her throat, guzzled cold water, and then suddenly fell backwards. Baekman came home to find her sprawled on the floor, arms akimbo, legs on the threshold, jaw agape. Just like that, their children were without a mother. Baekman wondered what sort of illness could have left her feeling so ravenous all the time, but years later it was his sister, Mageum, who explained that she had probably died of loneliness, as Baekman had not loved his wife tenderly enough. Baekman had no idea what she was talking about. Mageum moved in with Baekman's young family in Yeongdeungpo at first so she could find work in a textile factory, but she ended up staying to raise his two boys and support him, rather than getting married herself. Then, when it seemed she might be an old maid forever, she married a carpenter. As for Baekman, his continuing fascination with crafting metal trinkets may have been due to losing his wife early and never remarrying.

Baekman told his grandson Jisan time and again, 'The railroad was built from the blood and tears of the people of Joseon.'

Becoming an apprentice to a Japanese engineer and working for the Gyeongin Rail Works was practically a miracle, but then again, Baekman had clearly been born with an unusual gift for machining. That summer, the Japan–Korea Annexation Treaty of 1910 was signed, and the country was officially swallowed whole by Japan. The Gyeongin Line, which ran east–west between Gyeongseong and Incheon, and the Gyeongbu Line, which ran north–south from Gyeongseong to Busan, had already been in operation for a while. Construction of the Honam Line, which ran south-west to Jeolla Province, began that year, and the Amnokgang Bridge was built to connect Joseon and Manchuria the following year. He remembered that the Gyeongwon Line, which ran north-east to Wonsan, and the Honam Line both opened the year before his eldest son, Hansoe, was born.

During his apprenticeship, Baekman bunked in the rail works and took his meals at a hamba near Yeongdeungpo Station. The hamba, or workers' canteen, had been run by the same married couple for many years. Yeongdeungpo had originally been a poor farming village where dozens of households grew vegetables, but when construction of the Gyeongbu Line had started ten years ago, workers began to migrate there from all over the country. Civil engineers, office workers, supervisors, and labourers working on the railway flooded in, followed by merchants, innkeepers, restaurateurs, and prostitutes. As the number of Japanese with money to burn increased, Koreans crowded in as well and found work doing odd jobs, hawking items in the street, serving food, selling booze, and peddling vegetables. Then, as Yeongdeungpo became the hub from which the Gyeongin and Gyeongbu Lines departed, fancy newfangled buildings were built near the station, including a post office, telegram office, and telephone exchange. Directly across from the station plaza, a residential area for the Japanese sprang up. On the other side of this downtown area, the Yeongdeungpo Market appeared, and the streets branching off the four-way intersection filled with shops, restaurants, taverns, and inns.

The couple who ran the hamba were a forty-year-old woman known as Anyang-daek, after her hometown of Anyang, and her husband, whom everyone called Foreman Min, from Siheung. The hamba served over twenty workers from the rail works, along with other regulars who made their living around the market, which meant that the place was usually packed. The building itself was an ordinary commoner's hanok, with small rooms arranged around an open-air courtyard. Diners crammed in wherever they could find space: in the kitchen, the main bedroom, the smaller bedroom, the porch, or on one of the two wooden decks that had been placed side by side in the tiny courtyard. The entire family — husband and wife and all their children — would roll up their sleeves and get to work serving customers. Foreman Min never talked down to Baekman but used instead the familiar-yet-respectful register of hage-che, seeing as how Baekman had a respectable job despite being such a young bachelor. When the last of the lunchtime customers had ebbed away, the family could relax from two to four in the afternoon, and once the dinner rush had subsided as well, they would wrap up their day around nine in the evening.

After six months of eating there every day, Baekman had become like family and would simply go to the kitchen to grab his own refills. One day, he had missed lunch due to some overtime work. He headed to the hamba late in the afternoon and sat on one of the decks to wait for his food when a jet-black blur streaked past his feet.

'What on earth was that?' Baekman exclaimed, hurriedly lifting his feet from the ground and looking around wildly. Anyang-daek poked her head out of the kitchen.

'That wicked rascal is back!'

The offender turned out to be a black cat. Though Koreans enjoyed raising dogs, there were countless folktales and legends about how cats were such resentful creatures that they would nurse grudges long after having got even with those who'd wronged them and would continue to seek their revenge. Needless to say, cats weren't exactly beloved pets; Koreans preferred to keep their distance. And yet the hamba was bedeviled by not just one or two but throngs of cats that gathered every single night and let out the strangest, most awful wailing, disturbing their sleep. From the main bedroom, Foreman Min said, 'It's visiting from the Japanese village across the street.'

He added that the Japanese had a weakness for cats.

'They must be well suited to each other.'

Anyang-daek added knowingly that the women and children of wealthy families living in civilised cities enjoyed keeping cats as pets.

The cat tiptoed through the courtyard and off towards the back of the house, as if to see if it preferred it over there.

Anyang-daek remarked to her husband as she brought Baekman's food to him, 'The fish is so fatty today, I thought the stove was going to catch fire.'

'Makes sense. That scamp must've smelled it cooking.'

'I put some salted corvina out to dry, but it kept disappearing. I had no idea who was taking them at first. Those damn cats have been driving me crazy! Someone needs to round them all up and get rid of them.'

A couple of days later, Baekman finished another late shift and didn't make it to the hamba until nearly nine o'clock. Anyang-daek brought out a cloth-covered tray.

'I kept your food near the stove to keep it warm, but I'm re-boiling the soup. I'll bring that out in a jiffy.'

She disappeared back into the kitchen; Baekman could hear her fussing at her husband.

'Ugh, that smells disgusting! Stop boiling it already!'

'You have to boil it way down to make it into medicine.'

Baekman had just started eating when Foreman Min joined him with a small tray of his own. The tray held a bowl filled to the brim with soup, which Min blew on to cool it. Next to the bowl were two small saucers of doenjang, or fermented soybean paste, and raw garlic.

While waiting for his soup to cool, Min muttered, 'This is medicinal. Restores your energy. You know what they say: nothing like tiger-bone soup to cure your aching bones!'

'Tiger-bone soup?'

Min cackled. 'Well, cats are basically baby tigers, aren't they?'

'Who the hell eats cats?' Baekman asked with a frown.

'Hey! I said it's *medicinal*. People eat snakes and centipedes and cicada larvae as medicine, too.'

Hearing that reminded Baekman of a man from his childhood village who'd been suffering from tuberculosis. He'd seen the man catch salamanders and eat them. The man would search between the rocks at the edge of a stream and catch them with his bare hands, squeezing the wriggling creatures between his thumb and forefinger as he opened his mouth wide. He'd drop them into his mouth, still alive, and those little creatures would swiftly disappear down his throat. After gulping it down, he would turn to look at the neighbourhood children and smile at them innocently, as if nothing were amiss. Baekman understood all at once that the soup Min had been hunched over for hours as it slowly boiled down was made from the black-furred scamp that had scurried past his feet.

'How'd you manage to catch something that moves that fast?'

Min smiled. 'Same way I used to catch rabbits in the countryside. I set a trap.'

At last, he raised the bowl of cooled soup to his mouth and took several long swigs, then dipped a clove of garlic into the soybean paste and ate it, smacking his lips with pleasure. He paused for a long moment and then swigged the rest of the bowl in one long gulp before eating more garlic.

'Smells awful,' Min said sheepishly. 'I wonder if that's because it was a male.' He pulled the shoulder of his shirt open to show Baekman a deep scar that ran from his shoulder down to his chest. 'Check this out. That's from a sword. Only reason I'm still alive is thanks to my wife.'

'*Aigu!* What happened?'

'What do you think happened? It was all on account of my hot temper. I know I shouldn't say this to someone lucky enough to get a job on the railway, especially a job that keeps them well fed, but those Japanese bastards did all sorts of terrible things while laying those rails.'

Min began to explain how he'd earned the nickname 'Foreman'.

'Like most other Koreans back then, I started out as a farmer. If you worked hard, then all you needed at the time to keep your family fed were two majigi of fields and six majigi of paddies. My father was from the yangmin class, but having lost his parents at a young age, on top of being the only son for three generations with no uncles to lean on for help, he'd ended up wandering here from another part of the country and scraping by as a tenant farmer. He pulled himself up by his bootstraps and eventually managed to purchase a little land of his own. I didn't get married until the age of twenty, when I met that woman over there. We had kids together, and life got a little easier as we got older, but then in came that railroad. I walked for miles, all the way to Yeongdeungpo Station, just to see that train making its way between Incheon and Noryangjin. Now I'm no chicken, so I only jumped a little bit the first time I saw it and calmed right back down again, but the guy I walked there with was so terrified that he dove under an oxcart and refused to come out. Ha ha! Anyway, that train was a hell of a sight. Steam billowing, engine thundering, wheels rattling. Chugga chugga! I've never seen anything so beastly as that great hunk of iron tearing down the tracks like a bolt of lightning. Soon after, they were laying rail lines all the way south from Seoul to Busan, and then north from Seoul to the Amnokgang River and on to Uiju.'

The entire country was upended. Vast stretches of field, paddy, forest, and village were commandeered without warning for laying tracks. The Japanese and Korean governments had signed a treaty, but having already lost their national sovereignty, the Korean government officials were mere agents, tools of the Japanese colonisers. The Japanese railroad company didn't stop at seizing the land alongside the tracks, but also designated large areas of land around the stations as belonging to the railroad. They claimed at first that they would reward the landowners at one-tenth the cost of their land, but following their declaration of war against Russia, the army simply took the land without any further pretence. With the Japanese army at their back, the Gyeongbu Railway Company engineers, the Japanese civil-engineering companies contracted by them, and the rail workers themselves took the land needed for the railway by force. The land grabbing worsened along the Gyeongui Line. Everywhere the rails went, thousands upon thousands of common folk found themselves kicked off their land. It was theft, no question about it. Even the piddling compensation that was offered as hush money in the early days went instead to lining the pockets of provincial bureaucrats and petty government officials. The common folk lost not only their land but also their homes, forests, and even their ancestors' graves, for almost nothing in return. Laying the Gyeongbu rail lines was a way for Japan, which had only recently modernised, to make up for its weak capital base by plundering all that land for the rails.

'One day, me and some of the other villagers went out to the fields only to find them filled chock-a-block with Japanese soldiers and workers. They were digging up all our rice plants. Everyone was crowding forward, trying to see what was going on, but all we could really do was stand there and kick the dirt. Those arseholes were stomping all over our fields and hacking away at our crops. A few villagers stepped forward to try to stop them, but the soldiers knocked them down and beat them to a pulp with their rifle stocks. Meanwhile, the translator kept giving us this speech about how the land had been seized by the railroad and if we were mad about it then we could take it up with the government office.'

Min and his fellow villagers marched straight over to the county office, with the head of the township leading the way, but the office was guarded by a wall of Japanese military police armed with bayonets, and none dared try to cross that line. Rumour had it that the just-ripened grain the Japanese had been hacking out of the earth was being used to feed their war horses. Naturally, the villagers put up a resistance, but the MPs had been stationed in every corner of the countryside. People whose houses had been razed to make way for the rails and the military garrisons were made homeless, and those who'd lost their farmland could do nothing but go and cry about it to the powerless Korean government. Officials would order them to disperse, and if they did not obey the first time, then they were clubbed mercilessly and forced to turn back.

Initial manpower was supplied by Korean civil engineering and construction firms contracted by the Gyeongbu Railway Company. Dozens of these firms were created in response to the sudden demand for railroad construction, with the boards of directors filled mostly with high-ranking officials of the former Korean Empire. They supplied everything needed for construction of the railway, from the manpower to the materials, including wood, stone, and coal, and even the workers' daily necessities, such as tobacco, rice, and other food. Employed within the firms were the office managers and staff, and below them were the field managers, crew chiefs, foremen, and labourers. The branch offices had provincial officials and staff, along with those employed to supervise the onsite workers. Japanese firms worked with Korean firms initially, but during the Russo-Japanese War, construction of the Gyeongbu and Gyeongui Lines became rushed, and the Japanese firms began to beat out the Korean firms, who lacked the necessary skill and expertise, and took the lead on most of the construction work. As the Korean firms collapsed, the managers alone were absorbed by the Japanese firms and tasked with recruitment and supervision. During the early days of rail work, most of the workers were there voluntarily, to make a day's wage, and while clashes did happen, the cause was usually that those wages were too low. But as construction continued, the labour system shifted from voluntary employment to forced conscription.

'I was friends with one of the petty officials, so I pleaded with him to help me get one-third of the market rate for the paddies that were taken from me. Half went to him, for his troubles, of course. Not much I could do about that. The way the world was turning, you couldn't survive off the land anymore, so I sold all my fields. Lucky for me, it was hilly ground far from the tracks, so I got a fair price for it. This country is full of people who had their entire family's fortunes seized and were forced out onto the road, but we were lucky. I went to the branch office at a construction site, offered the crew chief four chickens, and landed myself the title of foreman. I was also given permission to run a food cart in exchange for splitting the profits. At first, the workers and labourers were mostly Koreans, so all they needed was rice, soup, and kimchi. My wife was happy about that and took over the cooking. Food and materials were handled by people directly selected by the subcontracted firms, so I guess you could say I was one of them, seeing as how the crew chief was watching out for me. Plus, I could read. Couldn't make head nor tail of Japanese, but I knew enough Chinese characters to be able to read documents. Though I never made it to the rank of crew chief, I was at least high-ranking among the foremen. And having steady work made up a little for losing my land. But then I started to notice that there were fewer and fewer Koreans in the branch office, until eventually they were all replaced by Japanese. Everyone from the branch manager to the crew chiefs were Japanese. Then — damn it all! — they started hounding me to quit, saying I was too old. In just one or two months, the place was overrun with Japanese employees. I guess they'd all but finished building their own rails back at home, and shifted the whole kit and caboodle over here. The good days came to an end overnight.'

Min had long quit farming, and with no land left there was nothing for him to go back to. Min and his wife took their children to Siheung, where they threw together a shanty house near the marketplace and set up a food stall to sell gukbap soup. Making their living in the streets also meant having an ear to the ground. Wherever railroad construction took place, Japanese officials would descend upon the local government office to bully officials of the crumbling Korean Empire into giving them railway sleepers and stone blocks. Each county was forced to cooperate in mobilising workers for railroad construction. Horses and oxen were requisitioned for transportation, and chickens, pigs, and grain were extorted from each village. Korean men were taken from areas not only along the Gyeongbu and Gyeongui Lines but from areas hundreds of kilometres away. Hundreds and thousands of men were mobilised, usually for more than six months at a time, because they were unlucky enough to live near sections that required the construction of a bridge or tunnel. Koreans were forced to work regardless of holidays, ancestral rites, and busy farming seasons. Some villages were completely drained of able-bodied men who ought to have been bringing in the harvest, leaving the fields in ruins.

Most of the rail work was done during the war, when the Japanese government was eager to finish construction as quickly as possible, which meant that the Japanese overseers were short-tempered and impatient with the workers. Insistence turned to violence, and they began arming themselves with guns and bayonets and treating the Korean workers like oxen or dogs. If the workers slowed even the slightest, they were beaten mercilessly with clubs and kicked when they fell. At every construction site, these innocent people who'd been forced into labour worked day and night under the watch of Japanese military squads. Clashes broke out, and not only soldiers but also Japanese civilian employees and labourers began killing Koreans indiscriminately. They murdered them with guns and bayonets or beat them to death with their work tools. Their fellow labourers would be gunned down on the job, too, with no warning, for having supposedly stopped for a smoke break.

Ghosts began to appear near construction sites. Min saw one once. At the time, the men were excavating a tunnel beneath some low hills that cut across an open field. After rigging some dynamite inside the tunnel so they could dig out the next section, the night crew signalled for everyone to retreat. All that was left to do was trigger the ignition and await a thunderously loud explosion and great shower of rocks and dust. But, just then, one of the Korean labourers at the back of the pack gave a shout.

'Wait! Wait! Someone's still inside!'

The Japanese engineer, looking exhausted, asked what he'd said, and the interpreter explained.

'Which idiot's in there slowing us down?' the engineer hollered, racing towards the workers as the interpreter rushed to keep up.

'I heard someone inside shouting for help,' the labourer explained, then turned to the guy next to him. 'You heard it, too, right?'

'I heard someone calling for their mother.'

The interpreter conveyed this to the engineer, who exploded in anger.

'That just means some arsehole is hiding in there because he doesn't want to work!'

He ordered the foremen to go in and drag the man out. Min took a couple of other foremen with him and entered the tunnel. Carrying torches made from sticks with oil-soaked rags wrapped around the ends, they had to move carefully to avoid scraping themselves on the rough dirt walls and stones sticking out. They made it all the way to the end of the tunnel, where excavation had paused, but they saw no hint of another person in there.

'What the hell? There's no one here.'

'Guess they're so hungry, they're all hearing things.'

The tension broken, they turned to leave when Min heard a sound. It was faint but clear: a voice behind them, calling, 'Help meeee. Please help meee.' He stopped. The others looked like they'd heard it, too.

Min turned and shouted, 'Who's there?'

He aimed the torch this way and that, but all he saw was the blank face of the dirt wall blocking their way. And yet there it was: the sound of a man sobbing near the wall. Min had no idea who was the first to run, but all three of them were scrambling and tripping over each other to get out of that tunnel. Needless to say, that put an end to the night's work.

Min's wife, Anyang-daek, had an encounter, as well. Hot days, cold days, sunny days, and rainy days alike, she never failed to show up at the construction sites with food for the men. Once the next location for construction was selected, she would purchase seasonal vegetables from the nearest village, make kimchi, and cook up a storm, then head out on those country roads with the old man who drove her oxcart for her. One evening in late autumn, when she was running late for the dinner service, the sun long set and the sky dark, a freezing rain began to fall. It was the kind of weather where the cold would find its way under your layers of clothes no matter how hard you tried to keep it out. The old man was perched on the front of the oxcart, urging the oxen on with gentle clucks of his tongue, while Anyang-daek sat in the back of the cart with the food, her legs hanging over the edge. In the distance, she saw someone walking towards the cart. The person appeared to be wearing a simple cotton skirt and top with a kerchief wrapped around their head. How is that woman walking so fast? she wondered. No sooner was the thought in her head than the woman had caught up to the cart and whipped past it! She thought she saw the woman eyeing her.

'*Aigooo*, what on earth *was* that?'

Startled, she leaned over and peered around the front of the cart, but there was no sign of the woman. She sat back up and there the woman was, back behind the cart and walking towards them again. Scared out of her wits, Anyang-daek called for the old man to stop the cart and, unable to explain what she'd seen, asked if she could sit up-front next to him instead. The story didn't end there. When the cart arrived at the construction site, the men lined up and Anyang-daek began dishing up their food. Theirs was one of ten food carts in total, so her work was over in only an hour. She was putting away the leftovers when someone suddenly loomed up out of the darkness.

'Pleeeease give me food.'

Anyang-daek looked up to see the woman standing just a few steps away. The same woman as before, with her white kerchief and soiled clothes. Unable even to shriek, Anyang-daek passed out from shock. When she eventually came to and got back up, the ghost had vanished.

There was one village, a large one, with 700 or so households in it. One day, the Japanese military showed up and tried to force the villagers to go to work for them, raping and killing as they went. The survivors all fled, and the place became a no-man's-land. But then rumours began to spread that the deceased had reappeared where the railroad was being built and had retaken their village. Workers out walking at night saw lights blazing in every window and heard whispers and raucous laughter, and floating above the thatched roofs were vague shapes that could have been smoke, could have been fog. Even after the tracks were completed, no living person returned to that village, and anyway the surrounding land was unusable after it had all been taken away. A few years later, a small train station was built there, along with a coal yard.

As the rails were laid, the common folk of Joseon — who'd had their land stolen, suffered as slave labour, and saw their family members slaughtered — began to rise up all over the country in tenacious opposition to the construction of rail lines and the operation of the trains. At the same time, the militias that had arisen in response to the nation's ruin and loss of sovereignty also made the railroads their prime target.

'Near Yeongdeungpo Station, people disguised as peddlers would pile heated roof tiles onto the tracks, causing train carriages to collide. We saw this happen with our own eyes. Anyone caught in the act was executed on the spot by firing squad. They also covered the tracks with gravel and planted gunpowder. At night, they would move the stone blocks from the construction site and place them across the tracks, causing the locomotive to detach from the coach carriages, derail, and fall over. In our county, as well, scores of Japanese soldiers were killed and injured that way.'

Toppling telegraph poles along the tracks and cutting the wires became an everyday occurrence, in response to which Japan proclaimed articles of war regarding the protection of electricity transmission and railroads: anyone caught sabotaging the rails or failing to report a saboteur would be executed; catching a saboteur would earn an award of twenty won; informing on and aiding in the arrest of one, an award of ten won; all villagers were responsible for protecting the railroads and telegraph lines that ran along them, but the village chief was responsible for assigning teams of two to patrol the rails; in the event that the rails or telegraph lines were damaged but no one was arrested, the team that had been assigned to patrol that day would be flogged and jailed instead; and in the case of secondary damage to part of the village, reports would be made to the Korean government and severe punishments would be imposed. However, these proclamations didn't stop the militia from forming troops of hundreds of men from every corner of the country and attacking the railway stations and railway construction sites.

Min told the story of how he'd ended up being stabbed in the shoulder.

'Construction of the Gyeongbu Line was almost done, so that must've been around mid-September. Ever since the start of construction, more and more people in Siheung County had been forced into labour every year. We were among those who'd been rounded up to work on the rails, and our wages and expenses were supposed to be split with the village. The amount we were ordered to collect jumped from a few hundred nyang to 3,000 nyang. That's not taxation, that's extortion. Meanwhile, the rumour mill was going wild: some were saying the army had gobbled up tens of thousands of nyang since they'd started recruiting farmers, others that the county clerks had pocketed the money that was supposed to pay for all the workers' daily food costs. Ten thousand people rose in protest after a clever neighbourhood official sent out a round-robin letter that inspired everyone to join forces. They marched to the county office in the afternoon, but the governor must have sent out an SOS, because the Japanese were waiting with their swords and iron batons at the ready. When the citizens raised their voices in protest at the governor, the Japanese began swinging their katanas and batons without any warning and attacking the Koreans. Those at the front were beaten and slashed and badly injured. One guy had his ear torn off, another got his skull crushed, and still another was stabbed in the shoulder and bled to death the next day. In the first wave of the melee alone, one died on the spot and nine were left injured. We were driven out of the county office, but we regrouped and rushed back in, throwing stones.'

'*Aego*, just the thought of those days makes me shake with fear all over again!' Anyang-daek said resentfully, clucking her tongue. 'I begged you not to get carried away, but you'd had too much to drink at lunch that day.'

The excitement in Min's voice faded.

'Anyway, if it weren't for her, I'd've died that day, too.'

Min was in the rear of the charging crowd. Those in the lead swarmed into the county office, killed the governor and his son, smashed up everything inside the building, and set it on fire. The seething crowd chased down the Japanese who were trying to flee and beat two of them to death. The other Japanese who'd hid when they were unable to escape at first took off running in the opposite direction only to be chased by the emboldened protesters. This was when Min grabbed a club and went off in pursuit. In an alley lined with neatly mortared stone walls, the Japanese suddenly doubled back, and Min came to a halt and glanced around to realise that there were only three or four others with him, not enough to stand their ground. Two of the Japanese who were armed with katanas rushed in for the attack. Min came to his senses and turned to run, but something seemed to flash past him like a burst of light. A second person was stabbed as well, which made the other two or three think twice about rushing in and gave the Japanese a chance to run away. Min was face down on the ground, bleeding, when his wife found him in the alley. She'd grown impatient and decided to go out in search of him. She tore a strip of cloth from the hem of her skirt and wrapped it around her husband's shoulder several times to try to stem the blood gushing from his shoulder, then pleaded for help from others to carry him to the doctor in the marketplace. The crooked gash was sewn shut and an ointment applied, after which he spent a month in bed waiting for the swelling to subside and the wound to heal. His collarbone must have been broken, too, because his left arm never was of much use anymore but just hung there limply. His badly healed shoulder plagued him for years. But thanks to his wife, he'd since become an old hand at running an eatery.

'Since I was at the rear of the march, I escaped with only this injury, but everyone who'd led the charge was arrested. An entire platoon of Japanese soldiers was sent in to capture and arrest everyone. That was just the start of their sufferings. In the end, they were all put on trial and not only imprisoned but also forced to pay damages, which left their families penniless. So what else could the railroad have been built from if not the blood and tears of the people of Joseon?'

3

The story of how Yi Jino's great-grandfather Yi Baekman met his wife, Juan-daek, was a curious one.

At eighteen, Baekman was still a trainee at the rail works in Yeongdeungpo, barely making enough to put food in his mouth. The rest of the family had moved from Jisan-ri to Incheon with his elder brother, Cheonman, who had recently married and found work on a coastal freighter. One day, Cheonman sent a telegram: 'Father very ill, come quickly.' Baekman showed the telegram to his Japanese foreman and received a two-day leave. As the breadwinner, Cheonman may have been on a freighter, but at the green age of twenty-two, he was a mere assistant to the engineer. The youngest of the three brothers, Shipman, was clever like Baekman and tried to pitch in by working as a clerk at a rice exchange. He later made money from running his own rice store and was the first of the brothers to establish himself.

By the time Baekman made it to the family's house at the top of the hill in Songnim-jeong, their father had already passed away. Mourners were scarce since they were far from their hometown. Apart from family members, one or two of Cheonman's fellow crewmen were there drinking soju. Mageum poked her head out of the kitchen to greet Baekman.

Their father's death had come unexpectedly in his middle years. He lost his wife early, but the man knew how to earn his keep. Even on days when he ended up without a penny, he never came home empty-handed. Recently, he'd been going to the fish market. A skipper he knew well from his days on a croaker boat had become a chief auctioneer there. He sold all the unwanted fish left over from each auction to Baekman's father for cheap. Every day, Baekman's father would load a few boxes of the leftover fish on his bicycle and head to bars or restaurants near the city's edge to sell the fish for slim margins. He got a kick out of it because although he made a pittance, that pittance came every single day, slowly fattening his wallet until it equalled a worker's monthly wage.

Two days before his death, the auction was almost over by the time he reached the market. The favoured fish was sold out and only a couple of boxes of rockfish, greenling, and pomfret were left, plus three monkfish. He couldn't help noticing that one of the three monkfish looked especially plump and juicy. Not long after he rode off with the boxes of fish strapped to the back of his bicycle, he heard a *splat-splat*. More *splat-splats* were followed by a *crrr-crrroak*. Baekman's father somehow suspected that the croaking was coming from the monkfish. Different ports called the fish by different names, including snailfish and scorpion fish, but regardless, a monkfish was a monkfish. He'd heard of bullheads grunting but never of monkfish croaking like a frog or toad. Upon arriving at his favourite bar, he began unloading the bike when he heard another *splat-splat* come from the box at the very bottom. He cleared all the other boxes on top and removed the lid from the bottom box.

The three monkfish lay in a row; the largest one seemed to be responsible for all the noise as it flapped its tail left to right against the sides of the box. Baekman's father muttered, 'You're one tough sucker, aren't you!' Then it occurred to him that eating this sucker might be great for boosting stamina. He thought of Cheonman, who always said he was tired, and his wife, who'd just given birth to their first child, not to mention Shipman, Mageum, and himself, drinking his days away on the brink of fifty. 'All right,' he thought, 'today I'll boil this sucker down to feed everyone and help my daughter-in-law's milk to come in.' He left the largest monkfish in the box and threw its limp friends into a different box of leftover fish.

After finishing his usual round of deliveries, he pulled up a seat at the bar, poured himself a large bowl of soju from a jumbo bottle, and drank it slowly with some rockfish stew. He spent at least an hour and a half at the bar before getting back on his bike to head home. During the ride, he heard more *splat-splats* and *crrroaks*. 'Huh, this sucker's a beast!' Baekman's father left his bike at the store at the bottom of the hill and walked the rest of the way with the fish. At the sound of an especially urgent *crrrrroak*, he put the box down and peeked under the lid. The monkfish with huge eyes on either side of its head broke into a wide smile. Baekman's father was taken aback but managed to catch his breath as he stared at the monkfish. When he told the family about the fish's smile, no one believed him. They said he must have been too drunk to see anything in the dark, but when Baekman heard about it later he thought there might be some truth to the story. After all, stranger things had happened before.

Back when he had lived in Jisan-ri, on Ganghwado Island, Baekman witnessed the old woman next door butcher a rooster, probably for a special occasion. She had come out to the front yard, holding a plump rooster by the wings in one hand and a knife in the other. She placed the bird on the stump used to chop firewood, aimed for its neck, and struck without hesitation. The head dropped, and blood sprayed with such unexpected intensity that the old woman leapt back and dropped the rooster. The headless rooster jumped off the stump and began to run around the yard. At the old woman's scream, her sons rushed out to chase it. The bird sprinted around the yard for a while then flapped its wings and flew into an apricot tree. It landed on a high branch and perched there without a stir, as if it were just taking a little break. And there it remained for three days, because no one could reach it. By the time one of the sons finally managed to borrow a ladder from far away and brought down the headless rooster, it was stiff as a board. No one in the family was willing to eat it, so the old woman found a nice sunny spot to bury it in.

Anyway, Baekman's father was staring at the monkfish when it suddenly moved its lips and muttered, 'Damn you, damn you, damn you.' Make no mistake, the fish swore at him. Out of shock, he grabbed it by the tail and slammed it down on the ground. The fish grew limp and again moaned, 'Daaaaaaamn you.' Mageum said she'd heard their father rustling about in the yard before he kicked open the kitchen door, dashed across the dirt floor, and thrust the black object he'd been clenching with both hands into the cauldron.

'Get the fire going now, hurry.'

He kept muttering 'more fire, more fire' as his arms pressed down hard on the cauldron lid, and rambling on about the strange monkfish to Mageum, who was pushing pieces of wood into the furnace to rekindle the flame. She couldn't help but giggle at the amusing tale their father spun as she squatted before the furnace. At any rate, she added sliced radish, minced garlic, chopped spring onion, and a dash of chilli powder to cook a tasty stew. But then their father said he wasn't feeling too good, and he went to his room to lie down and didn't get up even when the whole family gathered around the table for supper. Cheonman told the others not to wake him. He said nothing is more delicious than sleep to a tired man. When Mageum went to wake their father the next day, he wasn't breathing.

She didn't share the story with any of the mourners but whispered it to Baekman.

'The monkfish must have been the messenger of death. You know how they say those messengers can turn up as anything.'

The reason for bringing up Baekman's father's death and funeral, right in the middle of explaining how Baekman met his wife, is that one of the people who came to offer their condolences, saying he was an old friend of their father's, ended up becoming Baekman's father-in-law. The family had placed the coffin on the cooler side of the room, and without a nice folding screen to cover it, they instead propped a clothes hanger askew to drape a sheet in front of the coffin. Just as they were finished, a man five feet tall with wide shoulders and a habit of punctuating his words with a snort came in.

'*Hmph hmph*, so I'm, I mean, I'm a friend of your father's. Anyway, *hmph hmph*, this is so unexpected. I heard the news from the chief auctioneer yesterday at the fish market. Here today, gone tomorrow, *hmph hmph*. No wonder they say death lies just outside the gate, *hmph hmph*.'

The man never gave his name, so whenever Shipman talked about that day, he referred to him as Manny Ajeosshi, a nickname he had come up with since he couldn't quite wrap his head around calling this guy his brother's father-in-law. The nickname was supposed to rhyme with 'manhood' to joke that the man was no taller than a penis, but it also echoed the names Cheonman, Baekman, and Shipman, which made it sound like he was a genuine member of the family. Manny Ajeosshi used to work on the same fishing boat as their father, and when the two discovered they were the same age, they let go of honorifics and became friends. Manny Ajeosshi later landed a job at a salt farm in Juan. He lived just to the north, in another neighbourhood full of poor people scraping by on daily wages. After sitting quietly for a while, Manny Ajeosshi made an announcement to the three brothers.

'So, *hmph hmph*, I got paid today. *Hmph*, you know, I'm feeling down and not like my usual self, so, *hmph hmph*, I'll buy you boys a drink. Why don't we go now, get some barbecued meat, too? *Hmph*.'

Cheonman turned around and gave Baekman a look. Baekman took the cue and followed Manny Ajeosshi out. As they went down the hill, Manny Ajeosshi walked with a swagger in his shoulders that made him look like some kind of celebrity athlete.

'*Hmph hmph*, it's delivery day for a butcher shop in my neighbourhood. I mean, you know, they're getting a whole cow delivered from the slaughterhouse today, *hmph hmph*. It's close by, so we'll go there, *hmph hmph*.'

Baekman had no choice but to tag along. The shop was a hole in the wall at the edge of a neighbourhood to the north of theirs. The owner was an old man with a shaved head like any other butcher in those days. There were two tables made of wooden boards, and hanging from hooks above their heads were bright-red fillets, ribs, legs, and the like. Manny Ajeosshi didn't use honorifics to the muscular owner despite their apparent age difference.

'Is the, you know, special cut of liver available?'

'Special cut? Ah, that's been reserved, so you'll have to go elsewhere.'

'*Hmph hmph*, who reserved it?' asked Manny Ajeosshi with his head held high.

The butcher smirked as if to say, What's it to a small potato like you?

'Foreman Gang from the loading dock.'

Manny Ajeosshi grinned.

'Oh, he won't be a problem. We'll take it, *hmph*.'

'But he'll be here soon.'

Manny Ajeosshi hissed angrily through his teeth until the butcher stopped arguing and served them the whole thing. The glossy, supple lobe was the size of a small melon.

'*Hmph*, you can only get this, you know, when they butcher a whole cow. It comes from the side of the liver and tastes better than anything, *hmph hmph*.'

A knife, a cutting board, a dipping dish of sesame oil and salt, and a large bottle of cheap soju were also brought to their table. The lobe made a crisp sound as Manny Ajeosshi sliced it; it sounded more like slicing an apple than meat. Baekman would later say that he learned how to drink from his father-in-law, who had no doubt squandered his money on fast living but was resolute when he had to be. The Japanese referred to this type of person as 'assari'. The shop's wooden door slid open and a burly man appeared with two workers. When his eyes met Manny Ajeosshi's, he quickly bowed.

'Seongnim, you here for a drink?'

'*Hmph hmph*, what are you doing here?'

The man, who was big enough to fill the doorway, had greeted him with respect, but Manny Ajeosshi paid no attention.

'I heard you, *hmph hmph*, reserved this?'

'What? Uh, no, of course … not.'

'*Hmph*, I'm a regular here.'

'Yes, I see, we'll leave you to it and go elsewhere.'

The butcher watched their encounter in disbelief. He would have never expected to see a Goliath like Foreman Gang, who had the dock workers under his thumb, truckle to a David like Manny Ajeosshi. And yet, there's bound to be a match for everyone.

'*Hmph hmph*, get us a small cut of that, that thingummy, you know, the skirt steak, some neck chain, and, *hmph*, tenderloin,' said Manny Ajeosshi to the butcher, who still looked dumbfounded.

Without another word, the butcher got to cutting and brought the meat over with a grill laid over a charcoal brazier.

'So, I usually drink three litres of soju, but today let's just have two litres and enjoy some barbecued meat, *hmph hmph*.'

When Baekman was half-canned, he mustered the courage to ask Manny Ajeosshi how he managed to trump the brawny fellow he'd sent away from the butcher's shop.

'*Hmph hmph*, well there's not much to it. Small men like us have our own tricks.'

Big guys were used to wrestling their way to the top. In a neighbourhood fight, they would use their size to reach down and throw their opponent over. So all a little guy had to do was slide under quick and grab his opponent by the balls. One good squeeze, and all that muscle would turn to pulp. A couple of more squeezes and a 'Now who's your Seongnim?' followed by a 'You still thinking about coming at me again if I let go?' One final, mighty squeeze, and the strongman was sure to yelp and squeal in pain, 'Please, Seongnim, mercy!'

'*Hmph hmph*, I, uh, you know, taught him a lesson that way at the dock once.'

Baekman became completely drunk on the quality meat and all the liquor Manny Ajeosshi offered. Not only did he slur, but his arms and legs wobbled like the limbs of an octopus. He had to be propped up and nearly dragged to Manny Ajeosshi's two-room house. Around dawn, his eyes shot open to a bolting slap in the face. The room was brightly lit by candles. He was still hungover, but he could clearly feel the tip of a sharp knife being pressed against his throat.

'*Hmph*, wake the hell up, you son of a bitch, *hmph!*'

'*Egumeoni!*'

He heard a woman squeal right next to him. When he turned to look, a half-naked woman leapt out of bed and raced out the door, wailing in embarrassment, her face buried in her hands. Manny Ajeosshi's strength was unbelievable for his size — he already had both of Baekman's arms pinned down and a knife to his throat.

'Now that you've slept with my precious daughter, *hmph hmph*, will you marry her or not? *Hmph*.'

Baekman had no idea what was going on, but for now he had to save his own neck, so he choked out a yes. Satisfied with Baekman's answer, Manny Ajeosshi quietly slipped out of the room. Baekman tossed and turned until it grew bright enough outside to leave. As he was getting ready, the door opened and Manny Ajeosshi came in after his daughter, who carried a breakfast tray.

'Well, *hmph hmph*, after what's happened, there's no point in wasting time. I'll go meet your brother Cheonman today to break the news, *hmph*.'

Manny Ajeosshi then extolled his daughter's virtues. Despite growing up without a mother, the poor thing, she'd never given her father any cause to worry and was skilled at cooking and cleaning. He added that the couple should get a one- or two-room house in Yeongdeungpo with the money he'd been saving for marriage expenses so that they wouldn't have to waste money on room and board. That's how Yi Baekman ended up marrying Juan-daek. Though he never was able to bring himself to confess to his family that he'd been tricked into marriage while blind drunk.

Later, when Hansoe was born, Manny Ajeosshi confided in Baekman after knocking back a few to celebrate the birth of his first grandson: '*Hmph hmph*, I, uh, you know, marked you out as my son-in-law the first time I laid eyes on you. In times as tough as these, *hmph*, you did good to gain a skill, *hmph hmph*. That's why I got you drunk and brought you over, *hmph*.'

The newlyweds rented a place at the very edge of a cluster of two-room houses, built for working folk like them, that had begun to pop up around the marketplace intersection. Baekman was finally made a formal assistant at the Yeongdeungpo Rail Works a couple of years after Hansoe was born. It had taken a good five years for him to shrug off the label of apprentice. For the Japanese, graduating from a technical secondary school was all it took to get accepted as engineer trainees, and even if they only managed to graduate from primary school, they could still become engineers after a three-year apprenticeship. But Koreans were never promoted to positions of authority.

True to Manny Ajeosshi's word, Juan-daek was a resourceful woman. An assistant's wage was barely enough for one person to get by, so it was nowhere near enough to pay the rent and, with the addition of their baby, feed a family of three. Juan-daek started to make visits to her father every day. She didn't visit to ask him for money but to accompany him to the wholesale fish market in Incheon. There, she bought fish to sell, and in May and June she went straight to the boats docking at the pier to buy live shrimp that she pickled at home. She bought the salt that she needed for pickling in bulk from her father. Naturally, the house always reeked of fish. The Japanese liked to fry, braise, or stew fish for breakfast, so Juan-daek would sell them horse mackerel, grey mullet, herring, sardines, and pomfret. She also brought for her Japanese customers the pricier snappers and blowfish when they were in season, plus shrimp, crabs, clams, short-necked clams, and oysters. Five to six jars of salted shrimp were buried in the dugout hut in their yard until early winter, when it would be sold during the kimchi-making season. At first, Juan-daek went door to door, selling fish out of a basket she carried on her head, in the Japanese neighbourhood beside the train station. Later, she began taking orders instead and hired a young man to deliver the fish, using a large A-frame carrier strapped to his back. Before long, she secured a spot in the market and opened a fish stall.

Long after Juan-daek passed, Baekman would sometimes share stories about her talent for sales, which was the inspiration for Hansoe's wife, Shin Geumi, to start a clothing stall in the market. Apart from Baekman, the only family members who remembered Juan-daek were his sister, Mageum, and his father-in-law, Manny Ajeosshi, who showed up once every few years whenever there was an occasion to celebrate. Only when Uncle Manny stopped visiting did the family belatedly learn that he had passed. Juan-daek was thereafter remembered simply as Hansoe and Dusoe's mother, but it was Mageum Gomo, or Aunt Mageum, who talked about her the most. Mageum Gomo was the one who told Geumi as well as Hansoe and Dusoe about how Juan-daek died from choking on sweet potatoes she'd snacked on in the middle of the night.

Many years later, after finishing his training at the railway academy, Hansoe moved into the rail workers' housing, but Baekman was reluctant to join his son. He was uncomfortable with the fact that most of the residents were Japanese and some were former supervisors. Besides, he'd grown fond of the Willow Tree House. Standing at the end of an alley behind the marketplace intersection, the house was the very place he and his wife first rented as a couple. The willow tree, which had been there before the house was built, grew lusher with each year in its spot next to the gate. The house had a maru — a common room in the centre with one side open to the courtyard — with a bedroom on either side, and next to the front gate was the outhouse and a tiny room where workers could stay, which Juan-daek had added onto the house when she opened her fish stall. Although there was barely enough space for one worker to lie down in that eight-square-metre room, the salt jar was always kept there. The dugout where salted shrimp jars were buried took up half of the courtyard. Anyway, Juan-daek eventually bought that house with the money she made from selling fish and salted seafood. Anyone visiting the house would be told to look for the willow tree at the corner, and the family took to calling the place the Willow Tree House.

Manny Ajeosshi was small but scrappy, with nerves of steel and balls of iron. He also possessed a formidable gift of gab. Edifying his son-in-law on the art of combat was his ongoing project.

'*Hmph hmph*, it doesn't help much to, *hmph*, keep your mouth shut when you're fighting. Every fight is half fists, half words. If your opponent is holding a knife, be cool and say, *Why are you waving that little thing at me? Run on home and use it to peel some fruit for your kids instead, huh?* Just tell yourself, if he's waving a knife around then he's only got one hand free. Even if you get knocked down, don't give up. Just look for an opening from the ground. If he tries to kick you, grab his foot. If he grabs you by the collar to pull you up, go for a headbutt. And while you're at it, keep the trash talk coming. *Your luck's run out today, boy, 'cause I can tell, you're scared as shit.*'

Juan-daek, on the other hand, was a woman of few words. She towered over her father by the time she was ten. Her broad shoulders and long, muscular limbs were accustomed to lifting and moving jarfuls of salted shrimp, a task most men would struggle to perform on their own. Her husband gained permission from his co-workers at the train station to let her ride the freight trains on the Gyeongin Line. She'd leave at daybreak and return in the afternoon, travelling back and forth to Incheon once every two or three days. When all she had to carry was an empty basket, she'd sometimes take a passenger train to Incheon and return on a freight train.

A porter for freight trains once told Baekman about an accident he'd witnessed. Small cargo bound for the trains could be moved around on two-wheeled carts, but large cargo had to be brought all the way into the station and right up to the trains with the help of a mule. One day, as Juan-daek waited on a freight train with an empty basket on her lap, a wagon drawn by a mule with muscular legs and a bristly mane approached. The driver parked the wagon, placed rocks against the wheels to keep them from moving, and waited for the porters to load the cargo onto the train. The porters flocked to the wagon. One of them climbed onto the wagon to hoist the cargo onto the other men's shoulders. Startled, the donkey stamped its feet in agitation and tried to pull away. The driver clucked his tongue and tightened his grip on the reins, but it was too late. With a loud creak and a groan, the axle cracked, tipping the cart to one side and sending the porter tumbling to the ground. The mule jumped in surprise. The driver broke into a sweat as he pulled harder at the reins. Another porter tried to wedge a rock under the other wheel, which was also starting to wobble, but the whole thing gave way and the wagon collapsed onto him. Some of the cargo had already fallen off, but the weight of what remained must have been considerable. His legs kicked and flailed and then went still, as if he'd passed out. That's when Juan-daek rushed in. She got down on one knee, tucked a shoulder under the end of the wagon, and hoisted it right up off the ground! The other men grabbed their friend by the legs and pulled him free.

'Your wife turned a bit red in the face, but other than that, she just stood there propping up that wagon. She looked as calm as a toad after it snags a fly,' said the porter who told Baekman the story.

Baekman wasn't surprised at all. Back when the couple were newlyweds, living in their tiny, one-room rental, they were going at it one night, Baekman on top of his wife, pounding his way to the finish line, when he heard a loud thud and a crash from behind and the door fell on top of him. Juan-daek, who'd been writhing beneath him, had grown so aroused that she'd lifted both legs high and kicked the door down. Anyway, Baekman wasn't used to talking much at home and Juan-daek was also a woman of few words, so their place was usually as tranquil as a temple. After Baekman took to spending even his days off crafting and polishing small items at home, Juan-daek grew even quieter. She took to fattening herself up instead, stuffing her mouth full of whatever she could get her hands on. She would lift one bum cheek and let out a long, luxurious fart. Mageum Gomo could never talk about it without giggling first and adding how Juan-daek's farts would make the paper weather strips around the door tremble.

When he was growing up, Yi Jisan had heard stories about his father, Ilcheol, going out to the Hangang River with his grandfather Baekman to look at the water — later, Jino was told the same stories, too. The stories, of course, concerned the five or more years of flooding along the Hangang, including Saetmal. Most people found it hard to believe that a place could flood so badly so many years in a row, but Jisan's family had witnessed it firsthand.

Yeongdeungpo was originally sandy land that became waterlogged during the summer, leaving the ground in a muddy state nearly all year around except for the winter. No wonder the residents of Yeongdeungpo had long called the area Jindeungpo, or 'Mud-deungpo', from the days when straw sandals were their only option. In fact, Jindeungpo was a mild nickname compared to Jukmaru, or 'Mush-maru', inspired by the way the rain turned the dirt roads into porridge. Once factories began churning out rubber shoes, rubber boots, and Japanese split-toe jika-tabi boots, men would joke that you could survive in Jindeungpo without a wife but not without a pair of boots.

The year before the first of the big floods, the March 1st Independence Movement broke out nationwide. The district of Yeongdeungpo was one of Gyeongseong's key hubs — the Gyeongbu and Gyeongui Lines crossed paths there — so its streets were always teeming with people and goods. Rumours from all over the country tended to reach the area within a day or two. Word about the simultaneous protests in downtown Gyeongseong and around Gyeonggi Province spread like wildfire throughout the street market. Folks itching for revolution, as well as those itching simply for a spectacle, journeyed across the footbridge over the Hangang to meet relatives or friends living in downtown Gyeongseong and came back to confirm the rumours by sharing what they each saw or heard. In the ten years that Baekman had spent in Yeongdeungpo, Koreans had lost their country, but pockets of armed resistance continued to appear. These 'righteous armies' fired on Japanese troops and sometimes set bombs, only to be captured and killed or end up taking their own lives, leaving behind deeply painful memories for the Korean people. Those memories, however, would slowly fade with the seasons until they drowned in a stream of ordinary, uneventful days. The same went for natural disasters. Like the flooding of the Hangang, which happened every summer like clockwork.

As spring turned to summer, people would be reminded of the coming monsoon rains and start to worry about the safety of their homes. After work, Baekman would eat supper and take Hansoe by the hand to head out to the riverside at dusk. There, the water would reflect the glow of the setting sun bouncing off Bukhansan Mountain and Namsan Mountain in the distance, the western sky behind Seonyudo Island flaming a deep red. The Hangang forked around Yeouido Island, sending a strand of itself called Saetgang along the edge of Yeongdeungpo, before rejoining its waters at the Yanghwa Dock. To the west was the Anyangcheon Stream, which flowed into the Hangang and divided the district from Yeomchang at the lower end of the stream called Omongnae. Which meant that Yeongdeungpo was sandwiched between two streams and the river they fed into. The northern banks of the Hangang, lining the districts of Mapo and Yongsan, were likewise mostly sand. When the rain began to come and go and the sky to cloud over and clear again, it meant the monsoon season had arrived. The sound of raindrops falling from the eaves didn't bother young Hansoe. Instead, their cozy rhythm lulled him to sleep.

But that night, thunder and lightning boomed as if the world were being turned upside down, and the sky unleashed sheets of rain until morning. Baekman kept a worried eye on the sky on his way to work, the wind making it impossible for him to stay dry. It was a time when the only available options were a bamboo hat or a straw cape. There were umbrellas made of oil paper, but those were only for Japanese women, and raincoats had not yet been introduced.

Hansoe was eight and Dusoe was six. Hansoe didn't start primary school until he was ten, so before that he passed the time playing with other kids in the neighbourhood and looking after his brother while their mother was out selling fish. Juan-daek's affection for her boys was such that whenever it rained, snowed, or got too windy, she'd stay at home with them instead of going to work. This was why Hansoe would be in an especially good mood on rainy days. Not only did they get to spend the whole day with their mother, but she'd cook all sorts of treats for them, in addition to their regular meals, and snack with them all day until their father returned home. She made millet pancakes and potato pancakes, grilled or steamed corn, sweet potatoes, and pumpkin, and she pounded sweet rice to make injeolmi and jeolpyeon rice cakes. In the evening, unaware of why the boys would stop eating their suppers after only a few bites, Baekman would check the boys' foreheads for fever and rub their bellies. Hansoe kept quiet because of the promise they'd made to their mother, but Dusoe sometimes spilled the beans.

'We ate tteok.'

Baekman nodded at the confession as if he'd suspected as much, and chided his wife.

'You're spoiling them. And you need to be more frugal. Wasting perfectly good rice to make tteok when it's not even a special day? What will the neighbours think?'

Juan-daek would silently scoop huge spoonfuls of rice into her mouth to keep from having to answer. All the while glaring at Dusoe.

With that, Baekman would say no more and head over to his workshop to bury himself in his metalwork.

'One of these days, I'm gonna throw all those damn scraps of metal away,' Juan-daek would mutter, not caring whether the kids heard her or not.

But the rain that day was no ordinary monsoon rain. It poured without a single break or pause all through the night and into the next day, sending bucketloads of water down on them. Their house was at the dead end of an alley where the sunlight only made brief visits, so it was difficult to notice what was going on out there beyond the alley. Juan-daek wasn't too happy about the fact that her husband went to work like a straight arrow instead of staying at home with his family on such a day.

'Stubborn man, I wonder where he expects to find us if we get swept away with our house,' she griped.

Little did she know her words would come true. When the rain wouldn't stop and the sky grew darker in the afternoon, Juan-daek made up her mind to find out what was happening. She dragged an empty jar over to the wall of the house, balanced a log on top of it, and used that to clamber up onto the roof. She crawled up to the ridge, careful not to break any roof tiles, and took a look. An alarming sight awaited her. Though their alleyway was still safe, probably because they were on slightly higher ground than around the market, everywhere else was knee-deep in muddy water. If it continued to rise, they would be trapped there in the alley. Juan-daek quickly made her way back down.

'I'll be right back. Stay here and watch your brother,' she said to Hansoe.

By the time she left the alley and reached the main road at the marketplace intersection, all she could see was muddy water. People spilled out into the streets in a panic, carrying bundles in their arms or on their heads and calling out to their families. The water came up to the knees of adults but up to the bellies of children. And it was likely to rise further, possibly over the heads of those children.

On her way back, Juan-daek wracked her brain to figure out where they could flee to. They had to go someplace high. There were two options nearby and another closer to where her husband worked. She could think of an even safer place further away, but they risked getting trapped somewhere or drowning along the way if the water overtook them. Her little boys were relying on her to keep them safe. The closest places were to the north-east. One was Onggimal, where she bought the earthenware jars for her salted shrimp. It had two pottery mills and only ten or so houses. The hilltop neighbourhood didn't become populated with tile-roofed houses and a church until Hansoe was in secondary school. On the other side of Onggimal, toward the river, was a taller hill called Dangsan where there were several old gingko trees. The other closest option was to go past the marketplace intersection and head south towards Singil-ri, to the hill in front of the Bangagot Ferry Landing. There, on the side of the hill towards the river was Gwisinbawi, or 'Ghost Rock', a spot with a deep pool and boulders where children would swim in the summer and sometimes drown. Juan-daek decided against that spot, as the swollen river might swallow the bottom of the hill before they made it there. Near the rail works was still another hill, called Wondangsan, which she assumed her husband would head to if he couldn't make it back home in time.

She decided on Onggimal and rushed the boys out of the house. She'd searched for anything that would float, but all she found was a small wooden tub. The tub happened to have handles, so she tied a straw rope to one of them and pulled it behind her down the alley, which was already beginning to flood. Thankfully, it was easier to pull over water than bare ground. People were coming from all directions and sloshing off wherever they saw fit. The water was deeper in some places than others. Juan-daek was hustling her boys along when the water was suddenly at Dusoe's chest. He fell with a startled yelp. His mother had to snatch him by the wrist to help him back onto his feet. Dusoe broke into tears as he coughed up muddy water. Hansoe put Dusoe on his back and grabbed the tub from his mother. Ever since he'd been little, Hansoe had loved spending his summer days playing with the other neighbourhood kids in the Saetgang River and had learned how to dog paddle. While pushing the tub ahead of him, he lifted his feet off the ground now and then and cheerfully kicked them in the water.

By the time Juan-daek reached the foot of Onggimal with her boys, she could see that a fair number of people were heading for the same destination. They went up the hill toward one of the pottery mills. The ground was littered with pottery shards and broken crockery, and the mill with its two kilns was just an open workspace with a few pillars and a roof. Still, the layout of the workspace — like a long, squared horseshoe — was enough for many to take cover from the rain. The rain continued to fall as hard as it did overnight, and darkness fell far earlier than usual. There was no news of Baekman, nor did he suddenly join them. By then, not even the strongest man in the world could have found his way through that mess.

To help each other get through the disaster, the pottery-mill workers lit some bonfires around the mill and, as it was already past dinnertime, cooked some rice and made rice balls for everyone. About thirty people had taken refuge there; with the pottery-mill workers, there were at least forty people on that hill. The water kept rising and coming closer and closer to the foot of the hill. They slept shoulder to shoulder, and in the bright light of dawn they looked down and saw they were now in complete isolation. A vast sea of rain unfolded before them. The floodwaters covered everything except Onggimal. Juan-daek could barely make out the black tips of the roofs in her neighbourhood. The Saetgang, which had spread far beyond its banks, rumbled past. The only things in sight were the old gingko trees jutting up from Dangsan to the north and a couple of chimney tops among the factories to the west, but there was no telling just how high the water had risen.

That day, Juan-daek pulled off a feat that made her a legend.

Three days of nonstop rain had turned the Hangang to mud and wiped out all of the low-lying areas along the banks. As the day turned to afternoon, the rain seemed to thin, but bubbly, muddy torrents still surrounded Onggimal. Toppled houses, trees, a half-submerged clothing chest, and all sorts of flotsam and jetsam bobbed past. The evacuees looked anxiously down at all of it. Just then, as if struck by a thought, Juan-daek hurried back up to the pottery mill and began looking around.

'Do you have any rope?' she asked the owner.

'What for?'

'To catch me some of that floating treasure,' Juan-daek answered with a sheepish smile.

'What? You'll get yourself killed! Do you even know how to dog paddle?'

'I grew up on the shores of Jemulpo — the sea was my front yard,' Juan-daek replied with a grin.

His curiosity stoked, the mill owner found some strands of straw rope and skilfully braided three of them together. Once he had two thick ropes, Juan-daek was about to take them down the hill when the owner came after her with a bundle.

'Try this, it's a casting net for when we go fishing in the river.'

Juan-daek glanced at the bundle and said with delight, 'That's perfect!'

The owner and a couple of his workers followed Juan-daek. She tied one end of a rope around her waist and handed the other end to the workers.

'Pull me in when I say so.'

From the edges of the water, Juan-daek looked for a target and then jumped in without hesitation. The rope trailed behind her as she swam toward a bunch of watermelons. She gathered a few in the cast net and called out. As soon as she delivered the watermelons, she jumped right back in to collect chamoe melons, cucumbers, and the like. The task became so routine that she was soon bringing back anything and everything she could grab. She fished out a board, a rafter, even a bundle of chopped wood. Then two squirming pigs came floating along. One was as big as Juan-daek and the other was half as big. Juan-daek swam toward them, looped a noose around the big pig's neck, and locked her arm around the small pig's neck before she called out. At the workers' shouts for help, all the spectators standing nearby reached for the rope and started to pull. The big pig kicked, too, as if it knew the rope was its best chance at survival, and let itself be towed in. With the small pig tucked under one arm, Juan-daek kicked and paddled with her free arm. That afternoon, they feasted on watermelon, chamoe, and kiln-roasted pork, and the story entered local folklore and grew larger than life, as such stories do. For years, people spoke of the strongwoman known only as Juan-daek who swam like a fish and pulled dozens and dozens of pigs from the floodwaters.

The legend of Juan-daek did not end there. The epilogue to her heroics was her journey to the rail works to save her husband, Baekman. The tale was told by Mageum Gomo to her nephew Ilcheol, and from there it made its way down to his son, Jisan, and further on, until it reached the ears of his grandson Jino.

On the first day of the flood, Baekman had gone to work at the rail works. Most of the Japanese managers chose not to come in, whereas a few engineers had clocked in along with most of the section chiefs, assistants, and day labourers. Matsuda-san, an engineer on the lathe team, was worried about flood damage to the generator and other machines. But this was heavy equipment, much too heavy to be moved. No sooner had everyone arrived at work than they were stacking sand-bags in the entrance. As the water rose, they stacked the bags as high as their heads. They were on relatively higher ground to begin with, so the fact that the water had reached them meant the rest of the district was already flooded.

When the water was halfway up the sandbags, they began to evacuate. The plan was to head to Yeongdeungpo Station, because it was at the foot of a low hill called Gochumalgogae. The station had been built on a slope to help the locomotives start and stop. There were tracks from the rail works to the station, so they hitched three passenger carriages to a locomotive, and everyone boarded. A few assistants, including Baekman, agreed to stay behind to keep an eye on the works. The train carefully departed along tracks that had already disappeared under water. Still, the water only reached the bottom of the platform stairs and was yet to spill into the passenger carriage.

There were about ten people in total left at the rail works. They were determined to stay put and only escape to the roof if they had to, but one side of the sandbags suddenly collapsed and water rushed in. Baekman and his colleagues hurried up the emergency ladder to the roof. The roof was only slate tiles on wooden beams, which meant it could cave in if they sat too close together, so they all spread out and squatted near the eaves. The rain soon had them soaked to the bone, and even though it was summer, they were unlikely to withstand the chill at night. Someone who was familiar with the neighbourhood suggested that they flee to the rail workers' housing up on Wondangsan. It wasn't far — they sometimes ate their lunches on that hill under the shade of the trees. But with night falling, and no idea of how deep the floodwaters were, they were hesitant to make a move.

Everyone was forced to stay up there all night in the rain. Convinced they'd die of hypothermia if they fell asleep, they sang songs and slapped each other awake. They made it through to the next day, starving and exhausted as they held on to each other. The rain fortunately stopped, but the water kept rising. When it began to rain again around noon, someone emerged from the mist.

After demonstrating her talent in scooping up pigs, Juan-daek had rummaged through the items she'd gathered and built a raft using the rope and the boards and rafters and whatnot that had come off of toppled houses. She pushed the raft into the water and used a long pole to punt her way toward the rail works. Someone really should have stopped her, since she was jumping into flood currents. But who were they to question her after seeing her feat with the pigs? Her raft sped off toward Dangsan. People later said she drove the pole into the water so fast and hard that it looked like she was dancing.

By then, the roof was the only part of the rail works still above water. Juan-daek parked the raft right at the huddled workers' feet and ferried them to the foot of Wondangsan. Since the raft couldn't fit more than one at a time, she would've had to make at least ten trips. But on Wondangsan, with its shrine and handful of houses and other evacuees, they would be able to build a bonfire and even get something to eat. In any case, Juan-daek ended up saving more than a few lives.

After another day had passed and the floodwaters had nearly subsided, Juan-daek walked with her husband to Onggimal to retrieve their children and returned safely home to the Willow Tree House.

Although Baekman chose not to say anything about the legend surrounding his wife, he had a soft spot for his grandson Jisan and once said this much to him: 'Your great aunt's always been full of hot air.'

Baekman may have been dismissive of his sister Mageum's flair for the dramatic, but Jisan would always talk about how disappointed he was by his grandfather's reaction. If Juan-daek did in fact fish out those pigs, why couldn't she have also built a raft and guided it through a flood to save dozens of lives? The tale had to be true in order for the story of Juan-daek's appearance during the later flood of 1925 to make sense, which was years after she'd passed away.

Mageum Gomo may have been prone to tall tales, given her lifelong gift of gab, but Jisan believed that all her stories about his grandmother were factual. The flood of 1925 was the last and worst among the floods that hit them at least five years in a row. By then, Juan-daek had passed away and Mageum Gomo, who had come to Gyeongseong in search of work at a textile factory, decided to help her widowed brother take care of his kids.

This is how Mageum Gomo recapped the events of those years. The flood survivors took to preparing themselves in early June, before the arrival of the monsoon season. They made raincoats out of oil paper for each and every family member and built flood shelters in their homes. Those with houses built around a courtyard constructed temporary platforms on their roofs by laying rafters from one wing to the other and covering them with boards. For houses with wide-open yards, they built stilted huts instead.

With a skilled craftsman in the family, Baekman's place had the sturdiest-looking shelter in the neighbourhood. As befitting the name Willow Tree House, a stout crossbeam was hoisted up, with one end resting in the tree and the other on top of the workers' quarters. Crisscrossing rafters were installed above the crossbeam and covered with boards. It looked like a tiny attic, and had just enough space for two adults and two children to huddle inside. Hansoe and Dusoe remembered that small treetop shelter for a long time, often describing it as the world's coolest fort.

The area flooded every year, but in that first year after the big floods, the water only came up to the bottom of the maru. The market and its surroundings, of course, were submerged. The construction of embankments along Yongsan and Yeongdeungpo Districts began in 1921 and was completed the year Juan-daek passed away. As to whether Mageum Gomo came to Baekman's house before or after Juan-daek's death remains uncertain. Considering the way Mageum Gomo talked about how Juan-daek stuffed herself to death with dozens of sweet potatoes, she must have come before her sister-in-law passed away. According to Baekman, however, that, too, was just another of her tall tales. Baekman said that his wife didn't die of indigestion but because something went wrong while she was carrying their third and that both she and the baby died, which was why he had to stay home for a couple of days to take care of their boys. In other words, his version meant that Mageum Gomo came to Yeongdeungpo after Juan-daek had died. Mageum Gomo remembered many details about the flood of 1925, so, either way, she was definitely in Yeongdeungpo that summer, when Juan-daek was already gone.

Criticised for its poor response to the flood of 1920, the Japanese Government-General of Korea tried to fix things by rushing the construction of an embankment even in the middle of another flood the following year. The work, which took just under a year to complete, was clearly flimsy. As in the previous years, two heavy downpours occurred in 1925, delivering a one-two punch. An early-July typhoon and its torrents of rain was followed by another that hit the west coast in mid-July, before the floodwaters from the first had even receded, and caused an enormous flood that started from the upper reaches of the Hangang and engulfed every low-lying area in Gyeongseong and the towns of Goyang, Gwangju, Yangju, Gapyeong, Siheung, Gimpo, and Yangpyeong, knocking down the barely finished embankment and turning the capital's districts of Yongsan, Mapo, and Yeongdeungpo into swamps.

Baekman's family, who had grown accustomed to the yearly deluge, would take to their shelter in the willow tree and stay there for two or three days until the worst of the flood had passed. That year, as well, when the rainy season began, they placed their jar of drinking water in the shelter, thatched the roof with extra straw, and tied the ropes down extra tight. Thirteen-year-old Hansoe was in his third year of primary school and eleven-year-old Dusoe was in his second. When it started to rain, the school sent the students home right after roll call. Seeing as how Juan-daek had passed away the previous winter, Mageum Gomo must have been there, at her second brother's house in Yeongdeungpo, since the spring.

Baekman had struggled through the winter to take care of his two sons. He didn't approach his sister, Mageum, for help. When her sister-in-law passed away, Mageum had come to Gyeongseong with their brother Shipman and helped with the funeral. The eldest, Cheonman, couldn't make it since he was aboard a ship off the coast of Haeju. Mageum then caught rumour of a girl her age in her neighbourhood who'd found a job at a textile factory in Yeongdeungpo, and figured this was her shot. She would move to Yeongdeungpo to help her brother with the kids and house and get a factory job for herself if an opening presented itself. Baekman showed little reaction when Mageum appeared on his doorstep. Yet he must have been glad she came because as soon as he received his salary the following month, he bought some fabric and handed it to the neighbourhood tailor to make a new set of clothes for Mageum.

By the time Mageum Gomo joined them in the spring of 1925, Hansoe and Dusoe had, as grown-ups would say, developed a mind of their own and were capable of taking care of themselves. The day they were sent home from school because of the downpour, Baekman came back early from the rail works and was relieved to find everyone at home. The lowlands had begun flooding in the afternoon. Mageum cooked three times more rice than usual and made rice balls after supper. She'd already wrapped plenty of crispy rice crusts in paper as emergency rations. As the floodwater began to creep into their alley, the family decided to bear with it and stay indoors until it reached the maru. The last few floods had inundated the alleyways but only thigh-high, and so they'd merely watched with concern as water flowed into their yard but did not take refuge in their rooftop shelter.

The sky cleared for two or three days, and then another heavy downpour came and destroyed parts of the embankment, sending a wall of water into the whole of Yeongdeungpo. The water in their yard rose waist-high and breached the maru. Finally, they went up to the shelter. Thunder and lightning kept them awake as they huddled in the dark and watched the water continue to rise. Since their courtyard and now maru and both bedrooms were flooded, the water in the lower-lying areas around the marketplace intersection must have been over people's heads.

All through the night, the rain came down and the floodwaters rose. According to later reports, the embankment's collapse left the flat Yeongdeungpo area completely submerged. Houses disappeared from sight, and three metres of water inundated the train station. All that remained above water was Wondangsan, where the rail workers' housing was located. Wondangsan was the same hill Juan-daek had ferried factory workers to a few years earlier with a raft and pole. It was dead of night, the water not yet at its peak, when they heard someone knocking at their gate. According to Mageum Gomo, they were not about to jump down into all that water and swim over to open the gate. Baekman was still dozing off; Hansoe was the first to wake at the sound.

He told Mageum, 'Eomma is here.'

'*Aigo*, we better open the gate then,' said Mageum in a daze, before remembering that her sister-in-law was dead. 'No wait, that's just the wind. No one's there.'

'But Eomma appeared in my dream and told me she'd come.'

With a loud crash, the gate flew open and Juan-daek sloshed in wearing a straw cape and a bamboo hat.

She looked up and said to Mageum, 'Agassi, get down here already, and bring my boys with you!'

The shock jolted Mageum fully awake. Hansoe was the first to climb down to his mother, followed by Dusoe. Baekman was still snoring away.

'Oppa, wake up,' Mageum said to Baekman. 'Eonni has come for us.'

Baekman finally woke and followed his sister down into the yard. When they came out to the alleyway, a raft was waiting for them. Once they were all aboard, Juan-daek stood up in the back and pushed off. The raft zigzagged past several alleys until it reached a larger body of water most likely flowing over the marketplace intersection. The current grew stronger, making the raft pitch and roll. The rocking raft headed south-west and within just a few minutes arrived at Wondangsan. Juan-daek dropped her family off on the hillside and disappeared into the dark on her raft.

Baekman later gave a different account of what happened that night. Ever since she was little, Mageum Gomo would often get lost in daydreams and then believe those dreams to be true. That day, all employees were told to go home and evacuate to the rail workers' housing because a typhoon was on its way. Baekman insisted that he went home and took Hansoe, Dusoe, and Mageum straight to a community centre near the rail workers' housing where they all stayed for three days until the water receded.

The problem was that Mageum wasn't the only one who remembered being helped by Juan-daek. Hansoe firmly believed that his mom had come to their rescue. He even remembered receiving a delicious, freshly steamed piece of red-bean rice cake from her. He insisted that he did not eat it on the raft but outside the community centre in the rain, where she had summoned him and his brother out to give them each a piece.

'I'll bring tteok every day that you're here,' he swore she said.

Hansoe would get excited as he told the story, even though his aunt squinted at him to remind him not to talk about it in front of his father. Considering that at the time he was thirteen and in primary school and thus on the verge of mastering the liberal arts and sciences, when he told the story later to his wife, Geumi, and their son, Jisan, they had little choice but to believe that there was more than a grain of truth to his version.

Despite being two years younger than Hansoe, Dusoe took his father's side. Then again, no one ever paid much attention to what Dusoe had to say. Because Dusoe never really cared much about what happened at home. After all, he ended up hanging out with communists and spent the rest of his life running from the Japanese police or stuck in prison.

Mageum Gomo loved making up stories about Juan-daek with Hansoe. Juan-daek even appeared in the story about how Mageum met her husband. Mageum had tried everything she could to find work at a textile factory. She asked her brother Baekman to put in a good word every time a job opening came up, and stashed away money to buy gifts of cosmetics for the foreman's wife, but all to no avail. How could she expect to get a job, they asked, without so much as a primary-school diploma? And at her ripe old age of — seventeen, was it? Eighteen? She should be getting married and starting a family, not starting a career! One day, she'd made it all the way up to the interview only to be turned down again for the same old reasons and was heading home, in tears, when she saw Juan-daek standing in the courtyard, pounding rice in a mortar.

'My goodness, Eonni, what are you doing here?' asked Mageum.

'Can't you see? I'm making tteok for my boys,' Juan-daek replied as her stout body shook with each pound of the pestle.

'Let's just make supper. Oppa will get mad at us for wasting rice on tteok on an ordinary day.'

Juan-daek smirked and kept pounding as she said, 'Agassi, I'll finish this and leave before that stubborn man returns, so you do the rest with the steamer.'

Mageum went in to change, and by the time she came back out,

Juan-daek was gone. Leaving behind plenty of finely ground, snow-white rice powder in the mortar. So Mageum steamed tteok before making supper. When the boys came home from school, they wolfed down the sweet red-bean tteok that they usually only got on holidays. Mageum cleared all traces of the tteok away before her brother returned. She then prepared doenjang stew and grilled fish for supper. The boys put on a convincing act as they told their father they'd eaten their supper early. The next day, without much to do in the afternoon, Mageum took a nap. When she woke, she found Juan-daek sitting on the edge of the maru.

'Agassi, there's some place we need to be,' said Juan-daek.

Mageum followed Juan-daek to the market entrance. Two men, one older and one younger, were building a shopfront onto an existing house. They had just finished erecting wooden pillars and attaching rafters to support the roof for the shop. Mageum looked over at Juan-daek but she had vanished. Mageum paced back and forth until finally the younger carpenter barked at her, 'Get out of the way. Can't you see we're working?'

The words came unbidden. 'I would like to ask about getting some repairs done at our house.'

'Oh, you must mean that place the other woman mentioned earlier, the Willow Tree House in that alley,' said the older carpenter.

He told the young man, 'Run along and check the place out. We can start working on it tomorrow morning.'

Mageum had the young carpenter follow her back home, where she pointed out things as if she'd known what she was going to say.

'The floodwaters got to everything. All the rooms leak when it rains, and several of the pillars are crooked.'

The young man nodded.

'You were lucky. Most of the other houses collapsed. Let's see what we have here.'

He examined a crooked pillar set in a cornerstone, knocked on a few pillars further indoors, and inspected the leaky ceilings Mageum pointed out.

When her brother came home from work, Mageum told him about how Juan-daek appeared in her dream to tell her to repair the house. She said she'd arranged for the work to start tomorrow, but Baekman didn't say much. The next day, he waited for the carpenters to come, agreed on the terms, and paid them before leaving for work a bit later than usual. The repair took ten days to complete. All the while, Mageum prepared lunch and snacks for the two carpenters, who were father and son. The father later asked Baekman for Mageum's hand in marriage to his son.

Juan-daek had practically played matchmaker from the grave, which Mageum couldn't tell anyone except for two people: her nephew Hansoe, aka Ilcheol, who'd always been on her side, and later his wife, Geumi. Juan-daek continued to appear to Mageum and Ilcheol from time to time, and after Geumi joined them, the three would whisper about their experiences to each other.

For instance, there was the story of that snowy November night when Ilcheol was working as a stoker for a freight-train driver and his assistant. The driver's job was to keep his eyes ahead and his hands ready at the reversing lever and break valve. His assistant's job was to pay attention to the terrain and speed as he shovelled coal into the firebox. Ilcheol's job was to squat in the coal bunker behind the driver's compartment and break the coal into pieces. Brown coal mixed with loads of mortar to increase heating power would freeze in the cold and had to be broken up to fit into the firebox. Ilcheol used a long iron rod that looked like an icepick to do this. Whenever the train had to accelerate or go uphill, the assistant and stoker would take turns shovelling coal from the bunker and feeding it into the firebox. Travelling across flat terrain, on the other hand, meant less-frequent feeding, which allowed the driver and his assistant to take a break and gave the stoker more time to break up the coal.

That night, Ilcheol was crouched inside the roofless bunker in his raincoat, breaking coal and being pelted with snow. The heavy labour left him hot and thirsty despite the snowstorm. He had a water jug nearby, which was usually filled with makgeolli. The rice brew gave him a boost, so he'd take a swig every once in a while as he worked. The snow was thickening. Ilcheol was lifting the iron rod and driving it down toward a lump of coal when he noticed a thick grove of fir trees race by in the dark. Ilcheol had a good sense of direction and knew the grove lay at the foot of a slope. If coal wasn't fed nonstop at that point, the train would lose momentum on its way up and be forced to backtrack before they could accelerate again. He glanced ahead and saw that the driver and his assistant had dozed off in their seats. Ilcheol dropped his rod and was about to rush toward the firebox when a dark figure blocked his way, opened the firebox, and began shovelling. The figure seemed to dance as it twisted to scoop more coal and twisted back to toss it into the fire. When he was first assigned to the locomotive, he had been trained for over an hour on how to shovel coal before the train could depart, but this person who had just appeared out of nowhere was more skilled with the shovel than any stoker he had ever seen. All at once, he realised it was Juan-daek. She was dressed in her usual baggy floral pants and head scarf. Ilcheol snapped to attention, picked up a shovel, and went over to help her. The assistant woke up.

'*Aiiikuna!* We almost lost momentum!'

The assistant scrambled for his shovel, and Ilcheol headed back to the coal bunker. The driver woke as well and raised the steam pressure as the locomotive began its ascent and huffed and puffed over the hill.

4

Yi Jino had been skipping breakfast for a while now. A solidarity movement was underway to create a shelter to support the daily needs of struggling labourers. The news was that money had been raised to purchase and refurbish an old building in an alley downtown. That meant a base camp could be set up for Jino's support team to stay and take turns helping with his sit-in. Although Jino was confined to a space that was sixteen paces in circumference, he wasn't doing any backbreaking work, so it made little sense for him to eat three times a day. More importantly, skipping breakfast would give his colleagues more time to take on part-time jobs or pick up day labour to help make it through their lay-offs. The Metal Workers' Union provided support but only in terms of publicising the situation or joint activities against the company. When it came to making ends meet, Jino's colleagues were on their own. Since they took turns looking after Jino on their days off, skipping breakfast seemed to have lessened their burden quite a bit.

It had taken Jino two months to adjust to life on the chimney top, and now he was starting to feel at home. He was like a floating spore that had landed on a barren rock and got cozy there, basking in the sunlight, drinking in the dew, being buffeted by the wind, until it grew into a little patch of moss. Best of all, he overcame his boredom. Now he crawled out of his tent at sunrise and paced back and forth on the catwalk for an hour to warm up. Then he did burpees. He was up to sixteen and intended to reach twenty just like his trainer had recommended.

Once the rainy season passed, sweltering heat struck. The cement chimney's temperature rose to over fifty degrees Celsius, sometimes sixty degrees at midday. Eggs could be soft-boiled in temperatures that high. To work out, Jino had to get up at around five in the morning and finish at around six or seven at the latest. Afterwards, he'd pour drinking water into a camping pot to splash a little water on his face, brush his teeth, and wash his scalp. He'd requested an electric hair clipper at the start of the hot weather so he could shave his hair off, and since then he'd switched to using a razor on both his face and head. At night, he'd strip down to his boxers, but during the day, wearing a long-sleeved shirt and pants made from a sweat-wicking fabric helped him to keep cool better. Jino could see why nomads in the desert chose to completely cover their faces and bodies. It made the sweltering heat far more bearable despite the sweat that continued to dribble down his chest and bum.

Lunch arrived. Jino had got the hang of using the pulley and, with the help of rubber-palmed work gloves, could hoist everything up in just three or four rounds. He looked down and saw that Kim Changsu, a fellow longtimer at the union chapter, was on kitchen duty today. They waved hello. Jino's phone vibrated and he heard Changsu's voice on the other end.

'We're planning a small event to celebrate the hundredth day,' said Changsu.

'What, don't you think it's a bit early to celebrate?' Jino said sheepishly.

Without the slightest change of tone, Changsu replied, 'The decision isn't yours to make, it's up to the union. Your job is to hold the fort up there.'

'Well, I'm just saying ...' But Jino ended up saying nothing at all.

The company had given them no response whatsoever. With the union's support, the workers had tried protesting in front of the company's headquarters, demanding to meet with the president, but no one would come out of the building to talk. Their efforts were only so much street noise.

'Anyway, the shelter has officially opened. From now on, your meals will be delivered from there.'

The news gave Jino hope that he'd finally be able to eat something closer to home cooking. As grateful as he was for all their help, the truth was that the food they'd been throwing together for him wasn't much better than camping food, and it had taken only three days for him to grow tired of it. He opened the lunch box and took out the ssamjang sauce he'd requested. The lettuce had grown so well that each plant was still lush with leaves despite how many he'd already eaten. His plan was to hurry up and finish them off, with the help of the ssamjang, before the scorching heat wilted them. Tender leaves were budding near the bottom of the stalks. He would eat them once they grew tall enough or bury them if they happened to wilt. They, too, had left the earth behind, yet were managing to survive on just a few drops of water.

News from all around still found its way to Jino. In a city down south, a taxi driver had been occupying a crane for almost a year now. Female train conductors had been protesting for over a decade to be reinstated. Teachers had taken to the streets for years, asking for extra-legal unions to be brought back into the system. Somewhere out there, cleaners were getting injured, killed, or fired. Somewhere, temporary workers were facing the same. For them, the clock had stopped. Jino and his eleven colleagues had been protesting for over three years without knowing when it would end. The voice of an elderly worker who'd shouted in the middle of a bar echoed in Jino's ears.

'Yes, capitalism is terrible! But what's the alternative? I don't know. I don't know shit about alternatives, but I do know that capitalism is bad!'

After lunch, Jino was standing before the railing when he heard his mobile phone vibrate. It was his wife.

'It's me. How've you been?'

'Enjoying the three pleasures of life: eating well, sleeping well, and pooping well!' Jino kept his voice chipper to reassure her. 'How are the kids?'

'They're fine and doing okay at school. Kim Changsu told me to come tomorrow.'

'Why? Don't you have to go to work?'

'No, I'm on the night shift tomorrow.'

'Why keep a supermarket open all night? Do people really shop that late?'

'It's the same at all the other supermarkets. By the way, your mother's coming with me. She says she wants to.'

While Jino was protesting to be reinstated, his wife had stepped up as breadwinner by finding a cashier job at a large supermarket. Jino's mother, Yun Bokrye, had long ago closed and sold off the clothing shop Shin Geumi Halmeoni used to run in the market. After the word 'Traditional' was added in front of 'Market', all the locals had disappeared, and newcomers who'd just arrived from the provinces took their places. When the family lived at the Saetmal House, Bokrye had brought home extra cash through the tiny corner shop she ran at the neighbourhood entrance, but she'd had to quit after the newfangled 'grocery stores' began to appear. The one good thing about having to sell everything was that it enabled Jino's family to purchase an eighty-square-metre apartment.

'Don't bother. It won't be worth it.'

'The folks doing some cultural project said they want us to say something for their video.'

'Why is everyone so worked up over the hundredth day? The company won't give a hoot.'

'I know. Hang in there.'

'Thanks. You, too.'

Jino pulled out the markers and fabric from the lunch basket Changsu had delivered. He was going to make a banner. The afternoon rays pricked at his skin, but the breeze made it bearable. He unrolled two arms' length of the fabric and braced one end with his foot and the other with a bottle of urine that had turned brown.

One Hundredth Day of Sit-in
Jo Taejun, Uphold the Agreement You Broke
Talk With the Union

Five words on the first line, seven words on the second line, and four words on the third line. Jino pressed down hard on each letter. Jo Taejun was the one who'd fired them and sold off the company. Jino and his colleagues had shouted his name hundreds of times over the past five years as they protested for their reinstatement, and yet he was a faceless stranger who they'd never met. They knew him only as a name on paper. According to books, names like that were no more than abstract symbols of capital, silently fulfilling the role society gave them. Jo Taejun did not belong to boyhood or adulthood or old age or any of those places. He inhabited a time entirely different from that of Jino and his fellow labourers, living a life disconnected from theirs, and probably had no memory of them at all. To him, they were no more than a tiny, familiar mark on the wall that catches the eye for a split second but not long enough to disrupt his life. Jino finished the banner with red and blue markers and tied it to the railing.

With the markers still in hand, he paused to think for a moment and then looked down at a row of empty plastic bottles nearby. He felt a sudden urge to give those objects names as powerful as Jo Taejun's. With a grin, Jino wrote a name on the plump torso of a bottle. Little Clippers. He picked up each of the others in turn. Juan-daek. Geumi. Then he noticed that the red marker had left smudges on his thumb and index finger. Like blood from a cut, he thought. He wrote 'Yeongsuk' and paused. Another bottle was named Jingi. Why, look at them, they're all here. Little Clippers, Jingi, Yeongsuk, Juan-daek, and Geumi. Come to think of it, they were all dead. If Geumi, Juan-daek, and Little Clippers were names from his past, then Yeongsuk and Jingi were names from his present. He took the bottles he'd given names to and hung them from the railing away from the bottles of urine.

That night, the moment the sun went down, Jino brought Little Clippers' bottle over to his sleeping bag and tried talking to it.

'Hey, Little Clippers, long time no see. I still think about you now and then. I wanted to go play at the Ghost Rock and the Saetgang like we used to. I also wanted to go to Yangmalsan Mountain and Bamseom Island with you.'

A twelve-year-old boy tiptoed over and sat at the tent's entrance. Jino pretended to be surprised as he crawled out to sit with him face to face.

'Saekki, you know I hate high places. You actually live here?' Little Clippers asked as he glanced about.

'Inma, why would I live here? I'm just having fun. Can't you tell?' responded young Jino, sounding just like his friend.

'Hey, let's go dig up peanuts,' Little Clippers whispered quickly. 'This is the best time to eat them.'

'Just the two of us?'

'What, is there someone else up here I should invite?'

'Fine, let's go.'

The moment Jino said yes, Little Clippers set a condition, as always.

'There's a field only I know about. The peanuts should be ripe by now. I'll take you there if you give me your pop gun.'

Ah, the pop gun. It had a wooden grip made by inserting the screw from a bicycle spoke into a stick. Jino's father had made it in his free time at Great-Grandfather's workshop. The gun looked pretty real, with a trigger and a firing pin. It used lumps of candle wax capped with paper firecrackers as bullets. To fire the gun, you had to fix a lump of candle wax to the screw, stick a paper firecracker on top of the lump, light the firecracker, and pull the trigger. The hot lumps of candle wax stung when they hit you.

'But I like that gun.'

'No deal, then, saekki. I'll get going. Have fun by yourself.'

'Okay, okay, it's yours.'

In a flash, Jino was down from the chimney and on the banks of the Saetgang River. He walked along the tributary where wild reeds — mureoksae, galdae, dalbburipul — brushed against his waist. Where the tributary narrowed into a stream, a good row of stepping stones appeared. On the other side was a dirt road dotted with puddles; Little Clippers led the way, excitedly pointing here and there and calling out the names of the different plants. 'Lots of cogon grass grows there, and over there is knotweed, and I found a bunch of sunberries in the snake grass over there. This is my secret spot. It's full of stuff to eat.'

The two boys arrived at the corner of a peanut field where Yangmalsan Mountain loomed in the distance. Small oval leaves grew thick on the ground; Jino and Little Clippers groped beneath them in search of the stalks and then followed those down to sift through the sandy soil and ease the roots out. A row of peanuts, dangling like small sacs, emerged. They plucked the peanuts and moved on to the next section. In no time, each boy's lap was piled high. They decided to have a taste before digging up more. They blew the dirt away and carefully bit down on the shells. The kernels they dug out were moist, sticky, and covered with a flimsy, soft skin. They tasted slightly sweet and a little raw but also savoury. The texture was mushy, as if the kernels had been boiled. Jino and Little Clippers filled their pockets and took off their singlets to carry more. They'd be in for a scolding if they got caught, so they had to eat it all before heading home. The boys climbed up the embankment overlooking Yeouido Airport and sat on an oil pipe, carefully tossing shelled peanuts into their mouths.

'Are you gonna go back up that chimney?'

'I guess so.'

'Is it fun up there?'

'No, but I made a promise.'

'To meet someone?'

Little Clippers seemed to have one too many questions on his mind.

'Yeah, you!' said Jino, smiling and pointing at Little Clippers.

'You tellin' me I have to climb up there every day?'

'No, just hang out with me like this if I call for you.'

Little Clippers thought this over for a moment and said, 'Inma, everything has a price. There's lots of cool stuff at your workshop.'

'None of it is mine.'

'Come on, there's nothing your great-grandpa can't make. I lost my bugle mouthpiece. If you can get him to make me one, I'll do whatever you say.'

Jino gave in and said, 'All right, I'll try to ask my dad or great-grandfather.'

And just like that, Jino was back in his tent, lying on his stomach with his chin resting in his hands. Little Clippers' bottle stood quietly before him. He put the bottle back next to the others.

The sun rose on the hundredth day of the sit-in. Jino found it hard to get excited about the scheduled events. The whole thing felt premature. Other labourers had to protest for at least a year before the public noticed and began to take an interest. Conscripted policemen filed out of an armoured bus and surrounded the chimney. A truck delivered a rescue cushion. It was inflated and placed beside the chimney in case Jino happened to jump. He almost wanted to go for it, just to test the cushion's resilience.

Policemen were lined up in front of the power plant's main gate. Jino's colleagues, fellow union members, and civic-group members gathered at the tent outside the plant's walls. Jino heard a megaphone being turned on, and Changsu began to read a statement. Jino had no idea how many reporters had come, but he knew the press hadn't shown much interest. With videos and so much technology available these days, the union members had no choice but to take matters into their own hands to gain publicity. If they kept trying to spread their story, it was bound to have some effect. They hadn't reached the stage where they could request a meeting with the company's owner, so Jino had no intention of repairing the ladder he'd loosened. He assumed the folks down there meant to use today's event as a declaration that the sit-in was only beginning.

His mobile phone rang.

'Jino? It's Eomma. Why aren't you eating breakfast?' asked Yun Bokrye.

'Geez, why did you come?'

'I came to see you, but they won't let me in. Aren't you going to answer me? Why skip breakfast? Nothing is worth going hungry.'

'All I do is sit around up here. I'll get sick if I eat three times a day.'

'I saw your grandmother in my dreams. She told me to make you pat-sirutteok. She said your grandfather loved it. You do, too, right?'

'Sure, that'd be great.'

'Picketing has always been in the Yi family's blood. Remember, you're not doing it to line your own pockets, you're doing it so all workers can live decent lives.'

Bokrye's sage, uplifting words had Jino feeling choked-up with emotion.

'You're r-right.'

'Don't even think about coming down any time soon. So many have died for the cause already.'

She was echoing the words of Jino's great-grandfather Baekman, grandfather Ilcheol, and father, Jisan. She had believed in those words her whole life, and so did Jino.

'I brought you some homemade sikhye, in case you get thirsty. Think of today as the day you were born at the top of a chimney, and drink it as a birthday treat.'

Bokrye handed the phone over to Jino's wife, who told him that she and Bokrye were both in good health and that their children's grades were improving. She also asked him to pretend he was at work if his mother-in-law called because she hadn't told her about the sit-in. She then added that his mother had made a cameo on the video and spent the whole time bragging about him.

The hundredth day event ended up being a brief, quiet affair.

From that evening on, Jino also got to enjoy much better meals, prepared for him by the cooks at the shelter. He received two text messages from them. He knew one of the women well. She was a former member of the textile union who'd been laid off. After working at a textile factory for a long time, she had quit a few years earlier to be a full-time homemaker, but decided to volunteer at the shelter because she missed her old colleagues. The other was a woman about his age who had also been laid off from a factory. She was reinstated after a drawn-out solo demonstration in front of the factory only to lose her job again when they falsely declared bankruptcy and relocated overseas, just like the factory Jino used to work at. The union as well as various sponsors had pitched in to create and operate the shelter. Other union members helped with grocery shopping and cooking, and when the food was ready, Jino's colleagues took care of its delivery. In the dinner basket was an insulated box and bottle, a container of banchan, and a note that read, 'Happy One Hundredth Day! You're practically a newborn still, so let's make it to your first birthday!' Sure enough, the meal of warm rice and seaweed soup, jeon fritters, stir-fried pork, and seasoned greens was fit for a birthday or holiday. But their encouragement for him to stick it out until his first birthday confirmed what he knew: he needed to stay atop the chimney for at least a year. Now and then, there were aerial sit-in protesters who couldn't take it anymore and jumped to their deaths — their photographs were captioned with the word 'martyr' and then promptly lost among the countless others and buried in the passage of time.

Jino doused an already sour-smelling towel with water and wiped the sweat from his body. Even at night, the heat showed no sign of abating. Sweat turned into water, and the moisture the towel gathered from wiping his body turned back into sweat. After an early supper, Jino was starting to feel hungry again at around nine. He took the pat-sirutteok left over from the afternoon and ate it with the now lukewarm sikhye. The tteok was still soft and chewy. But it would spoil by morning and have to be sent down in the bag with his waste. He took another bite and struck up a conversation with Shin Geumi Halmeoni's plastic bottle.

'I wish I were eating the tteok you used to make, and a refreshing bowl of your nabak kimchi.'

There was no answer. The bottle just stood there against the railing and said nothing. Jino couldn't help feeling a little disappointed; just yesterday he'd had such fun digging up peanuts at the stream with Little Clippers. He went to the end of the catwalk to take a leak behind the canvas curtain. When he finished and turned around, he saw a familiar face. Geumi Halmeoni was standing there, in the same clothes she'd always worn, beckoning him to follow.

'Let's go home and have some nabak kimchi.'

They took turns leading the way through the dark.

Instead of the old Saetmal House, Jino followed his grandmother to a place he'd only heard stories about: the Willow Tree House in the alley behind the market.

*

That fact that Yi Ilcheol graduated from primary school after four years and enrolled in a five-year secondary school was an ongoing source of pride to his father, Baekman. Unlike Baekman, who'd had to teach himself how to read and write and picked up Japanese and learned a trade while working as a clerk and day labourer, Ilcheol was following a formal curriculum guaranteed to make him an educated man.

Baekman wanted his son to become a train driver. Ever since he first laid eyes on a train and was drawn to its grandeur, Baekman had dreamed of sitting in the driver's seat of a powerful locomotive. While the family was living at the Willow Tree House, Ilcheol was accepted into the training school for railway workers. The school, which had previously been entrusted to the management of the South Manchurian Railway, was reopened under a new name when the Japanese Government-General took over direct management. Baekman had always felt aggrieved by the fact that, up until that point, there was not a single Korean train driver, nor were Koreans even allowed to work as the driver's assistant, stoker, or coal hauler on passenger carriages running on the Gyeongbu and Gyeongui Lines. But after the reopening, they were put to work as stokers and coal haulers on branch lines, and Koreans began to be admitted into the reopened training school.

In his third year of secondary school, Ilcheol applied to the training school's full-time program. His father helped him secure a recommendation from a Japanese manager at the rail works. Belying the claim that Koreans were welcome to enrol, there were only two to three Koreans for every ten Japanese. Applicants had to have completed up to the second year of secondary school to be eligible. Once accepted, they had to complete the full-time program in three years. The children of the Railway Bureau's employees were given priority, which meant Ilcheol was more than qualified for enrolment. He took out a twelve-won student loan and moved into the school dormitory in Yongsan.

Whenever Ilcheol showed up at the marketplace intersection in his school uniform and cape, Baekman would take him out for drinks as if he were a friend. Ilcheol sometimes claimed the reason he and his father knew how to hold their liquor was because Baekman had learned how to drink from Manny Ajeosshi and Ilcheol had learned how to drink from Baekman. Ilcheol's brother, Icheol, on the other hand, could never hold his liquor, because he'd got his introduction to alcohol from binge drinking with the other guys at the textile mill. But at least Icheol managed to do one praiseworthy deed: he saw that Shin Geumi would be a good match for his older brother and introduced her to him.

Shin Geumi was the only daughter of a middle-class farmer in Gimpo. She had five older brothers; by the time she was born, her father was fifty, which was considered a ripe old age back then. Her mother was forty-eight. The age gap between her and her brothers was so great that her closest sibling could have already been a father himself. Three of her brothers were married and living elsewhere, while the eldest and youngest brother lived with Geumi and their parents. Even in those days, when daughters didn't count for much, her parents had always said they wanted a sweet girl of their own. And thus, Geumi's word was law in their family.

Once when a visitor came over, Geumi gave the person a long look before warning them, 'Beware of dogs!' Then immediately forgot that she'd said anything at all and went right back to playing. Her mother scolded her for talking nonsense, but a few days later they found out that the visitor had indeed been bitten by a dog. To another visitor, she blurted, 'Be good to your grandma!' and a few days later the visitor's grandma passed away. Her family tried to stop her from saying such things, but Geumi always managed to open her mouth only to immediately forget what she said.

One day, Geumi surprised her father by slowly reading the words in a Korean newspaper ad. This convinced him to give his daughter a modern education. He enrolled Geumi in the county's four-year primary school, which hadn't existed when her brothers were growing up. Upon graduation, she assumed her father would send her to a secondary school for girls. There were a few private girls' schools in Gyeongseong and a couple of other cities, but as it turned out, Geumi's father had no intention of sending his only daughter away from home. He wouldn't hear of it, no matter how many times Geumi's primary-school teacher explained that she'd be safe in the dormitories. Like any other father back then, he believed it was time for Geumi to stay at home and learn some housekeeping like a good girl, as she was nearly fifteen and would soon be coming of age. Her mother felt sorry for her daughter, who shut herself up in her room and refused to eat.

Geumi's mother then heard a rumour from her youngest daughter-in-law, who was from a village called Yeomchang-ri. According to the daughter-in-law, one of her hometown friends had done good for herself by going to work at a textile factory, where she received an education and training and rose to the position of team leader. She earned a decent salary, married an engineer at the same factory, and was now living comfortably in Yeongdeungpo. Geumi's mother put together a gift basket of fabric and pricey dried fish, and had her daughter-in-law lead the way to her friend in Yeongdeungpo. They managed to catch a boat departing Haengju Dock when the tide was high, so it took them only half a day to sail past Yeomchang to Yanghwa Dock near Seonyudo Island. When she heard that Geumi had graduated from primary school, the friend assured them that Geumi was as good as hired. She told them that Geumi could study while working because the factory offered a three-year night-school program.

With the number of mouths they had to feed, Geumi's parents had barely made ends meet over the years despite working hard in the three and a half acres of rice paddies they owned in Gimpo. Farming was all they were able to teach their children, which was why their sons struggled just as much to support their own families. The new world they lived in valued money over rice. Graduating from primary school gave Geumi a considerable advantage, as it meant that she had been educated in the 'national language', Japanese, which the older folk still struggled with, and could speak, read, and write in it fluently. And so, Geumi went with her sister-in-law to Yeongdeungpo, where she stayed with her sister-in-law's friend for a month, paying for her room and board with rice.

Geumi found a job at a textile factory and moved into the dormitory. Each tiny, four-tatami-mat-sized dorm room had four to five women crammed into it. The meals in the dormitory cafeteria consisted of thin doenjang soup and salted greens, with an occasional chunk of fish. After work, Geumi would head to the factory classroom for two to three hours of night classes. Her only day off was Sunday, when she could go out in the afternoon as long as she returned by eight in the evening. That much she had expected, but the rest was not what she'd been told. The work days were ten to thirteen hours long. She'd get up at six in the morning, eat a quick breakfast, and start work by seven. Lunch was at noon, then she was back on the factory floor by one, where she worked straight through until six. By the time she made it to night classes, she'd doze through the lectures and fall into bed exhausted around ten at night. Backlogs meant she had to work overtime until nine or even later. The dormitory's strict rules forbade workers from going anywhere except on Sundays and from visiting any room other than their own. Still, they were envied by the workers who assisted them. The assistants were hired for short contracts only, were paid by the day, and were assigned to the most backbreaking, menial tasks. If they made any mistakes or showed any signs of dawdling, they could be fired on the spot. In two years, Geumi completed her apprenticeship and became a weaver. After finishing the three-year night program, she was moved up to team leader in charge of her own loom and two assistants.

The Mukden Incident occurred when Ilcheol was in his second year at the railway workers' training school. The teacher came into the classroom and introduced a military instructor who had been sent to explain what had happened at Liutiao Lake in Manchuria. The instructor started with a brief overview of an earlier incident between the Chinese and Korean migrant farmers who were building an irrigation ditch near Wanbaoshan. The Chinese had refused to acknowledge the Korean farmers' right to irrigate, saying the farmers' leases were invalid anyway because the Chinese landowner hadn't obtained the permission that he was supposed to receive from the authorities in order to lease to foreigners. This led to a minor clash between the Japanese police and the Chinese army, after which Japan, having regarded these Koreans as settlers sent ahead of its advancement into Manchuria, sensationalised the Wanbaoshan Incident through Korean newspapers as a case of Chinese oppression of Koreans. Believing the reports to be true, outraged Koreans in Gyeongseong as well as other areas attacked Chinese-owned restaurants, shops, and farms. Korean civic organisations, however, learned of the truth behind the Wanbaoshan Incident. They urged people not to be deceived by Japan's propaganda and stressed the importance of friendship between Koreans and the Chinese. Ilcheol, of course, was shut away at school and so focused on his training that he didn't learn about all of this until much later. Meanwhile, Japan had already finished laying tracks all over Manchuria and established the South Manchuria Railway Company. The Kwantung Army was stationed in Manchuria under the pretext of protecting Japanese people and property. To execute their invasion of Manchuria, the army staged an attack on a section of railway line near Mukden and framed the Chinese for it. The military instructor's face was flushed as he wrapped up his briefing of the latest developments in Manchuria.

'In only five days, our fearless, valiant Kwangtung Army of the Great Empire of Japan took over most of Liaodong and Jilin Province, finally liberating those areas from China's grasp.'

Ilcheol was still at the training school when Manchukuo's founding was proclaimed over winter break of the following year. Puyi, the last Qing emperor, was installed as a nominal regent. Manchuria was now completely in Japan's hands.

After graduating primary school, Ilcheol's younger brother, Icheol, went to a smithy nearby to learn how to operate a lathe like their father and then went to the rail works as a day labourer. To work his way up to full employment, Icheol had to be as skilled and diligent as his father. Though he could not match his brother's academic performance, he proved smart and quick-witted enough to handle an assistant's job. Icheol worked a lathe under an assistant engineer who was Baekman's colleague.

One day, the disgruntled-looking head of assistants sent Icheol to the casting division to check whether a mould's original measurements were correct. Icheol took a casting with him. The assistant at the casting division checked the measurements and started badgering the day labourers who were pouring molten metal into the mould. One of the day labourers raised his hand.

'All we did was pour metal into the mould we were given and take it out when it cooled. Isn't it possible that the mould was measured incorrectly in the first place?'

'Whatever the case, the team that stuffed up needs to take responsibility and make up for the loss.'

The casting-division assistant handed a piece of paper to the day labourer, who checked the measurements written on it and nodded.

'Someone messed up the mould.'

Another day labourer raised his hand.

'How many defective goods are we talking about?'

'Seven,' answered Icheol.

'I'll pay for them.'

The assistant stared at him.

'Hey, all of us here are Koreans,' the labourer said, 'so let's help each other out. It'll take about twenty minutes to create a new mould and then we can make seven more as replacements. How does that sound?'

The casting-division assistant, who had started at the bottom just like them, said nothing for a while, then asked, 'Would it be okay to deduct the loss from your wages today?'

'Sure, just don't fire me,' the labourer replied with a grin.

The assistant also broke into a grin as he said, 'Fire you? Nonsense ...'

All at once, the tension broke. Icheol was impressed. On his way home after work, he saw the labourer walking ahead, shoulders swaying, lunch box dangling from his belt. Icheol hurried to catch up with him.

'Where do you live?' asked Icheol.

'Well, look who it is! You're the turner's assistant, aren't you, sir?'

'Please don't call me sir. You're obviously older than I am,' Icheol said cheerfully.

The labourer waved his hands in refusal.

'You think I don't know that? Aren't you Yi Baekman's son? I'm just a lowly drudge.'

The labourer said he was staying at an inn in an alley behind the market. Icheol told him it wasn't that far from his place and proposed they go for a drink. Lots of eateries and pubs had opened up around the market and were usually bustling with customers by the end of the day. Married men would pick up a fish or two in the market for supper and hurry home, assuming it wasn't the weekend, whereas single men who had nothing to look forward to but a shared room in a hostel would get together with friends and pool their money to buy bottles of makgeolli or soju and generous plates of cheap bar food for dinner. Icheol and the worker stood at a bar table eating the bindaetteok pancakes and grilled herring they'd ordered with a kettle of makgeolli.

'My name is Bang Wuchang. I moved up here from Cheonan in Chungcheong Province.'

'I'm Yi Icheol, and I was born in Yeongdeungpo, although my father is from Ganghwa.'

'I see bumfluff on your face, so how old are you?' Wuchang asked with a smile.

'Eighteen.'

'Well, you're a grown man if you're eighteen. I just turned thirty, so I guess that means I've got one foot in the grave.'

Icheol asked the question that had been on his mind from the beginning.

'Why did you take the blame today? Hardly anyone ever does that.'

Wuchang grinned again as he said, 'Yesterday was no different from today, and today will be just like tomorrow. So I can just pretend today never happened.'

Wuchang added, 'If the lathing and casting divisions started butting heads over who messed up, we *all* would've ended up squabbling with each other and one of us would've been fired. That's exactly how Joseon fell. Cunning Japan has been playing with the Korean people the same way.'

'You silenced everyone when you said all of us here are Koreans,' said Icheol, sounding truly impressed.

Wuchang took a long swig of makgeolli from his bowl before saying, 'We tend to forget what really matters and quarrel among ourselves. This is our land, Korean land.'

Wuchang dropped the honorifics once he was good and drunk.

'What do you do on your day off?'

'Oh, I just loll around the house.'

'I have plans to go fishing with some friends if you want to join.'

'Sounds nice. Should I bring anything?'

'Bring a bottle of liquor. Leave the rest to us.'

Three days later, on Sunday, Icheol bought a large, four-litre bottle of cheap soju at the market and headed to the embankment with it tucked under his arm. The embankment was a stone's throw away from the market; as soon as he reached the top, he saw Wuchang and two other men waiting beside the Saetgang River. Wuchang introduced Icheol to his friends Mr Hong and Mr Ji. They were from other divisions at the rail works. Wuchang said that one more person was supposed to come, and soon enough, a stocky, swarthy, youngish-looking man appeared. He had a rolled-up cast net slung over one shoulder. The rest knew him well, so Wuchang introduced him to Icheol. He was Mr Ahn, a first-grade worker from the freight-carriage division. The works had various divisions for handling tasks such as alloy moulds, electrics, freight carriages, finishings, painting, and steel plates. A first-grade worker was someone recognised for his technical skills and was about to become a probationary assistant. Mr Ahn seemed to be in his late twenties to early thirties. As Wuchang introduced him to Icheol, he threw in a joke about his name: Ahn Daegil.

'Daegil means "very lucky", but that darn family name of his, Ahn, sounds like "not".'

Daegil nodded as he laughed good-naturedly.

'What use is a good given name when Ahn comes in front to contradict it?'

'He makes the best cast net in our neighbourhood, though,' said Hong.

Wuchang cut in with, 'Forget his last name. Let's just call him Cast Netter.'

Patches of fluffy clouds floated overhead, and the sun was warm. Everyone took their shirts off and crossed the shallow Saetgang toward a large pool. They left their cooking gear on the sand and gathered stones to make a little stove where they could set their pot.

Someone said, 'I'd rather be making noise and having fun with a regular fishing net. This cast net makes me feel like some kind of monk.'

Daegil walked alone into the water until it lapped at his knees, and gazed down at the surface for a moment before casting his net. It unfurled into a perfect circle as it swooped down on the water. After three throws, their basket was filled with freshwater fish of all sizes. They threw back the small fry. About an hour later, the basket was teeming again with catfish, mandarin fish, carp, and minnows. They were even lucky enough to catch two of the famous Mapo freshwater eels. While the fish porridge was boiling, they grilled whole eels, sprinkled salt over them, and lifted their first glasses of soju. After enjoying the soju and porridge, they splashed about in the water to cool off and then sat in the shade of a sacred tree nearby. Unlike the others, Icheol was new to this sort of gathering and was treated to some surprising stories.

Icheol knew Wuchang was from Cheonan, but he didn't know Wuchang had taken part in the independence movement back in the day. When he was little, Icheol heard stories about the movement that occurred not only in Gyeongseong and Gyeonggi Province but all across the country. He'd heard rumours about people who were killed, injured, or captured and tortured in prison, but he was surprised to learn that Wuchang had been among them. It stunned him to hear that 3,000 people had gathered at a marketplace in Cheonan to chant for independence, but more so to learn that dozens of them had been shot dead by Japanese troops. Wuchang's mission at the time was to go up a mountain to light a signal fire when needed. He stuck to the mission all through April until he was arrested at the marketplace. The military police beat him half to death and kept him in prison for six months.

What Daegil told Icheol was even more unexpected. He said that chanting slogans in the street was unlikely to bring independence, and that for labourers like themselves and landless farmers, they and their children — and their children's children — had no hope of escaping poverty. He explained that they were like frogs trapped under a heavy pile of rocks. And that they were doubly oppressed by Japan and capital.

'What's capital?' asked Icheol.

'In simple terms, money.'

'Then all we have to do is work for it.'

'With our bare hands?' Daegil said. 'Land and factories are a means of production, in other words, money. If the people who work the land and the factories own them together, then we all live equally, but instead they're owned by a handful of men who take advantage of workers like us. In the old days, they were in the hands of the king and his officials, and passed down within their families for generations. Now the Japanese have taken over the whole country and are bossing us around, too.'

'Our young Yi here graduated from primary school,' said Wuchang.

'That must mean you can read and write in Korean and Japanese.'

'Not anything too advanced.'

The conversation wasn't the easiest to follow, but it made sense to Icheol. In Russia, the people had risen up to oust the tsar and establish a government of the people, and in Manchuria, countless Korean patriots were arming themselves to fight Japan. A revolution was therefore necessary for Joseon to break free from Japan and establish a new country. He said that socialist ideas seeking freedom and equality for the people had made their way into colonised Joseon and, for the past ten years or so, had prompted more than a thousand tenancy disputes in rural communities all over the country as well as fights for workers' rights at factories, mines, and ports. But the fight was impossible without collective organisation, and being organised did not mean having some well-read intellectual giving orders from above like it had in the past, but rather the workers themselves coming together to improve their lives, choosing representatives and leaders from among their own ranks, and achieving that highest level of organisation possible: the party.

Icheol didn't find out that their gathering was part of this effort to form a party until a few months later. The Joseon Communist Party had been established years ago, but its members had been arrested by the Japanese within a matter of months. Socialists had been launching one attempt after the next to revive the party. Just as there was more than one route up a mountain, there was more than one way to carry out an independence movement, and accordingly, ideologies and political views differed. But the fiercest fighters were those with nothing to lose: the property-less proletarians with a socialist streak. Daegil never went into such details, but Icheol came across them in a notebook Wuchang secretly handed him. In it was a collection of very specific statements written by multiple contributors.

> Freedom to go on strike, i.e. absolute opposition to police and military suppression of workers' strikes. Freedom to organise, e.g. form labour unions. Absolute opposition to all evil laws aimed at suppressing workers, especially the Maintenance of Public Order Act, Publishing Act, and Violence Control Act. Immediate release of all political prisoners. No death penalty. Workers' rights of free speech and assembly. Freedom of political assembly and demonstration. Freedom to establish management committees. No feudal dormitory curfews or restrictions. A seven-hour workday and forty-hour work week. Minimum wage for married workers. Absolute opposition to bourgeois industry rationalisation, e.g. aggressive workload increases, worsening labour conditions, wage cuts, and stretchouts. Equal pay for equal work. No indentured servitude or sale of women and children. Unionisation of workers by industry Gyeongseong-wide and nation-wide.

The notebook also included a chronological collection of Korean newspaper clippings dating back to 1925. The Joseon Communist Party had been formed in April of that year, but a few months later in November, scores of socialists were arrested during the Sinuiju Incident. Every year, over the next five years, between the first and the fifth Communist Party Incidents, a total of 12–30,000 Koreans took part in hundreds of labour and agrarian disputes all over the country. The independence troops continued to fight Japanese forces in Manchuria as well as around the border between Joseon and China, clashing nearly 500 times early on and then about 100 times per year. The most recent events were the fifth Communist Party Incident and an anti-Japanese movement started by students in Gwangju, which went nationwide. The Mukden Incident prompted Japan to reinforce the Maintenance of Public Order Act, which led to the dissolution of Singanhoe, an anti-Japanese coalition of Korean socialists and nationalists. Three thousand or more were arrested over the next ten months, filling the prisons to capacity.

Icheol was surprised to learn that such extraordinary events had taken place so recently. Over here in Yeongdeungpo, life had gone on as usual, while over there a fire had been raging. Apart from the newspaper clippings, he also read a couple of pamphlets in Japanese that Daegil and Wuchang gave him. He went over difficult passages several times and when he met with them on Sundays, he asked questions about sentences he'd underlined. He read a transcribed copy of Marx and Engels' *Communist Manifesto* translated from Japanese to Korean. The thin notebook that began with 'A spectre is haunting Europe' and ended with 'Workers of the world, unite!' grew to three copies with the help of his own transcription. He assumed the copy he had received had been transcribed the same way. He was able to understand parts of a Japanese copy of *Capital*, but *Materialism*, by a Japanese scholar, was too difficult from the outset. Someone had pencilled notes in the margins of *Capital* and signed them, in very tiny letters, 'Yu'. Their notes were far easier to read, so Icheol made copies for himself. Also easier to understand than Marx's *Capital* was Lenin's *The State and Revolution*. The part about the duty of the proletariat made his heart race. Over the course of a few months, Icheol took in all these new ideas like sandy soil soaking up water. And because he himself was a worker and one of the people of Joseon under the yoke of Japanese imperialism, everything he read seemed to call out to him personally.

One evening, Icheol returned home after meeting with Daegil and Wuchang. It was only he and his father in the Willow Tree House now, and with the lights already out in his father's room, the house was so quiet that it felt abandoned. He couldn't even hear his father snoring. Icheol had the other bedroom to himself since Ilcheol was living in the training-school dormitory in Yongsan. He tiptoed into the house and was about to open his bedroom door when Baekman coughed.

'Is that you, Dusoe?' asked Baekman.

'Yes, I, uh, just got back.'

'Come in for a bit.'

Baekman turned the lights on and sat up. He waited while Icheol sat on the floor at the far end of the room with his knees up.

'What are you up to these days?'

'Up to? I met some friends after work.'

'Did you drink?'

'Just some makgeolli,' Icheol said, trying to sound casual.

'What kind of friends are they?'

Baekman's unexpected question left Icheol briefly speechless.

'I noticed guys coming over to your workspace and you stepping away a lot these days. Your brother will be a formal employee of the Railway Bureau when he graduates from the training school. Shouldn't you work harder to polish your skills so you can move up to being a full-time assistant?'

'Don't worry, I'll find my own way in life,' Icheol mumbled, looking away.

'How? Do you intend to live hand-to-mouth forever?'

'I have plans of my own.'

Icheol made to leave, when Baekman raised his voice.

'Stay seated! I'm not done yet.' Baekman sighed. 'I've heard rumours about the ways of the world these days. They say people have been protesting and going on strikes all over the country. You think that can free us? You think the Japanese will let go that easily of the country they devoured? You think I don't know the socialist games you and your friends are into? Every Korean knows our country must be independent. But we have to get past this hump first. I've been lucky enough to find a job and make a living to this day.'

'Lucky? What's so lucky about your life? Those bastards own you, they're your masters! I mean, what I'm trying to say is that, no matter whether we're Japanese or Korean, we shouldn't live like slaves barely surviving on whatever scraps we're given, we should be compensated properly for our work. When *that* day comes, then our country will be free.'

To his surprise, Baekman nodded in agreement.

'Okay, let's pretend what you're saying is true. It takes power to change the world and gain independence. But when has our family ever owned any land or boats? Eighty per cent of Koreans are no different from us. Take your brother, for instance. Do you think he buried himself in his studies because he's not as smart or rational as you? You have to be able to stand on your own two feet first.'

At the mention of his brother, Icheol lost his cool and raised his voice.

'Abeoji, enough! For as long as I can remember, all you and my aunt and uncles ever talk about is Hansoe. You showered him with praise whenever he brought back his report card. When he became an honour student, you slaughtered a chicken for him. I enjoyed a chicken dinner, too, thanks to him, but I was never praised no matter how hard I tried, even when I helped out at your workshop. You've got him, so why worry? Forget about me. I can take care of myself.'

Baekman's anger suddenly subsided, and he lowered his voice.

'If you're so determined to go down that road, then go ahead. There's bound to be someone like that in every family, so you might as well be that person in ours. I won't go along with it, but I won't stand in your way either. You're old enough to fend for yourself now. In exchange, leave me out of whatever it is you and your friends are up to at the rail works. I just wish we didn't work at the same place.'

With that, Baekman said no more and went back to his usual gruff, expressionless mien. Icheol jumped to his feet and left the room. He lay in the dark of his own room until he heard his father snoring and knew he was asleep. Instead of turning the lights on, Icheol lit a candle and lay on his belly. He opened his notebook, used a pencil to draw a thick line under the subtitle to a brief commentary, and went over the passage again. When he reached the part about ways to go on strike, he began adding his own comments based on the discussions he'd had with Daegil and Wuchang.

Up until then, Icheol had no idea who was running the group outside of the rail works, and only had a vague idea that Daegil was a 'reppo', a type of liaison. He did not know that there were handlers on the outside dedicated to running the organisation just like those inside the rail works. Such handlers must have been connected to other factories throughout Gyeongseong. Icheol was aware that political parties in Joseon never made it more than a few months before being pulverised by the police. Pretend intellectuals kept forming cliquish factions only to disband, and would hurriedly throw together yet another group armed with nothing more than slogans, so impatient were they to connect with industrial workers and peasant farmers without making any actual changes to their lives, and would immediately find themselves arrested again. The Comintern's December Theses, released a decade prior, lambasted the petit-bourgeois intellectuals for their factionalism and their abstract approach to organisation, and called for all previous groups to be disbanded and consolidated. Daegil provided Icheol with an overview of the difference between nationalist reformism and the Red Labour Union movement. Icheol greatly sympathised with Daegil's explanation of how, after learning about the nationalist right wing's expectations of autonomy from Japan, socialists in Singanhoe decided to completely denounce the right wing's opportunism and lean toward the coalition's dissolution.

The events of those days stayed with Shin Geumi for the rest of her life. She used to tell the stories of the early days of her and Ilcheol's marriage to Jino over and over again. By then, she was past ninety and had been separated from her husband for more than five decades, since the Korean War. Fortunately, her son, Jisan, had lived to tell his own tale of how he went to find his father and narrowly survived the war. But it seemed as though Geumi was clinging to her memories of her husband as a young man.

'Back then, your great-grandfather was still living near the market. After we got married, your grandfather landed a job at the Railway Bureau, so we moved into the rail workers' housing in Dangsan-jeong. We must've stayed there for three or four years. Your great-grandfather missed his workshop so much that we decided to move to Mageum Gomo's place in Saetmal. Your great-aunt had already gone to Manchuria by then.'

'So how did you and grandfather meet? Through a matchmaker, or was it a love marriage?'

'There was no matchmaker around since we weren't living in the countryside. But we didn't meet by chance on the street and fall in love either,' said Geumi with a bashful smile.

'Then, how?'

She covered her smile with her hand.

'Let's just say it was a bit of both.'

She meant that their marriage was half-romantic and half-arranged. When Jino kept pressing her, she brought up her husband's younger brother, Icheol.

'You've heard that my brother-in-law used to be a communist, right?'

Jino didn't understand what this meant until he was all grown up, and by then he had come to the bitter realisation that his future had already been decided for him, with absolutely no room for any other possibilities. He'd been given no choice but to live the life of a manual labourer. After all, his grandfather had defected to the North, and his father had followed, only to return as a wounded prisoner of war. And before that, his grandfather's brother was a communist who died in prison before liberation from Japan. Had his grandfather's choices also been made for him in advance? Perhaps even his great-grandfather Baekman's gruff, expressionless neutralism had been predetermined long ago.

5

Back then, Shin Geumi began attending church every Sunday. Having jumped at the chance to work at a factory — lured in by the claim that she would be able to complete an entire secondary-school education through night classes alone — she was still determined to learn something. She envied the fact that professional-school students and those studying in Japan learned how to converse and read in English. So when a friend asked if she was interested in joining an English Bible study at their church, she jumped at that chance, too. The pastor himself was Korean, but the church had an American missionary couple posted there. The wife, Mary, was in charge of the Bible study. The group met for an hour after the Wednesday evening service and for an hour after the Sunday morning service.

By then, Geumi had more time to spare, as she'd already completed the factory's intensive three-year secondary-school curriculum. She'd also become a full-time weaver heading her own team, which meant she was now allowed to live outside the factory if she wanted. Nevertheless, she chose to stay in a double room at the dormitory. It was a little inconvenient, but with room and board taken care of, it helped keep her living expenses down. The dorm supervisor had Geumi bring a written confirmation from the church before giving her permission to go out.

The church was a fair distance from the factory. It was in a new brick building at the foot of Onggimal, past the marketplace intersection and Yeongdeungpo Station. Later, when the church opened a kindergarten, she regretted not being able to send her son, Jisan, there. Anyway, on

Sundays, Geumi would leave the factory to attend the morning service and the afternoon Bible study. Then she'd grab a bite before returning to the dormitory, or stop by the theatre near the market to watch a movie, or a play featuring Japanese sinpa or a samurai drama. The Wednesday-evening Bible study, however, usually ended a little after nine, which meant she had to rush back to make the ten o'clock curfew. At that hour, the streets were mostly empty except for the square in front of the train station. During the summer, at least, there were always plenty of people out walking or enjoying the night air in the alleyways outside their houses, but when the weather was bad or winter was near, then the stillness and silence that greeted her gave her the chills. But then again, ghosts were not nearly as frightening as people.

One day as she was leaving the church, Geumi noticed a dark shadow had begun to follow her from a distance and slowly close in. When she reached the marketplace intersection, where there were a fair number of people out, she came to an abrupt stop and waited. The person approaching was a young man in khaki work clothes buttoned up to his neck. He looked like he had just got off work nearby. Instead of walking past, he stopped five or six paces behind her and turned around. He took out a cigarette and lit it, as if stalling. The ever-plucky Geumi walked right up and confronted him.

'Why are you following me?'

'Wh-what?' stuttered the young man as he snatched the cigarette out of his mouth and took two steps back. 'Y-you know Seonok, don't you?'

'You mean my assistant, Bak Seonok? What's she to you?'

'Well, uh, I'm not quite sure where to begin, but I actually work at the same factory.'

Just then, a grey vision appeared briefly before vanishing into the dark. Black stripes had been drawn over the dark outline of the man's body. Geumi shook her head to chase the vision away.

'I've never seen you before.'

The young man scratched his head as he answered sheepishly, 'I've only been there a month.'

'In which section?'

'I'm a day labourer in the power and electricity department.'

Geumi couldn't help but smile. If this was true, then he was pretty much at the very bottom of the ladder and getting paid by the day with no guarantee that there'd be a next day, on top of which, a month was barely enough time for him to have learned the ins and outs of the factory.

'You should focus on getting better at your job so you can make something of yourself.'

The young man nodded and said, 'Yes, I plan to do so. I actually got fired before from the rail works.'

Years later, Geumi would recall that, from the moment she'd laid eyes on him, he hadn't struck her as a typical day labourer, and the vision she'd had weighed on her. She mentioned it more than once to her son, Jisan, and grandson Jino. According to Geumi, the vision had been an omen of her brother-in-law's future prison sentence. She was well aware of the strike hundreds had gone on at the rail works. In fact, there wasn't a soul in Yeongdeungpo who hadn't heard about it. Many were arrested and temporarily detained. It sparked labour disputes at an electrics company, a rubber factory, a flour mill, and a rice mill, leaving Yeongdeungpo and Incheon in turmoil. The young man slowly began to walk with Geumi toward the textile factory. The reason he wanted to talk to her was to invite her to a book club that a few workers at the factory were running on the outside every Sunday. Her assistant Bak Seonok was the one who had secretly recommended her.

'I couldn't talk about it back then, but that was when the younger communists were just getting started. They'd watched the older ones mouth off in restaurants and cafes, declaring themselves a party but doing nothing else, only to get arrested and disbanded, so they took a different approach. They got jobs in factories and tried to organise from the bottom up. Backing them was a legendary activist known only by his family name of Yi. Back then, your grandfather didn't even know what he looked like. Oh, and all those factions! There were people forming their own groups while fancying themselves as belonging to the

Comintern, the International Party, but not us! We spoke as one and pleaded for the same thing: to please join forces, to wake up and see what was happening to Koreans.'

The Yeongdeungpo Rail Works declared that the Mukden Incident and worldwide economic depression made a temporary shutdown necessary for restructuring. In protest, a hundred or so Korean workers went on strike. The company hit back by firing 200 employees, including both full-time workers and a large number of day labourers. This prompted nearly 300 more workers to join the strike, which completely shut down the factory. Seven or eight workers, including Ahn Daegil, Bang Wuchang, and Yi Icheol, formed a secret strike committee. Directions came from a central body on the outside that Daegil was in contact with. The committee held a workers' assembly and openly elected five representatives. The impact was felt immediately, as there had never before, in all the strikes held in colonial Joseon, been a strike organised in which every single employee of the factory participated. The hardline tactic of firing 200 workers had backfired and brought the workers together instead.

Icheol never forgot that morning when all the workers stopped their machines and gathered in front of the factory. Everyone was there, including the 200 who had been fired, as well as foremen, team heads, engineers, and assistants. Most were Korean, although there were a few Japanese foremen and assistants here and there. Icheol could see his father's lathe at the far end of the factory. When the workers filed out, their machines grinding to a slow stop like water ebbing from the shore, Baekman's lathe was still spinning. At last, it stopped, too, and he sat at his workbench for a long while. Then he slowly made his way down the rows of machines.

Icheol was standing beside the wide-open factory doors. When his father, the last to leave, finally exited, he slid the rail doors shut.

'You got a cigarette?'

Icheol pulled his pack from his shirt pocket, handed one to his father, and took out a match to light it for him. The front yard was already ringing with the sounds of workers clapping and responding to the rallying cries of the strike committee's chairman. Baekman took a long draw from the cigarette before speaking to his son.

'Since it's come to this, give it your best shot. I'm on the lay-off list with the rest of the 300, but it's probably just a threat. They won't be able to run the factory without us, so what choice have they got? But brace yourselves, because you've got nowhere to hide now. They know what you're capable of.'

And so father and son joined the strike. It took only a few days of work stoppage for the conflict to be patched up with a minimal number of arrests and lay-offs. But that was only the beginning.

After rescinding the lay-offs as a gesture of appeasement, the Japanese authorities launched a close investigation of the five representatives, as well as Icheol, who had publicly led the rally. They all strongly denied any connection to seditious organisations and were released with a warning. However, when Ahn Daegil and Bang Wuchang's covers were blown, everyone was brought back in for questioning. Daegil and Wuchang ended up being arrested, and Icheol was fired along with Hong and Ji, who had served on the strike committee.

After taking a break for six months, Icheol found work as a day labourer at the textile factory. The central body was still operating actively on the outside. A middle-aged female day labourer whose affiliation was less exposed was sent to visit Daegil and Wuchang in the holding cell. She deposited the food money the factory workers had chipped in for them, and continued to visit by pretending to be Daegil's sister-in-law, up until they were transferred to a detention centre. After one of her visits, the woman passed on a message from Daegil to Icheol. Wuchang would be released soon enough, but Daegil was going to have to do some hard time. Daegil suggested that Icheol visit the small restaurant his mother ran near Singil-jeong. Icheol had barely taken his first step as an activist, but he sensed that there must be a purpose behind Daegil's suggestion.

Hong said he'd been there before and led the way. They walked past Yeongdeungpo Station and over Gochumalgogae Hill toward Singil-jeong, where new streets had appeared, branching off either side of the main road, which was also new. Decades ago, the area had become a foreign concession. Japanese shops had appeared, and the Maruboshi factory moved in, making the neighbourhood as bustling as that near the marketplace, with plenty of eateries and taverns and inns. Most of the people who flocked to the area were labourers hoping to find work in a factory or with Japanese merchants. And they all needed a place to sleep at night, regardless of whether they were employed regularly somewhere or sold their labour piecemeal or got by doing odd jobs. From cheap rooms to hole-in-the-wall eateries, the area was teeming with young men. A cluster of cheap Korean brothels emerged from shacks built in the countless alleyways along the tracks, while the Japanese prostitutes plied their trade in the officially licensed red-light district near the station, complete with proper signage. Hong and Icheol arrived after lunch; Daegil's mother was busy doing dishes. At their words of comfort, she looked away, her eyes brimming with tears.

'What would I know? I guess he's doing it for a great cause,' she said, smiling helplessly.

'Hyeongnim told us to visit you and talk things over,' Icheol said gently.

Daegil's mother gazed at them for a moment before nodding.

'Come back in three days. I might have a message for you.'

On his next visit, Icheol was given a time and place. He walked across the bridge to Yongsan on the other side of the Hangang River and stood waiting by a tram stop at six as the sun began to set. He held a folded newspaper askew against his face, pretending to shade himself from the sun. A man tapped Icheol's shoulder as he passed by.

'You from Yeongdeungpo?' he asked as he kept walking.

Icheol started to walk with him as he replied, 'I received word from the inside to visit his mother.'

'What's your name?'

'Yi Icheol.'

They continued down the tree-lined footpath toward Yongsan Station.

'I heard you were fired. It's not good to be out of work for long. Find a job.'

The man advised Icheol to form a group with two comrades he could trust completely. The three of them would discuss matters among themselves while also forming other groups of three at their respective workplaces. This would keep the direct points of contact to a minimum while broadening their network: their group of three times three each would make nine, three times four would make twelve, three times five would make fifteen, and so on. Later, this would come to be called the 'troika hitch', after the sled pulled by three horses. Daegil's role as reppo to the central body was passed to Icheol, putting him in charge of all reppos in Yeongdeungpo. Communication with higher-ups could be done at two rendezvous points: the primary one being the restaurant in Singil-jeong, and the secondary one being the Samgae Gukbap restaurant at the Yongsan Market entrance.

*

Icheol had learned how to operate a lathe from his father and from his job at the rail works. And although his skills weren't refined enough yet to make delicate parts, he was a capable machinist. When he applied for a casual position at the textile factory, he was asked where he'd worked previously. He replied that he'd worked at a machi-koba, a small Japanese workshop, after graduating primary school. He was immediately hired and assigned to the machinery section.

Even though Icheol was only an assistant, the full-time employee he was there to assist would give him detailed instructions on whatever machine had come in needing repairs, watch just long enough to feel reassured that Icheol knew what he was doing, and then would take off on a cigarette break or to chat with co-workers. Within a matter of days, Icheol had befriended almost all the team heads and foremen at the workshop and went out for drinks with them. A month into his new job, he started a book club. Unlike the rail works, most of the workers at the textile factory were young single women, and the supervisors and trainers were all middle-aged women.

Shin Geumi followed her assistant Bak Seonok to where the

book-club meeting was being held. It was in a neighbourhood near the embankment, just a stone's throw north of the marketplace. Geumi and Seonok passed various shops and stalls beyond the market before arriving at a small hanok with a tteok shop in front. Seonok's maternal grandparents sold tteok there with the help of a young man from the countryside. On a display stand out front were rice cakes of all types and flavours, still hot and steaming from the stove: sirutteok, baekseolgi, jeolpyeon, garaetteok, baramtteok, songpyeon. Inside was the family's living space, and in the very back was a storage room half-filled with straw bags of grain, rice-cake mallets, rolling pins, wooden bowls, and wicker trays, but with enough space left over for several people to gather as long as they sat against the wall. Six people came to the meeting; Icheol was the only man. Apart from Geumi, the rest were assistants or day labourers. They began taking turns reading aloud from magazines or pamphlets edited by revolutionary figures. They also read short stories, poems, and social-science articles. It was Seonok's turn to read.

'Pro … propeller …' Seonok stammered.

'Proletariat. A propeller is like a pinwheel,' Icheol corrected her with a smile.

'This word keeps coming up. What does it mean?' asked Seonok.

Icheol explained that the proletariat were the have-nots, another name for labourers like themselves. He shared what he'd heard from Daegil: that the word originated from the ancient Romans, among whom the lowest social class had nothing to offer the state other than their own offspring, who would be slaves like them.

The members usually found it hard to focus for more than an hour or two, so they'd read and discuss for an hour and spend the rest of the time getting to know each other better. They agreed to look for others at the factory who were prudent and good-natured enough to make good additions to the book club. Geumi brought two friends who had taken night classes with her, and Icheol found a male team head. He was a full-time worker named Jo Yeongchun. Five years older than Icheol, he'd graduated from primary school and studied for two years at a technical secondary school before dropping out. He still hoped to finish his studies one day and would often talk about going to Japan to get certified as an engineer once he saved enough money. But after studying the notebooks like Icheol had for a few months, Yeongchun became conscious of his position as a colonial labourer.

Icheol, Yeongchun, and Seonok became the main organisers — or 'orgs', as they called them — at the textile factory. Through communication with the central body, they learned that industrial unions had to take the lead in showing solidarity, and that solidarity was already being formed between sections within the metal, chemical, and publishing industries. Icheol further found out that at least seven or eight to as many as ten or more members of Red Labour Union preparatory committees were connected with each silk factory — from filature to spinning to weaving. The chemical industry had rubber factories in every city throughout the country, and the textile industry had dozens of factories in Gyeongseong and three to four in most major cities. A majority of the workforce in these industries were women, married and unmarried alike. In a sense, compared to the countless other Korean girls their age who weren't even allowed outside their front gates let alone inside a school and sat around waiting to be married off to men their fathers had chosen, the factory girls were poised to boldly pioneer new lives for themselves. They were far more revolutionary than their male colleagues. Though Geumi had been introduced to socialism under Icheol's guidance, something very personal happened to her around the same time.

Icheol had been fired in the autumn and had begun the book club the following spring. By the autumn of that same year, the number of club members had doubled and had to be split into two groups. An affiliated group was also started at a neighbouring silk filature, bringing the total to three. Icheol's plate was already full, so Yeongchun led the book-club meetings with Seonok. Geumi joined Seonok, Sohn Yeongsun, and friends from the filature when they went on picnics or to see sinpa plays. Yeongsun had been a close friend of Geumi's since taking night classes with her at the factory. Once Geumi introduced her to the book club, Yeongsun became more eager than anyone at recruiting members.

At twenty-one, Yeongsun was older than Geumi and Seonok. As she grew close to Geumi, she confessed that she'd left her son with her parents in Chungcheong Province. After finishing school, she had married at seventeen to a boy three years her junior. While she was pregnant, her husband went boating and fishing with his friends one summer day and drowned in the Geumgang River. Yeongsun went back to live with her parents. Not long after giving birth, she learned from a relative that she might be able to find work at a textile factory. Geumi shared a room with Yeongsun for three years at the factory's dormitory; in the middle of eating or while lying in bed, Yeongsun sometimes fell silent, her mind clearly somewhere else. In her tear-filled eyes, Geumi would catch an image of a baby with big eyes and wispy hair, and say, 'Ah, you miss your little boy.' Yeongsun would put her hand over her eyes and cry.

One day, Geumi, Yeongsun, and Icheol went to a book-club meeting while Seonok was at a different meeting with Yeongchun. To accommodate their rising numbers, one group gathered at Seonok's grandparents' tteok shop and the other at Icheol's Willow Tree House. They were taking turns reading and sharing their thoughts when the door burst open and they saw a figure standing there.

'Close the door,' Icheol said casually.

The person was wearing a black school uniform with gold buttons fastened up to his neck. His cap with its metal insignia was pulled down so far that only the lower half of his face was visible. He closed the door without a word.

'Who is that?' Yeongsun whispered.

'My hyeong.'

According to Geumi, she was sitting beside the door at the time. She only caught a glimpse of a bandaged hand when she peeked sideways out the door. Ilcheol later brushed it off as an injury from training, but Geumi couldn't stop talking about the impression that bandage had left on her. It made Ilcheol look like a fearless warrior returning from a battlefront or an injured man with a dark, violent secret. No wonder it was so trendy for such a long time for secondary-school boys in sports clubs, like soccer, judo, or kendo, to walk around with bandages on their perfectly uninjured hands, necks, or forearms. Secondary-school girls who wanted to look cool, on the other hand, would bandage their neck or cover a pimple with a small star-shaped adhesive bandage. After the meeting, Icheol approached Geumi.

'It's Sunday. Would you like to go see a movie?'

'Is there anything good?'

'There's a Korean movie people have been talking about.'

Geumi looked at Yeongsun for consent and Yeongsun nodded. The three had stepped down to the courtyard when Ilcheol poked his head out of Baekman's workshop.

'What's that about going to the movies?'

'Tag along if you want.'

At his brother's invitation, Ilcheol rushed to put his shoes on.

'As a matter of fact, I've been wanting to see that one myself,' said Ilcheol.

The four headed out of the Willow Tree House and walked down toward the marketplace intersection. Icheol introduced his brother to Geumi and then Yeongsun. Naturally, when this story was told to them later, the whole family wanted to know what vision Geumi had the first time she saw Ilcheol's face. Surprisingly, she insisted that she saw absolutely nothing. But wasn't that more ominous, they wondered, given her uncanny sixth sense for knowing exactly what others were going through regardless of whether she knew the person or not. She didn't have any visions until after they were married, the most famous of which among their family was the one Geumi had at the railway inn in Onyang where the couple spent their first night. Actually, it wasn't even night yet — the sun was still blazing high overhead when she stepped into that room at the inn, luggage in hand, and saw a naked baby boy sprawled out on a blanket on top of the tatami mat, giggling and waving his arms and legs. Geumi even saw the brown wart beside the boy's belly button that looked just like the one his grandfather Baekman had on his shoulder blade. Wasn't it curious indeed for someone, whose gift was so strong that she could see her own son well before he was born, to have seen nothing when she met her future husband? Whenever her son Jisan, daughter-in-law Bokrye, or grandson Jino asked her about her first encounter with her husband, Geumi stuck to the answer she always gave.

'There was no need for a vision, because it was already decided that he would be my husband.'

When Geumi looked at Ilcheol for the first time and saw nothing, her heart began to pound. Ilcheol, too, later bashfully stuttered as he described Geumi's cute forehead and bright, twinkling eyes.

'What movie are we watching?' asked Yeongsun.

Icheol said, '*The Ownerless Ferryboat*,' at the same time that Ilcheol asked, 'How about *Arirang*?'

Geumi and Yeongsun shook their heads.

'Don't tell me you've been ditching work to go to the movies every day,' Ilcheol said to his brother.

'What's your excuse?' Icheol retorted.

'It's just been in the papers a lot.'

Ilcheol offered to buy all four tickets, but Geumi refused. Students don't have that kind of money, she said, they were all employed and could pay for themselves. Icheol sulked that his brother should be the one to pay, seeing as how he was a student of the Japanese Government-General, getting paid to study and live in their government dormitory. In the end, it was decided that they would each get their own ticket but would let Ilcheol buy them dinner after.

The movie's final scene was of an old ferryman killing an engineer on the construction site of a railroad bridge and then madly hacking away at the bridge itself. A train barrels towards him, blowing its whistle, and after the ferryman dies, his house burns with his daughter in it. All that's left is an empty boat floating listlessly on the river. When they came out of the theatre, Geumi's and Yeongsun's eyes were red from crying, and Icheol was boiling over with anger.

'The Japanese have ruined everything! We have to overthrow them. Those pig-footed bastards should all be wiped out!'

Ilcheol said little until they were seated in a Chinese restaurant and waiting for their noodles to come out.

'A boat will never beat a train, just like a horse and cart will never beat an aeroplane.'

'So what are we supposed to do? Just sit on our hands for the rest of our lives?' asked Icheol.

'My plan is to pick up a skill,' Ilcheol said. 'I only hope that I'll be able to put it to good use for my fellow Koreans.'

After they were home, the brothers kept talking as they lay in their room.

'I heard you quit the rail works for a textile factory?'

'I was fired. I had to take whatever job I could find.'

'Abeoji says you've turned communist, is that true?'

Icheol didn't answer and Ilcheol didn't push.

'When I finish school, I'll be hired by the Railway Bureau. I'm training to be a driver. I'll look after our family, so you don't have to worry about that. But in exchange, I hope you can keep your affairs out of the house.'

The brothers confirmed where they each stood and promised to respect one another's wishes. And they did their best to keep that promise. It went unbroken until after Liberation, and by then Icheol had long since passed from this world.

Icheol wasn't expecting a strike to happen any time soon. Class consciousness was key, and the few months they'd spent meeting in secret wasn't enough time for the dozen or so book-club members to understand what they should be doing. Moreover, Icheol had only just started forming connections with other textile factories and did not yet have a grasp of their situations. He stopped by the restaurant in Singiljeong and learned that Bang Wuchang had been released after three months. He was now working in the street as a porter and living in a rented room nearby. Icheol didn't tell Wuchang that he had been put in charge of communication for the movement in Yeongdeungpo.

'How's your health?' Icheol asked, out of polite consideration for Wuchang, who was old enough to be his uncle.

Wuchang stroked his haggard cheeks and chin as he said, 'Well, seeing as how my indictment got suspended and they let me out in three months, I can't say I really suffered.'

'What about Ahn Hyeong?'

'He was tortured a lot. I heard he was sentenced to eighteen months. If he manages to pull himself back together, I guess we could say he came back from training.'

When Wuchang was arrested, he feigned ignorance. He pretended to be illiterate, begged for mercy, and — as they had agreed beforehand — laid all the blame on Ahn Daegil. His torturers forced water laced with chilli pepper down his throat and strung him up naked and beat him unconscious to try to get information out of him, but all he did was cry and beg for his life. He flashed Icheol a happy-go-lucky smile and said the problem was that playing stupid only works once. If he were implicated in another case, his punishment and prison sentence would be twice as bad. Wuchang didn't tell Icheol everything. He left out the part where he met a certain someone from Shanghai while in lock-up. Wuchang told Icheol he planned to take a break from organising and would stick with working as a porter for a while instead.

*

At the end of the month, Icheol went to the Samgae Gukbap place at the entrance of Yongsan Market a little before six in the evening and waited for his contact from the central body. After ordering a bowl of gukbap soup and taking a seat near the door, he tried to remember what the man he met last time had looked like. But he couldn't picture his face at all. A few minutes past six, a man in work clothes and an old bucket hat came in and plopped down before Icheol. He ordered another gukbap for himself and smiled.

'Let's eat and get out of here.'

The man in the hat appeared to be the one Icheol had met last time. His voice sounded familiar, and Icheol was pretty sure he recognised the way tiny wrinkles formed around the man's eyes when he smiled.

'I heard you've been working hard,' said the man.

'What? Who —'

Icheol caught himself, figuring there was no point in asking about each other's connections. They stopped talking, hurriedly finished their food, and left. As they walked, Icheol talked briefly about the book club, and the man asked a few questions. They went up the wooded hill near Cheongyeop-jeong.

'Haste makes waste,' the man said. 'Keep up the good work with the book club. A strike or dispute can wait until you have as many workers as possible ready to go into action. Never bring up revolution or anything big like that when you're talking to the working masses. The trick is to raise questions about everyday life, about the things that are closer to them.'

From the top of the hill, they could see a few lighted windows among the houses below. They walked in circles, all the way back down to the bottom and up again. The deserted woods were quiet except for the crunching of dried leaves underfoot. Someone appeared in the dark and began to follow them. The man in the hat tapped Icheol on the shoulder.

'Let's sit for a bit,' he said quietly.

The man sat first, and Icheol followed suit, feeling unsure of himself. The person who'd suddenly loomed out of the darkness like a shadow immediately came over and sat beside them. He was wearing a Japanese yukata like a rickshaw man. The man in the hat had probably arranged for them all to meet there.

'I've heard a lot about you from Comrade Ahn Daegil. I'm Yu,' he said to Icheol.

It was the name Icheol had seen pencilled in his notebooks.

'I hear you're doing good work in Yeongdeungpo,' Yu said cheerfully.

Icheol gulped. 'It's just baby steps.'

'We're all taking our first steps just like yourself. Since we don't have much time, let's go through the essentials. There's no distinction between activists and the masses. No one should always lead or only follow. As both individuals and the masses develop class consciousness, they start to learn from each other. A party without people is nothing more than an idea. The worse Japanese oppression grows, the more the masses are bound to lean to the left, and all the more reason for us to keep our heads on straight. We have to stick to our principles yet keep an open mind, and protect what must be kept hidden. And, of course, we must be careful not to do or say anything that's out of touch with the lives of the masses.'

Icheol asked a question that had been nagging at him.

'Are the independence movement and class struggle different from each other?'

'That question has always weighed on me, too. We're bound in two heavy shackles: Japanese colonial oppression and bourgeois social order. I believe that we can solve both problems naturally while fighting the Japanese and inspiring the working masses to strike.'

The conversation continued as they discussed the book-club membership and talked about their contacts at other factories.

'We should minimise the number and range of our contacts and let each group decide what's best for their particular workplace. Your approach, Comrade Yi, can be applied to other workplaces to gradually broaden our reach.'

Two things were left etched in Icheol's mind that day: while no good could come from rushing, they also had to keep up with rapidly changing circumstances; and they had to have faith in the autonomy and leadership abilities of the working masses. To be an activist was to support the people while being constantly guided by them. After their meeting in Cheongyeop-jeong, Icheol never talked directly to Yu again. He held on to the hand-copied pamphlets Yu gave him. They were highly theoretical and difficult to grasp, but the instructions Yu had personally added were much more specific:

> When moving on foot, hide larger objects like books under your clothes in the summer or inside your coat or under your scarf in the winter. As for smaller objects, like letters, hide them in your shoes.
>
> When taking a tram, always board through the back door and

get off through the front door. Pay for the ticket as soon as you board. If you're carrying belongings, sit at the front and place them behind your legs. Stay alert at every stop and get off immediately if a policeman boards.

Arrive near a meeting point one or two minutes early to scan the surroundings first.

Once you succeed in making eye contact with the other person, follow them. Maintain your distance when walking along a brightly lit backstreet. When stepping into an open street, make eye contact and fall back behind the other person. When crossing a street, make eye contact and allow the person who fell back to cross first.

Act naturally and speak in a low voice so as not to attract the attention of others.

Display bourgeois literary works on a table indoors and bury important books in the yard.

Never doodle, especially names. Hide pieces of paper with writing on them in cracks or chinks around your room.

Yu had written these instructions in tiny letters crammed into the margins of the pamphlets he'd copied by hand. A few years later, the name Yi Jaeyu caused an uproar nationwide when it was splashed across the front pages of newspapers next to the words 'arrest', 'escape', 'undercover', and 'wanted list'. He went to prison for a long time. That's when Icheol realised that Yu wasn't his family name after all, but the second half of his first name. After Icheol died in prison, Jaeyu followed him a mere ten months before Japan's defeat.

The man in the hat who had arranged the meeting in Yongsan was not only from the same Yi clan as Icheol, but also an intellectual who had just returned from studying in Japan. They would cross paths again at Seodaemun Prison and at their preliminary hearings, but that was years away. First, the man in the hat decided that he would be Icheol's line of contact for the foreseeable future.

6

To hear Shin Geumi tell it, the big uprising at the textile factory wasn't planned at all but happened purely by chance. She didn't even know what was going on at first. Just, one day, Yeongsun told her assistant to take over and ran out of the factory, with the supervisor right on her tail, yelling something that Geumi couldn't make out.

'There was no overtime that day, and it was nearly six, so work was pretty much over. Yeongsun's mother had come all the way from her hometown with Yeongsun's four-year-old. The guard at the gate turned them away, saying no visitors were allowed. Yeongsun's mother tried to soothe her crying grandson and hung around the gate for hours. She tried to plead with the people coming in and out of the factory, but the only ones who could have come and gone as they pleased like that were either bosses or Japanese, so they just brushed her off and refused to listen. Fortunately, her plight caught the attention of a Korean engineer passing by with his Japanese colleagues.'

Once inside, the engineer passed word along to someone else. Upon learning that her son and mother had travelled so far and were waiting at the front gate, Yeongsun rushed out in a tearful flurry of joy and concern. Her supervisor, a middle-aged Japanese woman, didn't even bother asking what was wrong, and scolded her for leaving her machine without permission while still on the clock. Yeongsun dodged the guard trying to stop her, pushed through the side gate, and threw her arms around her mother and son. Panting angrily, the supervisor caught up with Yeongsun and seized her by the hair.

'*Baka, shine!* You're still on the clock!'

Shocked, Yeongsun's mother drummed her fists on the supervisor's back. The supervisor let go of Yeongsun's hair, turned around, and struck Yeongsun's mother on the face. When Yeongsun's mother staggered, the supervisor delivered another slap, with her other hand, and kept going, left and right, left and right, until Yeongsun's mother fell to the ground. Yeongsun pulled the kerchief from her head and cried as she used it to wipe the blood from her mother's nose. She tried to keep herself together as she declared to the supervisor who was already heading back into the factory:

'You'll pay for this!'

Instead of returning to her machine or dorm room, Yeongsun took off with her son and mother. She headed straight to the tteok shop, where Seonok, having returned from work, let them stay in her room. Geumi and Jo Yeongchun rushed over as soon as they received word from Seonok.

'Is your mother okay?' asked Yeongchun.

'I'm going to tear that place apart. If those arseholes fire me, I'll just go back home with my mother and my boy,' Yeongsun said through gritted teeth.

'You definitely can't let them get away with this,' said Yeongchun.

Yeongsun nodded. 'Let's go on strike. I'll take the lead.'

'We'll need at least two to three days to gather enough people,' said Seonok.

'We already have fourteen in our club,' said Yeongsun.

Geumi finally spoke up.

'You're in way over your head. Take it easy and stop talking about quitting.'

'Never mind that. Let's organise a strike committee. I'll contact the rest of our members,' said Yeongchun.

Later that night, Yeongchun met Icheol at the marketplace intersection.

'Whose decision was it to go on strike?' asked Icheol.

'Well, uh ...' Yeongchun hesitated before answering. 'Yeongsun, the team head, said she'd take the lead.'

'But no one can make that call without talking it over with everyone else first.'

Looking unusually excited, Yeongchun said confidently, 'That's why I've been spreading the word about holding an open meeting as soon as we clock in tomorrow.'

'A strike is a last resort. A lot of people could get hurt. It's like flipping the dinner table over before we've even finished setting it. Don't hold an open meeting. Let's meet after work instead. We'll need at least two to three days to prepare.'

Yeongchun threw his head back and let out a disheartened laugh.

'Come on, why are you ruining this for us? Everyone is stirred up over this right now, but in a few days it'll all blow over.'

'If it can blow over that quickly, then it's not worth pursuing in the first place. Three days is barely enough time to discuss, create teams, divide the work, draft statements, and get as many involved as possible in the strike committee.'

Yeongchun pulled out a cigarette, lit it, and sighed as he exhaled.

'The folks higher up seem to believe we should strike while the iron is hot.'

'Who? What higher up? We're supposed to act according to the circumstances of the working masses from where we each live and work.'

When Yeongchun stood up without answering, Icheol asked, 'Speaking of higher up, have you been meeting with someone recently?'

'So what if I have? You met with someone, too, didn't you?'

Icheol looked at him blankly.

'Go see Bang Wuchang,' said Yeongchun before he turned to cross the street.

The next day, Yeongsun went to work as usual. Having already heard the news, her colleagues told her to stay strong, and some assistants even left candy and senbei crackers at her work station. A tense, heavy silence filled the factory as another long day went by. One by one, the book-club members gathered at the tteok shop. With Yeongsun's mother and son staying in the already cramped smaller room, they had to intrude upon Seonok's grandparents' bedroom to hold their meeting. Twelve out of the fourteen club members showed up. Since everyone was aware of what had happened the previous day, they immediately began to debate whether they should go on strike.

Yeongchun argued that this was their chance to remedy the long-standing abuses in their factory, and that if they let what happened yesterday slide, they would only subject themselves to even more inhumane treatment. He added that tenancy disputes and labour strikes had become an everyday occurrence in all eight provinces on the Korean peninsula. And they weren't alone: a large-scale strike had been carried out at the Yeongdeungpo Rail Works, and the neighbouring silk factory had been through multiple strikes, just like the filature, spinnery, and silk manufacturer in downtown Gyeongseong.

Icheol admitted that while what Yeongchun said was true, their factory's treatment of its workers wasn't as bad compared to others, and the workers' class consciousness had not yet developed enough for them to jump right into direct action. Going on strike meant they had to be prepared for casualties, so they had to be sure of winning and gaining what they were after in order to make it worthwhile. Icheol said that while the battles you lose were just as important, waiting for the time to ripen could mean winning.

In the end, they decided to take a vote. Eight raised their hands in favour of a strike. With only four remaining, the decision was made. Yeongchun and Yeongsun had naturally voted yes, along with Seonok and Geumi. They were in no mood to back off when they felt just as much a victim as Yeongsun and her family. Icheol was among the outnumbered four. The decision made, everyone agreed to participate as a member of the strike committee. The next step was to elect a chairperson — whoever took that position knew they were likely to be fired and punished. Yeongsun was the first to volunteer, but Geumi tried to stop her, saying she would do it instead. Most of the people there suspected that Yeongchun and Icheol were connected to a network on the outside, so they didn't want either of them to serve in any position that risked exposure. While Yeongsun and Geumi argued, the rest of the members made a suggestion. Yeongsun could be chairperson and Geumi, deputy chairperson in charge of publicity. Seonok would handle coordination, and the rest of the committee members would take care of surveying and communication. Yeongchun agreed to support coordination efforts at the factory, and Icheol agreed to help with publicity and communication.

After the meeting, Icheol decided to pay Wuchang a visit. He couldn't shake off what Yeongchun had said the day before. Wuchang was living close to Ahn Daegil's mother's restaurant in Singil-jeong. Icheol headed to the restaurant first; he needed to get the word out about the new developments. By the time he arrived, the dinner rush had ended, and Daegil's mother was taking a break.

Icheol greeted her and said, 'I'm not feeling well. I need to get in touch with Uncle.'

'You ought to be more careful. Everyone catches colds more easily when the seasons change. Why don't you take a stroll around the block? He was here today,' Daegil's mother said casually.

'Really? When?'

'He came by earlier for lunch. He said he had some business to take care of nearby.'

'In that case, I'll come back in two hours.'

Daegil's mother waved this off and said, 'Not here. The alley behind the Maruboshi factory.'

Icheol stopped by Wuchang's room. Wuchang saw him coming and quickly put his shoes on. Labourers were returning from work, filling the yard with the sour stink of sweat and feet. Icheol joined Wuchang as he walked out without a word.

'We've decided to go on strike. By the way, do you know Jo Yeongchun?'

'Hmm, a little. I wasn't trying to hide anything from you, though.'

The two men came out of the alley and squatted in the gravel next to the railway tracks.

'I met someone from the International Party in lock-up,' Wuchang said. 'He's a student from Shanghai, and unless something comes up, he'll be out of prison in a couple of months. He put me in touch with his line, so I reached out. There seems to be several members in Yeongdeungpo.'

'Weren't we trying to rebuild a party locally based on the Red Labour Union? For convenience's sake, we've been calling it the Gyeongseong Troika.'

'The Comintern defined Korean parties as factions and sects years ago in their December Theses. The guideline has been to dissolve and rebuild.'

'I'm aware of that.'

'The task at hand is absolute integration.'

'We don't even know which side is factionalist.' Icheol's voice grew heated. 'The working masses don't give a damn about that stuff. They're fighting for their right to live. Shouldn't we be able to embrace anyone regardless of sides if they're willing to commit and contribute?'

'You're right about the masses. But we're the vanguard, aren't we? We can't ignore the International Party's instructions. What happened at your factory may have been impromptu, but the Yeongdeungpo-wide strikes were carried out with permission and instructions from the International Party. You should notify your higher-ups to arrange a meeting with someone from their line.'

'I'll send a message. But I'm telling you, we should each play it by the book.'

Two hours later, Icheol had arranged to meet Yi, the man in the hat, behind the Maruboshi factory. The location happened to be at the edge of a cluster of brothels. There were drunk men milling about, and prostitutes marching into the street to grab potential customers by the sleeve instead of waiting around behind their lattice windows. Icheol was uneasily looking around when a man in a loose, wrinkled suit jacket approached him, draped his arm over Icheol's shoulder, and slurred, 'Hey, let's go get a drink somewhere.'

He wasn't wearing a hat today.

'You see Ssangseongnu over there?' Yi whispered in Icheol's ear. 'Let's go there.'

At the Chinese restaurant, they sat in a corner seat partially blocked by a red curtain and a partition. With the dinner rush long over and no other customers coming in for drinks, they had the place to themselves. The man only nodded as Icheol quickly reported on the strike and the message he'd received from Wuchang.

'Comrade Yu always said we must never go abroad. We must stay in our own country and fight to the end. This is the land of the Korean people, this is where we make our lives, where we work and struggle. No one else can carry out our revolution for us. We may be poor and insignificant and inadequate, but we must trust in the strength of our people.'

Graduates of the Communist University of the Toilers of the East in Moscow would declare their intent to form lines or groups only to get caught the moment they crossed the border or arrested in the streets of Gyeongseong. More than once, one would show up and claim to belong to the International Party line and that they'd been dispatched by the Profintern or come at the order of the Comintern's Shanghai network. Yet, according to Yi, Comrade Yu and the local faction for party reconstruction were not rejecting international solidarity or instructions. What they rejected was the authoritarian approach that bore the Comintern's slogan but took advantage of the International line's authority to dominate the local movement.

Icheol relayed to Yi what he'd heard from Wuchang, and told him about Wuchang's connection to a worker, known only by his surname, Jo, who happened to be a member of Icheol's book club. Yi let out a sigh.

'International revolutionary organisations including the Comintern have failed to provide systematic, consistent guidelines on movements in colonial Joseon. Countless figures have come forward claiming to have been sent by the Comintern's Far Eastern Bureau, or received instructions from the Chinese Communist Party in Shanghai, or a graduate of the Communist University of the Toilers of the East, or sent by the Profintern's Far Eastern Bureau and participated in the Comintern's rep meeting, the Young Communist International's Eastern Bureau, the Chinese Communist Party's Manchurian Branch, or the Pacific

Labour Union. They have each claimed the Korean working masses as their own, created redundancies, and scrabbled for leadership. What they learn about Joseon outside the country is of no practical use to the movement inside the country. Meanwhile, the working masses here have been struggling just to survive and to rise up under the yoke of Japanese oppression.'

'What should we do? They're proposing a meeting.'

Yi nodded.

'It'll be risky, but a meeting will have to be held. Otherwise, we'll be accused of being a faction. I think those comrades are looking to test our capability this time around. My guess is that the strike won't be successful. The Japanese authorities are on alert because of the other strikes that took place in Gyeongseong and Incheon over the past few months.'

'The majority already voted. It's too late to back out,' said Icheol.

'Of course, if that's what everyone wants, then you have to follow through. Let's make it a solid give and take. Proceed as planned on site, and we'll arrange the meeting through Wuchang.'

Yi explained how multiple activist lines had made their way into Yeongdeungpo.

Yeongdeungpo was an industrial zone crowded with at least thirty different factories and over 20,000 workers — far more if you included all the casual labourers. They'd mostly come from other parts of the country in search of work; natives to the area were rare. Except for the few who found accommodation in factory dormitories, most boarded at private houses or inns, or made do in shacks or in temporary housing on construction sites. Permanent residence was all but unheard of, as was permanent employment, and all this frequent moving about made it relatively easy to evade the eye and the arm of the law. That was why Yeongdeungpo had become not only the heart of the labour movement and base for underground activism, but also an ideal hiding place. On top of which, it was only half a day by train from Yeongdeungpo to Incheon, the largest harbour on the west coast, where tens of thousands worked at the many loading docks and factories there. Yeongdeungpo, as Yi put it, had Incheon behind it as its base, and ahead was Gyeongseong as its front line.

'We might not have to push strikes as the be-all and end-all. If Red Labour Union members are embedded in each factory, labour actions could become an everyday thing,' Yi added.

That night, Icheol drafted a statement and made ten copies at home. The factory workers living in the dorm were scheduled to wake at six and begin work at seven. At 6.00 am, the fourteen book-club members on the strike committee entered the factory to post notices and inform team heads, assistants, assistant helpers, and day labourers of when and where to meet. Between half past six and seven in the morning, 350 or so workers gathered in the yard. As strike-committee chairperson, Yeongsun stepped up to the podium. Before reading the prepared statement, she relayed what had happened to her two days earlier.

'My mother took a long train ride from Chungcheong Province to come see me here. I'd left my four-year-old son at home with her and my father. My son had been crying and pestering them every day to come see me, so finally my mother put him on her back and set out from home. She never dreamed she would be prevented from seeing me. But what are the rules of our factory? We're strictly banned from receiving visitors or going out except on Sundays. I stepped away from my work station for only a moment to see my mother and son, but my supervisor Nakagawa came after me. She grabbed me by the hair and slapped my mother enough times to leave her with a bloody nose. We may be a people without a country, but does that mean we deserve to be treated like this? We can't work under someone like Nakagawa. She should be fired immediately. Forcing us to work thirteen hours a day is a breach of contract. Ten hours a day, from seven in the morning to six in the evening, is still too much compared to mainland Japan, and yet, we're working three more hours overtime for free.'

Yeongsun then read the statement Icheol had prepared. When she began chanting slogans, the workers lifted their voices to join hers.

> One, fire Supervisor Nakagawa immediately! We can no longer work under her. Two, reduce our working hours from thirteen

to ten and pay extra for overtime! Three, provide Korean workers with the same quality of meals as their Japanese co-workers! Four, revise the company's internal rules that forbid receiving visitors and leaving the dormitory! We hereby declare an indefinite strike until our demands are met.

The workers dispersed to head back to their division, but they did not return to their machines. None of the team heads or division chiefs pressed them to start working. The strike's main organisers took advantage of the opportunity to each go around with a petition; every single one of the workers happily signed it and added their thumbprint next to their signature. Assistants, assistant helpers, and day labourers alike sat around idly. Supervisor Nakagawa was summoned to the office upstairs, and the Japanese instructors were nowhere in sight. It was past lunchtime when a Japanese manager came down from the office with an instructor. He warned them that everyone would be fired if they didn't start working, but no one paid him any attention.

'Who's the representative here?' the manager asked, frowning.

'I am,' Yeongsun said and stepped forward.

Geumi followed suit. 'So am I.'

Seonok immediately joined in, as well. 'And so am I.'

'*Baka*, you can't *all* be representatives,' the manager muttered angrily.

The other female workers in the factory all spoke up at once.

'This concerns us all, so yes, we're all representatives.'

'Stop talking behind our backs, and give us a straight answer about how you're going to fix this.'

The whole day went by with no sign of a compromise. When the time came to clock out, the workers decided not to clock in at all the next day. This is how Geumi later described what happened.

'Yeongsun left to take care of her mother and son at Seonok's place, and Seonok went with them since they were guests of hers. Icheol and Yeongchun were men, so they couldn't go anywhere near the dormitory. A few people made a bonfire behind the factory and waited all night to hear from us. There were still six book-club members at the dormitory when I returned, so we stopped by each of their rooms and exchanged vows not to return to work until our demands were met. I had no idea where the dormitory's superintendent and instructor went, but those damn women were nowhere to be found. It took three full days for management to finally present a compromise to the entire staff in the auditorium. They said they could only meet two of our demands, the ones regarding meal discrimination and dorm restrictions. We said we wouldn't go back to work unless they met all four. The day after we failed to reach a compromise, I woke, washed up, and went down to the cafeteria. A policeman and two plainclothes detectives were waiting at the entrance with the superintendent. I was the first to be stopped by them. I asked what the problem was, and they told me they wanted me to accompany them to the police station. They also called for my roommate, an assistant helper who'd posted the notices around the factory with me. When they took me to the police station, the big one near the train station, Yeongsun and Seonok were already there. Fortunately, the police didn't seem to be aware of Icheol and Yeongchun's involvement.'

The papers reported that a compromise had been reached thanks to the intervention of the Special Higher Police — the Japanese 'thought police' — from Yeongdeungpo Police Station. Supervisor Nakagawa was to turn in her resignation for assaulting a staff member and the staff member's mother, thereby losing the workers' trust. As for working hours, workers would be notified in advance whenever they had to do overtime. An hourly rate for overtime was calculated based on a month's pay for back-to-back shifts. The Japanese authorities had been on edge because of all the strikes and disturbances that had broken out in different factories around the Gyeongseong area from early summer to late autumn. The Government-General's Police Bureau had even ordered a secret investigation into whether those strikes and disturbances were being instigated by communists.

The police advised management to accept the supervisor's resignation and fire the strike committee's chairperson, Yeongsun. She'd be allowed to work at a different factory, but only if she agreed to a six-month suspension first. The same terms were offered to Geumi, who'd been identified as the deputy chairperson. Geumi said she'd accept the terms if she and Yeongsun were the only ones to be fired. They wrangled over the terms for ten days, during which the two were kept in lock-up.

As core members who now had direct experience of labour struggle, Icheol, Yeongchun, and Seonok lay low for the time being.

The lock-up was divided into upstairs and downstairs. Geumi was separated from Yeongsun and held in a cell downstairs. A Japanese police officer in a black uniform and carrying a sword took turns guarding the place with a Korean police assistant. In the women's cell with Geumi were two prostitutes and a girl accused of stealing from the Japanese family whose baby she'd cared for. Geumi knew their stories the moment she laid eyes on them.

'Yaeya, you're here because of the ring, aren't you, dear?' Geumi said to the girl.

The girl's eyes widened, and she covered her mouth with her hands.

'*Aegumeoni!* How did you know?'

'I can see it as clear as day. You know the washroom in the house where you worked? The sliding door with the window? The ring rolled into the crack between the door and the wall. It's shining there still.'

The girl began to cry again over being wrongfully accused, waking the two prostitutes, who'd dozed off while leaning up against each other.

'What the hell are you crying for? Pipe down! You think you're the only one in here for no reason?'

'Why did you have to make her cry? What are you? Some kinda fortune teller or shaman?'

Geumi gave them a little smile and directed her attention to them, too.

'You're here because you thought you could pull in two customers at the same time and kept going back and forth between their rooms only to cause a fight to break out. And you're here because you snatched the hat of a student passing by to try to lure him in.'

'*Aiguna*, we really do have a fortune teller on our hands. So, tell us, when will we get out?'

'Don't worry, you'll be out after tonight. Isn't there a curly-haired man at your place?'

'Huh! That's our pimp.'

'He's going to pay your fine and get you out tomorrow.'

The two women, who seemed to be about Geumi's age or a bit younger, rubbed their palms together and prayed, bowing over and over until their foreheads touched the floor. Geumi quickly befriended them, especially after hearing that one of the women used to work at a silk factory, too, before the bottom dropped out from under her.

The silk factory Geumi worked at was a large one that housed both a filature and a spinnery. The management and engineers had been dispatched from the company's headquarters in Japan, which meant the conditions there were far better than most in Gyeongseong. But forcing Korean employees to work an average of thirteen hours a day for less than half of what their Japanese counterparts were paid still amounted to gross exploitation. Small factories, including independent filatures, operated under even more-backbreaking conditions because they subcontracted for larger factories.

For a commission, local government offices and police stations recruited girls from the countryside on behalf of Japanese and Korean businessmen. The girls were sold for a mere ten won to contracts that bound them for ten years, and with no way out. Luck alone determined whether they started out in a factory or a brothel. Later, the Japanese would use this well-established routine to kidnap Korean women into forced labour and sexual slavery during the war. Young girls ready to throw themselves overboard to save their starving parents withered in the agony of having their flesh sold in brothels and died as interchangeable parts in factories.

The stories of the prostitutes Geumi met in lock-up were no different. They were first sold off to factories, and then were told they were learning too slowly, their debts were growing too quickly, and just like that they were handed over to another hellhole where they had to sell themselves. Since time was money for prostitutes, their pimp paid their fines quickly so they could be put back to work.

The babysitter was sentenced for theft and taken away to prison.

Geumi had been getting by on meagre portions of rice and beans, pickled radish, and bean sprouts, and on soup that was little more than salted water, when she suddenly started receiving meal deliveries from the outside. One day, after she'd finished her lunch, an officer appeared and unlocked her cell.

'You have a visitor.'

'Who is it?'

'How should I know? He says he's your fiancé.'

Geumi came out of the dingy lock-up and stepped into the visiting room. A dark figure was standing with his back to the sunlight pouring in through the window. She couldn't make out the face, but she'd had a hunch it was Ilcheol from the moment the police officer said 'fiancé'. The officer stood watch as they sat down across from each other.

'I just found out yesterday, after I got home,' Ilcheol said, his voice soft and slightly hoarse.

Geumi would later say that was the moment she decided to marry him. It was fate, she'd realised. She was meant to keep him.

'Don't regret what you did for a friend,' said Ilcheol.

'I didn't do it for anyone,' Geumi answered in a deliberately coy tone.

'I heard they plan to fire you but will let you work at a different factory.'

'I plan to quit.'

Ilcheol just sat there, as if he'd run out of things to say. His angular hat and cape draped over his school uniform made him look like he outranked the police officer standing watch. As the silence stretched out between them, the officer announced that the visit was over.

Before leaving the visiting room, Geumi quickly said, 'By the way, I'm expected to share food with the others. How about bringing some rice cakes, like injeolmi or jeolpyeon?'

Ilcheol must have taken the hint, because about an hour later a large bundle of tteok was delivered. Geumi passed them around to the ten or so folks locked up on both floors. She would brag about that day for many years to come: 'You could say I agreed to wedlock in lock-up. And since the prisoners all ate a piece of our betrothal tteok, they were witnesses. Ha ha.'

Yeongsun and Geumi were released after ten days. Yeongsun found that she was already unemployable. To get a job at a different factory and be in charge of a loom like before, she would have to receive a recommendation or certificate from her former employer, but she was now branded as having served as a strike-committee chairperson. Her only hope of employment was working as a day labourer in one of the filatures and spinneries outside of the capital, closer to her hometown. But she didn't let that bother her.

'I'll go back home and be a mum to my little boy and figure something out,' Yeongsun said bravely.

Geumi also had to find a place to stay since she could no longer remain at the dormitory after being fired. Men could hire themselves out by the day as manual labourers and bunk with others in rented rooms, inns, construction-site lodgings, or what have you, but women had to consider their physical safety and couldn't exactly walk the streets in search of work. Seonok invited Geumi to stay with her at her grandparents' place, so Geumi moved her things there. After a few days, Ilcheol and Icheol came to see her. Ilcheol stared silently at the floor, while Icheol bowed to her where he sat.

'I suppose I should address you as Hyeongsu now,' Icheol said, playing innocent. 'My brother already declared himself your fiancé on a government document, when he signed the visitor log at the lock-up, so there's no going back now.'

Geumi and Ilcheol were both too embarrassed to respond, so Seonok chimed in.

'That's right! I finally get to be free of my team head. Please take her away.'

To summarise the rest of what Icheol said, once Ilcheol graduated from the railway academy and was assigned to a position, he would take over as head of the household. As Ilcheol's fiancée, Geumi was welcome to move into their house right away, but because they had not yet formally sought their parents' permission, she was better off staying somewhere else until then, for propriety's sake. The plan was for Ilcheol and his father to visit Geumi's parents in Gimpo, at which time they could propose marriage. Then the wedding could be held the following January or February, after Ilcheol's graduation.

The usually lively, optimistic Geumi seemed suddenly lost and speechless when it came to her own future. Two days after the brothers' visit, Seonok was at work and Geumi was in the courtyard helping Seonok's grandparents to prepare rice for tteok when a woman burst through the side door to the tteok shop.

'Hey, are you Geumi?'

'Yes, who are you?'

'Who do you think? I've come to pick you up.'

Behind the woman with the loud, confident voice stood another woman beaming at Geumi. She was heavyset, and her hair was messy, like she'd just woken up. Now you'd think they'd have dressed a little more nicely, seeing as how they were there to meet the new addition to the family. But alas, they were dressed in plain Korean blouses with the baggy, Japanese pants that female labourers usually wore and, oddest of all, big rubber boots. The woman in front followed Geumi's alarmed gaze, scanning her own body up and down, and let out a hearty laugh. 'I'm dressed this way because I was helping out my husband at work before rushing over here. I'm Ilcheol and Icheol's gomo.'

Geumi later told the family she would've asked about the woman standing behind Aunt Mageum had it not been for Seonok's grandparents standing nearby. That was how Geumi first met Mageum, as well as Juan-daek, who always appeared around Mageum and Hansoe in important moments. In a slight daze, Geumi packed her things up and let Mageum lead the way. When they stepped out into the street, the other woman was no longer in sight. Geumi kept looking back to see if the woman was following them.

'What is it?' Mageum asked. 'Did you leave a fart behind in that house? Why do you keep looking back?'

'I was just wondering where the woman who came with you went.'

Mageum stopped short.

'The woman who came with me?'

'Yes, the tall, heavyset one …'

Mageum smacked her palms together and sighed.

'You must've seen my sister-in-law. There's no doubt! You were meant to join our family.'

Mageum stopped short again.

'Have you always seen folks like that?' she asked, knitting her brows as she gazed at Geumi.

Geumi had just been kicking herself for saying anything, as she might've been imagining things. Her family had warned her over and over, ever since she was little, to never reveal her gift to anyone, and now she almost never let it show. She hadn't held back in lock-up, because those girls were harmless strangers, but this person standing before her was her future husband's aunt.

'It depends on the situation,' Geumi said vaguely. 'It doesn't happen very often.'

To Geumi's relief, Mageum didn't press any further, and they started walking again.

'She's Ilcheol and Icheol's mother. Whenever something important happens in our family, she appears out of nowhere. She passed away while the boys were in primary school, and I moved in to help raise them. Icheol tends to keep to himself, so he never notices when his mother shows up, but Ilcheol is kind and cares a lot about others. I think he sees her sometimes.'

Mageum Gomo didn't mention the story of the remarkable deeds her sister-in-law had pulled off during the floods or the story of Ilcheol receiving tteok from his dead mother. She knew no one would believe her. In any case, she took a liking to Geumi. If Geumi wasn't meant to be part of their family, why would she be the only one to see Juan-daek? As they walked toward the Saetmal House, Mageum couldn't help but share a bit more about her sister-in-law.

'Like you said, it depends on the situation for me, too, but I met my husband thanks to her.'

She told Geumi about how Juan-daek showed up one day to pound rice in a mortar for her to make tteok for the boys, and appeared again the next day and had Mageum follow her to the man who would repair their house and later marry her. Geumi didn't seem at all surprised, nor did she say it couldn't possibly be true, but simply nodded as Mageum spoke.

'This was a secret only Ilcheol and I knew. Now that you know, too, we're all in cahoots!' Mageum giggled.

Geumi wondered why Mageum Gomo hadn't seen Ilcheol's mother, but figured the importance of the occasion — meeting her mother-in-law for the first time — meant that this appearance was intended only for her. She figured it was because it was her own first time meeting her mother-in-law. Or maybe Mageum Gomo had just pretended not to have seen Juan-daek. And although Geumi never let on, she believed she'd fallen for Ilcheol at first sight. That is, maybe she'd had no visions when she first met him because she was blinded by love.

When they arrived at the Saetmal House, Mageum Gomo's husband, Carpenter Kang, was out working, and their two children hadn't come back from school yet. It was a small, three-room house, but the courtyard was big and the wooden floors of the maru and the verandah that ran the length of the house shone from polishing. Mageum seemed to be a flawless housekeeper. The house originally had a thatched roof, but her husband had replaced the thatch with tiles after his father passed away. Mageum Gomo practically snatched Geumi's luggage from her and flung it through an open lattice door into a small bedroom.

'This is your room.'

Mageum explained that Ilcheol and Icheol had come over a couple of days earlier to clear away the spare carpentry tools that used to occupy the room, and to replace the wallpaper. Geumi went in and sat down, craning her head every which way to examine the newly papered walls, windows, and doors, and opening the chest with nickel decorations that surely had come from her future father-in-law's workshop. In one corner, a neatly folded floor mattress and blanket was covered with an embroidered cloth. At the centre of the freshly papered lattice door was a square glass window the size of her palm that offered a view of the courtyard as well as the front gate. Geumi inched up to the window and made a show of gazing outside.

'Our Hansoe Ilcheol is so kind and thoughtful,' said Mageum. 'He lined the door with two layers of paper and brought that glass all the way from the Willow Tree House so you won't feel too boxed in.'

Geumi noticed that gingko leaves had been placed between the paper along three sides of the window. The leaves caught the sunlight and glowed a brighter yellow. That must have been Ilcheol's touch, as well.

During her first two weeks at Mageum Gomo's house, Geumi went through the process of resigning from the factory as previously agreed in exchange for employment elsewhere. Ilcheol then took Geumi to his house to introduce her to his father. When the couple told Baekman they wished to marry, he turned his head slightly to wipe away the tears that welled up.

'I should've been there for you more after your mother died. You practically raised yourself. Anyway, I know you won't have a problem finding a job after you graduate, so what've I got to worry about? You don't need my blessings, but you have them.'

The hondam, or marriage talk, complete, they made plans for Geumi to go to Gimpo to share the news with her parents, and then Baekman and Ilcheol would visit three days later for the cheonghon, the formal proposal of marriage.

Although it was early winter, the morning was sunny and mild. Baekman and Ilcheol boarded a boat at Yeomchang Dock just in time to catch the ebb tide and reached Gimpo in the blink of an eye, leaving them plenty of time to get to Geumi's family's home right before lunch. As soon as they stepped off the boat, Geumi's youngest brother spotted Ilcheol's uniform and greeted them. He ushered father and son to the house, where Geumi's parents and eldest brother were waiting. When Ilcheol entered the courtyard, Geumi's parents couldn't help but gape at the tall student dressed in uniform, complete with cap and cape. Although they'd heard about him from their daughter, the man before them appeared to be a finer match than they'd expected.

They agreed to hold the wedding in February, when Ilcheol would be graduating. The ceremony would take place at the hall inside the rail workers' housing in Yeongdeungpo. Heo Sangwoo, Ilcheol's primary-school homeroom teacher from fifth grade, agreed to officiate. Mr Heo had also been Icheol's homeroom teacher, and had become a good friend to the family. A quiet, gentle secondary-school graduate, Mr Heo would later help Icheol by hiding him in his countryside home when Icheol was on the run. Ilcheol had always respected the middle-aged teacher and sought his advice from time to time. Later, Geumi would sometimes say that Mr Heo's death was one of the reasons her husband defected to the North. Though she sometimes revelled in retelling the details of her wedding day, she would usually only tell a few episodes before abruptly falling silent. As if talking too much about those good memories might make them fade and disappear.

'Growing up in the countryside, I'd tagged along with my mother to plenty of traditional weddings. The courtyard would be packed with relatives and neighbours, the table piled high with food like a jesa was being held, and the couple would get on their knees and bow all the way down to the ground and then stand up only to get back down again over and over and over and drink toast after toast after toast. Spending the whole day like puppets on strings, like they were being punished. That's why I like these new, enlightened weddings. Someone plays an organ — da duh da da! — and you march in, make your big entrance, the officiant declares you husband and wife, and you march back out arm in arm. Done!'

The highlight, though, was the photos. After the ceremony, the bride and groom came back in for a photo shoot, first just the two of them and then with their parents. They also took group photos with their relatives and friends. Back then, there was a long, comical routine to taking a photo. The photographer would set the camera upright on its legs and cover it with some sort of cloth that was black on the outside and red on the inside, and then stick his head under that cloth and spend what felt like hours making adjustments of some sort. Then, after a few more minutes, he would pull his head out at last, and holding a small corded bulb in one hand and a big metal plate in the other, he'd say something like, 'Now everybody smile,' or, 'Please look at the camera,' and then there'd be another very long wait, and when he finally seemed satisfied, he would ignite the magnesium on the metal plate and squeeze the bulb at the same time. At the bright flash of light and sudden loud pop, everyone would shut their eyes in shock, and immediately worry that they'd ruined it, but later, when they saw the photo, they would realise it wasn't half bad, even if their faces were a bit stiff. Of course, some did have their eyes closed, or half-closed, or wide open and bulging like startled rabbits.

When Geumi posed with her parents and father-in-law for the first time, she spotted Juan-daek sitting right there in the front, dressed in an all-white Korean blouse and skirt. Both of Geumi's parents stood with the bride, while the groom had not only his widowed father but also Mageum Gomo next to him, presumably because she had filled in as his mother all those years. Geumi watched as Juan-daek stood and walked over to Mageum Gomo, slipping in quietly between her sister-in-law and her son. She held her spot at the groom's side even when it was other relatives' turns, including Cheonman and Shipman and their wives and children, to be photographed with the newlyweds. Of course, she was nowhere to be seen in the actual photos. The day after the ceremony, the couple headed to a railway inn near the Onyang springs, courtesy of the Railway Bureau's employee-welfare department — and the story of their honeymoon was always how Geumi saw the future newborn Jisan the moment they stepped into their room. But, in fact, Ilcheol had also gingerly confessed to his wife that he, too, had spotted his mother among the wedding guests. Later, when they compared their stories, Mageum Gomo also admitted she had seen her sister-in-law in the front row that day.

It had, after all, been no ordinary day. Mageum said she'd had no doubt that Juan-daek would show up. And Mageum was very pleased to find that Geumi shared something in common with her. That was why she believed the three of them — herself, Ilcheol, and his wife — had a special bond of trust.

As soon as Ilcheol graduated from the railway academy's full-time program for drivers, he was appointed as an engineer's apprentice and sent to work on the Gyeongin Line. Being a rookie with no experience, he started on freight carriages instead of passenger carriages. They had no way of knowing which line he'd be assigned to after his six-month apprenticeship. Ever since the Japanese Government-General had taken back control of Korean railways, having previously entrusted management to the South Manchurian Railway, its policy was to give preference to graduates of its own railway academy for every post in Joseon. This was also a declaration of sorts that even the remotest of areas would be manned by those who'd received a proper, Government-General-approved education. The Gyeongin Line had originally ended at Noryangjin, on the southern bank of the Hangang River. But after the Hangang Railway Bridge was built, Namdaemun became the last stop. Nevertheless, Yeongdeungpo was where the Gyeongbu and Gyeongin Lines crossed paths. As dozens of factories opened and demand for industrial freight trains increased, the Honam Line, originally created as a branch of the Gyeongbu Line, came to pass through Yeongdeungpo as well. Scores of warehouses popped up, and the rail yard became a tangled mess. The tracks linking the factory district and rail works had long run through the centre of Yeongdeungpo. With its terminus in Incheon, a major port city that was rapidly industrialising with more and more factories opening, the Gyeongin Line became a major freight route, second only to the Gyeongbu Line, which terminated in the southernmost port city of Busan.

There were freight trains in operation during the day, of course, but they were busiest after hours, coming and going all through the night, when there were no passenger trains running. Having just begun his apprenticeship, Ilcheol was mainly assigned to night shifts. He'd come home when the sun was already high in the sky, half-heartedly shove a few spoonfuls of breakfast into his mouth, and sleep like the dead.

Ilcheol's six-month apprenticeship was also Geumi's introduction to newlywed life at the Willow Tree House. Baekman gave the main bedroom to the couple and moved into his sons' old bedroom. He went on with his life as an ordinary mechanic on weekdays, and spent his weekends and holidays absorbed in metal crafts in his workshop. Around the time his grandson Jisan enrolled in primary school, the family moved into the rail workers' housing. Since he couldn't have a workshop of his own there, Baekman had to give up his hobby until the family moved to Saetmal. He once confessed to his grandson that their time at the rail workers' housing was the most boring days of his life.

When his brother married and his father switched rooms with the newlyweds, Icheol quietly moved out to a room he rented in Singil-jeong. At first, he came by the house every couple of days, but his visits grew more infrequent, stretching to barely once a week. When his cover was blown, he'd left the textile factory for a job at an electrics company, continuing to take positions as a mechanic's assistant. The family could only guess that he was still working as an activist.

It was early summer when Geumi's belly was growing bigger with Jisan inside. Out of nowhere, she suddenly craved hobak kimchi. Hobak kimchi was made from squash or pumpkin, usually in the late autumn, and could be boiled with seafood, even before it was fully fermented, to make a delicious stew. Geumi shook her head in disbelief that she was already missing the food back home after less than a year of marriage. Just then, the gate squeaked open and Mageum Gomo stepped into the yard. Geumi quickly put her finger to her lips before Mageum could launch into her usual racket, because Ilcheol was fast asleep after another night shift. Baekman was gone for the day, so the two took a seat inside his workshop. Mageum untied the bundle she'd brought to reveal a small jar, which gave off a tart scent when the lid was removed.

'Why, what's this? Isn't this hobak kimchi?'

'How did you know? My friends and I have always made this. There's nothing better when you've lost your appetite.'

'This is unbelievable, Gomonim. I was craving this just now.'

Mageum clapped her hands and Geumi raised a finger to her lips again to shush her.

'Ha, I knew it. It's like that saying: if you hear a snap, of course it's the sound of a hobak falling from your neighbour's roof. In Ganghwa, we add crabs to make stew with this.'

'In Gimpo, we add big-eyed herring or small hairtail.'

'The folks in Hwanghae Province add fish sauce.'

Mageum Gomo gave Geumi a small wave that meant she should wait there a moment, and darted out the gate. She was back in a flash, bearing three small hairtail strung together. The two women fired up the portable stove and made a stew out of the hobak kimchi and hairtail, which was all they needed to enjoy a tasty lunch. Mageum was in a good mood because Geumi felt like a kindred spirit.

'Now that we're full, how about a walk?' asked Mageum.

'We could head down to the Saetgang to take in the breeze.'

'Hansoe will probably sleep until dinner time, right?'

'Yes, but ...'

Mageum said they were going someplace close and that she'd lead the way. Geumi followed her, but she began to slow down because she hadn't a clue as to where they were headed.

'Where are we going?'

'It's a place I stumbled upon over there by the tracks.'

By tracks, Geumi assumed she meant somewhere beyond the marketplace intersection, near the bend in the road leading to Saetmal.

'Are we meeting someone?'

Mageum nodded with a smile.

'She's a clairvoyant.'

The two women went into a small house near the tracks. It was one of those gabled houses with glass windows, neither strictly Korean nor Japanese in style, that had begun to crop up around that time. A shoe shop selling work boots and gomushin, a new type of rubber shoe modelled after Korean shoes, occupied the ground floor. A steep, rickety ladder led up to the attic. A girl waving a fly swatter slowly nodded when Mageum asked, 'She in?' Geumi carefully climbed up the ladder behind Mageum. In the attic with white papered walls, an old lady sat before a large table.

'What do you want? I was about to take a nap,' the old lady said.

But even as she said it, her gaze went straight to Geumi, who was just stepping into the room behind Mageum, and stayed there. For some reason, Geumi didn't feel like avoiding the old lady's stare when they locked eyes, so she glared back at her. The old lady slowly lowered her gaze and would only look at Mageum after that. Geumi noticed a little girl, maybe three or four years old, sitting beside the old lady. The girl was wearing a short mongdang skirt and jeogori blouse, and an old vest too warm for the season. She smiled bashfully at Geumi.

'I brought my niece-in-law with me today,' Mageum Gomo said. 'Please tell us what you see.'

'You don't need me for that. She can see far enough herself,' the old lady muttered as she threw a handful of rice at Geumi.

'Why are you throwing that at me?' Geumi asked, brushing rice off her chest.

'Because your chi is too strong.' The old woman added, 'You can see my taeju, can't you?'

Mageum grinned as she scooted over to give Geumi a better view.

'Didn't she die of smallpox? She's your granddaughter,' Geumi said.

Completely unruffled, the old shaman shook her cluster of bells and yawned repeatedly, her shoulders rising and falling, until she suddenly shuddered and began to speak in a little girl's voice.

'Oh, you're having a boy! He's smart and handsome. His father will make something of himself without much trouble. But I see a split. Parent and child torn apart and then brought back together. Ajumeoni, you'll have to get your whole family through this rough world all on your own.'

The girl in the vest was looking straight at Geumi as she spoke, but though her lips moved, the sound was coming from the old lady's mouth. The old lady rattled on about this and that until finally Mageum pounded on the table.

'Enough already, enough!' Mageum shouted. 'Sounds like your sight's a little off today.'

The old lady let out a sigh, and her eyes, which had been rolled back up in her head, returned to normal.

'That was great,' Geumi said with a hearty laugh. 'Thank you for telling me that I'm having a son and that my husband will have a successful career.'

Mageum seemed a bit down as she left the house with Geumi.

'That old lady's off her game today.'

'I looked right into the eyes of her myeongdu or taeju or whatever she called her, the little girl,' Geumi said cheerfully.

Mageum clapped her hands together and said, 'Of course! Why bother taking a clairvoyant to a clairvoyant? I don't see things like that.'

'My brother-in-law calls it superstition, but I think it's just something I was born with. That's how the world works — all sorts of crazy things all jumbled together.'

'The old woman told me I'll live in a strange land far from home and be so well off I'll want for nothing,' Mageum said sullenly. 'Though she did say it'll be a bit lonely.'

Always an optimist, Geumi smiled and said, 'If my future really is predetermined, then I'll just take it as it comes and enjoy myself instead of fussing and fretting.'

The following year, Geumi gave birth to a healthy baby boy, as predicted. A straw rope threaded with chillies was hung across the gate until the baby turned a hundred days old. Ilcheol finished his apprenticeship with a Gyeongin Line engineer and was assigned to a Gyeongbu Line freight train. Perhaps his quiet, hardworking ways had found favour in the eyes of the Japanese managers. Or perhaps he had his father to thank for faithfully serving as an assistant at the rail works for so many years without ever causing trouble. Either way, being assigned assistant engineer on the Gyeongbu Line, the main line that connected the capital to the continent, instead of being stuck on a branch line hauling minerals or puffing away deep in the mountains — as all of Ilcheol's older rail colleagues wasted no time pointing out to him — was a huge stroke of luck.

7

It had been nearly seven months since Jino went up the chimney, and according to Changsu, his 200th day up there was just three days away. Winter had already arrived with the first snow of the season a few days earlier. To prepare for the cold, Jino wore winter hiking clothes, a padded jacket, a woollen hat and socks, and winter boots. He laid a tarp over the cemented part of the catwalk floor. On the tent floor, he added an aluminium foam mat and a synthetic-fibre blanket beneath his padded waterproof sleeping bag and placed an extra blanket on top. The union had procured the winter items for him with support from several civic groups. The clothes and food containers were all mountaineering equipment. It was still bearable during the day, but once the sun set, the temperature began to drop sharply so that, by daybreak, it was already as freezing cold as midwinter. Living outside at that altitude felt like clinging to a cliff.

But he had been through something similar at least twice before in his life. One was the two winters he spent at a guard post along the front during his military service. The winter equipment provided back then was similar to what he was currently wearing, and even the conditions were pretty much the same. Actually, that wasn't true. He had it easier better back then. His late-night and early-morning shifts at the post lasted only an hour or two until the next guard arrived to relieve him, on top of which he only had to do it a couple of times a week, because the guards rotated between day and night shifts. And the post wasn't as exposed on all sides like it was up on the chimney. It had a roof and a wall connected to a bunker along a ridge. A mask and goggles made it cozy enough to fall asleep despite the wind coming in through the observation hole. Jino would usually poke the muzzle of his rifle through the observation hole and drift in and out of sleep until his shift was over. Other than the quartermaster butting his nose into everything and making his life hell, those winters weren't so bad.

The other time was when Jino had been serving as a union branch chief. He went to prison for six months for violating the law on assembly and demonstration. People say there are no seasons behind bars. In prison, there are only the two sentences of summer and winter. Summer begins in May and ends in September, while winter begins in October and ends in April. Jino was unlucky enough to get put away in October, which meant he lived through an entire winter sentence. October was the start of winter because that was when the prison staff did facility inspections and the inmates got their clothing and bedding ready ahead of the cold. The longer an inmate had been inside, the earlier and more detailed were his preparations. They'd put in requests for vests padded with synthetic cotton and stitch them to the insides of their uniform shirts. They bought wool socks to wear or cut them to fit over their heads like beanies so they could stay warm at night. The cotton in their blankets was usually wadded and lumpy from age and frequent washings. When inmates left their cells for work, solitary inmates were sent in to remove the blanket cover, carefully split and even out the cotton lumped like snowballs inside, and then sew the cover back on. The cells began to grow chilly from the end of October, and by midwinter the dampness kept seeping up through the floor, which was just wooden boards laid directly on concrete. You had to cover the floor beneath your bedding with cardboard or else the sponge mattresses would get too wet to sleep on. There was so much condensation created by the difference in temperature between body and floorboards that, come morning, the cardboard looked like it had sat out in the rain. You would wake to find the cement walls white with frost and the ceiling dripping. The water drops were your own exhaled breaths that had turned to frost on the ceiling overnight and melted one by one. Military-issue ammunition boxes were one of the most highly valued items that outgoing prisoners would pass down to others; their metal sides and rubber linings made them perfect hot water bottles. But only the most well-connected inmates were able to use those. If you couldn't secure an ammunition box, you had to get a hold of two or three thick plastic bottles. On cold days, with the guard's permission, you could fill the bottles with boiling water from the kettle on the stove in the corridor. If you wanted the warmth to last longer, you needed a pouch for the bottles, which could be made by stitching together two pieces of cloth from a worn-out blanket. You'd put the bottles in the pouch and bury the pouch under the blanket near your feet, trapping the warmth inside until it was time to wake up.

Here on the chimney, Jino couldn't ask his colleagues to send up hot water, nor did he have to. Because a thing called heat packs had long been invented. Before going to bed, he'd stick a pack on each foot and two more on his neck and shoulders to get through the night. The bottle of drinking water froze if he left it near his head, so he kept it inside his sleeping bag. As the sun set earlier and the nights grew longer, he'd get hungry around nine, just like in prison. But while the long and bitterly cold nights lasted, he had no intention of setting foot outside his tent before morning. To make that possible, his foremost rule was to relieve himself right before going to bed. That way, he didn't have to wake in the middle of the night and leave the sleeping bag after having taken forever to adjust his bedding, find a comfortable position, and finally fall asleep, warming the inside of his sleeping bag with his body heat alone. Before crawling out of his tent, Jino put on his padded jacket, zipped it all the way to his chin, and drew the hood over his woollen hat. He waddled over to the catwalk railing and lifted the many layers on his torso to unzip his winter pants. The part of him that had been tucked away and cowering from the cold shot out a stream of urine on reflex. He managed to gauge the direction of the wind first, and was relieved to see a north-westerly gust pushing his stream to the left. With a shiver, he turned and headed carefully back to the tent, keeping his body as close to the wall of the chimney as possible, one hand on the railing, moving one step at a time. Something caught his foot. When he looked down, he saw that one of the plastic bottles that he'd written names on and lashed to the railing was sticking out. He bent to pick it up and crawled back into the tent. His torch revealed the name 'Jingi'.

Jino slipped out of his padded jacket and winter boots but left his thick woollen hat and socks on. He slid into the sleeping bag. Outside the tent, the wind had sounded like a high-pitched whistle, but inside it was more like a low rumble of waves crashing onto a shore. Sometimes, the wind moaned as it circled past the hollow chimney. Jino thought about the plastic bottle now sitting next to his head. Jingi was a friend he'd met at a Metal Workers' Union assembly. Despite being at least three years younger, Jingi had always brazenly used banmal — the informal register — when talking to Jino, and would say things like, 'Hey, Jino. We're just vermin surviving on metal dust, aren't we? We could be crushed under someone's boot at any moment.'

Jingi was a short man. When they stood face to face, Jino had a clear view of the top of Jingi's head, where there was already a bald patch the size of a table clock. Because their names were similar, their colleagues called them brothers and used the old movie title *All the Brothers Were Valiant* to tease them. After being fired from an automobile factory, Jingi occupied a factory chimney for almost a year. The protest, however, failed, and one by one, twenty-two fired workers committed suicide. Jingi was the ninth to take his own life. He'd had two sons and a daughter, and his wife had struggled to support the family by working at a restaurant for years after he was terminated. Jingi had a good singing voice. Once, he was picked to represent his hometown on the TV show *National Singing Contest*. He'd received a notification telling him to report to the provincial government building at the end of the month for the contest, but he never made it, because he'd been, in his own words, 'liquored up to his eyeballs' the day before. Whenever people talked about Jingi, Jino would smile faintly and shed a few tears that he tried to cover with a fake yawn. Whenever he'd asked Jingi why he had to go and get liquored up to his eyeballs the night before such an important day, Jingi had given the same ridiculous answer. *Because my sweet doe told me she'd always be there for me.* That was his embarrassing nickname for his wife, no matter the time or place.

'I can't get you out of my mind,' Jino murmured.

A voice spoke right beside him.

'Then buy me a bottle of soju. Let's go to my in-laws' food stall!'

'Wait, what the hell are you doing all the way up here?'

Jino turned to see Jingi lying on his side and looking down at him with his head propped on his hand. He looked the same as always, with his usual bristly stubble covering his top lip and chin because he was too lazy to shave. And, as always, he acted like he was older than Jino.

'Inma, when your hyeong comes to see you, you should be the one to say let's get a drink. Do I have to do everything myself?'

'Look at this kid trying to pass himself off as my hyeong! I've seen your ID.'

'You may be three years older than me, but I went up a chimney way earlier than you, and that makes me your seonbae.'

'Fine, you win this round, Seonbae. Let's go get you a drink.'

Arms swinging, Jino led him away from the chimney and down an asphalt road overgrown with weeds on each side. They could see lights ahead from factories working through the night. The industrial complex was on the south-eastern edge of a provincial city in the south, and the factories where Jino and Jingi had worked were about a block apart. Clustered at the entrance to the complex was what passed for a main street, with apartments, row houses, studio flats, convenience stores, restaurants, and bars. Many of the workers had moved there with their families, but there were still plenty of others who'd left behind families well-settled in other cities to move there for work and either lived alone or shared rooms with two or three other workers. Jino had come by himself because he and his family were natives of Yeongdeungpo, whereas Jingi had relocated his family there back when the complex first opened. Jingi's in-laws ran a food stall that served 'pig scraps'. Jingi introduced the place to Jino, who soon became a regular, stopping by whenever he felt like a drink. Jino remembered what he'd said to Jingi the first time they went there.

'Really, chief, pig scraps? That sounds disgusting.'

Jingi laughed as he said he'd thought the exact same thing at first. Back in the day, when pigs were slaughtered, the better-selling cuts were carved out first, and the bits and pieces left over, which turned out to be the tastiest, were tossed aside. Those trimmings were enjoyed in the back of the butcher shop by peddlers who gathered there after work.

'It used to be that the best parts of the pig went to the folks who did the hardest work. But that's all ancient history now. These days, they call those scraps "choice cuts" and charge extra for them,' Jingi had explained.

Having arrived at the food stall, the two men ordered 'pig scraps', placed the meat on the grill, and cracked open a bottle of soju. They poured each other shots and dipped the cooked meat in coarse salt.

'How long ago'd you get fired?'

'Almost three years now, but you knew that.'

Neither of them wanted to talk about how they'd managed to survive the foreign-exchange crisis, but their long silences were hint enough. At the time, it had felt like someone picked up a large shovel and jabbed away mercilessly at a once-peaceful ant colony. Factories were dismantled, and vague words like 'flexibility' and 'restructuring' were tossed around as a reason for firing labourers at random. Those lucky enough to avoid retrenchment or 'early retirement' were shipped off to factories in other parts of the country where they had no choice but to eke out a living for what was left of their unhappy lives in the precarious positions of contractors and temporary workers. And just when they thought the storm had passed, factories began to pack up and move overseas to countries with cheaper wages while throwing around more big words like 'globalisation' and 'unlimited competition'. The automobile factory Jingi worked at had moved a division overseas and laid off a huge chunk of its Korean workforce. The laid-off workers swore to defend their jobs and organised a sit-in on the factory's roof, but their protest was brutally put down. As union chief, Jingi would've been at the forefront of the action, but he only suffered a few burns.

Jingi filled his glass with soju and downed it.

'Damn, where's the fire?'

'Why, you worried about the bill? It's been a while, I can't help it if alcohol tastes so sweet.'

Back then, Jino had heard some unsettling rumours about his factory as well, but nothing had happened yet. He'd made up his mind to buy Jingi a drink since it was pay day, but the way Jingi was acting that day made him anxious. After knocking back several shots in a row, Jingi was half-canned and his eyes finally softened.

'Shit, I think the liquor is catching up with me. Hey, big-shot branch chief, want me to sing for you?'

'Here? We're not even at a noraebang.'

'Must I take a robot like you to a noraebang to show off my skills? And without my sweet doe?'

'Where is your wife?'

'She's at work, man. Hey, I said I'll sing for you.'

He began to sing, his voice unexpectedly low and mellow. He slurred the lyrics, but that somehow made it sound better. Since when did he sing so well? When they first met, Jingi was marching behind Jino at a rally. Jino could hear Jingi humming and thought he had a pretty good voice for a labourer living on metal dust. He didn't know the name of the song Jingi sang at his in-laws' food stall, but he remembered the first few lines:

Walking with my eyes closed,
Walking with them open,
All I see is misery

When he was done singing, Jingi hung his head for a while, then looked up again and leaned across the table toward Jino.

'Jino, I'm gonna go up.'

'Up where?'

'Up the chimney. Where else? Shit, where else can we go?'

Jino said nothing. Many of the workers had already left the city, but Jingi stayed. As the sole breadwinner, he was holding out with his family in their seventy-two-square-metre flat, waiting to go back to work someday.

'I went to a funeral yesterday,' said Jingi. 'You know there's been a string of them in our union, right?'

'Again?'

'Five, so far. This time it was one of my older colleagues, a guy with really specialised skills who'd also worked as a union rep. He jumped off a fifteen-storey apartment building.'

The week after Jingi had been laid off, Jino went to see him climb up the chimney of the shuttered automobile factory. A vertical banner with the words 'Dismissal is Murder!' written in bright red hung down the front side of the chimney. The workers would spend the next three years in the streets or up chimneys, transmission towers, and pylons. The protests went on after Jingi passed, but they solved nothing. Then the factory Jino worked at was shut down and sold, though it was later revealed that it didn't so much go out of business as change its name and move its money. The workers' numbers had dwindled to twenty to eleven to five, barely managing to keep their high-altitude protest going.

Suddenly, Jino was back inside his sleeping bag, squirming like a caterpillar in its cocoon. Jingi had followed and was lying sideways in the one-man tent, crammed into what little space was left.

'I didn't make it to your funeral,' said Jino. 'I was in the middle of a sit-in in front of the company's headquarters.'

Jingi chuckled. 'You think you can change the world? Things are only getting worse.'

'I survived — I'm trying to inch my way forward. Maybe if I keep inching forward, things will change, bit by bit.' He looked up at the tent ceiling and added, 'I'm still alive, so I might as well do what I gotta do.'

In the past, workers had doused themselves with petrol and set themselves on fire, one after the other, as if the idea were contagious. Now what shattered workers wasn't rage but despair — a mighty, terrifying enemy that slowly gnawed away at them day after day. Another protest assembly would end, and the workers would be on their own. Even after returning home to their waiting families, they were alone. The world has always been as indifferent as the universe. It is lonely, still, and silent. Tedious, worthless everyday life crushed them all. Dismissal was murder.

Jino had visited Jingi's family ten days or so after his funeral. He'd talked things over with his old co-workers who'd worked in the union with him, and collected a small amount of condolence money. They'd agreed that Jino should be the one to make the visit, as he'd been the closest with Jingi. Jino's next trip from the chimney took him back to the day of this visit. Swaying like smoke, Jingi hovered around Jino, pacing him on the walk back.

'I wasn't sure I'd remember your place,' said Jino, 'but isn't that it?'

'Let's see if you can get it right.'

The four-storey buildings were showing their age: the original white paint bore chips and stains and blotches of black mould.

'Your building was at the very front, second entrance from the left. But which floor …'

'I like the smell of grass and soil.'

Of course, the ground floor. Jingi's kids used to open the living-room window and jump into the tree standing right outside. Jino made an immediate right inside the building and rang the doorbell. He rang once more, waited, and was about to ring a third time when the door cracked open.

'Hello, I'm Yi Jino.'

'Oh, the union branch chief.'

Jingi's sweet doe looked as though she'd just woken up. Jino couldn't tell whether she was still in a daze from grief or always looked that blank. She stepped aside without a word, and Jino entered, hesitantly, feeling like an uninvited guest. Their children were seated around a low table in the living room; they each greeted him and swarmed off to another room. Their mother turned off the TV and offered Jino a floor cushion.

'Please make yourself comfortable.'

Jino sat down awkwardly.

'We couldn't make it to the funeral because we had a labour action scheduled for that same day,' he said. 'It was just so unexpected, I really don't know what to say.'

With no one to call her a sweet doe anymore, Jingi's wife had gone back to being a tired mother. She kept looking up at the wall behind Jino. Jingi had vanished after accompanying him to the front door, but Jino couldn't help glancing back to see if he was there. Instead, he saw a round digital clock hanging on the wall. She'd been checking the time.

'Do you need to be somewhere?'

Jingi's wife gave a faint nod and said, 'Yes, I'm on the overnight shift today. I stopped by to fix dinner for the kids.'

'Oh, then I should get going.'

'No, it's okay. It's a small sewing factory in our neighbourhood. I used to work there before.'

She even managed a small smile. Maybe ten days was enough time to look okay on the outside. She was probably exhausted. The sweet doe's tone suddenly changed and she started talking fast.

'That dwarf had us all fooled, you know. He did it while I was working and the kids were at school. I was still at the factory when my daughter's class ended and she came home and found him. She ran all the way to tell me. There was a bottle of parathion pesticide next to him, froth coming out of his mouth, vomit all over the floor. It looked like he'd struggled.'

The difficult part over, she heaved a long sigh and dabbed the teardrops from her skirt with a fingertip.

Jino was back in his sleeping bag before he knew it. Jingi didn't seem ready to leave any time soon, as he was still lying on his side next to Jino.

'Hey, how does a brave man like you kill yourself?' Jino asked.

Jingi smirked.

'Why dig into the past? I guess I had nothing left to live for. What of it?'

'Inma, what about your sweet doe and the kids?'

'Even if I'd stuck around, nothing would've changed. The kids will still end up just like me.'

'What's wrong with them going up the chimney like us or creating a world of their own?'

'I guess I wanted too much,' Jingi mumbled feebly.

Jino choked up as he asked, 'Too much? How could you want too much?'

When he heard no answer, Jino looked around to find nothing but the tent wall trembling in the wind. Jingi was gone.

As the sun began to rise, light snuck in through the tightly closed door of the tent, turning the dark canvas a brighter red. Although he always woke around then, Jino usually waited in the sleeping bag for his mobile phone to vibrate with a message letting him know food was on the way. Between half past eight to nine o'clock in the morning, one of his colleagues would arrive at the bottom of the chimney with his breakfast. These days, the sun rose at 7.30, 7.40, or even 7.45. He'd stopped eating breakfast during the summer, but come winter, it grew very difficult to stand the cold on an empty stomach. He'd decided to lean on his colleagues and volunteers at the shelter again. He'd also stopped shaving his head when the temperature fell, and now his hair touched the rim of his ears. A small pair of craft scissors sufficed to keep his beard trimmed. Jino tried to stick to his own set of rules; sit-in or not, he couldn't just let himself go entirely. He kept the bottle of hot water sent up with dinner inside his sleeping bag overnight, then used the water to wash his face and brush his teeth the next morning. Sometimes, he used a small hand mirror to check his face. His cheeks looked a little gaunt but not too bad. He'd pared his workout routine down to one round of push-ups and squats in the afternoon.

Jino believed these efforts had meaning. What could have been the meaning his great-grandfather, grandfather, and father tried to pass down to him? It may have been the belief that, no matter how hard things get, life goes on. You just had to take it one day at a time.

Jino slipped out of his sleeping bag at 8.00 am. He washed his face and brushed his teeth with the lukewarm water he'd saved. The temperature had dropped to twenty below Celsius. He wiped the moisture off his face and quickly put on his hat and gloves. He did three sets of thirty push-ups and three sets of thirty squats. Sweat beaded along the band of his woollen hat. At 8.35, his mobile phone vibrated. He picked it up.

'It's me.'

He knew from the voice that it was Jeong. Jeong had told Jino ten days ago that he'd volunteered to deliver breakfast. He'd found a temporary position at a construction site nearby and could stop by the shelter to pick up Jino's food and drop it off on his way to work in the morning. Lunch would be delivered by the youngest, Cha, or occasionally one of the women who volunteered at the shelter, and dinner by Changsu after he got off work in the evening. Among the final five dismissed workers, Bak had found work on a vegetable farm and could only manage weekend visits with the others, despite wanting to do more. Jino tried to cheer Bak up by telling him to work hard and hang in there.

'You know the day after tomorrow is the 200th, right?' asked Jeong.

'Yes, Changsu told me yesterday.'

'We're holding an event for it.'

'Why not play it down this time and go big on the 300th day?'

There was, of course, no guarantee of reaching an agreement, but 300 days was enough to at least attract people's attention. That's when the real fight would begin, either up on a chimney or down on the ground.

'All you have to do is wave at us, and the union and folks from civic groups will take care of the rest down here.'

'In this weather? Tell them to take it easy.'

Jino put his empty containers in a backpack and sent it down. Jeong sent up drinking water and thermal containers of food.

By five in the afternoon, dusk was falling; in thirty more minutes, the sky would be dark, and the streetlights and the Hangang Railway Bridge would already be aglow. Dinner was supposed to be sent up at six, but it often arrived anytime between 6.00 and 6.30, most likely due to rush hour. Changsu usually picked up the food in a backpack and took the subway or hitched a ride with one of the visitors at the shelter. Today, he managed to arrive at 6.40. While the police inspected his backpack, Changsu cupped his hands around his mouth and yelled, 'Hey, how's it going today?'

Jino leaned against the railing and yelled back, 'Good, thanks.'

Jino tied the lunch backpack to the pulley and sent it down in exchange for the dinner backpack. The evening delivery usually contained more than just dinner: a book, two to three bottles of hot water, occasionally lantern batteries. It sometimes took two or three trips to pull it all up. When Jino was done, his mobile phone vibrated.

'The day after tomorrow, we're going to visit the National Assembly to explain why we're protesting and urge them to help resolve the situation. Then we're doing an ochetuji march: we're going to prostrate ourselves all the way here,' said Changsu.

'I thought you said this was a festival?'

'The civic groups will take care of the festival part while we crawl. We might even keep going and crawl right up the chimney to meet you.'

'Isn't it too far? Plus, it's cold.'

'It's a piece of cake. For your 300th day, we plan to crawl all the way to the Blue House.'

'Don't wear everyone out.'

'You're too soft. Management hasn't even batted an eyelid yet. All you have to do is keep doing what you're doing: eat, poop, persevere. Leave the fight to us.'

Changsu left.

Jino sealed the tent firmly to keep the wind out and ate his dinner. The rice was still warm, but as the soup quickly started to cool, bits of hardened fat clung to his lips. The tender inner leaves in the freshly made kimchi were delicious. Now and then, he came across raw oysters that had been added to the seasoning. A separate container of the kimchi filling had been included; he placed a large scoop of it onto his rice and mixed it together. Oh, if only he had a few drops of sesame oil to add, as well! When he was growing up, his grandmother would always have a bowl full of seasoned shredded radish in the kitchen around this time of year. He'd wake in the middle of the night and look for it, tossing radish and rice together in a large brass bowl with a spoonful of gochujang and a swirl of perilla oil: the resulting combination was so mouth-watering that he'd catch himself looking around the room before digging in, as if to invite others to dig in as well.

After finishing his dinner, Jino packed the containers back up, drank some water, and stood at the railing, wind biting at his nose, to gaze at the distant lights of downtown Seoul. When the weather was nicer, he'd sing now and then. He picked out 'Geumi' from the row of bottles along the railing and sat back down inside the tent. There was something so young and sweet about the name 'Geumi' that it brought back childhood memories of playing with friends; in fact, it felt so much like the name of a close friend that he'd unconsciously left off his grandmother's family name when he labelled the bottle. As a child, Jino had spent a lot of time at home with his grandmother. She was so knowledgeable and had so many stories to tell, along with a few strange old songs that she'd taught him. Whenever he hummed a song he'd learned from his grandmother, his wife and colleagues would clutch their stomachs with laughter and exclaim, 'Which ancient tune is that?' The songs he learned from his grandmother included the 'Bride Groom Song', the 'Yakgwa Song', 'One Shot Two Shots', and 'The Internationale'. When he asked her who she learned 'The Internationale' from, she said her brother-in-law Icheol had taught her and that Jino's grandfather and father knew the song as well. Jino turned the lantern on and hummed away as he lay in the tent.

Up-down, up-down, bobs the child-groom's topknot
This-a-way, that-a-way, sways the horse carrying him to his wedding
Hurry, hurry, let's make fun of him!
Yes, yes, let's make fun of him!
Young groom, straw sack, what a sad sack, in a big hat, just a little brat
Young groom, straw sack, what a sad sack, in a big hat, just a little brat

There goes the bride, the ugly old bride, big and round as a crock
Riding a palanquin with her eyes closed, she's off to meet her groom
Hurry, hurry, let's make fun of her!
Yes, yes, let's make fun of her!

Old bride, boo bride, boo-hoo bride, rolling down the hill, round
as a basket bride
Old bride, boo bride, boo-hoo bride, rolling down the hill, round
as a basket bride

Jino belted out the last word. At some point during the song, Geumi Halmeoni had arrived and was sitting across from him, tapping her knees to the rhythm and singing along as he launched into the 'Yakwa Song'. *To the village across the way we went / to see a festival one day / we were given a piece of yakgwa, sweet yakgwa / but when my mother and I took a bite / the damn dog snatched it away.*

The next one was a counting-out rhyme sung in the winter. Everyone would gather at the warmest spot on the ondol floor and put their legs under a blanket. They would count their knees, and the person whose knee came last got a penalty. Jino murmured, *One shot, two shots, three and a-four shots, crunching over the snow, here comes the hawk, the falcon, the hunter, and* pop!

'I used to have no idea what the lyrics meant when I sang along with you, and my mother would yell at me to stop.'

'Which song are you talking about?'

'The Internationale.'

'Can you sing it for me now?'

Jino hummed the melody first. The song should have felt like a roaring wave sung by a crowd, but instead Jino's whispered rendition sounded sad and fragile. Like that song about walking with your eyes closed that Jingi used to sing. Still, Jino felt heat start to rise within him.

Rise, oh people, cursed into a world of hunger and slavery
Our boiling blood drives us into the ultimate fight
Let us uproot oppression and build a new world
Owned by all who've been mistreated and trampled

This will be our final decisive fight
With the Internationale, humanity will rise

This will be our final decisive fight
With the Internationale, humanity will rise

'But Halmeoni, I like today's version of "The Internationale" instead of the one that was sung under Japanese rule.'

His grandmother smiled softly as she said, 'They say history repeats itself. That seems to be true no matter how much the world, and all the people in it, change, or as customs change. I guess that's another way of saying that the way we live only looks different on the outside, but what's on the inside stays the same.'

Jino stopped singing, but the lyrics he'd belted out with colleagues at rallies lingered in his throat.

'You feel all alone up here, don't you?'

'You're with me, Halmeoni.'

Geumi took her grandson by the hand.

'Look up there, at all the stars. Millions and billions of people have come and gone, but they're all keeping an eye on you.'

Jino was a little boy again, holding his grandmother's hand as they headed to the Yeongdeungpo Market. The Willow Tree House was just as he'd seen it in his dreams. Jino's memory only went back as far as the Saetmal House, where the family had moved after living in the rail workers' housing, but he'd heard so much about the Willow Tree House from his father and grandmother that he could practically draw a picture of it.

8

Yi Ilcheol was made engineer's assistant on a Gyeongbu Line freight train and began driving from Yongsan and Yeongdeungpo Stations down south to Daejeon, with the occasional shift rotation that had him overnighting there and continuing further south to Busan, where he overnighted again, before returning. Which meant he was spending half the week away from home. When he walked into the engineers' waiting room at Yongsan Station for the first time, a gangly man in his mid-thirties, tall for a Japanese, was sitting by the stove, sipping green tea. The man stared at Ilcheol as he stepped in through the latticed glass door.

'You the rookie?'

'Yes, I've been assigned to freight.'

'Where did you apprentice?'

'The Gyeongin Line.'

'You've been lucky.'

The man asked his name but looked stumped when Ilcheol told him.

'I-I-I-roo-choo-roo? That's hard to say. Can I just call you Yi-san?'

'Sure, that's what everyone calls me.'

'Great, I'm Hayashi.'

Hayashi was an engineer. Engineers were required to clock in up to two and a half hours ahead of departure time. They first stopped by the central office to be assigned to a service section and receive any special instructions or precautions about the freight they were to transport. Then, they'd join their team at the engineers' waiting room. The room would bustle with engineers and assistants right up until departure, when everyone would swarm out to their own trains, leaving the building as empty as if no one had been there in the first place. Hayashi handed Ilcheol a pocket watch. All engineers and their assistants were given a watch with hands synchronised precisely down to the second. Freshly appointed engineers were charged with dividing and assigning locomotives to each line at large stations like the ones in Namdaemun, Yongsan, and Yeongdeungpo. They usually left the office with a small wooden tag engraved with the track number and locomotive number. Hayashi stood up.

'Yoshi!' he chirped in Japanese. 'Okay! Shall we get going?'

Hayashi and Ilcheol emerged from the waiting room, left the passenger-carriage platform, and walked across the tracks to where freight trains were queued in front of a row of warehouses. Hayashi knew exactly where they were headed. Workers were pulling items from one of the warehouses, carrying them over on a cart, and stacking them in front of the freight-carriage platform before loading the stacks into the train. A man dressed in uniform, complete with work cap and gaiters, stood up on the freight-carriage platform and came running toward Hayashi to greet him. He welcomed Ilcheol, as well, in Japanese.

Hayashi nodded and said to Ilcheol, 'Yi-san, this is the coal hauler. He'll be your right-hand man. What did you say your family name is?'

The man stood straight and answered loudly, 'It's Kim, sir.'

'Right, Kim-kun.'

Ilcheol had known at first glance that Kim was Korean. Locomotives had originally been assigned a staff of four: an engineer, engineer's assistant, stoker, and coal hauler. Once it was known that the job could technically be handled by the coal hauler with support from the engineer's assistant, the stoker was made redundant. The duties of Kim as a stoker-slash-coal hauler and Ilcheol as an engineer's assistant-slash-stoker may have overlapped, but there was an enormous difference in their ranks. After all, Kim was equivalent to a lowly day labourer, whereas Ilcheol was an assistant who would become an engineer in the future. Koreans were forbidden from speaking Korean on the job if even one Japanese person was present.

Hayashi was about to mount the locomotive's steel stairs, which looked even higher from directly below them, but he stopped and asked Ilcheol, 'You know what kind of locomotive this is, right?'

'Yes, isn't it a Mikado?'

'Uh-huh, it's an impressive beast. This is a new-and-improved version of the locomotives we used to import from America, made in the factory at our very own Kawasaki shipyard. What do you think of our homegrown train?'

Through his training at the academy, Ilcheol had grown familiar with the specifics of trains operating in Joseon. The Mikado was the largest of the freight locomotives. Weighing fifty tonnes, the Mikado could pull up to twenty tonnes, or ascend a one per cent–grade track at an average of thirty kilometres per hour with up to twenty-four railway carriages in tow. The Pacific type, or Paci for short, was like a brother to the Mikado. It was used to pull passenger carriages on the Gyeongbu and Gyeongin Lines. The international limited-express trains that travelled to Manchuria were pulled by larger tender locomotives. Kim stood at attention beside the locomotive.

'We'll check the bottom first and then the cab,' Hayashi said to Ilcheol. 'Starting next time, you'll be in charge of checking the outside.'

'Yes, sir.'

Ilcheol followed Hayashi as he approached the locomotive's massive wheels with a small hammer in hand. Hayashi checked the cylinders and compressed-air tank, tapping at them with the hammer, and examined whether the connecting rods and slide bars were properly and tightly engaged with the wheels. He also checked whether the compressor was aligned. Then, one after the other, the three men mounted the steel stairs into the cab. The engineer's seat was inside to the left, and the assistant's seat was to the right. In front of the seats was the brake, reverse lever, and regulator: a push closed the steam valve for deceleration, and a pull opened it for acceleration. In the middle of the cab was the boiler, and below that was the firebox. With the press and release of a foot pedal, the firebox doors slid open and shut. The brake had two levers: one for an independent brake for the locomotive only, and another for an automatic brake for all of the carriages. The engineer's seat offered a view of the left side of the tracks ahead, while the assistant's seat offered a view of the right. Behind the seats, the coal bunker sat on a water tank that fed water into the boiler through an injector. The coal hauler stood in the bunker to shovel coal to the front and took turns with the engineer's assistant to keep the firebox fed. A seasoned stoker could tell when and how much coal was needed just by looking at the fire, unless the train was accelerating or climbing uphill, in which case it had to be fed nonstop. Apart from serving as a part-time stoker, an engineer's assistant was expected to cover for the engineer during his break once the assistant had enough experience under his belt. While Hayashi checked the dashboard, Ilcheol climbed on top of the locomotive to examine the boiler's safety valve and the steam receiver's control valve. He also knocked on the sand dome to determine whether it was filled with enough sand for their journey.

At the scheduled departure time, Ilcheol looked out to see that the block signal had been cleared. This meant there were no obstructions ahead. Ilcheol raised his hand, and Hayashi opened the steam valve. The train let out a short whistle followed by a blasting hoot to announce its departure. Slowly, the train began to move forward. Ilcheol took a step out onto the steel stairs leading to the assistant's entrance with one hand holding onto an iron railing and the other stretched out. A staff member from the track division was waiting at the end of the platform to hand him a pass. The pass was inside a wallet attached to a leather band. It was a permit of sorts giving the train exclusive use of the track ahead during its operation. It also meant that each station had been notified via telegram of the train's schedule so that tracks could be switched and obstacles removed in time for the train to pass safely. A locomotive without a pass wasn't allowed to pull any freight or passenger carriages. The engineer's assistant had to snatch the pass from the other person's hand while the train was picking up speed. This marked the start of his shift, just as a stoker's shift began with the first shovel of coal. Each time he did this, the leather band whipped through the air and smacked Ilcheol hard on the forearm, leaving a bright-red mark. The engineers got a kick out of teasing him about that mark, saying it was his veins popping out from trying too hard. It took Ilcheol a month to finally get the hang of snatching the pass without getting smacked.

The pass allowed for travel to Cheonan Station, where the Chungnam Line branched away from the area that had long been known as the 'Cheonan Three-Way Intersection' and headed for the Naepo plain. The crew had to stand by there. Unlike passenger trains, freight trains could maintain a constant speed and did not have to stop at every single station along the way. The Mikado they were driving that day, with eighteen freight carriages in tow, was able to make good time at thirty kilometres, or eighty li, per hour. And despite it being the night shift, the benefit to the monotony of driving freight was that the fewer starts and stops meant the engineers experienced far less fatigue. They would reach Cheonan in three and a half hours.

About a month after Ilcheol joined the crew, Hayashi began taking breaks and having Ilcheol take his place in the driver's seat. Somewhere between the capital and the provincial cities of Anyang and Suwon, he would retreat to a low stool topped with a plush cushion and rest his head against the cab wall.

Most trains carrying passengers or heading to the continent were pulled by new locomotives with mechanical stokers, but freight trains running on the main lines were still hauled by old locomotives that required coal haulers and stokers to manually feed the firebox. Instead of being inside the coal bunker, the coal hauler Kim was up front, shovelling coal into the firebox. Each section of track required a certain amount of fuel, and Kim had already prepped the amount he needed so he could keep the fire stoked. If the fire were to die down, they would lose too much steam. Inside the firebox, the floor was shaped like a plate, flat in the centre and flared on the sides. Coal had to be thrown once to the right, once to the left, and once deep into the centre. To keep the stokers and haulers motivated, the Railway Bureau regularly hosted a coal-throwing contest, and the apprentices being mostly Koreans, play was just as important as work. They turned their shovelling into a dance. They began by standing sideways to the firebox, and with a big scoop of coal on one, they'd twist on two, throw coal to the left on three, to the right on four, then turn and face front on five, and throw a last big shovel of coal straight down the middle on six, their arms and legs loose, shoulders rising and falling in time with the beat, bodies moving as smoothly as if on strings.

Between Osan, Seojeong-ri, and Pyeongtaek, the tracks began sloping gently upward into two mountain passes and two bends. After that was a flat plain stretching long and straight from Pyeongtaek to Cheonan, giving the stoker a chance to catch his breath. Outside, an early winter rain began to fall. Normally, when the train began to climb uphill, Hayashi would slowly rise from his stool, stretch, and relieve Ilcheol of the driver's seat, but a month into working together, Hayashi had observed that his assistant was adept at handling the tricky section, and more often than not would continue to nap at the back. Ilcheol pulled the whistle cord to signal the start of the slope, the whistle blast surely loud enough to wake the driver, but Hayashi kept his eyes closed and did not budge from his stool.

'More coal!' Ilcheol reminded Kim.

Kim sang the 'Singo Mountain Taryeong' as he began his coal-throwing dance.

Singo Mountain shudders at the sound of a coal train leaving
The rubber-factory girl packs a bindle in vain
Uh-rang uh-rang, uh-huh-iya, eh-heh-ya, diora-ah
Everywhere I turn is my love
Uh-rang uh-rang, uh-huh-iya, eh-heh-ya, diora-ah
Everywhere I turn is my love

As the train began to chug and puff its way uphill, it would gradually slow to the point that a person running alongside could have jumped on. That's when the driver would pull on the regulator and push another lever to spray sand on the rails while the train picked up speed again. The sand helped to improve traction on rainy and snowy days. Once over the top, the train would head back downhill, and the driver would push the regulator to maintain a steady speed. When a bend came up, the width of the tracks slowly widened about ten millimetres from 1,435 to 1,445. The wheels would screech against the outside rail and spray metal shavings into the air — the crew called this 'the blind man': the fine bits of metal stung and made their eyes tear up and clamp shut; they would force each other's lids open to gently blow away the metal dust or blot it away with wet handkerchiefs. But once the hurdle of those two mountain passes and bends were behind them, Ilcheol would blow the whistle once more to signal their approach into the straight, level stretch between Pyeongtaek and Cheonan.

When the train approached the Cheonan Station freight-train zone, Hayashi would finally rise from his stool and take over until the train was parked. Then the three men would head to the waiting room. They'd stand by for an hour, waiting for passenger trains and other freight trains switching to main lines to clear the tracks.

From Cheonan, the train passed the Charyeong Mountains, racing between North and South Chungcheong Provinces, and stopped at Jochiwon and Sintanjin before arriving in Daejeon. Because there were so many tunnels, bridges, and slopes in that section, Hayashi remained in the driver's seat. The trip from Gyeongseong to Daejeon took six hours, including the time spent standing by in Cheonan. During the peak season, if they didn't change shifts in Daejeon, they could spend as long as twelve hours driving from Gyeongseong to Busan. Off-season meant six-hour shifts and overnights in Daejeon, but when the schedule was tight they would drive straight through and sleep in Busan instead, take the next day off, and depart for Gyeongseong at night. The two cities became quite familiar to Hayashi, Ilcheol, and Kim as they spent half the month in Daejeon and the other half in Busan. Over the course of a few months, the three grew close enough to feel like family and embraced the same customs and rules that other cab crews lived by.

At Daejeon, they'd lodge at the station dormitory, a sort of makeshift inn with a small tatami-lined room assigned to each crew. The wooden building resembled an army barracks with a toilet and shower room beside the entrance and a row of rooms on either side of a long corridor. At first, Hayashi slept there with his crew, but he soon began spending his nights elsewhere and would show up at the freight-train platform half an hour before departure. He was normally accompanied by one or two fellow engineers who worked on other lines, but one night as he set out he seemed to be on his own.

'Yi-san, care to venture out with me?' Hayashi quietly asked.

'Out, sir?' Ilcheol said, pretending to be clueless.

'Train drivers are like sailors. You gotta make the most of shore leave.'

'How do we do that, sir?'

'Follow me and I'll show you,' Hayashi said, letting out a hearty laugh and patting Ilcheol on the shoulders.

Past the train-station square was a main street filled with Japanese-style wooden houses. As Hayashi stood there looking around, a man approached him, said hello, and handed him an envelope before disappearing in a hurry. Hayashi headed toward the street across the square, Ilcheol following without a word.

'You can usually catch a rickshaw here, but I guess it's too late.'

Ilcheol pulled out his pocket watch and saw it was past two in the morning. Hayashi whistled as he strolled down a street to the right. Three or four blocks down, they arrived at the entrance to a street flanked by two cement lampposts.

'This is Haruhi-cho,' Hayashi said, glancing back at Ilcheol.

The cement posts marked the start of the district, but the street itself continued further back, to where lookalike two-storey buildings stood on either side with paper lamps hanging from their railings. Halfway down, Hayashi entered one of the buildings that resembled an inn. In the small tearoom by the entrance snored a middle-aged woman dressed in a kimono. She woke with a start.

'Welcome, Mr Hayashi.'

'How's everyone? Why don't you show us in?'

The woman led the two men into the parlour. She waited hesitantly until Hayashi said, 'Bring Natsuka if she's available.'

The woman bowed and left. Then a younger Japanese woman appeared, carrying a porcelain bottle of hot sake, cups, and an appetiser on a tray.

'Huh, I guess business is slow on weekdays. I brought my assistant Yi-san with me today,' said Hayashi.

Natsuka knelt and bowed to Ilcheol.

'Pleased to meet you, I'm Natsuka.'

'Now that we've all been introduced, show us some girls already,' Hayashi said.

Natsuka pulled a thin album out from under the tray. Hayashi pushed it toward Ilcheol and said, 'Pick one.'

Ilcheol hesitated. 'If you don't mind, sir, I'm pretty tired. I think I'll just have a drink with you and go back to the dormitory.'

'What? What kind of man are you if — Look, I'm ordering you, as your superior. We're sleeping here tonight.'

Natsuka smiled as she listened to the two men.

'We have Korean girls as well. Take a look at the back.'

Hayashi picked up the album and flipped to the last page.

'Right, there's five here. Pick one of them.'

Ilcheol squirmed in his seat, saying nothing, until finally Hayashi poured him a cup of sake.

'You called yourself a newlywed, right? Well, guess what, you're not. It's been over six months, which makes you an old married couple. Way past time for you to start whoring.'

Hayashi turned to Natsuka.

'Bring whoever's newest.'

'As you wish, sir.'

'The kotatsu's freezing, by the way. Why is it so cold in here?'

'I'm sorry, sir. It must be due to the late hour.'

'That's okay. We'll be in bed soon enough.'

Natsuka stepped out of the room. About three or four cups of sake later, she returned with a girl in a modernised hanbok. The girl was dressed in a full skirt that stopped just above her ankles and a quilted jeogori blouse that fastened without the usual long ribbon; her hair was bobbed, and she wore no make-up. Beoseon socks with upturned tips covered her feet, which she kept modestly pressed together. But even if she hadn't been dressed in that get-up, Ilcheol still would have known immediately that she was Korean.

Ilcheol said nothing while Hayashi marvelled at the girl.

'My, my, a wildflower! What's your name?'

Natsuka shot the girl a look, and she answered quietly, 'Ha-Haruka.'

Hayashi chuckled, 'Everyone in this place has "fragrance" in their name.'

Ilcheol almost laughed out loud to realise that the girl's Korean name must be Chunhyang, or Spring Fragrance, the name of a lowly courtesan's daughter from a classic love story, in which Young Master Yi, a magistrate's son, falls in love with her at first sight.

'Show Yi-kun here a good time,' said Hayashi. Then he and Natsuka exchanged looks and went upstairs.

Ilcheol and Haruka just sat there, not saying a word. Finally, struggling not to fall asleep, Haruka, or Chunhyang, broke the silence and addressed Ilcheol, the aptly named Yi.

'Why don't we go to bed, sir?'

Ilcheol felt embarrassed at the thought of being left alone in the parlour, so he stood and followed Haruka upstairs into a room at the far end of the corridor. The bedding was already laid out on the floor, complete with a long pillow for two.

'If you'd like to take a bath, I can show you the way, sir.'

'No, I'm fine.' He quickly added, 'I'm tired. I'll just sleep by myself.'

'I'll be scolded if you do,' Haruka pleaded. 'Please don't tell me to leave.'

Silence fell again, and they sat there until Haruka spoke up.

'I'll turn the lights off so we can go to bed.'

'Go ahead and lie down. I'll sit here for a while and then leave.'

Haruka stood on tiptoes to flip the switch to the light globe hanging above. She stripped down to her chemise and slipped under the blanket. Ilcheol sat where he was in the dark.

'I didn't want to wear Korean clothes,' Haruka mumbled. 'But they brought them and kept telling me to put them on.'

Ilcheol fought the urge to ask what difference it made whether she wore Korean or Japanese clothes.

'I wanted to work in a Korean house, but they told me those places are out past the underpass and are rougher than here.'

Was she feeling ashamed about being dressed up in hanbok and paraded around in front of a fellow Korean in a Japanese brothel? How had she ended up here anyway? Someone had probably gone to her family's farm during the spring famine and offered to take away their old maid of a daughter for a few coins, an advance on her wages. In a year, she'd be skilled, a seasoned prostitute, maybe even make a name for herself among the whoremongers as the Chunhyang of Haruhi-cho, or else she'd catch a disease, or simply remain a square peg, and find herself sold off at an even cheaper price to one of the brothels in front of the train station, where she would grow old and be sold again to a mining area or some remote island and die before the age of thirty. Ilcheol suddenly wondered what his brother was doing right that moment. Would liberating the nation mean a new life for people like her, too? From the soft, even sound of the girl's breathing, Ilcheol could tell she'd fallen asleep, so he picked up his jacket and tiptoed downstairs.

The next day, when it was time for them to depart for Gyeongseong, Hayashi showed up in the cab, clean-shaven and missing the coal smudges of the day before.

'Yi-san, *baka desho!*' he scolded Ilcheol. 'How could you just leave like that? I paid three won per person.'

'I was tired,' Ilcheol mumbled.

If Hayashi's complaint was true, then he had spent six won in the brothel. An eighty-kilogram sack of rice cost five won, so they'd figuratively eaten an entire sack of rice and then some in one night. Ilcheol's monthly salary as a Korean engineer's assistant was thirty won and would rise to about forty won once he became an engineer. Japanese employees were usually paid double their Korean co-workers, so Hayashi was probably earning at least eighty won a month. Even so, how could he afford to go out and spend money like that as many times as he had? Only later did Ilcheol find out that engineers traditionally made extra money by 'skimming coal'. A few days after that night in Daejeon, Ilcheol and Kim headed to the rail workers' dormitory while Hayashi went out with other Japanese engineers. Before leaving the train, Hayashi called Ilcheol aside.

'Take this and treat Kim-kun to a nice meal or some drinks when we get back to Gyeongseong.'

Hayashi stuffed a wad of neatly folded banknotes into Ilcheol's uniform pocket. Ilcheol pulled them out later to find three one-won notes. Skimming coal usually happened at stopover stations or the last station. For instance, if the final destination was Cheonan, then the best place to do it was right before the train entered the outskirts of Gyeongseong. That was when Hayashi would hand the controls over to Ilcheol and take the shovel from Kim. The locomotive's firebox was shaped like a huge furnace, and the ash naturally collected on the bottom. These ashes had to be disposed of and their water supply refilled whenever they were stopped in a station. A lever opened the bottom of the firebox and released the ashes onto the railway sleepers, which were then cleaned up by the track workers. And so, after the train departed and was coasting slowly to some prearranged location, coal would be shovelled into the firebox as if to pick up speed, but with the bottom of the firebox still hanging open. The coal would carpet the railway sleepers. A smuggler, who'd been lying in wait, would appear with some muscle to help him scoop the coal into sacks and lug it away in a cart. He would have already paid the locomotive driver while he was on stand-by at the previous station. This smuggled coal could be bought for half the market price, which was why merchants operating near train stations were keen to secure a deal with engineers. Merchants would even pay in cash on the spot or make monthly payments. If the drop was to be made near the last stop, the firebox was left open as the train entered the outskirts of the final city. Trains were supplied with coal at the departing station, where the amount of coal was usually determined by the locomotive type, the number of carriages the locomotive had to pull, and the weight of the cargo being transported. A Mikado, which could pull up to twenty-four carriages, tended to receive a generous amount of coal, especially since running out could cause an accident. The fewer carriages it pulled, the more coal was left over, which meant a tidy bonus for the engineer braving such difficult, dangerous, and often dead-of-night work. Engineers therefore had to habitually grease the palms of those in charge of supplying coal to the train carriages. Hayashi must have made an extra ten to fifteen won from skimming coal once or twice per trip. Outside the capital, most cities' main streets were centred on the train stations; in the pubs and gisaeng restaurants and red-light districts there, locomotive drivers were very popular among the ladies for what the Japanese called 'kimae' — their generosity — and were considered well educated and handsome, to boot. To others, they lived on the road and therefore naturally had wandering eyes. The most popular of all, though, were the engineers who drove back and forth to the continent, as their trains were big and their incomes even bigger; they had girlfriends at every station and were treated like kings in the dance halls and bars.

Yet the money made from skimming coal was pennies compared to what could be made from skimming carriages. Locomotives transported not only people but also supplies and regional specialties, connecting distant areas to each other. An item cheap in one place gained value as it moved. The greater the distance, the bigger the difference in price. There was more than one way to skim a carriage: one was to arrange directly with the owner of the freight to transport their goods off the books for half the cost. The more profitable way was to hire a local to procure scarce or popular seasonal goods, transport them using an unregistered carriage, and sell them in a different region. Skimming carriages could not be done often, so the one or two times a month it did happen brought in good money. Engineers with a head for business boasted about making double or triple the money in the colony that they would have back home in Japan, while those who drove the continental routes did so well for themselves that not even the highest ranking of government positions inspired their envy.

On days when Ilcheol headed to Daejeon, he'd go to work in the evening, spend the night in Daejeon, and come home the following afternoon. He'd rest and then spend the next day at home with his family before heading back to work in the evening. On days when he went all the way to Busan, he'd depart in the evening and drive the twelve hours there, arriving in Busan the next morning, where he'd sleep for the rest of the day until the train departed for Gyeongseong in the evening, getting him home the following morning. He would rest that day and the next. The long-distance trips essentially earned him an extra day off. When Hayashi skimmed a shipment of dried seafood and Gupo pears from Busan ahead of the holidays, he gave Ilcheol and Kim fifty won as a bonus, which meant he'd made nearly 300 won in profits. The bonuses from Hayashi left Ilcheol feeling ashamed and unsure of himself every time. He never knew what to say while handing Kim his share of the money. With coal skimming, the three or four won that found its way into their hands meant they could stop by a pub or a Chinese restaurant together after work and spend one won on a nice meal, after which they'd split whatever was left, telling each other to buy snacks for the kids or a gift for the wife on their way home. Splitting a bonus of fifty won was, however, a different story, because the amount was so much more than Ilcheol's salary of thirty won and a good five times more than Kim's salary of ten won. Their salary difference made it awkward for Ilcheol to take thirty won, worth a month's salary for him, and hand Kim the remaining twenty won, worth two months' salary for Kim.

Ilcheol had grown up learning how to handle money from Baekman. He decided that he and Kim should each take a month's worth of their respective salaries as a bonus from the skimmed carriages and split the rest, which meant thirty-five won for Ilcheol and fifteen for Kim. The money was a huge help to Ilcheol and a veritable windfall to Kim. After returning from a trip one day, they parted ways with Hayashi and exited Yongsan Station. Before splitting the coal-skimming bonus that Hayashi had given him, Ilcheol took Kim to one of their regular pubs.

'That Hayashi-san is real nice,' Kim said with a grin.

Ilcheol ignored this and asked, 'How did you end up joining the Railway Bureau?'

'Well, back home, my father worked on a private railroad for years. That's how I got my start as a day labourer on the Chungnam Line before coming here.'

They ate slices of boiled pork and drank makgeolli. Each time

Ilcheol refilled his cup for him, Kim took it politely with both hands.

'I've been thinking for a while now about who the railway belongs to,' said Ilcheol.

'What? What do you mean by who?'

'I mean I've been thinking about whether it belongs to Japan or Joseon.'

Without giving it much thought, Kim said, 'Seeing as how it took over management from the South Manchuria Railway Company, I reckon the rails belong to the Government-General.'

'I suppose. Which makes it Japan's?'

'I mean, you know, we don't have a country …'

Unsure of what to say next, Kim stared at Ilcheol.

'Japan began laying tracks in Joseon before we were born and snatched the construction rights from a falling country. And it cost almost nothing to complete because they simply took the land and forced people into labour. Doesn't that seem backward to you?'

'Stolen or not, either way, it's not ours anymore, is it?' Kim said. 'It's like if you own a house but lose all your money and so a different owner moves in. Not much you can do about it, is there?'

'Houses come and go, but can you say the same about land? This land is where Koreans have always lived. And it will be ours again.'

'Come on, when do you figure that'll happen?'

Ilcheol decided to enlighten him.

'Japan is like a thief placing a ladder against the wall so they can climb over and rob our house. Do you really think they built the railroads for us? From the very beginning, the tracks that lead from the peninsula up into the continent were called a military railway. That's how they were able to grab all that land and labour to build it.'

'Still, aren't we lucky to have these jobs? Times are rough.'

Ilcheol nodded helplessly.

'Yes, yes, we're lucky. Plus we get bribes from Hayashi-san. Anyway, the point I'm trying to make is that we should never forget that we're the true owners.'

They drank in silence for a while until Kim suddenly looked up and declared, 'Oh, I feel so much better now. We're the owners!'

'That's right. We may be serving others at the moment, but we're still the owners. Let's not forget that.'

Although it was only nine in the evening when they came out of the pub, the streets were as quiet as the dead of night. From what was left after paying for their drinks, Ilcheol handed Kim a one-won note as his split. The two men looked as sheepish as ever about sharing Hayashi's bribes and quickly parted ways without saying goodbye.

*

Geumi had put the baby to sleep and was cleaning the yard and her father-in-law's workshop when she heard Mageum Gomo pounding on the gate and calling out to her.

'Jisan Eomma!'

Geumi dropped the broom and opened the gate to see that Mageum had brought someone with her.

'This is my niece-in-law,' Mageum said to the woman.

Geumi saw that the woman was wearing a black modernised-hanbok skirt paired with a white jeogori blouse on top. She had bobbed hair, pleasant eyes, and wide pursed lips that made her look smart. She bowed.

'Nice to meet you. I'm Han Yeowok.'

As always, Geumi narrowed her eyes and saw the woman's silhouette blur against the sunlight. She saw a smiling Icheol holding a baby. The baby raised its scrawny arms and wiggled its tiny fingers.

'What are you staring at?' Mageum asked, her voice both playful and admonishing.

Startled into her senses, Geumi said, 'Nice to meet you, too. I'm Jisan Eomma.'

'She's our Dusoe's sister-in-law. His elder brother is her husband,' Mageum added with a giggle.

Geumi gave Mageum a questioning glance. Even though Geumi didn't say anything, Mageum knew she was asking whether the woman was Icheol's girlfriend, and nodded.

'Come on in,' said Geumi.

She showed the women into the main room.

At the sight of the napping baby, Mageum said quietly, 'My, just look at how well our Jisan sleeps. It'll be a delight to raise such a sweet-tempered boy.'

'It's been a while since he's seen his uncle. I wonder what he's up to these days,' Geumi mumbled as she stole glances at Yeowok.

'Dusoe brought her over a couple of days ago,' said Mageum.

Geumi had suspected as much. After all, she'd immediately recognised that the woman was with her brother-in-law and that the two would have a baby in the future.

'She'll stay with me for the time being as we look for a room for the couple and get it furnished,' Mageum added.

'She could stay here,' said Geumi.

Mageum Gomo quickly waved her hands as if to say she wouldn't dream of imposing on Geumi.

'No, that's out of the question. Your father-in-law is using the extra bedroom.'

'That room was originally meant for Icheol Doryeonnim.'

'Still, your father-in-law would have to move to the workshop. The tiny room you used at our place before you got married will do. She's agreed to stay there for the time being.'

Yeowok finally spoke up.

'I'm really sorry for the bother. Icheol and I have run into a bit of a situation, so we need to lie low for a while ...'

Geumi understood what Yeowok was getting at.

'Then you should find a place as soon as possible. What's Icheol doing now?'

Yeowok was too discrete to say anything, so Mageum answered for her. 'Well, he's something of a go-between.'

Some time back, Geumi had caught on to the fact that Icheol was managing communications for the Red Labour Union in Yeongdeungpo. She could only assume that the authorities had intensified their surveillance. With the baby keeping her housebound, she couldn't help them look for a place herself, so instead she slipped Mageum some money to help pay for the basic household items Icheol and Yeowok would need. She'd pitch in again once they found a room.

When Ilcheol came home from work in the evening, she told him his brother had found a bride and that the woman would be staying at his aunt's place for the time being.

'Icheol won't be able to stay here when he's on the run,' said Ilcheol. 'Let's look for a house they can rent somewhere in a more residential area.'

Geumi would always say this much to her son, Jisan.

'I'm sure your Aunt Yeowok is well and alive out there somewhere. She's a survivor.'

How Yeowok came to meet and be with Icheol was a story Geumi gradually pieced together as Icheol and Yeowok each shared the details with her over time.

*

Following the Comintern's release of the December Theses in 1921, there'd been a new awakening. The Comintern officialised the Joseon Communist Party's dissolution via letter, criticising the socialist movement in colonial Joseon for lacking class affiliation and being too factionalised, centred on intellectuals, ideologically chaotic, and idealistically distant from the masses. The new generation of activists therefore had to take a different approach than their predecessors. Instead of a few socialist intellectuals gathering to proclaim the formation of a party, the plan was for activists to infiltrate places where labourers and farmers made their livelihoods in order to awaken them, train them through protests, and thereby form a party from the bottom up.

This approach spread like wildfire throughout Joseon in the early-to-mid-1930s. In Manchuria, it was socialists, not nationalists, who emerged as the pivot of armed struggle. According to the one-party-state rule, however, Korean communists fighting in China had to be absorbed by the Chinese party, whereas those fighting in Japan were to be absorbed by the Japanese party. For communists in colonial Joseon, the most urgent task was to re-establish a Korean party. The foundation for revolution wasn't something a colonised nation could afford to lose after having been deprived of its sovereignty.

As a young man, Yi Jaeyu had worked to support himself through university in Japan and was involved with the Japanese branch of the Korean Communist Youth League until he was arrested and sent back to Joseon. During the long preliminary hearings, he met various activists in prison. These activists had put more work into creating grandiose names for their organisations — from the Joseon Communist Council, to the Joseon Anti-Imperialist Alliance, to the National Council for the Left-Wing Workers of Joseon — than they did building their actual organisations, only to putter out after printing off a couple of pamphlets and proclamations. Although they weren't yet connected to each other, socialist groups in different provincial cities all over the country had launched countless labour and agrarian disputes since the March 1st Independence Movement. Jaeyu believed that dedicated activists needed to be connected to each other. More than anything, he believed they should actively seek the poorest labourers and the farmers who'd suffered the most, those who were essentially fighting for their right to live.

As soon as he was released, Jaeyu and a few young men his age that he'd met in prison discussed how they would rebuild the Joseon Communist Party, which had already been uprooted four times. They each took different roles to help recruit members. Some went into secondary schools and universities, while others went into factories in Gyeongseong, Yeongdeungpo, and Incheon. They also decided on their principles and methodologies. The core group was made up of Jaeyu and the other new founding members, each of whom formed smaller groups of their own with members they'd recruited. Those recruited members then formed subgroups of their own.

Unlike in the past, their organisation had no name or manifesto. Each group read legally acquired books and gradually moved on to illegal copies or handouts distributed by the core group. Communication between the subgroups was kept to a minimum, and opinions were exchanged with the core group through a loose network of scattered individuals. Later, when the Japanese authorities caught on and began to apprehend them, the total number of members was reported to be almost 200, but just as many managed to avoid arrest and went on working or headed to the outskirts of town to lie low. The true number was probably closer to 500, which was more than enough to rebuild a party from the top down. Yet they humbly refrained from being openly associated with the socialists embedded among tenant farmers in the remote mountains of Hamgyeong and Pyeongan Provinces and the plantations between Pyeongyang and the Hwanghae plains to the north, or among farmers in Chungcheong and Jeolla Provinces and labourers in Gwangju, Mokpo, Daegu, and Busan to the south. The organisation wasn't ready to fight in solidarity; the best they could do was to keep track of who was doing what and where through minimal degrees of personal contact. Meanwhile, Jaeyu and other members of the Committee for the Joseon Communist Party's Reconstruction worked to grow their group into a more solid, promising organisation based in the capital, Gyeongseong, and this is what came to be known as the Gyeongseong Troika.

In any case, they were only in the early stages when Icheol stumbled across them. Over the course of almost a year and a half, they managed to organise walkouts at schools and partially succeeded in pulling off a series of linked strikes at factories around Gyeongseong, all while suffering some arrests but not to the point of having to curtail any of their activities. The colonial police noticed these tremors of unrest happening throughout the country and went on full alert by launching a secret investigation. They also began to mobilise Korean police assistants and spies. These undercover agents were poor labourers and farmers who'd been converted after being caught participating in communist activities or volunteers who were after money, goods, and financial security. Meanwhile, the activists switched to one-on-one meetings and contacts. They kept their real names from one another and only met after going through multiple secure channels of communication.

Lower-level members only responded to orders from above and picked up documents via dead drops.

When Ilcheol and Geumi married, Icheol moved to a tiny room in Singil-jeong and found a job as an assistant at an electrics company. Spending more than thirteen hours a day at the factory, however, made it impossible for him to handle communication with multiple activists scattered across different workplaces. Like Bang Wuchang, Icheol chose instead the flexibility of working in the street as a porter. Of course, he only made the decision after talking it over with Comrade Yi, aka 'the man in the hat', his sole connection to the core group. After working together for a while, the two grew to trust each other enough to share their full names. Icheol learned that Comrade Yi's real name was Yi Gwansu, a former secondary-school teacher who'd studied in Japan.

Icheol stopped by Bang Wuchang's room once every three or four days; they sometimes went out for food or makgeolli if they had the money for it. Icheol was getting by with his brother's help. Each time he ran out of money, he turned to Ilcheol, who would quietly hand him ten or sometimes fifty won.

'Wow, must be nice working for the Railway Bureau.'

Each time that Icheol made fun of his brother, embarrassed at having to accept such large handouts when he himself had no job and wasn't earning a penny, Ilcheol would calmly say, 'That money was stolen, so put it to good use.'

One evening, when Icheol stopped by Wuchang's place, Wuchang happened to be out in the front yard with the other boarders, who were drawing water to wash up after work. Wuchang quickly headed for the gate with Icheol in tow.

'I was just about to go see you. Something has come up.'

Although they met routinely, they made it a rule to discuss important matters only while walking. Icheol and Wuchang passed the Maruboshi factory and crossed the tracks toward the Saetgang River.

'A comrade dispatched from Shanghai wishes to meet with the core members of your organisation,' Wuchang said, choosing his words carefully.

Though Icheol and Wuchang maintained different contacts, they trusted each other because they belonged to the same circle of labourers in Yeongdeungpo.

'I'll ask and let you know what they say.'

'There's not much time. Could you get back to me by tomorrow?'

'It usually takes two to three days, but I'll see what I can do.'

After their meeting, Icheol walked over to the last tram station in Noryangjin, where he hopped on a tram headed for downtown Gyeongseong. Yi Gwansu lived in Changsin-jeong near Dongdaemun Gate. Their contact point was a cigarette shop at the entrance of the alley to Gwansu's place. Icheol stepped into the tiny shop and saw the old lady in her usual seat inside the small room to the back.

'I'd like some cigarettes.'

'What do you smoke — Jangsuyeon?'

'No. Sakura, please.'

As he picked up the pack, Icheol asked, 'Is Mr Yi home?'

'Go ahead. I don't think he's gone out today.'

Icheol went up the alley and gave the wooden gate a little push. It was already open. The small bell attached to the gate jingled. It was a simple, rectangular house with a gabled roof, similar to Japanese houses, and had a front yard so tiny that the house practically opened right onto the alleyway. Gwansu's room was at the far end and had a door fashioned from wooden planks. When Icheol stepped into the yard, Gwansu was peering at him through a crack in the door. He'd probably been watching from the moment he heard the bell jingle. He'd been making copies by hand at a low table. All documents distributed to small groups were hand copied instead of mimeographed. Icheol told him about Wuchang's request; Gwansu knitted his brows as he mulled it over.

'We're aware of who he is. We know those people have comrades working in ones and twos around the country, distributing leaflets and pamphlets one at a time like they're planting beans. Didn't we meet one of them over the last strike when they tried to establish a connection with us?'

'Yes, I remember. I was the one who reached out on their behalf.'

'The request was similar back then. They wanted Comrade Yu to meet a prominent International-line comrade from abroad.'

Gwansu always referred to Yi Jaeyu by the last syllable of his name.

'I guess they didn't meet back then.'

'Of course they didn't. During our discussion, Comrade Yu said that while it's fine to meet with a comrade wishing to discuss something specific related to the struggle, it would be a waste of time to meet with some petit-bourgeois type who would wash their hands of us after a single meeting. And we agreed with what he said.'

'Does that mean you're not going to meet this person?'

'No, I think we'll have to meet this time. All these different groups keep stepping on each others' toes, so I believe it's time to either join forces or make some changes.'

Icheol couldn't help but ask, 'So you know who this person is?'

Gwansu grinned as he replied, 'Of course, he's the reason police surveillance got so much worse. We were on edge every time he distributed leaflets. He's older and quite well known. I believe his name is Kim Hyeongseon.'

Kim Hyeongseon's group had printed up literature and mailed it north, where a local member mimeographed copies and forwarded them to factories around Pyeongyang and mines in North Pyeongan Province. From there, the literature found its way to more factories and mines and newspaper branches all over the country. Hundreds of copies were handed out in the streets of Gyeongseong and Incheon. The publication was titled *The Communist*, and the contents included reporting on the anti-war struggle, defences of the Soviet alliance, support for the Chinese Red Army and the Soviets, calls for imperialist wars to become wars of national liberation, and a continual call for the absolute independence of Joseon. One issue proclaimed, 'Down with the Japanese Occupation of Manchuria!'; another, 'Long Live the Red May Day!'

'We were caught off guard when they went public.'

Gwansu bemoaned the adventurism of overseas activists who grew distant from their country and people. He added that what was needed the most over there was armed struggle. In any case, he said it was necessary to find out what their intentions were.

He let out a long sigh and mumbled, 'On the other hand, we're fighting for freedom, so I guess we need all the help we can get.'

When Icheol returned the next day, Gwansu gave him a message from Yi Jaeyu. It said he'd agreed to meet, and named a time and place. The rendezvous location, however, had to first be cleared by Icheol and someone from Kim Hyeongseon's group. If either found anything even slightly suspicious, the meeting would be cancelled.

Kim Hyeongseon joined the socialist movement in Masan where socialism had been spreading rapidly since the early 1920s. He organised the Masan Communist Youth League and then the Masan Communist Party, which were dissolved 'for progressive reasons' the very next year, when the Joseon Communist Party was established, and restructured into Masan-based cells of the Joseon Communist Party and the Korean Communist Youth League. Kim Hyeongseon was one of the youngest promoters of the Hwayo Faction, alongside Pak Hon-yong and Kim Danya, when the first Joseon Communist Party was established. At a secret meeting in Sinuiju, a drunk young local got into a fight with a Japanese and boasted that he was a Communist Party member. This led to the young man's arrest and torture by the Japanese police, which unfortunately exposed the whole Joseon Communist Party. Authorities all around the country were suddenly obsessed with arresting communists, so Kim Hyeongseon fled to Shanghai with Pak Hon-yong and Kim Danya.

Since the publication of the December Theses, Korean communists in Manchuria had been criticising the idea of independently rebuilding a party in Joseon as domestic expansionism, and instead chose to join the Chinese Communist Party. Over the next two years, the Manchurian bureau and Japanese bureau of the Joseon Communist Party were dissolved and respectively absorbed by the Communist Parties in China and Japan, in keeping with the one-party-state rule. Kim Hyeongseon was ordered by the Chinese Communist Party to cut off his association with the Joseon Communist Party and all other groups in Shanghai.

After discussing it with Kim Danya and others, he left Shanghai for Gyeongseong in February 1931. The plan was to distribute leaflets and manifestos to labourers and farmers to educate them and prepare to build a party. Until the end of the following April, he communicated with Kim Danya several times and developed a campaign using the leaflets and written manifestos Kim Danya sent from Shanghai. He started receiving funds and issues of *The Communist* from a contact in Shanghai, and purchased a mimeograph to make copies for distribution. When the police began to make arrests again, he escaped to Shanghai and reported his activities to Kim Danya and others before returning to Joseon three months later. One by one, Kim Hyeongseon met members in different regions who had been involved in distributing literature. He chose the standard method of rebuilding a party in the early 1930s, which was to create a network of activists dispatched to major cities. This method, however, resulted in a generally weak popular base in each region. As Kim Hyeongseon's group based in Gyeongseong attempted to create a network of its own, it was inevitable for its members to run into activists led by Yi Jaeyu in the same city. In other words, they'd been aware of each other's presence for some time.

On the agreed-upon date, Icheol arrived near Ihwa-jeong fifteen minutes earlier than he was supposed to. It was seven in the evening, and the street, Daehangno, in front of Keijo Imperial University's main building in Dongsung-jeong was mostly deserted of students. The early summer sycamores lining the street were a lush green, and the setting sun glowed against the sides of the buildings. Icheol strolled down Daehangno from Ihwa-jeong. His plan was to walk to the start of the Hyehwa-jeong traffic roundabout and turn back, while carefully checking whether anyone was following him or staking out the area. This security check was supposed to be performed simultaneously by reppos from both sides. Afterwards, they would rendezvous midway at the front gate near the university's main building.

As Icheol made his way down the street, he noticed someone walking toward him. It was a woman. He'd figured as much since he'd been told that the person he was supposed to meet would be holding a parasol. She was in heels and a solid-coloured, Western-style dress, but her face was concealed beneath the sky-blue parasol. When they drew closer to each other, the woman tilted her parasol just enough for Icheol to take a sharp look at her face. As previously agreed, Icheol was wearing work pants, had the sleeves of his shirt rolled up, and carried a rolled-up newspaper in his left hand. The two locked eyes as they passed. Icheol was sure she was the one he was supposed to meet. When he reached the start of the Hyehwa-jeong roundabout, he crossed the street and made his way back toward the university's front gate where the woman with the parasol was standing. Icheol continued to walk toward her. He checked his pocket watch and saw that it was seven o'clock sharp.

As Icheol approached, the woman asked, 'Could you tell me the time please?'

'It's seven.'

After he made sure no one was within earshot, Icheol casually suggested, 'Would you like to walk with me?'

The two walking together was a sign that all was clear.

'It seems like there'll be a drought this year,' the woman said.

'I agree. It hasn't rained since spring,' replied Icheol.

Although they didn't openly look around, the two remained aware of their surroundings as they headed toward Hyehwa-jeong. Yi Jaeyu, wearing a ramie shirt and straw hat, came down from Naksan Mountain and followed them at a distance. When they drew near the Hyehwa-jeong roundabout, a man in a suit emerged from an alley across the street.

'He's here,' Icheol said, and threw away the newspaper.

The woman nodded as she folded her parasol, and said, 'Ours is here, too.'

They crossed the street, and Yi Jaeyu followed. They passed the man in the suit and turned left toward Changgyeonggung Palace. Yi Jaeyu joined the man in the suit as they walked toward Dongsomun Gate. After making sure that the two men had safely found each other, Icheol and the woman felt far more relaxed as they walked along the stone wall around the palace. They didn't ask each other's name or what they were involved in, but the fact that they were both members of activist groups fighting against Japan made them feel almost like family.

When they reached Wonnam-jeong, Icheol asked, 'Have you had dinner?'

'No, but I ate a late lunch …'

Icheol knew full well that she couldn't have had time for dinner, because they both had to arrive at the rendezvous spot on time.

'I'm starving,' Icheol confessed.

She pointed across the street and said, 'Looks like there's a restaurant over there.'

She crossed the street with him but stopped on the other side and said, 'You go ahead. I'd better get going.'

'Wait, I was hoping you'd join me.'

The woman smiled faintly, gave him a slight farewell nod, and walked in the direction of Jongno. The restaurant on the corner was a noodle shop. Feeling disappointed, he opened the glass door, found a corner seat inside, and ordered a bowl of kongguksu.

*

Yi Jaeyu and Kim Hyeongseon talked as they walked through Dongsomun Gate and up to the minigolf course in Donam-jeong. Hyeongseon began with his impression of the movement in Joseon.

'You've been in prison for years, so you may not be entirely familiar with everything that's happened. Japan has swallowed up Manchuria and advanced into mainland China. This will probably lead to all-out war. We Koreans are suffering more than ever from extreme poverty and oppression. People are desperate and their desire to fight is about to explode, but activists haven't been able to rise to the occasion. Instead of acting with the people, they keep looking to intellectuals to save everyone and let themselves get distracted by factionalism and idealism.'

Jaeyu listened without responding or reacting until Hyeongseon lost his patience and finally showed his hand.

'The left wing in Joseon is a mess, so the International Party sent me to straighten out the front lines.'

Hyeongseon argued that each domestic faction line had to be sorted out via proper connections with the International line, which would in turn expand and strengthen the movement in Joseon.

'I haven't actually done anything yet,' Jaeyu said modestly. 'I'm just one powerless individual, but I'll do whatever the International Party asks of me if it's in the name of the movement.'

They agreed to meet again a week later at eight in the evening in the pine grove west of the Jungang Hangnim Buddhist seminary in Sungil-jeong.

*

Icheol arrived early and walked the route back and forth, running into the same woman from before. She'd just finished her own check of the area. The sun had nearly set, and it was growing dark. Once both sides gave the all-clear, Jaeyu and Hyeongseon headed onto the wooded trail across from the now deserted street. After watching the two enter the grove two to three minutes apart, Icheol and the woman slowly walked down the road toward Hyehwa-jeong like a young couple out on a date.

'I'm sorry about last time,' said the woman.

'Never mind that, I just thought I should treat you to dinner,' Icheol answered cheerfully.

'I'm a bit hungry today.'

'In that case, follow me. I noticed a place on the way here.'

While working as an activist, recruiting large numbers of people from the Yeongdeungpo factories for the book club and maintaining close relationships with them, Icheol had grown into something of a social butterfly. Then again, he'd always been the optimistic, outgoing type.

'You can call me Comrade Yi. That's my family name.'

The woman hesitated for a moment before replying, 'Mine's Han.'

They were supposed to use aliases with labourers and other people they met in the field. Icheol had two: Bak Cheol and Kim Yeong. As a general rule, sharing their real names even with other activists was forbidden. Knowing each other's names could become a burden. If any one of them were to be arrested and brutally tortured, there was no knowing whose name would be given up. Only comrades who were extremely close would reveal their real names to each other out of faith that their lips would remain sealed even under torture. It usually only happened with people from the same group working on the same task. The fact that Icheol and the woman revealed their family names to each other meant that a tiny bond of trust had begun to form while carrying out the same job. Before reaching the tram tracks that ran through Hyehwa-jeong, they turned down an alley and entered a seolleongtang restaurant.

'Uh, I guess ox-bone soup isn't exactly the place to bring a lady,' Icheol said as they sat down.

Comrade Han just smiled quietly.

As they ate, Icheol asked, 'Are you originally from Gyeongseong?'

'No, I'm from down south.'

'I don't detect an accent.'

Comrade Han smiled faintly. 'That's because I've lived in a lot of different places. Where are you from, Comrade Yi?'

'I was born in Yeongdeungpo, and I've never been anywhere else.'

After dinner, they parted in front of a tram stop. Icheol stood and watched Han walk away, her head down, until she disappeared from sight. He'd parted ways last time without a second thought, but this time Icheol found himself worrying about whether she'd make it home safely.

*

In the pine grove, Hyeongseon and Jaeyu didn't speak until they were sure there were no unusual sounds nearby. Then they found a rock to sit on and began their second conversation.

'I was so relieved last time when you said you would comply with the International line,' Hyeongseon said. He sounded relaxed, but as he continued, his voice took on a slightly firmer tone. 'A decision has been made. We want you to go to Hamheung.'

This time, Jaeyu kept a cooler head.

'Does the International line really think that's wise? I don't have a problem with going to Hamheung, but I can't leave without drawing the attention of the police. And I don't even know much about the circumstances over there. They industrialised early, and ever since the Wonsan General Strike, that whole area has really progressed, both ideologically and organisationally. The Pacific Labour Union's literature has made its way into Gyeongseong — the workers there take great encouragement from it. With so many excellent activists in Hamheung, they must already have an established line. I don't see why I'd be needed there.'

'So many have been arrested and put away for long sentences in Southern Hamgyeong that it has left a huge void in the leadership. Your presence there would be a great help.'

Jaeyu wasn't ready to back down just yet.

'If I absolutely must go, I'll need guidelines.'

'Guidelines? What sort of guidelines?'

'As a member of the International Party, I need realistic guidelines to take with me. Without a concrete course of action, how do you expect me to lead anyone?'

Hyeongseon was taken aback. He was accustomed to winning comrades over with the authority granted him by the International line. With no independent guidelines of his own, he had no choice but to improvise.

'The Korean committee of the International Party's Shanghai branch has a publication now. You should distribute it to draw in readers and recruit them into groups to work for the movement.'

The publication Hyeongseon was referring to was *The Communist*, which Pak Hon-yong and Kim Danya had launched in Shanghai.

'Is this publication more concerned with politics or theory?' Jaeyu asked.

'Both.'

'Either way, it must be flawed. If it's political, then they have to constantly address the political demands of the public back home, and if it's being published in Shanghai, then even if it manages to get through the multiple layers of surveillance, it would still take several months to reach Joseon, by which time everything in it would be old news. And if it's focused on theory, then its readership is bound to become the foundation of a revolutionary party, which is why building a movement of Korean readers and activists based on something published in Shanghai is simply unrealistic.'

Instead of attacking Hyeongseon, Jaeyu was trying to calmly persuade him.

'If that's the only guideline the International line can give me, while expecting me to completely change my field of operation, then I'm afraid I can't accept this order. When I asked for guidelines, what I meant was guidelines for dealing with different factions or suggestions on how to handle organisational or technical issues; in other words, explain your central, political course of action to me in detail.'

This had several implications. Jaeyu was criticising the reliance on overseas activists to rebuild the party; the blind, indiscriminate faith in the International line's course of action; the tendency to abuse the authority of said course of action to control activists instead of allowing them to act independently; and the very notion of a handful of activists building a movement from the top down without popular support. At a loss for a response, Hyeongseon tried to stall.

'Let's table this until after we have copies of the publication in hand.'

Jaeyu decided to make his intentions clear.

'I don't believe it's necessary to leave my comrades here and scurry off purely for the reasons you gave. Please understand that if I do ever find my way to Hamgyeong-do, it will be because the movement demands it of me, not because of an order from above.'

*

Their third meeting took place the following month, in early July. Having already ensured their safety several times, they decided on Tapgol Park. They also decided to go ahead without their reppos: they simply set a date and had their reppos talk the day before to confirm the exact time and location.

Icheol and Comrade Han agreed to meet in Yeongdeungpo, where contact had first been made. Icheol made the suggestion through Bang Wuchang, and Comrade Han sent word that she'd come. They were to meet at a crossroads near the Ghost Rock past Banghagot Ferry Landing. From there, the embankment began to the left, and across the Saetgang River and down the hill to the right was the poplar grove on Yeouido. Icheol was the first to arrive. Han would probably get off at the last tram stop in Noryangjin and walk over to meet him. He sat on a rock beside the road and looked down toward Daebang-jeong. He could see a few passers-by and a woman behind them. Even from a distance, he could tell it was her.

Today she was dressed like an ordinary Korean woman in a white jeogori blouse and shin-length mongdang skirt. As she drew near, he stood in the middle of the road for a moment to catch her attention. When she came close enough, he turned and walked down the hill ahead of her, glancing back to make sure she was following. He crossed the stepping stones over the Saetgang and headed toward the poplar grove. No one else seemed to be there. When she caught up with him, her forehead was beaded with sweat from the walk. She wiped her face and neck with a handkerchief. The cool breeze from the river greeted them as they strolled along the sandy path through the trees.

'The date has been set for tomorrow,' Icheol said, getting straight to the point. 'The time and place will be seven in the evening near the ten-storey stone pagoda at Tapgol Park.'

'Okay, seven in the evening near the ten-storey stone pagoda at Tapgol Park.' Then Han asked, 'Is it true that he's a factionalist?'

Icheol stopped.

'Is that what you heard?'

'Some of my acquaintances said so.'

Icheol had suspected as much. At other factories, he'd run into activists who had been working with the International line for a long time. During the previous year's strikes, he had even got into an argument with them in front of labourers who'd gathered somewhere in Gyeongseong to discuss what action to take.

'We already said we'd accept guidance from the International Party. Direct action, however, always takes place on the ground as the need arises. Lenin may have steered the Russian Revolution from Germany, but that doesn't mean the same will work for us. The International Party's role should be to keep an eye on the big picture — for instance, enforcing the principle that the party must be built from the bottom up, by the masses who made their way up through struggle and organised action,' he said.

'And do you practise what you preach?' asked Han.

'We're willing to join hands with any group. It's actually one of the most urgent tasks ahead of us.'

Han seemed to hesitate before finally saying, 'Please, let me join you.'

'What?'

'I worked in a factory until a few months ago. I started out with a book club and then got a job there, but all I did was hand out leaflets. And those leaflets weren't exactly …'

'Exactly … ?'

Han smirked.

'When you understand what you're talking about, your writing tends to be clear and simple, but those leaflets were nothing but big words, foreign words, Chinese characters.'

Icheol smiled and nodded.

'When leaflets like that come our way, we either throw them away or rewrite them before making copies and handing them out. But are you sure about this? Working with us, I mean.'

'No matter which side I'm on, I'll still be fighting for our country and the liberation of the working class. It's not as if I'm seeking fame and prestige. Oh, maybe it's because I'm not obsessed with hegemony like men are. Workers don't understand why the two sides are fighting over policies that are ultimately identical to each other. They'd join the fight against Japan if both sides supported them. And I agree with them. It comes down to choosing the right path and ignoring unrealistic goals.'

'I agree with you in principle, Comrade Han. But I also believe we have to follow through on the decisions made by leadership through organised discussions.'

Icheol chose that moment to share his real name with her.

'By the way, my name is Yi Icheol. But my family calls me Dusoe.'

Han covered her mouth as she laughed.

'Two Steel? I take it there's also a One Steel or First Steel in your family?'

'Yes, my older brother, Hansoe.'

'I'm Han Yeowok.'

Icheol later confessed to Yeowok and his sister-in-law Geumi that when Yeowok told him her name, a bolt of electricity ran through his heart and shook his shoulders. In that moment, they went from activists to individuals.

*

Hyeongseon and Jaeyu met at Tapgol Park and talked as they roamed through the maze-like backstreets of Nakwon-jeong. Hyeongseon had left their last meeting with a hard look on his face, his wishes having been directly criticised and rejected, but now he seemed glad to see Jaeyu again.

'We've accepted your opinion. Instead of distributing a publication from abroad, could you recommend groups or activists capable of creating one in Joseon?'

Jaeyu was happy to oblige.

'Of course, we've already been doing something similar,' Jaeyu said, and asked, 'According to the news, the Far East Anti-Imperialist Congress will be held in Shanghai. What does the group there plan to do about our situation here?'

'That would be up to our comrades in Shanghai to decide.'

'Our first task should be to raise awareness among the masses that the congress is being held in Shanghai. Otherwise, no matter who we send to speak at the congress, it won't have much meaning.'

Hyeongseon gave Jaeyu one last nudge about going to Hamgyeong Province, but Jaeyu remained steadfast in his refusal. He said he was needed here, in Gyeongseong, where the movement was just starting, and not Hamgyeong, where the movement had already been flourishing, and that he would only reconsider after the labour movement in Gyeongseong had reached maturity. Hyeongseon wasn't happy about this, but he couldn't exactly force Jaeyu to leave. The only thing they could agree on was launching an independent publication in Joseon, and as luck would have it, they never did manage to continue their discussion.

Hyeongseon felt an urgent need to check on his network in Yeongdeungpo. His local activity base was still weak, and if he was to join forces with Jaeyu to distribute a publication in Gyeongseong, he had to have a certain number of people on his side. The most promising areas to target seemed to be Incheon and the factory district in Yeongdeungpo, which was referred to as South Gyeongseong. The person who had put him in touch with Bang Wuchang in Yeongdeungpo was a young man named Jang. Jang had been a Communist Youth League member in Shanghai before he went to prison. Although he was eventually released when his indictment was suspended, he came to know Bang Wuchang from being housed in the same cell. Among the network of about thirty people in Gyeongseong who were involved in distributing copies of the publication, Jang and Han Yeowok were on the same team. Jang and Yeowok took turns communicating with Hyeongseon and acting as a reppo.

About two weeks after his third meeting with Jaeyu, Hyeongseon headed to Yeongdeungpo with Jang to meet Wuchang. He instructed Jang to drop by Wuchang's place and bring Wuchang back with him. Jang made it to the boarding house around eight in the evening, well past dinner time. He'd been to the place a couple of times, so he didn't hesitate to enter the yard, where labourers were washing up and chatting in the dark. He went straight to Wuchang's room. With summer at its peak, the doors to each room were left open by their occupants, who had stripped down to their underwear. Wuchang was lying shirtless when Jang appeared. As soon as he spotted Jang, he bolted to his feet, put his shirt back on, and rushed out of the house with him.

'Why didn't you warn me you were coming tonight?'

'Isn't it safer this way?'

They usually met on the first and last Tuesday evening of each month. If something came up, the rule was to notify each other in advance so they could change the time and date of their meeting. Wuchang's preference was to head for a quiet spot away from his neighbourhood, as if simply going for a walk, and talk there.

This time, Jang took the lead, saying, 'He's here. Follow me, please.'

Wuchang knew immediately who he was talking about. If it was someone from higher up the line, then they had to have been sent by the International Party. He said nothing as he followed Jang into the alley behind the Maruboshi factory. Their destination was the Chinese restaurant at the entrance to the red-light district. Everyone with experience knew that the place, tucked away as it was in a seedy part of town, was perfect for secret meetings. It was probably the same restaurant where Icheol had once met Yi Gwansu. The place got few customers outside the peak hours on weekdays, and the partitions between each booth made it seem safer. When they drew aside the curtain to a booth near the back of the restaurant, Hyeongseon rose to greet them. Once they were all seated, Jang calmly and covertly introduced Wuchang and Hyeongseon to each other. They ordered food and drinks and began talking. Right when they were deep in discussion, someone flung the curtain open and stuck his head inside.

'My, my, look who's here? Enjoying some Chinese food, are you?'

Wuchang sprung to his feet and headbutted the intruder right in the face; Jang kicked him while leaping out of the booth. With no time to think, Jang raced between the tables to the entrance, Hyeongseon right behind him. Wuchang went the other way, through the kitchen and past the toilet, toward the back door. As he elbowed his way past the startled cooks and ran out into the back alley, Wuchang heard the shrill sound of a whistle. He clambered over the wall at the alley's dead end, snuck across someone's yard, and emerged next to the railroad tracks stretching away into the dark. With the yells of the other men not far behind, he ran across the tracks toward the familiar territory of the Saetgang's embankment. He knew he couldn't go back to the boarding house or stay in Yeongdeungpo anymore.

Outside the restaurant, four plainclothes policemen were standing by. Jang charged toward them to enable Hyeongseon to escape. But they had been ready and waiting to make this arrest. One of them struck Jang on the head with a club as he rushed toward them, knocking him out instantly, while Hyeongseon was quickly pinned to the ground. They pulled Hyeongseon's arms back and handcuffed him.

'We lost Bang Wuchang.'

The man with his shirt covered in blood from his nose emerged from the restaurant and stomped on the unconscious Jang over and over in a fit of anger until the other men finally yanked him away. Another man, who appeared to be their boss, nudged Jang's head with the tip of his shoe to examine Jang's face, and said, 'Letting Bang Wuchang get away was a huge mistake.'

They had been surveilling Wuchang for the past few weeks. After the nationwide series of strikes the year before, the Government-General had been retracing the steps of local police investigation from behind the scenes, starting at square one. The Special Higher Police dispatched men to each police station to secretly investigate everyone who'd been involved in the strikes. While going over the latest developments, they began to tail people who'd been arrested and released for other cases. Wuchang, who had served three months for participating in a strike, came under suspicion for living in a neighbourhood brimming with factory labourers even though he was working in the street as a porter. He'd also made too many trips to downtown Gyeongseong and met too many times with factory workers.

The young man who had pushed back the curtain at the Chinese restaurant and pretended to know Wuchang was a police assistant. In fact, only one of the four policemen there that day had been a formal Japanese detective; the rest were all Korean police assistants. Not long after annexing Joseon, Japan had increased its ranks of police and military police and begun to hire Koreans. For the first five years after the March 1st Independence Movement, it was simple to become a police assistant, with one or two for every three applicants succeeding. But following this rapid growth, the success rate fell to one out of every ten applicants by the mid-1920s and to one out of twenty by the 1930s. Most Korean police assistants were spies, acting as informants on Koreans who were under investigation. Applicants who'd graduated from primary school, knew Japanese, and passed a background check were eligible to take the employment test. Those who passed the test received a certain amount of training before they were assigned to a military-police unit or police station. Sometimes, temporary informants who were used for specific cases could get hired as formal assistants if they proved to be skilled and trustworthy. By the later years of the Japanese occupation, more police assistants were being hired from among temporary informants than through the regular hiring process.

In truth, they hadn't been expecting to arrest a big fish like Kim Hyeongseon that day. Their original surveillance target was Wuchang because of his previous conviction for disrupting public order. A police assistant went undercover as a labourer staying at the same boarding house as Wuchang. One day, he spotted Jang visiting the boarding house and tailed Jang and Wuchang when they left together. After that, he observed Wuchang heading downtown to meet Jang on multiple occasions. His instincts told him that the person Wuchang was meeting was no ordinary labourer. To borrow the Special Higher Police's lingo, he'd caught a 'whiff of ink' from Jang, meaning that he seemed too educated to be who he claimed. When he reported this to his immediate supervisor, a Japanese detective, it was decided that he would call it in immediately the next time Wuchang's contact showed up, so that they could arrest him. That very day, the undercover assistant saw the same young man, and followed the two of them to the Chinese restaurant. As soon as the two went in, the assistant made a phone call to alert the team standing by near the train station. In less than ten minutes, a single Japanese detective arrived with two assistants. Because they were expecting to make an easy preliminary arrest, they pounced without calling for backup. When they realised they'd hooked a much bigger fish than they'd hoped for, the entire police network in Gyeongseong went crazy.

Wuchang hid in the tall grass along the Saetgang and let the mosquitoes feast on him until deep into the night. Then he made the bold move of heading back to Singil-jeong. The destination he had in mind was Icheol's place. Icheol lived in a poor neighbourhood where tiny houses were packed together on a hillside. Wuchang turned down an alley to Icheol's place and tapped lightly on his window. It opened immediately. Even in the dark, Icheol seemed to know from the look on Wuchang's face that something was wrong, because he quietly slipped out of his room and opened the gate. His room was right beside the gate, away from the main part of the house, so no one was likely to notice what was going on at such a late hour.

'What's wrong?' Icheol asked.

Wuchang quickly and quietly explained what had happened.

Nervous, Icheol asked, 'You'd better leave before daybreak, but where will you go?'

'I'm not sure, maybe Incheon.'

'I guess we'll have to declare an emergency.'

'Yes, send word to Jo Yeongchun.'

Yeongchun was still working as an org at the textile factory where Icheol and Geumi had once worked. Icheol nodded, and lifted up a corner of the flooring where he had stashed twenty won for emergencies. He handed it to Wuchang.

'You should get going.'

Wuchang gave Icheol's hand a hard squeeze. In front of the gate, he whispered, 'Don't do anything for a while.'

Wuchang disappeared into the dark. He had a twenty-seven-kilometre walk to Incheon ahead of him. At the break of dawn, Icheol walked over to Noryangjin and caught a tram to Dongdaemun Gate. He felt anxious. Everything now was a race against time. Activists went by an unwritten twenty-four-hour rule: arrest meant torture, so they had to hold out — and hold their tongues — for at least twenty-four hours, to buy the others time to flee. The authorities were well aware of this rule and used every means of torture they could think of to gain as much information as they could as soon as they had the person, to the extent that it was referred to as 'wringing them out'. The experience was so severe that some activists were broken by it and switched sides to become tools of the enemy, or else were mentally maimed for life, while those who held out until the end, provided they didn't die of their injuries later in prison, came out tougher and even more dedicated to the movement. Ultimately, any group of people is fundamentally a collection of weak, lonely individuals.

By the time Icheol reached Yi Gwansu's place in Changsin-jeong, it was seven in the morning. When he knocked on the rough wooden door to Gwansu's room, Gwansu jumped up and greeted Icheol with a tense look on his face. Icheol informed him of Hyeongseon's arrest and Wuchang's escape, and the two left the house immediately. Gwansu headed to Naksan Mountain alone. His job in these situations was to relocate Jaeyu's Dongsung-jeong agit hideout immediately.

Just a short while earlier, Icheol and Yeowok had finished their last scouting missions and spent several hours walking and talking. When they parted, Icheol had asked Yeowok the best way to contact her in an emergency. Worried that his question might spook her, he gave her his emergency contact. His was Wuchang; hers was at a cafe in Jongno. Now that an actual emergency was happening, Icheol couldn't help fretting over the possibility that Yeowok might drop by Wuchang's boarding house to try to reach him. He hurried towards the Umigwan movie theatre; she had said it was close to the cafe. He managed to find the place, but it was still too early; the small cafe didn't look like it would open until after 10.00 am. He found a seolleongtang restaurant in an alley nearby and took his time eating; when he got back to the cafe, it was still mostly empty except for a young man in a suit, perhaps because it wasn't lunchtime yet. Icheol took a seat close to the entrance. A waitress yawned as she approached him.

'What can I get for you?'

Icheol recited the code.

'Is your aunt around? I'm a family friend.'

The waitress glanced over at the man in the suit before saying, 'Why do you need to ...'

'Her mother is very ill.'

The waitress nodded, swiftly returned to the counter, and made a phone call. About half an hour later, Yeowok came in through the cafe entrance. She was wearing a polka-dotted summer dress. She took a quick look around, gave the waitress a nod, and left. Icheol followed. Instead of heading to the main street, she ducked into the long back street called Pimatgol. Icheol kept his distance for a while before hurrying to catch up with Yeowok.

'What's going on?' she asked.

'Comrade Kim was arrested last night in Yeongdeungpo.'

Yeowok stopped short in surprise.

'That doesn't leave us much time,' she said. 'I need to tie up some loose ends.'

'Just send word for now and move out of your place immediately. The comrade who scouted locations with you has been arrested as well.'

'Fortunately, he doesn't know where I live. But he does know which neighbourhood it is. You must have some loose ends to tie up yourself. Let's meet at five near Banghagot Ferry Landing like before.'

The two split, and Icheol hopped on a tram. He considered meeting Seonok and Yeongchun as soon as he returned to Yeongdeungpo. He was more worried about Yeongchun. Seonok didn't know he'd been communicating with Wuchang. But if Yeongchun's cover was blown, Seonok would be at risk, too. His thoughts turned to an org at a different electrics company. The company was fairly small and faced directly onto the road, making it perfect for calling out to someone inside. And because it was summer, the windows and gates all sat wide open. The noise from the machines inside was deafening, and waves of heat kept gusting out. Icheol loitered around the gate until a familiar face came running outside. It was Ji, who'd gone fishing by the Saetgang with Icheol, Daegil, and Wuchang.

'What's going on?' Ji asked, pushing his grease-smudged face close to Icheol's. He took out a cigarette.

'I'll take one, too,' Icheol said.

The two squatted next to each other and smoked. Anyone looking would assume they were co-workers on a smoke break.

Smiling casually, Icheol said, 'A senior member of the International line was arrested with his reppo today. Wuchang was able to get away.'

'Oh no! You think we'll be okay?'

'Can you clock out early?'

Ji scowled. 'It'll be a hassle, but I should be able to.'

Icheol told Ji to head straight to the textile factory and pass on the news to Yeongchun. Yeongchun had never been in direct contact with the International line, so he might be safe as long as Wuchang wasn't caught. However, if he had reppos in other subgroups, it would be necessary to tie up those loose ends.

Icheol went to Banghagot Ferry Landing to meet Yeowok at five, and together they hid in the poplar grove until dark. She'd changed clothes since they met in Jongno earlier that day and now looked like a completely different person. Dressed in a white cotton jeogori blouse and black cotton skirt with a small suitcase in her hand, she looked like a country girl who'd come looking for a job in the city. But Icheol liked this look better. As night approached and darkness began to fall, they crossed the embankment and walked past the marketplace intersection toward Saetmal. They were headed to Mageum Gomo's place. Yeowok waited in front of the house as Icheol hesitated before knocking on the gate. It cracked open without so much as a hello from anyone inside first, as if it'd been waiting for him.

'Dusoe, is that you? Come on in.'

This caught him off guard. It really did seem like she'd been expecting him.

'Uh, I brought someone with me …'

Without seeming the least bit surprised, Mageum Gomo opened the gate further and said, 'Yes, I see. Come in already.'

Icheol entered with Yeowok right behind. Mageum quickly shut the gate and placed her hand on Yeowok's back.

'I've been expecting you. Welcome, I'm so glad you're here.'

Mageum later told Geumi how she knew they were coming.

At the time, Mageum's husband, Carpenter Kang, was working as a site supervisor for a Presbyterian church elder in Yeongdeungpo who'd been subcontracted to build a hundred houses as part of a construction project to create 500 new housing units in Mullae-jeong near a cluster of textile factories, to address the housing shortage caused by the rapid influx of factory workers to the area. It was a Japanese firm, of course, that had done the subcontracting, and the houses were all boxy, modern, Japanese-style buildings. There was so much work that he spent half his nights sleeping at the onsite hamba, which doubled as a dormitory. As Mageum wasn't expecting her husband back home that night either, she'd had a late lunch, or early dinner, of cold rice and was sitting around with nothing else to do. She lay down with the hakko radio her husband had brought home beside her and was giggling at the jokes being told by the famous comedian Shin Bulchul when she thought she heard someone outside. She felt alarmed, but managed to swallow her fear. She had a hunch who it could be.

She slid the door open and murmured, 'Who's there?'

Sitting at the edge of the maru, facing the yard, was a heavyset woman.

'Eonni, it's been so long!' exclaimed Mageum.

Juan-daek turned her head and beamed.

'Yes, our Dusoe's coming, so I'm waiting for him.'

'Oh my, in that case, I better prepare some food.'

At her sister-in-law's words, Juan-daek stood and headed to the kitchen.

'Agassi, where do you keep the rice, and where's the, whatchamacallit, the mortar?'

'I'll take care of it,' Mageum said. 'By the way, rice is ground in factories nowadays.'

Juan-daek beamed again as she said, 'Dusoe's coming with the girl he's going to marry. I want to make tteok for them.'

'Okay, then let's make tteok and cook some other food while we're at it.'

Mageum brought out the sweet rice she'd stashed away in a jar and put both the sweet rice and some plain rice on the stove to cook. While she prepared doenjang stew and dished up some banchan, the sweet rice finished cooking. Although Mageum had said she didn't need help, Juan-daek squatted on the kitchen floor, spread the cooked rice in a flat mortar, and pounded it with a wooden mallet. Then she roasted soybeans in a dry pot, ground them into a fine powder, sprinkled it evenly across the square of rice cake, sliced it all into bite-size pieces, and just like that, she'd made injeolmi, Hansoe and Dusoe's favourite treat.

They'd finished cooking and were taking a break side by side on the edge of the maru when they heard a knock at the gate. Mageum rushed across the yard and welcomed Icheol and Yeowok inside. If Geumi had been there, she would've noticed Juan-daek and whispered as much to Mageum, but since Mageum was on her own, she struggled to pretend that no one else was around. Later, after Yeowok had got to know her in-laws better, Geumi and Mageum would let her in on the stories of Juan-daek's appearances, to which she would simply nod. She said that the first time they'd met, Mageum kept looking around the yard, unable to shake the feeling that she was being watched. She added that Mageum's gaze had kept drifting to a corner of the room instead of focusing on her, as if someone else was with them.

She'd even asked, 'Is there someone in that room?'

'Huh? Oh, that's my kids' room. Don't worry, there's another room for you two over there.'

Unaware that Yeowok had already sensed something, Mageum tried to change the subject by bringing out the injeolmi and nabak kimchi on a small tray. Juan-daek, who sat watching from the corner, spoke up in a voice only Mageum could hear.

'It'll be easier on the stomach if you take your time with the injeolmi and eat it with the kimchi.'

'Okay, save it, Eonni.'

Icheol caught Mageum turning her head away and mumbling as she set the tray before him and Yeowok.

'What? Save it? Who should?'

Mageum blinked at Icheol and tried to find a way out.

'I guess I'm so used to being alone all day that I can't stop talking to myself.'

Icheol realised what was going on and grinned. 'You still see my mother sometimes?'

'No! Why do you and your father always gang up on me?'

She meant that Icheol and her brother Baekman never believed a word she said. Icheol swiftly picked up a piece of injeolmi and stuffed it in his mouth.

With a laugh, he said, 'I'd say you, my brother, and Geumi Hyeongsu are the ones who gang up on *us*.'

After a delicious dinner, Icheol and Yeowok went to the spare room and were quite surprised to find that only one set of bedding had been prepared.

'Looks like my gomo has seriously mistaken our situation.'

'No, it's okay. It'll be weirder if we make excuses. I'll just sleep in my clothes sitting up against the wall.'

'I'll go bunk with the kids.'

Yeowok stopped Icheol.

'From now on, we're a couple. I don't know how long I'll be hiding out here, but I've seen plenty of comrades pose as married couples while staying in an agit. Some even wind up actually getting married.'

Icheol hemmed and hawed and then sat down near the door.

'You take the bedding. I'll stay here.'

But instead of going to sleep, the two sat down and kept talking for a while.

'You may not have noticed, but my gomo sees my dead mother sometimes. That's why she acted like my mother was with us when we were eating dinner.'

Icheol brought it up for fun, but to his surprise Yeowok took it in stride.

'How can you be sure your mother *wasn't* there? Maybe she's worried about her children.'

'But my brother and sister-in-law actually believe the superstitious nonsense that comes out of my gomo's mouth.'

'Why don't you believe it?'

'We're supposed to believe in science …' Icheol replied sheepishly.

Yeowok let out a laugh.

'You could just kindly embrace it. Wouldn't you say there's a lot more to this world than what we know?'

Icheol was impressed by how grown-up Yeowok sounded. He didn't fully graduate from his own youth until after he was arrested and did time in prison, and it was from that point on that he started opening up to his sister-in-law Geumi about the changes happening in his life. Icheol and Yeowok chatted a bit longer and decided to turn in. The moment they turned out the light, Yeowok quietly exclaimed, '*Omona!*'

Icheol asked what was wrong, but Yeowok only laughed softly in the dark. She had seen a woman slip out the door right when the light had gone out. Yeowok later discretely asked Mageum whether Icheol's mother had been as tall as a man, with broad shoulders and a thick waist. Mageum was stunned to learn that Yeowok had seen her mother-in-law's ghost for herself, and ended up telling Geumi about it time and again.

The incident convinced Mageum that Yeowok was meant to be part of the family. A few days later, Mageum took Yeowok with her to visit Geumi. With Ilcheol, Geumi, and Mageum's help, the couple were able to find a place of their own. They figured that a busy area would be safer for them than a deserted one, so they rented a two-room house in an alley near a row of shops that had recently opened along the railroad tracks on the way to Saetmal. It was one of the new, low-cost, urban homes being built at the time, neither Korean nor Japanese in style, with a gabled roof atop a boxy single-storey structure. The front room facing the street had its own entrance with a glass door so that it could be used or rented out as a retail space. To the back was a room with another door that led to the other half of the house, with a kitchen, spare bedroom, and maru.

Because it would appear suspicious if the couple didn't work, Icheol and Yeowok decided to set up shop in the front. After talking it over with the rest of the family, they agreed to sell tteok supplied by Bak Seonok's grandparents. Icheol bought a used cargo bike, loaded it with empty crates every morning, and peddled to the neighbourhood next to the embankment and north of the market. Icheol brought back all sorts of rice cakes that Seonok's grandparents had got up at dawn to make: sirutteok, baekseolgi, jeolpyeon, garaetteok, baramtteok, sultteok, songpyeon. Yeowok set up the displays and handled the customers. When they were first starting out, the tteok that didn't sell ended up being their dinner, and sometimes even the next day's lunch. But after a month or two, they started getting regulars and their business was doing well enough that they no longer had to worry about making ends meet. Mageum marvelled at the fact that the brothers Ilcheol and Icheol not only loved tteok like their mother but were born with the good fortune of never going hungry. On Sundays, the shop was opened to factory workers for their book-club meetings. Orgs from different factories managed several book-club groups of five or six members each. Icheol established connections between those groups as he supplied them with literature distributed by the core group of activists.

As for when Icheol and Yeowok went from being a pretend 'agit couple' to actually coupling, the rest of the family could only assume that a man and a woman sharing the same room long enough were bound to sleep together eventually. The truth of it, though, was that Icheol and Yeowok kept their distance initially. Even after moving out and finding a place of their own with the family's help, they slept in separate rooms for the first few months. Icheol took the front room attached to the shop, while Yeowok slept in the back room across from the kitchen. One day, after closing up shop, Icheol went out to a meeting while Yeowok stayed at home. She cleared the dinner table, spread out the bedding in both rooms, and sat in her room to make handwritten copies of some papers. She heard a rustle outside, and the next thing she knew, the door flew open and a bundle of bedding barged its way in. The same woman she'd once seen in the dark was coming in with an armful of blankets. Under the yellow thirty-watt globe, Yeowok watched the stout woman in baggy Japanese pants and a plain jeogori blouse step into her room with a smile on her face.

'Why are you two sleeping in separate rooms? Married couples should share a bed.'

Yeowok remembered talking about Juan-daek with Icheol, so she answered as if nothing was out of the ordinary.

'That's true, Eomeoni, except we're not really married yet. We just have to pretend to be for a while.'

Juan-daek grinned sheepishly and plopped down on the bedding Yeowok had set out earlier.

'Yeah, I know, but I don't care. I brought these blankets over anyway. So you can get started tonight, is what I'm saying. I want a grandchild.'

Yeowok shook her head to clear it. When she looked up again, Juan-daek was gone, and only the blankets she'd brought were still there. Yeowok turned the lights off, hoping that might bring Juan-daek back, and waited in the dark. But the only thing that greeted her was the cool breeze of a summer night with autumn just around the corner.

*

Yeowok grew up in a seaside home overlooking the wharf in Tongyeong. The original family house was an L-shaped hanok with a large courtyard and four persimmon trees that had been growing for years next to the stone wall surrounding the home. Yeowok's grandfather had practised herbal medicine, and her father had inherited the family business. As the sea route between Jeolla and Gyeongsang Provinces expanded, the wharf grew from fishing boats to ferries and freighters. The boom in population around the port helped the family business prosper. Yeowok's father added a modern, two-storey building in their yard to receive patients from other areas and islands nearby. The building's ground floor housed a dispensary and a reception area. The second storey was divided into multiple rooms for treatments such as acupuncture. Whenever Yeowok went into the clinic, there would be at least five or six people sitting in the reception area, while her father would be chatting with his friends over in the dispensary. He always sat towards the back of the room with a folding screen behind him and his gombangdae-style pipe in his mouth; on the other side of the screen, his assistant chopped herbs and prepared prescriptions. His guests would sit on cushions around a large table and play baduk, drink tea, or have lunch delivered from a restaurant by the wharf.

Yeowok graduated from primary school at fifteen. She wanted to continue studying at a secondary school in Busan, but like all established men in rural society at the time, her father believed that too much education brought nothing but bad luck to women. He was convinced that the best life for a woman was to stay at home and help keep house until a boy from a well-off family was found for her to marry. The people he socialised with everyday thought the same way he did, and they each had an eligible bachelor or two to recommend. Just as Geumi had, Yeowok bemoaned her frustration and misery to her mother, and as they spent most of their time in the same room every day, Yeowok's mother came to side with her daughter. The only place outside of home that Yeowok was allowed to visit was a Catholic church, which was where she met a foreign priest and nun and saw books and photos that opened her eyes to how the times were changing. And then something happened that caused her to run away from home.

Among her father's friends was a man who owned a couple of ships. The man's son had just returned, having graduated from a secondary school in Busan, and the two men agreed that their children were a good match and that it was time for them to marry. Yeowok had no intention of marrying nor could she imagine spending the rest of her life in Tongyeong. Plus, she had a bad impression of the man's son after passing him in the street. He was wearing a Japanese yukata hanging open over a pair of schoolboy shorts and was dragging his feet in geta sandals with a cigarette clenched in his teeth. To make it worse, he had a white-striped school cap cocked at an insolent angle on his head. Every soul on that wharf knew exactly whose son he was. The next time she saw the whelp was at the Chinese restaurant where their parents met to discuss their possible engagement, and she'd seen more than enough. With their parents sitting right there, talking and eating, he wouldn't stop leering and grinning at her like an idiot, and even stretched one leg underneath the table to brush his toes against her knees. Disgusted, she said she wasn't feeling well and took off even though her flustered parents tried to convince her to stay. It was on the way home that she made up her mind to leave. Her mother wept, begging her not to go, and she wept right back, begging her mother to let her go. In the end, the mother gave in and handed her daughter her stash of emergency money. Yeowok took a ferry to Busan at dawn and decided to keep going, all the way to the boarding house in Tokyo where her uncle lived.

A mere four years older than her, Yeowok's maternal uncle had gone to Japan after finishing secondary school in Joseon. After a two-year preparatory course, he had enrolled at university. Yeowok's mother's family in Masan was well off, of course, and even Yeowok's father helped out now and then with his brother-in-law's tuition. Yeowok had written to her uncle a couple of times over the years, so he wasn't too surprised when his niece showed up on his doorstep. The worried letter he'd received from his nuna, Yeowok's mother, added to his sense of duty.

Yeowok was an independent woman. She was determined to work to help pay for her education instead of relying completely on the money her mother sent to cover her tuition plus room and board. Her uncle helped her find a job at a newsagency that he had worked at while in preparatory school. Every day, Yeowok rose at dawn and delivered newspapers by bicycle. Many of the delivery people were students, mostly young people from Joseon. Yeowok naturally heard about socialist meetings from them, and in less than a year, she joined the Communist Youth League under the Joseon Communist Party's Japanese division. Back then, a foreign student in Japan could read a book or two and consider themselves educated, but if they didn't know socialism, then they were treated like the class dunce. And Yeowok, ever thirsty for knowledge, was happy to quench herself at the well of new ideas. Leftist books were making their way everywhere, even into Korean prisons, so it stood to reason that in Japan, the so-called home country, countless revolutionary books were being churned out, from original editions to commentaries written by Japanese scholars. When Yeowok dropped out of school, she said it was because the tuition was too hard to scrape together, but the real reason was that the authorities had been cracking down on the Communist Youth League and large numbers of Korean students were being rounded up or expelled. Yeowok, being no exception, found herself on the wanted list.

Geumi used to say, 'Jangsan Eomma confided in me that she did what she did not out of love or romance but because she was desperate. One of her uncle's classmates was the son of a large landowner in Gunsan. He'd make generous donations to student groups, like he was their own personal International Red Aid. And he'd had feelings for Yeowok for a long time. Luck turned out to be on his side, as here was his chance to rescue a damsel in distress right when he was about to return to Joseon. Despite being unmarried, Jangsan Eomma went alone with the man to Shimonoseki, and from there the two made their way to Fukuoka, avoiding ferries, and then stowed away on a freighter to the port of Mokpo.'

Upon returning to Joseon, they bought a house in Gunsan and started living as a couple, even though Yeowok had yet to meet her in-laws. A year later, she found out that her 'husband' was already married. His parents had arranged the marriage when he was only in secondary school, his wife had already borne him a son, and now they were waiting for him to return from studying in Japan. Barely twenty years old, Yeowok didn't pick a fight but simply negotiated coolly, took the alimony, and set off for China.

No one knew exactly what happened to her there. But according to what Icheol told Geumi, Yeowok went to Shanghai first then Manchuria, where her experience with the youth league in Japan helped her join the Profintern. After the Mukden Incident and the bombing by a Korean named Yun Bonggil in a park in Shanghai, which led to the death of General Shirakawa and several other Japanese military officers, Yeowok went back to Joseon. The one-party-state policy of the International Party's Far Eastern Bureau may have also triggered other Communist

Youth League members like Yeowok to return to their homeland. It may have been the group's decision for her to go to Pyeongyang and then Gyeongseong, where she began working as a 'cafe girl' — essentially a modern-day gisaeng — but she turned out to be exceptionally skilled at the job, as if born to the role. She drank and entertained customers by chatting with them but stayed clear of any scandals.

Was she a withered tree that had never loved or been loved? Geumi remembered her as a sad soul who'd 'never had a chance at love'. And that was how she described her to her son, Jisan, and grandson Jino.

'Then again, sad women were a dime a dozen back in those days.'

*

After sitting in the dark of the agit with her eyes closed, Yeowok quietly rose and went out into the backyard. She filled a basin with water for bathing. The cold water ran from her head, down her shoulders, and over her stomach and thighs. When she was done washing up, she spread out the extra bedding Juan-daek had provided and placed two pillows side by side. She lay down, and just as she was about to drift off to sleep, she heard the glass door to the shop open. Icheol had returned from his meeting. She heard the door to his room open, and then a brief silence. Then she heard him tiptoe to the back of the house and pause in the kitchen, as if unsure whether to open her bedroom door or not.

'Do you have my bedding in there?' he finally asked.

Without getting up, Yeowok drowsily replied, 'Come in. You're sleeping in here tonight.'

After another brief silence, Icheol quietly opened the door, came inside, and sat next to the door. Yeowok lay waiting as Icheol hesitated before stripping down to his underwear. Once he was lying beside her, Yeowok turned over and put her arm around him. It's hard to say whether Jangsan was conceived that very night, but a few months later Yeowok whispered to Mageum and Geumi that she was pregnant. Icheol's older brother had named his own son after Jisan-ri, their father's hometown on Ganghwado Island. From that, Icheol borrowed the second syllable, declaring it the boys' dollimja, or generation name, and named his son Jangsan, after a mountain near Yeowok's hometown, and chose the Chinese characters *Jang* for 'long' and *San* for 'mountain'. This, of course, all happened the following year, when Jangsan was born under the care and protection of Mageum and Geumi, in lieu of his father. Icheol was locked away behind bars then, and by the time he was released, Jangsan had missed the chance to ever meet his father, as the child's life turned out to be all too short.

9

That day, Ilcheol drove the freight train all the way down to Busan and back. After finishing his shift, he took the Gyeongin Line home from Yongsan Station. The Chuseok holiday was around the corner, so he and Kim bought some meat, and Hayashi gave them each a box of Gupo pears left over from skimming carriages. With a box of pears on his shoulder and a packet of meat tied with string in his hand, Ilcheol walked out to the square in front of Yeongdeungpo Station. A passer-by suddenly stopped and called out to him in Japanese.

'*Oi!* Aren't you Yi Ilcheol?'

Ilcheol looked back. The man in a suit jacket, jodhpurs, and a flat cap seemed vaguely familiar, but Ilcheol couldn't place him.

'I am indeed Yi Ilcheol, but who are you?'

'Come on, it's me, Choi Daryeong. We were classmates in primary school.'

The name rang a bell. Over a hill near Yeongdeungpo Primary School was an old village with thatched houses that was called Moraetmal. Many of the villagers raised pigs; Daryeong's family had several. No matter the family, feeding the pigs was boys' work, and so the stench of the pigsty never left Daryeong's clothing. He was teased mercilessly for it by his classmates, and though Ilcheol himself did not remember, Daryeong insisted that Ilcheol had stood up for him more than once. The one incident he did remember had happened on a Monday morning. In the middle of performing a hygiene inspection, their Japanese teacher stopped in front of Daryeong, pinched his nose shut, and pointed his finger at the classroom door.

'Out!'

While Daryeong's face turned red and he squirmed with confusion about what to do, the teacher slammed the roll book down on his head.

'*Chikusho!* Go wash your clothes this instant!'

Ilcheol rose from his seat.

'His family raises pigs at home, sir. It's natural for him to smell a little.'

Surprised to see a model student like Ilcheol speak up, the teacher tried to calm his anger as he said, 'Oh-ho! So you like the way he smells, do you?'

'I was taught to be kind to people who don't have it easy, sir.'

No sooner were the words out than the flat of the teacher's hand was battering Ilcheol's face.

'*Yoshi!* You get out, too, you cocky little bastard!'

Daryeong rushed out of the classroom in tears; Ilcheol followed him. The two boys ran to the row of taps near the school fence. As he took off his shirt and pants, Daryeong muttered, 'Fucked if I'll ever feed those damn pigs again!'

Daryeong turned on one of the taps, threw his clothes on the ground under the falling water, and stood there looking down at them. Ilcheol took his shoes off, rolled his pants up, and began stepping on Daryeong's clothes to wash them. Daryeong joined Ilcheol. The two boys burst into laughter.

'I heard you got a job at the Railway Bureau,' the grown-up Daryeong said as he gave Ilcheol a pat on the shoulder.

Glad as he was to see an old friend, Ilcheol gave Daryeong a careful once-over. From the looks of what Daryeong was wearing, it was unlikely that he was a labourer. He probably had some sort of desk job.

'Where do you work?'

Daryeong paused for a moment. 'Huh? Oh, I, uh … work for Shokusan Bank.'

Ilcheol couldn't help feeling a little surprised, considering that Daryeong had barely passed primary school. Along with the Oriental Development Company, which was under the Japanese

Government-General's direct control, Shokusan Bank was a state-run organisation that oversaw the economies of Japanese colonies. Most of the executives were Japanese; for Koreans, it was all but impossible to get hired with anything less than a professional-school degree.

'Wow, good for you! How did you manage to get a job there?'

Ilcheol's admiration made Daryeong scratch the back of his head.

'Well, it's not a regular position, I'm just a kotsukai.'

Ilcheol smiled when he heard Daryeong refer to himself in Japanese as a servant or helper.

'Aren't we Koreans all kotsukai, wherever we work?'

'Listen, we can't just part ways after running into each other like this. Let's go have a drink somewhere.'

Ilcheol put the box of pears down for a moment and pulled his pocket watch out of his breast pocket. It was nearly seven, which meant the rest of the family should be just sitting down to dinner. But on the other hand, in their family, dinner was served at the time that best suited his father, which meant Geumi might already be clearing the table. She would understand, since Ilcheol's irregular schedule of night shifts and off days meant he usually missed mealtimes at home.

'A nice pocket watch, worthy of a train driver, I see.'

Daryeong strolled eagerly across the square and headed into a Japanese neighbourhood called Jungmaru. Ilcheol could count on one hand the number of times he'd been there, as he usually stuck to the main street right outside the station. Daryeong led him to an izakaya with a curtain over the doorway. As soon as they stepped inside, the owner shouted a welcoming 'Irasshaimase!' from the kitchen. Daryeong led the way to a table separated by a waist-high partition in a corner near the back. From the way he raised a hand in greeting to the middle-aged Japanese waitress, Ilcheol assumed he was a regular. When Daryeong took off his jacket to hang it up, Ilcheol noticed the pistol in the leather holster strapped under his arm. Ilcheol stared without a word.

'About this, I don't actually work at a bank. I'm a cop. Sorry I wasn't honest with you before.'

'What, you've become a big shot! I should watch out.'

Ilcheol wondered if Daryeong had taken his jacket off on purpose, just so he could tell him that. Ilcheol was alarmed but tried not to let it show. The first thing that crossed his mind was his brother, Icheol. He remembered his wife telling him that his brother recently had reason to be cautious. And he and Geumi had just found a place for Icheol to stay with the 'New Woman' he'd brought along. He decided it might be necessary to be on good terms with the friend now sitting before him.

Ilcheol had exaggerated his surprise, but Daryeong was no longer acting as playfully as he had when they bumped into each other on the street.

'I've seen you pass by a couple of times in your railway-academy uniform.'

'Why didn't you stop me then like you did today?'

'You know, being a Railway Bureau engineer is something that even the Japanese envy. Don't you think it's a bit seditious-sounding to say that all Koreans are kotsukai?'

Ilcheol scratched his head, at a momentary loss for words.

'I was just, uh … playing off what you said.'

Daryeong smiled and patted Ilcheol on the shoulder.

'I'm just kidding. Anyway, I suppose we've both done well for ourselves.'

'Mine's a dirty job. You're the successful one.'

Daryeong ordered some sashimi, a nabe hotpot, and two bottles of Masamune sake. After knocking back a couple of glasses, Daryeong said, 'How could I ever forget the time you and I washed pig shit off my clothes with cold water by the taps? After that, I considered you my only friend.'

'I'd forgotten about all that,' Ilcheol claimed. 'Thanks for thinking of me that way.'

'I knew it. I never forgot, but you? You never gave me the time of day again after that, not even on our graduation day.'

Ilcheol thought that not many were likely to remember every single thing they had done on the day they graduated from primary school. What did he do that day? There was a big group photo, and then some people had individual photos taken with family and friends by a photographer they'd booked privately. After that, everyone had gone their separate ways, either celebrating with their immediate families over Chinese food or, if they could afford it, inviting their friends home for beef bulgogi and jeon fritters, just like on their birthdays. As far as Ilcheol could recall, he hadn't asked Daryeong to take a photo together, nor had he invited him over to his house. Daryeong must have stood on the sidelines, watching everyone celebrate but unable to join in. It was very unlikely that a widower like Baekman would have invited his son's friends over to celebrate. It would have been just their family — Ilcheol, Icheol, Mageum Gomo, and their father — eating jjajangmyeon or udon noodles at a Chinese restaurant.

'A goody-goody like you would have no idea what hell I went through to get to where I am today.'

Hearing that made Ilcheol feel genuinely sorry.

'You really did have it rough. I didn't do anything special. Just obeyed the teachers and took the tests to get into secondary school the way they told us to.'

'Misfits like me have no choice but to drag ourselves up the ladder one rung at a time, all while getting spit on. But if you're loyal to your master and look up to him, he's bound to appreciate you.'

Ilcheol tried to change the subject.

'How are your parents doing?'

'My father passed a long time ago, and my mother lives in Dorimjeong with my sisters. One of them will be married soon, and I'm thinking of finding a job for the younger one. Say, what's your brother up to these days?'

'Icheol used to work in a factory, but now he's opened a shop.'

'What? I guess studying wasn't his thing, unlike his fancy Railway Bureau father and older brother.' Patting himself on the chest, Daryeong added, 'He should've taken the police exam like me.'

'You might be right, but then again, I hear the odds of getting in these days are something like twenty to one. And he doesn't exactly have your brains.'

Daryeong shook his head as he burst into laughter.

'Ha! You think I studied for it? The written test counts for nothing. They tell you that's the only way in, but there's also a shortcut called special recruitment.'

Since he'd already sat down with Daryeong, Ilcheol decided to give him his full attention for the night, and took his time pouring drinks.

Daryeong had actually been promoted from police assistant to policeman only a couple of months earlier. The promotion was the Police Bureau's award for a grand contribution he'd made to a case. Namely, on the day Kim Hyeongseon was arrested, the spy who had lived undercover in Bang Wuchang's boarding house and then tailed him was none other than Choi Daryeong. Lowly police assistants were not usually allowed to spy for the Special Higher Police, but Daryeong had been volunteering as a police informant since his teens.

After finishing primary school, Daryeong was struggling to find work because his father, a pig farmer who'd been barely making ends meet as it was, drank himself to death, leaving Daryeong as the sole male breadwinner for a household of women. Initially, his mother and two sisters, both younger than him, took over their father's work of raising the pigs, while Daryeong handled taking the fully grown pigs to market. Their father had always kept the pigs in the yard right next to the house, where they were tethered by a straw rope threaded through their ears, leaving the family to live in the constant stench of pig shit. But the newly responsible Daryeong appealed to the village head and asked to borrow a scrap of land on a hill downwind from everyone's houses. In exchange, he offered to donate a pig every year for his neighbours to feast on during the Dano festival. His offer was readily accepted, and Daryeong went about building a decent-looking pigsty by digging into the side of the hill to create a dugout and erecting a pine fence in front of it. His pigs soon doubled from ten to twenty. Daryeong also built a tiny hut next to the pigsty and stayed there day and night. Around mealtimes, his sisters took turns relieving him so he could go home to eat, or brought him steamed potatoes or sweet potatoes to tide him over. There were butchers near Yeongdeungpo Market and on the other side of the Dorimcheon Stream; whenever it was time, he had to take the pigs all the way there and pay for their services in either meat or cash.

It did not take Daryeong long to learn that he could make a lot more money if he did everything himself. He stopped selling the pigs to butchers at wholesale prices and started butchering them at home instead. He'd already figured out how to handle pigs by watching others. To drive the pig forward, you pulled on a straw rope tied to its tail with one hand and used the other hand to poke the pig left and right with a bamboo cane. The trick to keeping pigs from running amuck before castration or slaughter was simple. A pig could only muscle its way around by lifting its chin up and down and shaking it around, but if you bound its snout tight, it would instantly lose all confidence. Slaughtering a pig only required a bit of nerve. He couldn't do it near the pigsty or else the other pigs would never obey him again, so he would bring the one to be slaughtered a good distance away, to the front of the house. That also made it easier to draw water from the well nearby for boiling. He would leash the pig tightly to a post. By then, the pig knew it was going to die and would go into a frenzy, squealing, stomping its hooves, and shitting itself. He would get within handsreach of the pig, holding a sledgehammer with a head the size of a fist hidden behind his back. Then, without any further ado, he would take a deep breath and slam the hammer down on the animal's forehead. The pig would instantly collapse, its skull caved in, and he would swiftly slit its throat with a well-honed knife. The elder of his two sisters would bring large bowls and buckets to collect the pig's blood. Once the blood was almost completely drained, the dead pig was flipped over so that its belly was facing the sky. He would remove the head and make one long cut from neck to anus to remove the guts. Then, boiling water was poured over the skin while the hair was shaved off with a knife.

As rough as it was to raise and butcher pigs, the most important key to successful pig keeping was to supply the pigs with good feed. Daryeong had to collect all sorts of chaff from mills, corn and sorghum stalks, restaurant scraps, and soybean or sesame-seed residue from places that made tofu or sesame oil. He even stopped by the acorn-jelly manufacturer to collect acorn shells because they helped soften the texture of pig flesh. It wasn't too difficult for him to gather enough feed, thanks to the places his father had formed ties with before he passed, in addition to some new suppliers Daryeong found on his own; nevertheless, procuring feed required both diligence and business acumen. As a teenage boy, Daryeong had to pull a handcart around all day to gather pig feed from dozens of places. Whenever he could spare the time, he'd stop by those places to repay them with a box of cigarettes, a kilo or two of meat, or even a little cash in some cases.

What made him finally tire of pig farming and decide to wash his hands of it was Baeksun. Who was Baeksun? She was a sow he'd raised. Baeksun, whose name meant 'white', was the youngest of eight piglets born to a black sow named Geomdung. Baeksun had caught her master's eye because she was smaller, weaker, and a different colour than her siblings. If he'd tried selling her as livestock instead of meat, she would have been singled out and accused of not being a purebred because of her colouring. Normally, male and female pigs were kept in separate pens, and mothers were separated from their young. It was difficult to fatten pigs if they mated too often, and sows tended to eat less to make sure their young got more. Daryeong's mother and sisters would bring the piglets in just long enough to suckle and then separate them again. The boar that mated with Geomdung must have been a mixed breed from Japan because it had streaks of white hair on its belly and hind legs. Two of his eight piglets were born with patches of white hair: the male was average sized, but the female, Baeksun, was the runt of the litter. She was always getting pushed to the back by her greedy brothers and sisters and never got a chance to suckle. Daryeong would personally hold Baeksun up to her mother so she could eat, and after she was weaned he started taking her out of the pen and feeding her separately. After six months of loving care, Baeksun grew to be bigger and stronger than her siblings.

Maybe it was the attention Daryeong lavished on her, or maybe it was already in her nature, but Baeksun would respond when her name was called, and unlike the other pigs who squealed and went crazy as they rushed toward the trough whenever Daryeong approached with their feed, Baeksun would wiggle her tail and brush against Daryeong's legs like she was happy to see him. Then, one day, Daryeong realised that Baeksun really could understand him. It was a warm spring day, right around lunchtime, with the sun beating down and a heat shimmer blooming over the fields in the distance. Daryeong had just poured a mixture of ground soybeans, rice bran, and fresh water into Baeksun's trough and was leaning against the fence. As always, he started chatting with Baeksun.

'Enjoy your kongbiji. I picked it up this morning, so it should still be warm.'

Lifting her snout high, Baeksun smiled and said, *oink*, *oiiink*, *oink oink*. And Daryeong understood every word: 'Thanks, Papa! It's delicious.' He was certain that's what she'd said. He was so surprised that he kept talking to her. Of course, this story was told by Geumi, the family's gifted storyteller, who'd heard it from her husband, Ilcheol, and told it to her son, Jisan, and his son, Jino, and so it was bound to have been spiced up along the way. But there were folks who remembered Daryeong from the days when he pulled a handcart from place to place to collect food for Baeksun, so it couldn't have been complete nonsense.

'Baeksuna, it must be so boring for you to be trapped behind that fence all the time,' said Daryeong.

Baeksun oinked, 'Yes, Papa. Please take me with you the next time you go to the market.'

Daryeong was so amazed, bewildered, and delighted that he couldn't help wondering if butchering so many pigs had left him possessed by the ghost of a pig. As soon as his sister came to trade places with him so he could eat lunch, he told her the amazing news.

'Would you believe I just now learned that Baeksun can talk!'

His sister stared at him, dumbfounded, and shook her head.

'Oppa, this won't do. You need to quit raising pigs.'

She figured he was so worn out from doing such dirty, difficult work that he didn't know what he was saying anymore.

'Come see for yourself. I'll get her to talk.'

With a serious look on his face, Daryeong looked down at Baeksun and said, 'Listen to your papa now, and say hi to your sister.'

'What? That's some weird family tree. If you're her papa, how come I'm her sister?'

'Just wait a minute. Come on, Baeksun, say hi to your sister.'

Baeksun, however, kept her head down in the trough, happily slurping up her delicious meal of ground soybeans and rice bran.

Daryeong's sister said, 'Oppa, go get your lunch already. Hunger must be making your mind play tricks on you.'

Daryeong realised then that he could only communicate with Baeksun when they were alone. After that, he started letting Baeksun leave the pen without so much as a leash, and whenever he headed to the market with his handcart in tow, the half-grown Baeksun would trot behind him. They had to travel a fair distance from their village and past the train station to reach the market; jaws dropped the entire way at the curious sight of them. Children would sometimes tag along and try to play pranks until Daryeong yelled at them to scram. The pig who walked with a person just like a pet dog became famous all throughout Yeongdeungpo, and once folks at the market found out that the pig's name was Baeksun, they called out, 'Baeksuna, Baeksuna,' whenever the two of them showed up. Vendors offered sweet potatoes, squash, and whatever else the pig might like and clapped with joy upon seeing her happily feast on their offerings. If Baeksun was too full to eat, she'd keep the food between her teeth and hold it out to her father.

In a deliberately loud voice, Daryeong would say, '*Aigo*, you want to save it for later? Would you like your papa to hold onto it for you?'

This made the folks at the market clap and burst into laughter.

Then, one day, Baeksun wouldn't come out of the dugout. She looked as if she wasn't feeling well. When Daryeong stepped inside, he saw Baeksun lying on her side and panting with her hooves tucked together.

'Baeksuna, what's wrong? Are you sick?'

The pig groaned, '*Aego*, must be something I ate.'

For the past few days, the older of Daryeong's sisters had been trying to warn him that something was wrong. She'd told him that Baeksun kept rubbing her body against a post and scratching at the ground. Daryeong didn't think much of it, but now it seemed she might be really sick. He ran to another farm across the stream. The farmer was an old family friend who was skilled at raising livestock and owned dozens of cows and pigs; they had been helping each other out since before Daryeong's father passed. Daryeong quickly brought the farmer to his pigsty so that the man could take a look at Baeksun.

'Is this the one that follows you around?'

'Yes, she's smarter than a dog.'

'Must've eaten something wrong or caught an infection while out walking.' The farmer tilted his head and added, 'Haven't you heard? Foot-and-mouth disease has been spreading all over the province.'

'What should I do?'

'What else can you do? Kill it before it infects the others.'

'Kill? You want me to kill Baeksun?'

'You silly boy. What'd you go and name it for? Kill it now so you can at least sell the meat.'

The farmer chuckled as if it was no big deal and left. He didn't offer to butcher the pig in exchange for a cut of the meat like he used to, because he knew the boy could do it himself. Daryeong's sister worriedly peered at Baeksun and said, 'Oppa, you got to hurry up and kill her.'

'Shush! Watch your mouth! How could you say that in front of her?'

His sister looked up at the sky and laughed in disbelief.

'Are you kidding? How are you going to support the family by raising pigs if that's how you feel about it?'

After Daryeong's sister turned on her heel and headed home, Daryeong sat next to Baeksun for the longest time. Then he fetched his tools and dragged his handcart over to the pigsty. His worried sister picked up a bucket and followed him. Baeksun was even more listless than before and was frothing at the mouth.

Before loading the pig onto the handcart, Daryeong whispered, 'Baeksuna, I'm going to have to let you go.'

The pig, who'd barely stirred until then, moved her head, wiggled her tail a couple of times, and said, *oink oink oiiink*. To Daryeong's ears, Baeksun seemed to be saying weakly: 'Papa, please don't kill me. I promise I'll get better.'

'Hey, hey, lift her hind legs.'

While Daryeong lifted the pig by the front, Daryeong's sister grabbed the pig's hind legs, cursing and grumbling the whole time. Together, they struggled to load the pig onto the cart.

'*Aigo*, I guess it's a relief she's not any bigger. What would we have done then?'

They brought the pig to the yard and laid her down on the ground without bothering to tether her or knock her out first with the hammer. Daryeong plunged a long, sharp knife into Baeksun's throat and pulled it sideways. Baeksun slumped over without a squeal, while Daryeong's sister grabbed a bucket to collect the blood. Daryeong threw his knife down and walked away. His sister had seen him work enough times that she was able to finish the job with the help of her mother and younger sister. After that, Daryeong couldn't bring himself to raise any more pigs or even go near one, and he never ate a single bite of pork again, either.

At the end of his funny yet tragic story, Daryeong said to Ilcheol, 'Jitsuyo. I learned that word too late.'

He added, 'Jitsuyo honi, that's what Japanese bosses are always saying: keep it practical. What they mean by that is compassion, loyalty, and all of that are garbage, a waste of time. If you can rid of yourself of that nonsense, then your mind will be as clean as an empty room.'

Ilcheol stared silently at Daryeong.

'To enjoy a good life,' Daryeong said, 'isn't that what we were born to do? Why is that a bad thing? I decided that I had to be strong, and made that my first priority.'

One day, Daryeong went to see a Japanese detective named Mori at the police substation beside the train station. Daryeong had been caught once for breaking butchery regulations while out delivering meat to one of his regulars. Even before the Japanese occupation, it was customary in rural areas to slaughter a pig or chicken to share with family and friends on occasions like weddings, birthdays, funerals, and village rituals. A single person couldn't butcher large livestock like cows on their own, but anyone could butcher a pig or a goat. Butchering and selling meat to the public without a licence, however, was strictly forbidden. Pig farmers had to choose between handing their pigs over at wholesale prices to licensed butchers or hiring such butchers to process the meat they planned to retail themselves. But this pushed the farmers' margins down by two-thirds, so many farmers broke the law instead. Daryeong used to go out in the dark wee hours, cover the pork in his handcart with a straw mat, and make his rounds through the market until, one day, he was caught by Detective Mori in front of a haejangguk restaurant. Though his pronunciation wasn't precise, Mori spoke fluent Korean, at least as fluent as the Japanese that Daryeong had learned in primary school.

'I've looked the other way so far, but I can't today. I'll have to confiscate all of this and send you to jail.'

'Please look the other way just one more time, sir. I swear I'll repay you.'

Mori shoved his face into Daryeong's and yelled, 'Yeah? And how exactly will you repay me?'

'Th-there's a place that sells moonshine,' blurted Daryeong.

Mori didn't seem too impressed by this.

'Lots of places sell moonshine,' Mori said flatly. 'What we need are the bastards who're making it'.

'They make bootleg soju.'

Moonshining was a far more serious offense than unlicensed butchery. Koreans traditionally brewed liquor communally for village rituals or individually at home for family events. After Japan occupied Joseon, however, liquor, salt, and cigarettes were turned into monopolies. Moonshining in particular came to be strictly regulated. Ever since the Mukden Incident, Manchuria had been unofficially at war, and with a campaign going on in Joseon to boost rice production, rice and yeast were not to be wasted on brewing liquor. The authorities were especially strict about soju and cheongju because these required more rice to make compared to makgeolli. But drunks all clamoured for soju, claiming that makgeolli made them too full and didn't go well with meat and fish. And so, moonshining soju was both very profitable and a serious offense tantamount to tax fraud.

'Show me.'

Mori took with him a Korean assistant on duty at the police substation and followed Daryeong to the riverside neighbourhood. The neighbourhood was to the north-east of the market and had grown to add a tofu factory, bean-sprout processing plant, rice mill, vegetable-oil manufacturer, distillery, and other businesses of all sizes as the market expanded. As he led the way, Daryeong felt a brief surge of regret, but he shook it off. The distillery was where his father used to pick up leftover malt for the pigs, and Daryeong, too, still stopped by every few days. In exchange for the malt, Daryeong cleaned the distillery, washed all the jars and crocks, and moved them out to the yard to dry in the sun every time he visited. He also sometimes brought pig parts for the workers at the distillery to enjoy over drinks. He owed them nothing, he told himself. When they arrived, Mori called the owner and three workers out to the yard and ransacked the place with his assistant. The distillery was divided into one large workspace and two smaller partitioned spaces, but they didn't have to search much before finding the spot where soju was being distilled. They also discovered stacks of wooden crates filled with jugs of cheap soju.

Daryeong had taken off immediately after pointing out the distillery; it stayed closed for nearly a month afterward. Curious as to what had happened, he passed by the police substation one day and snuck a peek inside. Mori must've spotted him right away, because he called out to Daryeong as he was turning to leave.

'*Oi*, get over here!'

When Daryeong stepped inside the police substation, a sergeant in full dress uniform was sitting all the way in the back, then there was Mori in plainclothes and a uniformed policeman, and two assistants sitting on a long wooden bench by a window. It looked like they'd just finished a meeting of some kind. Only the sergeant and Mori were Japanese; the rest were obviously Korean. Mori introduced Daryeong to the sergeant.

'This is the boy I told you about. Say hello to our substation chief.'

Daryeong bowed from the waist.

'What's your name, kid?'

'Choi Daryeong, sir.'

The sergeant tried to pronounce Daryeong's family name but only got as far as Ch-ch.

'Give him a new name, why don't you?' he said to Mori.

'Where did you say you live?' Mori asked Daryeong.

'Dorim-ri.'

'At the bottom of that one hill, right?' He mulled it over for a moment and said, 'From now on, you're Yamashita.'

'How old are you?' asked the sergeant.

'Seventeen, sir.'

Mori and the sergeant seemed to have already talked about the Korean boy who had exposed the distillery's moonshining operation. They nodded to each other.

'Yamashita, we'd like to offer you a job,' said Mori.

'What? What job?'

'Starting today, you're our errand boy. Fifteen won a month. But there are other perks and bonuses, so you'll really be making about thirty won a month. What do you say?'

Daryeong thought it over, juggling a few different things in his mind very carefully. When he didn't answer for a while, Mori took some banknotes from his breast pocket and handed them to Daryeong.

'Here's twenty won, a reward for your help last time. Do good again and you'll be rewarded accordingly.'

The moment the cash was in his hand, Daryeong blurted out, 'Yes, sir! I'll do my very best, sir!'

Thirty won a month as a police assistant was supposed to only be possible for those who had graduated from primary school and aced a police exam that only one in twenty were able to pass. Daryeong later found out that none of the Korean police assistants at the substation had been hired this way. Like Daryeong, they'd all started out as informants and were eventually called assistants as they got older, but on paper they were never more than temporary hires. And yet, while out on duty, they wielded more power over Koreans than the actual cops did. They were called apjabi, ggeunapul, and even yeowu — 'narks', 'tattered strings', 'foxes' — by other Koreans, while those who openly ran pro-Japanese groups and oversaw informants were called ggweong, or 'pheasants'. To the public safety agencies, they were simply spies.

Right after Japan annexed Joseon, there were 3,000 military policemen, 2,600 policemen, 4,800 military-police assistants, 3,000 police assistants, and 3,000 official police spies in the colony. Since both military and civil police assistants were mostly tasked with espionage, that brought the actual number of spies up to 10,800. And since each MP and cop had at least two personal spies in his neighbourhood, then the national total was a cool 25,000. The number would have jumped into the hundreds of thousands if every blunderer who'd tried and failed to pass the police exam had actually landed their dream job of informing on their fellow Koreans. So as much as there were those who abandoned their family and worldly goods and risked their lives to fight Japan, others were more than happy to help the enemy for a few bucks and an ounce of power.

There were four types of spies, more or less. The first were paid informants, people like Daryeong who were lured in by the promise of salaries or bonuses and made a full-time job out of it. This group included both those who were hired by organisations, such as the police, the military, or Japanese intelligence, and those hired by individual policemen to serve as their personal spies. The second type were temporary informants commissioned for specific cases and for only as long as was needed to gather information. They, too, were in it for the money. The third were snitches, or quasi-spies. They differed from the first two types in that they passed on information out of spite or to ruin a competitor, and in most cases only did so when asked. The fourth were military or civil police who went undercover for investigations. They either disguised themselves as civilians or activists and infiltrated places directly, or sent their personal spies in and obtained information indirectly. Some even hired spies to spy on their spies, in order to verify the intelligence they'd received. Of the four types, the most common were the first two, the hired and temporary spies. Some became such big shots at it that they could be called professionals. These were either heads of pro-Japanese groups like the Iljinhoe or former independence activists who sold out their compatriots for the commission money they would get from the Police Bureau or the Japanese Foreign Ministry.

Although Daryeong belonged to the police substation next to Yeongdeungpo Station, his range of activities weren't limited to Yeongdeungpo. Depending on the case, he went up to Noryangjin and Yongsan to the north-east, Bupyeong and Incheon to the south-west, and even Siheung and Anyang to the south on the other side of Gwanaksan Mountain. And he disguised himself differently depending on whether he was going on a stakeout, tailing someone, or infiltrating a group. For the first two years, Daryeong mostly helped with criminal investigations as Detective Mori's personal spy. He followed the direct orders of Mori, but as he grew more skilled and experienced, he gradually hunted for targets of his own and even personally profited from them on some occasions. He teamed up with a junior police assistant and had him tail gambling rings. When the spring fish market opened, Daryeong snooped around the shipowners' gambling dens near Yeonan Pier in Incheon, and during the winter off-season he raided the dens of wealthy farmers in Siheung, Gimpo, and Goyang.

Gambling rings were criminal organisations made up of professional gamblers with criminal records who'd been chosen for their particular skills. The kisha's job was to use sleight of hand to switch or hide cards and sweep the table after making a player raise his bet by supplying him with a tempting combination of cards. Playing the rube and goading the others on in order to help the kisha maintain his ruse was the joshu. The location and seed money were supplied by the shujin. And the oya was in charge of bringing in dedicated gamblers with money to burn. Three or four people were usually enough to fill these roles, though it could go as high as seven or eight. These rings were heavily influenced by Japanese gamblers when the native Korean gambling games of gabo japgi and tujeon were replaced with Japanese hwatu following Joseon's 'enlightenment'. Daryeong profited at first by shutting down gambling dens and confiscating the money, but after a few of these raids he began making deals with the oya. After a full night of gambling, the money would be piled high by dawn, which was when Daryeong would swoop in. He'd seize all the money first and let the gamblers go, or chase the gamblers away first and then collect and share out the money. Meanwhile, the gambling ring would be allowed to keep operating. In other words, the police were in cahoots with the rings. Daryeong began to embrace the directive to 'keep it practical' and paid Mori off after each raid.

After three years of this, police headquarters caught wind of Yamashita's abilities, promoted him to the position of assistant police officer, and sent him to work for the Special Higher Police. Since then, two more years had passed.

In his first year with the thought police, Daryeong exposed and crushed a rebellious walkout before it could happen at a silk factory in Saok-jeong, Yeongdeungpo. The thought police carried out surveillance in industrial districts like Yeongdeungpo precisely to detect strikes and other acts of resistance in advance and weed out communists. By the 1930s, armed struggles had grown routine in Manchuria, and tenancy disputes and strikes led by socialists were spreading across rural areas and factories all over Joseon. Although Daryeong was only an assistant police officer, he was appointed to lead a surveillance team of three other police assistants. Daryeong reported to a Japanese inspector named Matsuda who headed the Special Higher Police in Yeongdeungpo. Daryeong spent most of his time away from the police station. His team would split up to surveil different parts of Yeongdeungpo and meet in the evening to put together the information they'd gathered.

Daryeong wasn't stupid enough to actually roam about Saok-jeong, where at least three different silk factories were clustered. Even if he'd wanted to, he would have stood out among the all-female factory workers and be run off as a creep. Compared to other textile factories, subcontracted silk factories had terrible working conditions, but the workers were older and experienced and their pay was therefore a little better, and so the entire Yangpyeong-jeong neighbourhood in the district of Yeongdeungpo was filled with female silk workers who hung out in groups of two or three and split tiny rooms in flophouses with each other. Daryeong set up a stall selling chrysanthemum bread at the entrance to the neighbourhood.

The surveillance team made up of Daryeong and three other police assistants used the stall as cover for their stakeout. Groups of women would stop by the stall and eat the small, chrysanthemum-shaped pastries right there or buy a sackful fresh out of the cast-iron moulds to take home and enjoy later. The team's primary mission was to listen in on the women's conversations. Sometimes, if they picked up what seemed like important information, one of them pretending to be an assistant at the stall would follow the workers to find out where they lived and creep up against their window late at night to eavesdrop on them some more. That was how Yamashita's team found out about the book-club meetings. Through further investigation, the team identified not only book-club members, but each of their positions at their respective factories, and learned there were at least three book clubs centred on the silk factories. Just one month into the stakeout, the team grew confident that focusing on the very first book club it uncovered would lead to the exposure of others.

Chief Inspector Matsuda ordered Mori, who had once again become Daryeong's direct supervisor after being promoted to sergeant, to round up the factory workers of the first book club. The team had already figured out exactly when and where the meetings were being held. Around seven on a Saturday evening, Mori, Daryeong, and his three teammates each went into position, ready to pounce on a meeting at a house in Yangpyeong-jeong.

This particular silk-factory book club didn't belong to the same line as Icheol but rather had been hastily formed using the papers, manifestos, and publication that Kim Hyeongseon distributed. It was a mere cell, or yacheyka, started up by the other International-line organisations that had been connected to Jo Yeongchun and Bang Wuchang ever since they crossed paths during the textile factory strike that Icheol was involved in. If the book club had had ties to the core, or if it had been loosely managed, then the arrest of its members could have been like harvesting a potato plant: one good pull on the stem and a whole row of potatoes emerges from underground.

Daryeong and his team split up as they entered the alley to the house. Mori stood at the alley's entrance, smoking a cigarette and checking his watch as if he were waiting for someone. The first assistant went around to stand behind the neighbour's house, just in case someone tried to hop the wall to escape. Daryeong inched up to the window facing the alley and listened carefully; he heard a low, rhythmic voice, like someone was reading something out loud. It sounded like a recital of some kind. When Daryeong gestured with his chin, the second assistant approached the gate. Daryeong and the third assistant took positions on either side of the gate, then the second assistant knocked. The recital stopped, and after a brief silence, a woman's voice asked, 'Who is it?'

'I have a telegram for you, ma'am.'

It grew quiet again, then they heard someone approach the gate. The moment the gate unlatched and started to open, the three men pushed their way inside. Mori joined them as well. Daryeong and the two assistants shoved open the door to the room next to the gate and jumped in without bothering to take their shoes off. There were six female factory workers inside; the police quickly scanned the room for other exits, but there was only the one small window. One of the women could have attempted to run to the inner courtyard to climb over the wall into the neighbouring house, but they never had the chance. They were cornered, like rats in a jar. All six women were handcuffed and tied to each other. All their papers and books were seized, too, since there was nowhere to hide them in the first place.

Mori went over to question the landlady, who lived in the inner wing of the house. The fifty-something-year-old woman trembled and pleaded, 'The only thing we're guilty of is renting a room to factory workers, just like everyone else in this neighbourhood.'

'You rented it to subversive elements, so you have to be questioned.'

A backup vehicle had been on stand-by for half an hour, so the seven handcuffed women including the landlady were put in two cars to be taken to the police station by Mori and Daryeong. The rest of the team stayed behind to search for other dangerous literature that might be hidden around the house.

Most of the Japanese police top brass had started out in the military police prior to Governor-General Saito's policy of 'cultural rule', and even after the police force was restructured, the torture and violent punishment of Koreans in police custody was passed down intact. This tradition of wanton cruelty, in which the military police could do whatever they wanted to Koreans they arrested, from floggings all the way up to summary executions, without the benefit of a trial or even so much as asking whether the crime merited serious punishment, never changed. After the Maintenance of Public Order Act was announced, if Korean defendants changed their confession during trial or objected that the charges in the police report had been falsified through torture, they'd be taken back to the torture chamber. Trials and judicial justice were nothing more than formalities. The Maintenance of Public Order Act also allowed the authorities to prolong the detention of Korean defendants convicted for taking part in the independence movement even after they'd finished serving their sentence.

The police were well aware that the first twenty-four hours after arresting an activist or other seditious element were crucial. If the prisoner could hold out for at least twenty-four hours, their comrades could take advantage of that time to destroy evidence or flee. That was why torture began immediately upon their arrival at the police station. The heavier the charges, the more pressing and barbaric the torture became. Prisoners were only kept alive for the sake of extracting information, and no one took responsibility even if they were crippled or they died in prison from the after-effects of their torture. Plus, given the callousness towards anyone affiliated with socialism, the rule during investigations became 'Who cares if a communist dies?'

As Japanese officers were mostly in the position of receiving written reports and would only bother attending a torture chamber in person if they'd landed an especially big fish, the actual torture and interrogation were left to Korean police officers or assistants, who better understood how their victims' minds and emotions worked. It took a fellow Korean to discern the subtle differences between an 'uh' and an 'ah'. But most of all, the Japanese benefited from turning Koreans against their own.

The womens' arrest had the police station buzzing with excitement. Like lions returning to their den with fresh prey, they were ready to feast. Whenever they arrested women, the first thing they did was strip the prisoners of their clothes. Men were stripped as well, but for women, their naked bodies were an unbearable shame that took away their ability to mentally brace for the violence to come, and it broke them.

Torture took many forms, regardless of gender: a group of men with clubs beating the victim senseless; whipping their naked body with a flogger strung with lead weights; placing a block of wood behind their knees and making them kneel while their thighs were stomped on. There was the 'roast chicken', in which the victim was suspended face down with their limbs tied behind them to a pole, and then beaten or left to hang all day. The 'Hangang Railway Bridge', where the victim was tied across the gap between two desks and beaten or stomped. The 'maeuntang', or 'spicy soup', i.e. hanging them upside down and pouring a kettle of chilli-pepper water in their nose. The 'water ghost', in which they were tied to a chair with their head pulled back and their face covered with wet cloth before water was poured over their face. Bamboo needles under the fingernails. Clubs and electrodes inserted into genitals. Searing the skin with hot iron. Perverse tortures of every variety are recorded in activists' memoirs. The lightest torture involved winding a crank-telephone wire around a wet finger and turning the crank. These tortures that were inflicted on political opponents for decades after Liberation were the legacy of the Japanese Empire.

What the police were most frantic to extract were names: who suggested or ordered the book club's creation, who supplied the reading material, and who else from the factory or any other factory was involved? The prisoners were first separated, then locked up, tortured, and interrogated, one by one. All to prevent them from 'getting their stories straight'. Every group was bound to have a leader. The book-club members knew they'd be asked, so they gave up a name right away. The circle tightened, something new was revealed, and everyone was questioned again, separately of course, to confirm it. Yes, someone did supply the reading material. But they vanished right after making the drop, they came by the factory without warning, there was no way of knowing what they did or where they lived. His family name was Kim, Yi, Bak. His given name was So-and-so. It was probably an alias anyway. Everyone knew activists never, ever gave their real name or revealed where they lived. Then one of the members confessed something new. She was growing weak, she was scared, she was starting to cave. She remembered what she'd been told when she was handed some literature for a meeting one day. They said it was from the International Party. Brutal torture resumed. What did she mean by International Party? Meanwhile, the police already knew that *The Communist* was published in Shanghai and was being distributed all throughout Joseon. The book-club leader said all she meant was that the person who gave her the literature said it was sent from the International Party and they would have to find that person if they wanted to know anything more. The torture continued for two days, and three women lost consciousness, but the investigation made no further headway. The only other information they got was that the book-club members had handed a few copies of a manifesto to a few co-workers they were hoping to recruit. That, and the name of a different book-club member at another factory, which sent the police running to make more arrests.

The police arrested fifteen book-club members from two out of the three silk factories in the area. The leader they'd already arrested turned out to be responsible for running both clubs. Maybe the plan all along was to have whoever was arrested first bear all the responsibility. Most of the rank-and-file members chose to write statements apologising for and renouncing what they had done — they didn't understand what they were reading, they would work hard and be true and loyal subjects of the empire, they deeply regretted and repented for having joined the book club — in exchange for having their indictments suspended or being released with a warning. Some among them, upon receiving new instructions or happening upon the activist network again, took the risk of rejoining the movement. The book-club leader was beaten to a pulp, fired from her job, turned over to the courts, and sentenced to up to three years in prison.

For his team's meritorious service in going undercover and apprehending the Red Labour Union's book clubs, Choi Daryeong received an excellent review from the Special Higher Police. It was concluded that more surveillance of those leading or taking part in strikes in Yeongdeungpo was urgently needed.

While flipping through some documents related to a past case, Daryeong came across the names Ahn Daegil and Bang Wuchang. Daegil was serving his sentence, while Wuchang's whereabouts were unknown. Daryeong discretely asked around about Wuchang and sent his spies out to track him down. Daryeong had begun referring to himself as Yamashita, so he was now called Yamashita-san by everyone at the police station, from his Japanese superiors to the Korean assistants.

An informant he'd embedded in the neighbourhood around the Maruboshi factory found out where Wuchang was staying. The informant was a day labourer who helped load and unload the freight trains at the station. He had been in prison for theft a year ago, and said that he'd spotted a communist he met on the inside at a local hamba. He said that he was a nice guy and that everyone in prison had respected him because whenever he received food from outside, he shared it with everyone in his cell equally, and it was a real shame that someone as good as him should have to stoop to manual labour to survive.

Yamashita memorised Wuchang's face in the photo in his file and then combed through all the hambas in the neighbourhood. Since there were only four, it only took him a couple of days to spot Wuchang. Yamashita changed into worn-out work clothes, hung a dirty towel around his neck, and took a room at the boarding house where Wuchang was staying and began surveilling him. When Kim Hyeongseon's reppo dropped by one day, Yamashita sensed an opportunity and decided to follow Wuchang. That's how he was able to score a big shot like Kim

Hyeongseon, who was at the core of the International line. And with that, Yamashita was no longer an assistant police officer, but a detective with the thought police.

10

One early winter day, Ilcheol noticed that his name was missing from the freight-train schedule at the Yongsan Station central office. Flustered, he asked a staff member at the carriage division, who shuffled through the papers on his desk in confusion.

'Oh, here you are. Go to Namdaemun Station. You've been reassigned to the Gyeongui Line.' The staff member pulled out a paper to show Ilcheol, and asked, 'Isn't Hayashi Taoro-san the engineer you work with?'

'That's right.'

'He was notified a few days ago. I guess he forgot to tell you.'

Ilcheol went to the tracks and waved down the first freight train he saw bound for Namdaemun Station, one stop to the north. The station's name was actually Gyeongseong Station, but the employees still called it by its old name, Namdaemun Station. It wouldn't come to be called Seoul Station until after Liberation. Ilcheol went to the central office at Namdaemun Station and confirmed that he had indeed been reassigned to a Gyeongui Line freight train along with Hayashi. Luckily, he wasn't late for his shift: the rule was to clock in two and a half hours ahead of departure. He went straight to the platform where the freight trains were parked. When he opened the door to the engineers' waiting room, Hayashi was nowhere in sight. As he stepped inside, feeling out of place, a middle-aged man sitting with a couple of other engineers asked him, 'Are you Yi-san? On Hayashi's team?'

'Yes, sir.'

'I'm the engineer of the route you'll be taking over.'

'Pleased to meet you, sir.'

'Hayashi-san is a seasoned engineer, I'm sure he'll do a good job. I heard you graduated from the Government-General's railway academy. Which line did you ride?'

'The Gyeongin and Gyeongbu Lines, sir.'

'Well, with that much experience, you might as well be an engineer yourself!'

Maeda was kind and gentle, perhaps because he was older. About half an hour later, Hayashi walked into the waiting room.

'Oh, I'm sorry, Yi-san. I should've told you about the reassignment at the end of our shift the day before yesterday. I guess you've already met Maeda-san?'

The three men went out to the freight-train platform and headed to a locomotive standing by. What awaited them was a Tehoi, a large tender-tank locomotive, instead of a Mikado. The Mikado that Hayashi and Ilcheol used to drive on the Gyeongbu Line weighed fifty tonnes. The tender-tanks that pulled the majority of freight trains along the Gyeongui Line weighed up to eighty-eight tonnes, though their hauling capacities were little more than that of the Mikado. The Tehoi, along with the Mater, or 'Mountain', that was later put into service, was a large locomotive fit for long-distance transport along mountainous routes. Both types had an automatic coupler, air brake, and air pump. Most large tender-tank locomotives also had an automatic firebox door and reversing lever, which kept the engine crew safe and reduced their workload while greatly improving the safety and precision of the drive. The automatic coal feeder was a new feature that eliminated the need for a stoker to stand watch and manually shovel coal. It channelled coal from the bunker to the firebox using a pipe fitted with a spiral wheel on the inside. As the wheel turned, coal made its own way into the firebox. The express passenger train on the Gyeongbu Line was named the *Akatsuki*, which meant 'dawn'. The *Akatsuki* could travel as fast as 110 kilometres per hour. It could also maintain an average speed of seventy to ninety kilometres per hour to get passengers to their final destination in just six hours. Freight trains took about eight hours to travel the same distance: though they didn't have to stop as often as passenger trains, their goal was to transport cargo safely rather than quickly. It therefore took about ten hours for a freight train to travel from Gyeongseong to Uiju. Freight trains also usually ran at night, which meant trickier work for the engineers. Hwanghae Province was mostly plains, but Pyeongan Province was mountainous with lots of bridges and tunnels.

Maeda went over the features of the Tehoi-class locomotive and how it differed from the Mikado. Hayashi and Ilcheol could see how advanced the mechanisms had become. After the locomotive was supplied with coal and water, Maeda adjusted the regulator to slowly steer the locomotive toward the freight-train platform. With a clang, the locomotive connected to the freight carriages. Maeda blasted the whistle, and with a long burst of steam, the train began to move forward. Ilcheol stepped down onto the stairs to the right and stretched his arm out as he eyed the end of the platform. He could see a staff member from the track division holding out a pass. He skilfully snatched the pass up by its leather band. Behind him were the days when he'd grab the pass the wrong way and end up being teased about the lash marks on his arm. The pass allowed them to travel to Pyeongyang, where another would be issued for the next leg to Uiju. The Tehoi-class locomotive with its fifteen freight carriages crossed the border of Gyeongseong and entered Goyang at a speed of sixty kilometres per hour. By the time it reached Munsanpo, the sun was setting beyond the Hangang River. After crossing the Imjingang River, it would reach Gaeseong Station in about an hour.

The three men had dinner at Gaeseong Station. The rain that began to fall in the early winter evening turned to sleet by night. They stopped by the carriage division's waiting room first to wash up and change out of their uniforms. Built in the Western style, Gaeseong Station was a fairly lavish two-storey wooden building with a clock tower in the middle. The second storey had a sloped ceiling and dormer windows like an attic. There was a cafe and restaurant in each wing of the building. Run directly by the Railway Bureau, the Station Grill could be found at every major station in Joseon. It served Japanese dishes such as bento boxes and sushi, and Western-fusion dishes, like omurice, curry rice, hayashi rice, tonkatsu, and hamburger steak.

Ilcheol thought how nice it would be to go for some warm soup on such a chilly day, but Maeda led the way straight up to the second storey with Hayashi right behind him, leaving no chance for Ilcheol to suggest one of the many Korean places just outside the station. Since it was slightly past dinner time, Ilcheol expected the Station Grill to be empty, so when they walked in, he was surprised to see how many seats were taken. There were young couples, along with some older customers, about twenty in total. Some were eating bento boxes or one of the rice dishes, while others were drinking beer or sake. After looking around for a moment, the three men reluctantly sat at the only empty table, right in the middle of the restaurant. Surrounded by those already seated along the edges of the square space, it felt like all eyes were on them. Everyone else was dressed up, the men in suits, the women in skirt suits, complete with leather shoes and nice coats.

'Are they all tourists?' Maeda whispered.

Hayashi perked up his ears for a moment and then shrugged.

'I hear both the national language and Korean.'

Ilcheol listened carefully and added, 'I agree, it's a mix of Koreans and Japanese.'

After a more thorough scan, Ilcheol said, 'They don't seem to be tourists. Maybe they're performers?'

'Performers? What're you talking about?'

When a waiter came to take their order, Maeda quietly asked him, 'Who are all these people?'

'Oh, don't you know, sir? They're actors with the famous troupe Cheongchunjwa, from Gyeongseong.'

While the three men were sipping beer and waiting for their food, a middle-aged man from the table next to theirs spoke to them in Japanese.

'Excuse me, but how far are you travelling?'

'We're going to the last stop.'

'Oh, you mean all the way to Hsinking?'

Instead of answering, Maeda looked back at Hayashi and Ilcheol. The man appeared to be Korean, so Ilcheol responded in Korean.

'We drive a freight train on the Gyeongui Line.'

The middle-aged man shouted in Korean to the rest of his troupe.

'These folks here say they're engineers!'

The man turned back to Ilcheol.

'I had no idea Koreans were allowed to drive trains. We're all part of a troupe on our way to perform in Manchuria. After our performance in Gaeseong, we'll go to Pyeongyang next, and then Antung, Fengtian, and Hsinking before we finish in Harbin.'

After bragging about all the places they were going, the man asked Ilcheol, 'Will this be your first time to Manchuria?'

'Third.' Then Ilcheol corrected himself. 'I mean, it will be my first time going there. These Japanese seonbae here are the engineers. I'm still just an assistant.'

'Well, I'm sure you'll be driving your own train someday. Manchuria is neither China, nor Japan, nor Joseon. It's international. You'll see what I mean when you get there. It's very modern.'

When the conversation kept flowing in Korean, Hayashi gave Ilcheol a warning.

'What are you two talking about? Don't you think you're being rude to Maeda-san?'

'My apologies, sir. These folks say they're travelling all the way to Manchuria to perform. They were just saying what an international place Manchuria is and that Hsinking is very modern.'

'You have "go zoku kyowa" to thank for that,' said Maeda.

'That's a mouthful. What does it mean?' asked Hayashi.

'It's Japanese for "five races under one union": Japanese, Koreans, Han Chinese, Manchus, and Mongols working together to build a peaceful country. It means that anyone of any race from any country is welcome to help settle Manchukuo. Japan, of course, has been taking the first step.'

Hayashi chuckled as he said to Ilcheol, 'Did you hear that? The Japanese Empire's Kwantung Army is bringing peace to Manchuria.

And the railroad is at the forefront of it all.'

Their food arrived before the conversation could go any further. Ilcheol couldn't help but be reminded of how cynical Hayashi usually was.

The three men returned to the waiting room after dinner. About half an hour later, they were told to resume service and soon departed from Gaeseong. Ilcheol took the driver's seat to let the two engineers rest until they reached Pyeongsan. As they passed Myeoraksan Mountain, Hayashi took over and drove through Bongsan and Sariwon. Maeda's shift began at Hwangju and continued until Pyeongyang Station. Every time they passed a bridge or tunnel, Maeda pointed out the key features of the terrain and things that Hayashi and Ilcheol needed to pay attention to. It was around midnight when the freight train arrived at Pyeongyang Station. The locomotive would be replaced there once it was refilled with coal and water. The three men left the train in the carriage division's care and took a break in the waiting room. Although Hayashi and Ilcheol were used to night shifts, they felt more tired than usual, perhaps from taking on an unfamiliar route.

For the last ten years, Chinese labourers had been flocking to major Korean cities, and large vegetable farms run by Chinese farmers had been appearing on the outskirts. The sensationalisation of the Wanbaoshan Incident had resulted in numerous attacks on Chinese living in Pyeongyang and North Pyeongan Province, and the wounds from the falling out between Koreans and Chinese back then had not yet healed. The Japanese had kept their distance; because they mostly resided downtown, where the train stations and administrative agencies were located, they were unlikely to come into direct contact with Chinese labourers. Korean labourers, on the other hand, had to constantly compete with and live alongside their Chinese counterparts, causing tension to grow between them. The border city of Sinuiju was practically neighbours with Antung across the Amnokgang River, and the people living there shared the same food and cultural customs despite fighting like cats and dogs. Chinese labourers would ferry or walk across the frozen river to enter Joseon without papers and work for lower wages than Koreans, which is why Japanese business owners sometimes chose Chinese labourers over their unrulier Korean counterparts. Only later did the Government-General realise that the presence of Chinese labourers was a hindrance to its colonial governance and ban their employment in Joseon. Japanese farmers and business owners, however, didn't care at all about the ban. In Manchuria, the Chinese looked down on Koreans and called them a ruined people. Nevertheless, young Chinese and Koreans supportive of armed resistance against Japan organised a regiment to join forces and fight together. Meanwhile, the Korean middle class in Manchuria, which included technicians, teachers, bureaucrats, and merchants, knew full well who ruled the area and tried their best to be like the Japanese in body and mind.

After the locomotive was replaced, Maeda, Hayashi, and Ilcheol ended their late-night break and sped toward Sinuiju. The sun rose as the freight train crossed the rail bridge over Cheongcheongang River and passed Jeongju, Gwaksan, and Seoncheon. Once the train reached Sinuiju Station and was handed over to the carriage division, the three men went out for a drink before heading to the railway inn, as engineers usually did when they arrived at their final destination. Maeda led the way to a Chinese restaurant, since he knew not only Sinuiju, but Antung, Fengtian, and Hsinking across the Amnokgang like the back of his hand. Maeda ordered in Chinese then turned to Hayashi and Ilcheol.

'I'm leaving for Hsinking tomorrow morning. After you spend the next few years getting the hang of the route between Gyeongseong and Sinuiju, you'll be promoted to the Continental Line like me. You might even get to drive a passenger train. Word is that the number of Japanese railroad workers is decreasing.'

The engineers all referred to driving express passenger trains as the crowning glory of the rail. Hayashi looked excited.

'Is, is there really something to that rumour?'

'They're saying the war will get bigger. Since rail workers are all educated, they'll be made officers when the draft comes.'

Hayashi snickered and said, 'And that'll mean more job openings in the Railway Bureau. And no guarantee that I'll get to keep driving trains.'

'Come on, aren't you in your mid-thirties already? They won't send old fogies like you into battle until the war is almost over.'

Hayashi nodded and looked at Ilcheol.

'I guess there will be more opportunities for Koreans like you, then.'

The next day Hayashi and Ilcheol ventured across the Amnokgang to Antung to check out the exotic scenery at the threshold of Manchuria. They hitched a ride back to Gyeongseong on a freight train driven by a different engineer departing from Uiju. From there, they continued to work on the route between Gyeongseong and Uiju. Engineers on that route rode the South Manchuria Railway's Continental Line every year as part of a two-week training in case they might be reassigned to the line in the future.

*

Icheol and Yeowok's tteok shop grew in popularity, drawing customers all the way from Yangpyeong-jeong and Saetmal. With the increasing number of regulars, the supply from Seonok's grandparents was no longer enough to meet demand. The couple talked it over with Mageum Gomo and decided to start making their own tteok. They prepared the necessary equipment, including three large cauldrons, three steamers, patterned stamps, a pounding board, a mortar, a pestle, bowls, sieves, and rolling pins. Thankfully, times had changed for the better, and they had more than one rice mill to choose from at the market. Once every few days, they took rice and other grains to one of the mills for grinding and prepared ingredients for fillings, including red beans, mung beans, sesame seeds, honey, and oil. Mageum Gomo rolled up her sleeves and went to work for them, saying there was no point in her just idling away at home when she could use the extra income to help pay for her two kids' monthly school fees. Yeowok was pregnant with Jangsan at the time and getting bigger by the day. As for Icheol, he started to feel bad about leaving whenever he wanted to attend meetings, and cut back to just once or twice a week. He sold and delivered tteok during the day and spent the evenings preparing products to sell the next morning. He also took care of the heavy lifting, while Yeowok and Mageum handled the delicate work of cutting, shaping, and filling the tteok. That day, Yeowok and Mageum were sitting in the shop's back room as they stamped patterns onto tteok and cut them into squares, while Icheol was busy placing rice powder in steamers, drawing water to pour into the cauldrons, and carrying wood out to feed the fires.

'We've got a problem!'

Startled, Icheol and the women in the back room all turned to see Seonok rush into the shop. After starting out as Geumi's assistant at the textile factory, Seonok had served in a yacheyka, a cell, for the Red Labour Union for about two years, during which she was not only put in charge of her own team of weavers at the factory, but also learned the ins and outs of activism well enough to become Icheol's org. In other words, Seonok was one of Icheol's closest comrades in Yeongdeungpo.

'Look at this.'

Seonok was holding a newspaper. It was the evening edition and smelled like it had come fresh off the printer. Splashed across the front was detailed coverage of Yi Jaeyu's arrest and escape.

*

The Police Bureau had been vaguely aware of Yi Jaeyu's underground organisation. With strikes erupting one after the other across Gyeongseong, the workers who had led the strikes at each factory were interrogated until they gave up the name of someone close to the core. The Seodaemun Police Station and Yongsan Police Station in charge of the case seized a large volume of documents, including some papers that contained the same sort of guidelines. The police intensified their interrogations in order to uncover the Red Labour Union's core. By 'intensify', of course, what they really meant was torturing their captives to the brink of death. And one worker did die during interrogation, followed by two who died in prison during their preliminary trials.

The Police Bureau discovered that, according to their archives, Jaeyu had previously been arrested in Japan and transported to Joseon, and that his profile was a perfect match for the testimony of a former Red Labour Union member. It didn't take them long to confirm that he was indeed the person they were looking for; secret instructions were sent to the Special Higher Police divisions at every police station in Gyeongseong. A promotion and a huge cash prize awaited the lucky officer who made the arrest.

Jaeyu had a female reppo, Hong, a student posing as a factory worker and living in her own place near his agit hideout, who handled all of his communication. The day Kim Hyeongseon was arrested, Jaeyu and Hong moved into a new place together to pose as a couple. To avoid suspicion from their neighbours, Jaeyu went to work in road construction. The 'agit couple' made it a rule to always come home by an agreed-upon time. They were also vigilant every time they came and went. Before Jaeyu left for work, Hong would first check the alley and walk all the way out to the main road to see whether the tram stop was safe. On his way back home from work, Jaeyu would get off one stop early to scan the streets on foot. Upon reaching the alley where their room was located, he'd look at the house for the all-clear signal. A piece of white laundry hanging over the wall meant it was safe to come home, and no laundry meant either go somewhere else and wait or be on alert. Black laundry meant run and never come back.

On the way home from work one day, Jaeyu saw that there was no laundry hanging over the wall, so he went to visit a trustworthy comrade who worked as a central org for the factories in Yongsan. The comrade's nickname was Jang Mansu. As a labour activist, Mansu had been an org in Jaeyu's first Red Labour Union alongside Ahn Daegil and Bang Wuchang. They'd all been committed to rebuilding the Joseon Communist Party from the bottom up, despite the previous failed attempts at reconstruction by others. Mansu had been working at a factory while living in a small rented room in a working-class neighbourhood on the side of a hill in Malli-jeong, behind Gyeongseong Station.

But he, too, had been forced to quit after being put on the wanted list for his involvement in the serial strikes, and was now working as a handcart puller in the streets around the train station while staying in touch with the organisation. Jaeyu waited nearby until after dark. Luckily, Mansu was already home from work, so Jaeyu told him about the warning sign and asked if he could find out what was happening.

After a sleepless night, Mansu went to meet a female reppo at the factory to have her look into the situation. Meanwhile, Jaeyu went up Namsan Mountain to kill some time, then headed to the tram stop in Jungnim-jeong where he was supposed to meet Mansu at precisely three o'clock. Fifteen minutes went by without any sign of Mansu, but Jaeyu decided to wait until half past three, figuring his comrade was just a little late. And in doing so, Jaeyu broke a cardinal rule: if your reppo was more than ten minutes late, that meant run.

The police had found out where Jaeyu was hiding and arrested Hong. They'd learned everything they needed to know about Hong, including that she was most likely Jaeyu's reppo, from a female factory worker they'd arrested during the previous strike — she had been re-arrested and tortured for this information. Figuring that they could also uncover Jaeyu's whereabouts from Hong directly, they went ahead and pounced without staking the place out first. Meanwhile, they learned from the landlord and neighbours that Hong appeared to be married, and confirmed that Hong's supposed construction-worker husband was indeed Jaeyu. They knew, too, that she was the one who'd been helping him hide out from the cops. The timing of her arrest meant she wasn't able to send the all-clear to Jaeyu, so the police kept the dragnet up and went into stakeout mode. Detectives disguised as peddlers loitered near the alley.

If only Mansu had gone back to the agit hideout himself, he would have recognised it was a stakeout even from far away. But instead, wary of being wanted by the police, Mansu thought it less risky to send an ordinary looking woman who could pretend to be a former colleague of Hong's. But the police were far more cunning than that. They let the woman approach the house, ask where her eonni was, confirm that she'd been arrested, and walk away nervously. That was when they began tailing her. They followed her to Gyeongseong Station and arrested Mansu, who'd been waiting for her while posing as a porter out front.

The Seodaemun Special Higher Police knew exactly what to do with people like them. They focused their torture on Mansu. For revolutionaries facing interrogation, if the twenty-four-hour rule proved difficult, they could resort to giving random names and addresses or fake locations and times to throw off the investigation. But the thought police, with all of their training and experience, were not so easily fooled. Information not directly related to Yi Jaeyu, and even true confessions that smacked of falsity, led to even more torture. They inflicted the cruellest of punishments, guaranteed to convince Mansu that he would be left crippled right then and there, or else die in bewildering agony. The first two hours were particularly crucial. Mansu caved after three. Or rather, he did not entirely cave. In exchange for giving false information, his fingernails were pulled out and he was electrocuted. That compelled him to admit to having let Jaeyu stay the night, and he gave them his own address. But he managed to keep secret the fact that he was supposed to meet Jaeyu at three in the afternoon at the tram stop in Jungnim-jeong. Surely, he thought, this would give an experienced activist and leader like Jaeyu plenty of time to make his escape. And so he held out until three o'clock.

The purest of Joseon revolutionaries did their best to keep true to the twenty-four-hour rule. Of the many legendary activists, a dozen or so had actually succeeded, though all but the very strongest ended up dying in prison from the effects of torture. Most lasted a few hours or so. If you've ever held your breath, then you know how long two or three minutes can be. A fistfight on a battlefield is over in about five. Five minutes can feel like a lifetime, can feel like enough time to change the course of history. At any rate, the only real information Mansu gave them was his own address. The problem was that the path to his home on Mallijae Hill would take the police right by the tram stop where Jaeyu was waiting.

That winter afternoon, a bitterly cold wind had driven everyone from the streets. Shop windows were white with frost, and white smoke billowed from every chimney. Only the occasional tram or car passed by. Figuring he would wait for this one last tram and then go, Jaeyu stood and watched it pull in from Namdaemun. Sparks leapt from the overhead wires as the tram bent around the curve toward the stop. It appeared to be packed. Having shivered outside in the cold for half an hour, Jaeyu hurried over in the hopes of greeting Mansu among the passengers getting off. Just as he drew close enough to make out the conductor's face, he saw a group of men crowding one of the exits. Detectives. Normally, detectives on a stakeout were disguised as labourers or peddlers and were therefore difficult to spot. But these detectives looked as though they'd come straight from the police station to make an arrest. Jaeyu could tell at once by the way they were dressed — flat caps and fedoras, suit jackets, jodhpurs and gaiters, not to mention the gold-rimmed glasses and moustaches — that they were from the thought police. He turned and immediately started walking back toward Bongnae-jeong, gradually picking up his pace without looking behind him. But it was all too easy to spot him there, approaching the tram in the middle of a deserted street and then suddenly turning heel and rushing away. Several of the detectives alighting from the tram began to follow him. Jaeyu's steps grew even more hurried.

When he made it onto the Bongnae-jeong Bridge, six more detectives were walking toward him from the other end. They were a different team, on their way to Mansu's address. There was no turning back now. Jaeyu let out a long breath to calm his nerves and kept his eyes forward as he walked, trying to look casual. They, too, seemed to be in no rush, as if they hadn't noticed who he was. The ones in front scrutinised him as they drew near. Meanwhile, the ones in back had nearly caught up. The moment he walked past the detectives on the bridge, they sensed that he was the man they were after. One of the detectives, a Korean, spun around and hooked his arm around Jaeyu's neck. They tumbled to the ground. The rest swarmed in and pinned him down by the arms, legs, and neck.

'You must be Yi Jaeyu.'

'Yi who? I'm Kim, from the Railway Bureau. You've mistaken me for someone else,' Jaeyu declared breathlessly.

The detectives handcuffed him and tied a rope around his waist.

'Let go, you filthy Japanese bastards!'

Jaeyu shouted as he kicked and rolled, trying to not get dragged away. As an activist, it was one of his duties to let people, especially Koreans, know that a fellow Korean was being taken. But the other Koreans on the street didn't dare come near them and instead watched from afar or scurried away, pretending not to have seen anything. The detectives took their time beating and kicking Jaeyu into submission and then cheerfully dragged him off.

Ahead of Jaeyu's arrest, many activists had already been brought in by the police. Jaeyu's organisation supposedly had about 200 members in Gyeongseong and 160 in areas outside the capital. The police charged Jaeyu for conspiring with contacts in Shanghai to establish a nationwide organisation, and began to torture him viciously to extract a confession. This is how one publication described his ordeal:

> They beat him, kicked him, forced water down his throat, and hung him from the ceiling, and then later heated an iron rod over a fire and burned his thighs with it. But our noble Comrade Yi was willing to die to protect his beliefs and defend the movement. Impatient with his refusal to speak, the police dragged Comrade Yi, who was already unable to eat or walk on his own, into another room, where they subjected him to electric-shock torture. He later told his comrades that he 'was prepared to die from the unbearable torture'.

In charge of Jaeyu's torture were two notorious Korean detectives from the Seodaemun Police Station. They stripped him to the waist, lay him down on a long, narrow wooden bench, similar to the kind used in weightlifting, and tied his hands and feet so that he couldn't move. One of them straddled Jaeyu's chest like they were sitting on a horse, forced his mouth open, and gagged him with a towel, making it impossible for him to swallow or breathe through his mouth. The other detective changed out of his shoes and into a pair of rubber boots, pulled a chair up close, pinned Jaeyu's head between his knees, and poured a kettleful of water down Jaeyu's nose. With his mouth gagged and water running down his nose, Jaeyu couldn't draw a breath. Water filled his lungs, and his stomach felt like it would burst. The towel in his mouth prevented him from killing himself by biting off his own tongue, and so he writhed in pain until he passed out, only to come to and writhe in pain again. When the water torture didn't work, they wrapped the wires from a crank telephone around Jaeyu's wet body and turned the crank to electrocute him. When they burned his thighs with a hot iron, Jaeyu smelled his own flesh burning and screamed. His was a relatively easier interrogation, as those who'd been arrested before him had already confessed to his organisation's involvement in the serial strikes. The only thing Jaeyu could do was to give false statements when asked about members of his organisation. To shave time off their sentences, he said they were unwitting friends or acquaintances who didn't know the first thing about socialism.

When Jaeyu refused to give in to their torture and perversities, the police opted for an extended interrogation that would allow them to draw out his physical and mental suffering in their quest to extract a confession. Instead of a regular jail cell, he was kept in a separate room in the Special Higher Police office on the second floor. The stated reason for keeping him in solitary was that he had beri-beri and a terrible fever, but really they wanted to hide the signs of his torture, and for another reason, as well. They were worried that putting him in with other political prisoners would enable the activists to match up their stories, or expose what was being done to them and get the public in an uproar.

Then came a rainy night in mid-March. The detective, exhausted from another long and tiring torture session, had dozed off. Jaeyu grabbed this opportunity to climb out the window and jump down to the street below. Staggering from the effects of his torture and illness, he headed toward Gwanghwamun, alternating between running and walking, trying to put as much distance between himself and the police as possible. By the time he reached Jeong-dong, he could already hear police whistles and shouts. A firewood peddler appeared just as he ducked down an alley, so he took cover by helping the man push his cart. As the chase tightened, he hopped a wall and found himself inside the US consulate, across the street from the courthouse. Without a clue as to what the place was, Jaeyu crawled under the eaves of the wall to take shelter from the rain. Suddenly relieved and overwhelmed with fatigue, he passed out.

Before long, he was jolted awake by a loud noise and saw white men in military uniforms pointing rifles at him. He was taken to the guard house, where he tried to explain in what little English he knew that he was a political fugitive in need of protection, but the soldiers pretended not to understand. The American consul called the police to say that they'd caught a thief and to come and pick him up. The Japanese police disregarded these calls at first, as they were frantic to track down Jaeyu and couldn't care less about dealing with some thief, but the consulate wouldn't stop calling and so finally they sent someone to check it out. Looking thoroughly annoyed, the officer they sent to pick up the thief was shocked to find himself beholding none other than the man they'd been looking for, and he made an enormous scene as he called for backup.

Jaeyu drifted back into unconsciousness on the way to the Seodaemun Police Station and could only be revived with an injection. The police beat and mocked him mercilessly for trying to flee to a communist country, mistakenly assuming that he'd sought asylum at the Russian consulate only to accidentally end up in the American consulate instead. The torture this time was so brutal that it wiped away all thought of survival and left him with only the hope of suicide. He was bound hand and foot, with metal cuffs on his wrists, and a ball and chain shackled to his ankles. They strung a bell from his waist so it would ring with his every move and wake anyone who might doze off while watching him, then locked every possible door and had Yoshino himself, chief of the Special Higher Police, take the key home with him after work every night. And that was the story of Jaeyu's first, failed escape attempt.

No one could have ever imagined that Jaeyu, who'd been beaten to a pulp and could barely walk, who was kept under such strict surveillance, would actually try to get away again. But sure enough, a month later, in the dead of an April night, he slipped through their iron grip and made his second attempt at an escape. The police went on high alert. Officers were dispatched like a swarm of ants across Gyeongseong to search every station and route out of the capital. Uniformed police and plainclothesmen alike went door to door, combing the city as if for lice, in search of Jaeyu. They even searched the mountains — from Namsan to Bugaksan, Inwangsan, and Naksan — hoping to ambush him, but to no avail. Chief Yoshino was forced to resign, and the case was handed over to the Gyeonggi Provincial Police. A bounty of 500 won was placed on Jaeyu's head.

This is how the escape was described in the prosecutor's records. Twelve days before his escape, his ankles were still shackled, but his handcuffs were removed for the guards' convenience. The moment both hands were free, he immediately began plotting. About a month prior, he'd been moved from solitary to another room on the same floor where six or seven other Korean political prisoners, including a man who went by the surname Kim, were being kept. They were not cuffed and were allowed to use the toilets on the ground floor, but Jaeyu was given a portable toilet to prevent him from taking even a single step outside of the room. The milk given to the inmates was delivered in glass bottles, the caps of which were made of tin. Jaeyu mashed up grains of rice and stuffed them into the keyhole of his shackles to make a mould, and then bent a tin milk cap into the shape of the key. To his surprise, it actually worked. The lock opened easily. He hid the key in a crack between the wooden floorboards beneath his bunk. The inmates were allowed to store personal belongings under their bunks, so that was where Jaeyu kept his coat and a nail clipper with a tiny blade attached to it. The coat he'd been wearing when he was first arrested had some cash sewn into the lining in case of an emergency. He cut out a different section of the lining to make a mask. One by one, he made these preparations in secret at night while everyone else was asleep. On the day of his escape,

Jaeyu deliberately didn't finish his supper, and offered his leftovers to Kim, who was suffering from dysentery. Kim happily accepted and gobbled them up. Around midnight, Kim started to beg the policeman on watch to let him go to the restroom. Eventually, at 4.00 am, the officer gave in to Kim's repeated pleas and took him downstairs. Jaeyu swiftly unlocked his shackles with the key he'd made and put on the mask, then put on his coat and hat, pulling the brim down low, and confidently walked out the front door. The policeman guarding the gate thought he was a detective and bid him good night. Jaeyu told the policeman to keep up the good work and hopped into a taxi. With the money he'd stashed inside the lining of his coat as cab fare, he changed taxis several times as he sped toward his ultimate hideout.

The version told by activists after Liberation differed, however, from the prosecutor's official version. According to those activists, while he was being held captive in the Special Higher Police office, Jaeyu had befriended a rookie Japanese policeman on the night watch. Among the young Japanese men who applied to join the force, some did so with the pure intention of hoping to protect the good and apprehend the bad. The bright, selfless Morida was one of them. Each time he came in for another night shift, Morida, who was not a socialist but 'disliked the Japanese imperial cult, embraced democratic ideas, and was quite interested in communism', always wanted to talk with Jaeyu, who declared with such confidence that he'd 'become a socialist for human equality'. They weren't able to chat when Jaeyu was first brought to the police station, because a team of two were initially assigned to the night shift. As the police relaxed their vigilance, Morida was placed on duty alone, so he struck up a conversation with Jaeyu in Japanese. It was said that Jaeyu's knack for agitprop swayed Morida and won him over, and that Morida was moved by his 'revolutionary passion, intelligence, and rich humanity' into helping him escape. Jaeyu told Morida that the imperial system was a mental shackle created by capitalists and men of power to control the people, and that the only way for Japan to achieve absolute human equality was to abolish the imperial system and ultimately embrace socialism. According to Jaeyu, Japan's imperialist encroachments into the rest of Asia and its victimisation of Joseon were an inevitable result of capitalism, which could only sustain itself through endless expansion. With the same look of passion and conviction he wore as he spoke to his fellow revolutionaries, Jaeyu explained to Morida that everyone, whether male or female, Eastern or Western, deserved to live in freedom and equality. And Jaeyu said he was more than willing to give up his own life to make that dream come true. Jaeyu's words inspired Morida. The two men continued their conversation deep into the night. Morida took notes and eagerly expressed his agreement. Every night that he came in for his shift, they shared intense conversations and eventually grew so close that they felt they could tell each other anything. One night, after they had been talking for a while, Jaeyu made a careful, yet casually worded, comment to Morida. 'It'd sure be nice to get out of here and be free to do what's right.'

Morida lost his smile. His voice deadly serious, he replied, 'Cherry blossoms that were in full bloom outside always wither when they come in here. But who can stop a flower once it begins to bloom? It'd be lonely around here without my friend. But I'm not one to complain about it. At least not until my tea goes cold.'

That night, Jaeyu unlocked his shackles, stuffed a bundle of clothes under his blanket to make it look like he was still in bed, and slipped out the window. Thirty minutes later, Morida blew his whistle and yelled that an inmate had escaped. The policemen asleep in their quarters leapt out of bed and ran around the building, while the half-dressed mounted police caused an enormous ruckus as they dragged out their sleepy horses. Police cars and motorcycles swarmed from their garages. Chief Yoshino, who'd rushed straight over from home, stomped around his office like a mad man with his gun in his hand. A few hours after the commotion had started, Morida, the very man responsible for letting Jaeyu escape, went to the room where the Korean political prisoners were kept. Unlike the other Japanese policemen, Morida, the rookie cop who was barely over twenty, was kind and pure of heart, and had always had a secret soft side for the Korean prisoners. The whole station had been turned upside down because of the runaway, but Morida looked serene, albeit a little tired from his night shift. With his usual smile, he stood before them and offered to sing them a song he'd written the night before, borrowing the melody of a Japanese song.

'In the cherry orchard, some blossoms have withered while others have just begun to bloom.'

The Korean prisoners complimented him on his songwriting, clueless to what was going on outside. Morida only gave them a sad smile in response. After a rigorous interrogation over the events in question, Officer Morida was demoted to a substation in the backwoods of Hamgyeong Province, far away from Gyeongseong.

Once he'd cleared the police-station grounds, Jaeyu grabbed a taxi and travelled to Hwanggeum-jeong. He walked a block, grabbed another taxi, to Dongsomun, and from there travelled on foot over Naksan Mountain to Dongsung-jeong. His plan was to evade the police's frenzied search by going to the home of someone of high standing, someone the imperial police would never, ever suspect.

Ever since Jaeyu had foregone the methods used by his more ideological predecessors of the petit-intelligentsia and focused instead on building the party from the bottom up, nearly all of the local activists had been embedded in factories. But as much as he cared about labourers, he also cared about student activists. Though they were not pushed to the edge of survival the way labourers were, they were pure of heart and eager to accept advanced social ideas, and even when arrested or beaten down for protesting, many found their way back to the picket lines. Once the student movement began to spread nationwide — especially after the Gwangju Student Independence Movement against the Japanese — national independence became their focus for the next few years. The one in charge of overseeing student movements ever since the core was first formed was Jeong, a Keijo Imperial University graduate who chose activism over money. Jeong was one of many Korean students who had been taught by Professor Miyake. Before coming to teach economics and Marxism at Keijo Imperial University, Miyake graduated from Tokyo Imperial University and went to study in Germany, where he took part in socialist movements. He was introduced to Jaeyu through Jeong, and after a couple of discussions about Japanese imperialism, Miyake and Jaeyu came to trust one another. Jaeyu believed that he'd be able to buy himself some time if he could hide out at Miyake's place.

In Dongsung-jeong, he climbed over the wall to Professor Miyake's house and sat in the garden in the dark, waiting for daybreak. Once the sun had fully risen, he brushed the dirt off his clothes, took off his mask, and rang the doorbell. The maid came to the door. He gave her a fake name and told her he was a student of Professor Miyake. Miyake came to the door, puzzled, trying to place the name. When he saw Jaeyu on his doorstep at that early hour, dressed in a suit, tie, and coat, he guessed that something was wrong and quickly ushered him into the living room. Jaeyu told him about his middle-of-the-night escape from the Seodaemun Police Station and asked whether he could hide there for a while. Considering that his first escape attempt had made the papers only a month ago, Miyake was surprised that Jaeyu had tried again and so soon.

By coincidence, Jeong dropped by the same morning to visit Miyake. Jaeyu asked him to look for a proper hiding place for him, along with a change of clothes and shoes to help him travel incognito. The only other people living in the house at the time were the maid; Miyake's wife, who was currently hospitalised; and his mother, who was visiting from Japan and, as luck would have it, was at the hospital with his wife that very morning. Jaeyu suggested it might be safer not to keep the maid around, and Miyake fired her the same day. After spending the night in the living room, Jaeyu asked Miyake for his help renting a room somewhere to hide out in, but with the police on alert all over Gyeongseong, it was too risky to set foot outside the house. Making matters worse, a notification arrived that day, 12 April, from the Dongdaemun Police Station, letting Miyake know that his house's spring hygiene assessment was scheduled for 15 April.

Miyake calmly made a suggestion, which turned out to be one of the most unexpected, bizarre ideas in the history of the Korean independence movement.

'How about hiding under the floor?'

Jaeyu and Miyake pulled back the tatami mat and removed the floorboards. The bare ground underneath was made up of soft, sandy soil that looked easy enough to dig. Jaeyu went to work with a shovel. Unfortunately for him, while the whole area was indeed sandy, as it was built on the banks of a stream, it was also very rocky, which made for backbreaking work. Jaeyu dug from eleven in the morning until ten at night. Miyake carried buckets of unearthed soil and rocks out to the garden. At last, they had a pit large enough for him to lie down in and a passageway. They dug an air hole beneath a window facing south and decided to use that gap for supplying food, too. They lined the bottom of the pit with a thick layer of newspapers and covered it with bedding and clothing. Jaeyu's meals consisted of bread, hardboiled eggs, and mandu dumplings; fruit, like apples and mandarin oranges; and emergency rations of canned goods. To relieve himself, Jaeyu dug small holes and filled them back in when he was done.

On 20 April, Miyake's wife was released from the hospital and came home with Miyake's mother. The following day, Miyake's mother went back to Japan. The only thing left for them to worry about was the fact that Miyake was scheduled to leave for Manchuria on 22 April for a field inspection in Gando, and would return ten days later on 2 May. The trip was Jaeyu's idea, after having heard updates on the manhunt from Jeong. Jaeyu thought that sending the owner of the house away on business would keep the place off the police's radar.

'It'll be easiest for you if you leave ten days' worth of food under the floor,' Jaeyu said.

Miyake shook his head. 'I can't bear to do that. I'll tell my wife the truth and ask for her help.'

'Your wife?'

'She's been a true comrade of mine since my days in Germany. I can't keep lying to her.'

Miyake called his wife, Hide, to the living room and introduced her to the now heavily bearded Jaeyu.

'This is Mr Yi, a Korean revolutionary and fellow communist. I have a duty to protect him. If you love and trust me, please help us.'

Her eyes brimming with tears, Hide nodded heartily.

'Thank you for trusting me. I'll do as you wish and protect Mr Yi.'

While her husband was studying in Germany, Hide had attended the Congress of the League Against Imperialism held in Berlin and kept company with German socialist groups, so she was familiar with their ideas and fond of ideological activists. During her husband's ten-day absence, she faithfully carried out her mission by delivering food to Jaeyu in the dugout below the living-room floor.

Jaeyu stayed there for a total of thirty-eight days, until Miyake was arrested on 21 May. The very reason Jaeyu became known in Joseon and all the way over in Japan was because of the story of his camaraderie with the Keijo Imperial University professor Miyake and his taking refuge under the floor of Miyake's house. While hiding out, Jaeyu bore a chopstick-sized hole in the floor next to the coffee table and used it to exchange written messages with Miyake. Jaeyu used a torch to read the books Miyake brought him, and occasionally emerged in the middle of the night so he could bathe. He also discussed with Miyake the general direction of Joseon's anti-imperialist activities, which had been put off due to the arrest of himself and others. Together, they reviewed the movement's policies, which had remained in draft form since the tense serial strikes, critiqued past activities, and considered the movement's future. They earnestly discussed what the general approach for activists in Joseon should be and which theory had been dictating the affiliations of the Pacific Labour Union in Wonsan and the rest of Hamgyeong Province, since they reportedly received instructions from the Profintern's Far Eastern Bureau. Meanwhile, through Jeong's introduction, Miyake also held discussions about policy with a Gyeongseong communist group affiliated with Kim Hyeongseon. He tried to form a connection between that group and Jaeyu's organisation. For these purposes, Miyake reviewed with Jaeyu an unauthorised copy of the *Theses of the Comintern's Thirteenth Plenum*, a publication called *Proletariat*, and the *May Day Manifesto*.

Then, on 17 May, Jeong was arrested. Miyake's arrest followed three days later. Miyake asked the police to postpone his interrogation by one day. He claimed it would help him get himself together to write a confession of his own accord. It wasn't until the evening of 22 May that Miyake confessed to having harboured in his house the fugitive named Yi Jaeyu, who'd escaped from the Seodaemun Police Station. Miyake had, of course, minded the activists' rule and stalled as long as possible to buy time for Jaeyu's escape. From the day Jeong was arrested, Jaeyu was fully prepared to flee at any moment. He suspected that Jeong wouldn't last long since he was an intellectual and that he'd confess other details in addition to those about Jaeyu. Still, Jeong managed to hold out for three days.

Before Jeong's arrest, Jaeyu was wearing the suit and shoes that student activists had procured for him, and Miyake had given him a pocket watch and thirty-six won in emergency money. As soon as Hide told him about her husband's arrest, Jaeyu slipped out of the house, crossed Naksan Mountain, and fled toward Jongno. By the time the police raided Miyake's house, the only thing left for them to find in the dugout beneath the living room floor was a handful of mandarin oranges.

Miyake was sentenced to three years in prison at the Gyeongseong District Court for violating the Maintenance of Public Order Act and harbouring a criminal. In prison, he issued a statement titled *Reflections* and renounced his beliefs. After his arrest, Miyake's students from Keijo Imperial University helped Hide open an antique bookstore in Byeongmok-jeong. Later, with the help of Korean activists, she opened another antique bookstore, called Kameya, or House of Turtle, in Myeongchi-jeong, so that she could support her husband while he did his time. Upon his release in 1937, the couple closed the shop and returned to Japan. Barred from his original teaching position, he grew mushrooms at the foot of a mountain until the war ended and he was able to go back to teaching. He continued to lecture at several universities up to a year before his death at eighty-two. His old books were donated to the Tohoku University in Sendai as the 'Miyake Collection'.

11

Yamashita's surveillance team had moved on to a new mission. With Jaeyu's escape stirring up the whole country, the Special Higher Police in Gyeongseong had been on emergency alert for more than two months but to no avail. The concentration of factories made Yeongdeungpo an area brimming with tens of thousands of factory workers, not to mention a large transient population of day labourers and porters. The police figured out that Yeongdeungpo and Incheon were practically in the same belt: workers in Incheon would relocate to Yeongdeungpo and vice versa. Both areas had a concentration of similar factories, from textile, machine, chemical, and electrics, to milling. Most factories were run by large companies headquartered in Japan and also had ties with the continent. Chief Inspector Matsuda came back from a Police Bureau meeting with new instructions. The Yeongdeungpo Police Station's interrogation of Kim Hyeongseon and the Seodaemun Police Station's interrogation of Professor Miyake, as well as the interrogations of Jaeyu's fellow activists, revealed that local Communist Party reconstructionists had been seeking to join forces with International Party members sent from the continent. The reading materials seized when Yamashita's team arrested the female factory workers' book club were obviously copies that Kim Hyeongseon's faction had brought over to reprint and distribute in Joseon.

'The arrests suggest that members of the International Party are still active here,' said Matsuda. 'Communicating with them is likely to be a top priority for the reconstructionist leader Yi Jaeyu. That's why we have to uncover subversive groups with ties to the International Party.'

'We suspect that Bang Wuchang may have run away to Incheon,' said Yamashita.

'Are you sure?' asked Matsuda.

'We're sure that he's not in Yeongdeungpo,' said Mori. 'Considering that he left from here, he would have to be in either Gyeongseong or Incheon. But labourers from Yeongdeungpo don't usually go looking for jobs in other parts of Gyeongseong. The factory district does extend into Yongsan, but the chances of being exposed are too high. The Railway Bureau and other facilities are right there. The shanty town is also risky, because it's much smaller than those in Yeongdeungpo and Incheon. That's why we need to focus on Incheon.'

Matsuda nodded.

'Bang Wuchang and Ahn Daegil were booked for the same case. Ahn Daegil will be released soon. We need to track his movements, sir,' Yamashita proposed.

'All right. Then let's send a surveillance team over to Incheon.'

'Shall I put in a request for cooperation?' asked Sergeant Mori.

In a scornful tone, Matsuda said, 'Look, the Incheon police have probably never even heard of the name Bang Wuchang. Why not just ask them to catch him for us while you're at it? We need to keep this operation secret.'

'We'll do a stakeout like last time, sir,' said Yamashita. 'We can set up a trap and release the bait.'

'How?'

'We'll pretend we're members of the International Party.'

Matsuda and Mori immediately approved Yamashita's plan. As usual, Yamashita took three assistants and headed to Incheon. The team set themselves up at a two-room house in Haincheon near the harbour. The files they brought along included confiscated documents and pamphlets as well as newsletters originally published on the continent. They also brought along a mimeograph machine to print a hundred copies of a leaflet. But the copies weren't meant to be handed out randomly in the streets, since they didn't want to risk attracting the attention of the local police. The team spent the next two weeks figuring out where workers at the textile factory, machine factory, and rice mill lived, ate, and drank. Then they split up to individually approach young workers over bowls of naengmyeon noodles and gukbap soup or while swigging makgeolli. Yamashita had his eyes on two factory workers at a pub he'd been frequenting for a couple of days. The two men had finished their first kettle of makgeolli; by their second kettle, their voices and laughter grew louder.

'Someday, I'm gonna kick that foreman's Japanese bloody arse.'

'That son of a bitch! He slapped me twice.'

Yamashita quietly told the boy passing by his table, 'Hey, young man, bring another plate of pork suyuk.'

The boy was puzzled, as Yamashita's own plate was still half-full.

'Sir, are you sure you'd like more food?'

'No, yaeya, give it to the table behind me, but put it on my tab.'

A few minutes later, the boy brought a steaming plate of boiled pork-belly slices to the other men's table. The young workers, who'd been slowly picking away at some bindaetteok pancakes that had already gone cold, looked confused.

'Wait, we didn't order this.'

'The customer there sent it over.'

Yamashita turned to smile at the men, who'd turned as well to steal glances at him. They began whispering to each other.

'Do you know that guy?'

'Nope.'

Yamashita turned all the way around in his seat.

'Sorry to interrupt, but I couldn't help overhearing your conversation, and it seemed interesting. I was hoping you might let me join you …'

'Oh, you're here alone.'

'Yeah, it's not much fun drinking by myself.'

'Then go ahead and join us.'

Yamashita introduced himself first to make them feel at ease.

'I'm Choi. I work on a ship.'

'I'm Kim, and this is Oh.'

'We both work at a machine shop.'

'Wow, so you're technicians.'

'Not really. We've been assistants for a few years now.'

With introductions out of the way, the three men began chatting like old drinking buddies. They talked about their hometowns, still being single, and how life was treating them.

'I steam back and forth to Shanghai. I'm a ship engineer's assistant,' said Yamashita.

He ordered more drinks and food. The two men were now pleasantly drunk.

'The foreman I heard you talk about earlier, I guess he's Japanese?'

'Aren't those bastards always the boss, wherever we go?'

'I guess so. It's the same on ships.'

'The Japanese come over here, take everything away, and act like they own us, too, don't they?'

Yamashita sensed an opening.

'When something's not right, the only way to fix it is by talking about it together and joining forces to make your voices heard.'

'How do we join forces?'

'We'd have to put our heads together first to see if we all share the same goal.'

He said no more.

When they were nearly done with their drinks, he pulled a leaflet out from his inside pocket.

'I came across this,' he said as he handed it to the puzzled men. 'My blood boiled when I read it.'

Before parting ways outside the pub, he added, 'Our ship leaves in a few days. If you'd like to chat some more, meet me here again tomorrow.' The men responded with a smile.

Yamashita's team gathered back at the house to share what they'd each worked on that day. They had all distributed leaflets and were hopeful that they'd managed to lure a few others in, though none had made actual plans to meet again like Yamashita had.

The next evening, Yamashita was waiting at the pub when the two factory workers came in looking for him. He waved. Looking hesitant, the two men joined him at the table. Yamashita asked the waiter to bring some food and a kettle of makgeolli.

'Were you surprised by what you read yesterday?'

'Well, it said we should drive the Japanese out and gain independence …'

'It also said labourers should stick together.'

One of them glanced around before asking, 'Brother, do you really work on a ship?'

Yamashita beamed. 'I told you I'm from Shanghai,' he said, avoiding the question. 'The mood there is completely different. There, young Korean men are ready and willing to fight the bastard Japanese.'

'We have a lot to learn from you.'

Yamashita told them he was actually an independence activist and that he was recruiting members for a book club. Eager to be educated, the two young men volunteered. Although they'd left their hometowns for work, their innocence had not yet been tainted by the hucksters of the world. Yamashita gave them a time, date, and place and spent the rest of the evening drinking with them until they parted.

In total, Yamashita's team succeeded in recruiting six members for their fake book club. To host the meetings, they rented another two-room house, not far from where they were staying. Yamashita and one of the assistants attended the meetings, while the other two stayed back. Over the course of a month, they met four times and doubled the number of members.

Yamashita mimeographed the material he'd prepared. The book-club members would read the handouts together and discuss them. Every time they met, Yamashita asked the members to invite co-workers they trusted to join the club. Oh, who worked at a machine factory, brought his crew chief, Yun. Yun was in his thirties; he'd started out as a day labourer and endured a long apprenticeship to become a generator engineer. Not only was he now treated like a foreman at the factory, he was a veteran whose words carried weight among the day labourers and apprentices.

Among the dock workers in Incheon were a few activists associated with the Pacific Labour Union. In less than a year since coming down south after the strike at Wonsan Port, they managed to form ties with activists working at various factories who'd come to Incheon from Gyeongseong, Gangwon Province, and Gyeonggi Province. Naturally, the dock workers also came into contact with Kim Hyeongseon's International line and received their publications and handouts. Some dock workers even had connections with Communist Party reconstructionists in Gyeongseong. Bang Wuchang was one such contact.

As soon as Wuchang fled to Incheon, he discussed his situation with Foreman Jo, a senior Pacific Labour Union associate working at the dock. They concluded that going to work was the best way for a fugitive to hide. Foreman Jo introduced Wuchang to a rice mill that was one of the oldest factories standing across the street from the dock. Wuchang had been a lathe operator at the Yeongdeungpo Rail Works, so he headed straight to the rice mill to demonstrate his skills. When he easily finished the machine parts he was asked to make, the Japanese owner and mechanical engineer were happy to put him in charge of his own lathe.

Once a week, he'd meet with other activists at a pub nearby to brief each other on recent developments. One day, Yun, a crew chief at a machine factory, reported that he'd heard news about two of his crew members joining a book club. Naturally, Wuchang had to know which line the book club belonged to. Vladivostok was home to Pacific Labour Union affiliates, while International lines all led back to Shanghai. The two groups may have been heading in different directions, but they'd both originated from the International Party. Although nearly 200 Communist Party reconstructionists, including Yi Jaeyu, had been arrested, many whose cover hadn't been blown still remained active. Once their core went into hiding after the arrests, International Party members attempted to absorb the remaining activists under the pretext of integration. Labourers, however, were less nitpicky about lines and believed that factionalism had to be overcome. This was why Foreman Jo agreed that Yun and Wuchang should look into the new book club. Yun decided to tag along with his crew member to the next meeting.

Two o'clock on a Sunday afternoon was a precious time for factory workers. Those who were married would pack rolls of kimbap and go on a picnic to the amusement park on Wolmido Island or visit their parents or relatives. Those who weren't married would change into something more charming than their greasy work clothes to go on dates or spend the afternoon playing soccer or volleyball. Yun, on the other hand, accompanied his colleague Oh to a book club. There, he was introduced first to Yamashita and then the rest of the book-club members before the meeting began.

'I brought Yun, the head of our factory's generator crew.'

Trying to sound as unremarkable as possible, Yun said, 'I don't know the first thing about any of this stuff. I'm just frustrated because I don't know what's going on in the world. I hope to learn a lot from you.'

With the sharp eyes of a spy, Yamashita studied Yun. He seemed like an ordinary labourer in his white short-sleeved cotton shirt and work pants. With an unguarded look on his face and a smile lingering on his lips, Yun looked around at the young men as they engaged in heated discussion. It looked like most of it was going over his head. He even appeared to grow bored as he flipped through the handouts excerpted from *The Communist* resting on his knee. He seemed to be skimming through the headings instead of carefully reading the mimeographed copies. When the meeting ended two hours later, Yamashita decided to ask Yun a couple of questions, which is what Yun had been hoping for as well.

'How was it? I mean, what's your impression of the book club?'

Just as seasoned as Yamashita, Yun kept a smile on his face as he replied, 'Honestly, I couldn't even say. I'm pretty ignorant when it comes to this stuff. I was just sort of hoping that the wages at our factory could be raised a bit.'

'You'd first have to gather others who agree with you. It's not something you can achieve on your own.'

'May I ask which factory you're working at?'

Oh, who was sitting beside Yun, said, 'Didn't I tell you before? He works on a ship. He's from Shanghai.'

Yun smiled good-naturedly again and nodded.

'I see, Shanghai. Then you must not be familiar with the circumstances around here.'

Yamashita had no choice but to say, 'I'm just a middleman. I was asked to pass on news from Shanghai to the local labourers.'

The look on Yun's face changed as he lowered his voice.

'It's dangerous here.'

Yamashita figured it would be better to give Yun a peek at the cards in his hands.

'The other day, I saw in the papers that someone from the International Party named Kim Hyeongseon was arrested.'

The slow-witted look returned to Yun's face.

'Folks like us are so busy trying to make ends meet that we never notice what's going on in the world.'

After the meeting, Yamashita went back to the house where his team held their daily check-in. At the end, he wrapped it up by saying, 'Yun can turn out to be one of two possibilities: a run-of-the-mill veteran labourer who's politically ignorant but wants to be treated better at work such as with a raise. If that's the case, then he'll be most concerned with his own self-interest, which would make it easier to bring him over to our side. On the other hand, he could be an activist who's infiltrated a factory and is checking us out in return. Either way, we have to keep an eye on his movements.'

Meanwhile, Yun attended the weekly activists' meeting and shared his impression of the book club with the five key members, including Foreman Jo, Wuchang, and Kim Geunshik, who was associated with the Red Labour Union. Yun showed them the pamphlet he had brought back from the book-club meeting.

'The text seems to have come from the fourth issue of *The Communist*.'

After flipping through it, Wuchang said, 'This is from the original that Comrade Kim Hyeongseon asked us to reprint, so there's nothing new in it. How did they get their hands on this in the first place? If it's been reprinted, the remaining members of the organisation in

Gyeongseong might be involved. But if it came from Shanghai, the next issue should be available as well.'

'Let's wait until we're sure which side they're on,' said Foreman Jo.

A member of Yamashita's team set up a peddler's stall near the machine factory where Yun worked. A few days later, the team members began to take turns tailing Yun. Before the next book-club meeting took place, they figured out almost all the routes Yun regularly took. Yamashita left his team in Incheon and went to the Yeongdeungpo Police Station to report on their progress. The report naturally led to the conclusion that the surveillance team was in need of new reading material from Shanghai. Yamashita put in a request with the Police Bureau and managed to get his hands on the latest publications.

After a ten-day absence, he returned to Incheon. His team members informed him of some new details they'd uncovered while he was away. Yun had indeed turned out to be no ordinary labourer. After work, he'd go home and read books. On days off, he met other factory workers at Manguk Park, Munhaksan Mountain, the harbour construction site, or Wolmido Island to hold more book-club meetings.

When Yamashita showed up at the next fortnightly book-club meeting hosted by his team, Yun was sitting there with ten other members. Yamashita passed around mimeographed handouts that included an excerpt from a Communist Youth League magazine published in Shanghai, an essay from the fifth issue of *The Communist*, a manifesto on the May Day struggle, and a manifesto against imperialist wars. As always, Yamashita gave security instructions regarding the handouts. It was fine to individually carry manifestos around, but if anyone was caught by the authorities with one in their possession, they were to claim that they'd picked it up off the street or that a stranger handed it to them. The members were allowed to take the handouts home to study them only if they promised to return them at the next meeting. If they were caught with the handouts at home, they were to claim that someone had left them on their doorstep. Yamashita, who was known to the club as Choi Gapsik, announced that the two manifestos would be discussed at the meeting that day while the rest of the handouts would be covered through the next meeting after the members finished reading them on their own at home.

At the weekly activists' meeting the following week, Yun presented the handouts to his comrades and said, 'This Choi Gapsik person wasn't lying about sailing back and forth to Shanghai. These appear to be from the latest International Party publications.'

Foreman Jo and Kim Geunshik could tell at once that the text had been authored by the party. The content communicated views from Shanghai that were in accord with the party's guidelines and the general direction of its activities.

'It shouldn't be necessary for all of us to meet them. I think you should take charge of winning them over,' Wuchang said to Yun.

Through one of his team members, Yamashita learned that Yun regularly met with a couple of people at a pub near Haincheon. About a month later, in mid-August, Yamashita waited across the street from the pub until he saw Wuchang show up for the meeting. Ever since Wuchang had got away from him in the alley behind the Maruboshi factory in Yeongdeungpo the previous year, Yamashita had not forgotten his face. The moment he saw him, Yamashita was itching to pounce. Instead, he pulled out a cigarette to calm himself down. After taking his time to finish the cigarette, he turned to the police assistant who'd led him to the pub.

'We need to find out who they are, what they do, and where they live. This is exactly what we came here for. Leave Bang Wuchang to me.'

Yamashita headed straight to Yeongdeungpo to give an update, after which Chief Inspector Matsuda personally came over from the Police Bureau to confirm the contents of Yamashita's report. Instead of apprehending the activists right away, they decided to wait until the activists came into contact with their comrades in Gyeongseong, so they could take them all down together.

Ahn Daegil finished serving his sentence and returned to his mother's restaurant in Singil-jeong. Daegil stuck to the rules of activists who'd been arrested for disrupting public order. Unless they were core members, most could declare that they'd had a change of heart during the investigation or trial. Labourers would typically claim that they only did what they were told without knowing what their actions meant, thereby shifting the political blame onto the core activists who'd been arrested. Then they'd turn in a statement vowing to live as good, loyal subjects of the Japanese Empire. Right before their release, they'd confirm their vows by turning in a pledge stamped with their thumbprint to the prison authorities. Core activists, on the other hand, sought to take responsibility for propagating and inciting the masses. They'd confess the ideas they believed in, and refused to waver. At the same time, they argued that since they'd been caught making preparations, they were only guilty of attempting to take organised revolutionary actions. In Daegil's case, he had played a leading role in a strike, but because no associations with the Red Labour Union had been uncovered, he received a relatively short sentence. Before his release, Daegil signed a pledge with his thumbprint. Once out of prison, core activists weren't supposed to rush to reconnect with their comrades. They were expected to rest and avoid any excitement in order to heal from their prison ordeals. Above all, it was important to do whatever they could to make a living. In other words, they had to get a job. Having a job would draw them back into normal society, where they wouldn't be spied on as much. If the organisation needed to contact them, a reppo would be sent. Until then, all Daegil could do was wait. If there was anything urgent to communicate, he had to make sure to send word through a reliable reppo and wait for instructions.

Daegil set up a routine for himself. He woke at dawn to draw water for his mother to use at the restaurant and waited on customers all day. Once the dinner rush was over, he'd hang a towel around his neck and head toward Saetgang to wash up or go for a walk. He stuck to this routine like clockwork. Keeping track of subversives like Daegil was a task usually given to rookie police assistants. After tracking the same, boring routine for an entire month, the police assistants watching him and the detective they reported to would start to drop their guard. Meanwhile, those who were waiting to get in touch with Daegil were bound to be keeping an eye on him as well to figure out when and where would be best to approach him.

Icheol knew the exact date of Daegil's release and watched his mother's restaurant from a distance to confirm that he was out. He decided to approach Daegil through Seonok. Daegil was well aware of who Seonok was and could easily guess who was trying to contact him through her. Although Seonok worked at the textile factory, she often shopped at the market for her grandparents before going to work. Once Icheol and Yeowok opened their tteok shop, they took turns in going to the market early in the morning just like anyone else who owned a small shop along the streets and alleys of Yeongdeungpo. One early morning, Daegil was pushing his bike along the stalls in the bustling market. When he stopped by one stall in particular, Seonok came and stood beside him. Daegil recognised her at once. For a moment, a cheery smile flashed across Seonok's face. Meanwhile, Yeowok was on the other side of the wide road, peering at the people around Daegil and Seonok as she pretended to choose something from a fish stall. With her experienced eyes, it was easy to spot Daegil's tail. His loose suit jacket, stovepipe trousers, and gaiters made it glaringly obvious that he was a police assistant. Even Daegil was probably aware that he was being followed.

'Oh my, I see the new crop of beans is finally out!' exclaimed Seonok as she grabbed a handful of beans and let them run through her fingers.

Standing beside her, Daegil casually asked, 'Is this good?'

'Of course, it's good with rice and for making powder to coat tteok.'

After asking for two kilos of beans, Seonok muttered, 'How come it's so hot when the Chuseok holiday is just around the corner? It'll be close to midnight before the womenfolk can bathe at the Ghost Rock.'

Daegil caught the hint right away and confirmed.

'The day before Chuseok is best for a bath.'

Once she'd bought the beans, Seonok walked away from the stall. Daegil purchased some greens and potatoes and loaded them onto his bike. While he was still shopping, Seonok and Yeowok met at the market entrance and walked side by side.

'The meeting's been set for midnight at the Ghost Rock the day before Chuseok.'

Seonok had breezed through her mission. Yeowok went back to deliver the news to Icheol.

Since Jaeyu's arrest and escape, Icheol's only contact with the core had been Yi Gwansu. However, when Jaeyu escaped once more after hiding at Professor Miyake's house, Gwansu moved and Icheol lost touch with him. Icheol assumed that Gwansu must be hiding somewhere near Gyeongseong. The harder things got, the more Icheol believed in the importance of holding true to their activist rules and keeping everyone together. It was the duty of those who evaded arrest. And because Daegil and Wuchang had started out as a troika with Icheol in the Yeongdeungpo network, they were important to him.

Yeowok told her husband of the rumour about a group under the International line led by a Gwon So-and-so. The group had initially come to check out Gyeongseong, but now it was reaching out to labourers, claiming it was the only group qualified to succeed Jaeyu's group and rebuild the Joseon Communist Party. Icheol had also heard rumours about how the group was claiming that the Gyeongseong Troika were in fact factionalists and that their outmoded operations had to be eradicated. Icheol had matured enough as a communist to be able to overlook such rumours. He believed folks in the field had to help each other out as long as it was for the right cause. Some argued that doing so would allow the organisation to be usurped by those who claimed to be International Party members, but Icheol didn't care.

When the fourteen-day-old moon, almost fully round with only a bit left to go in the corner, had reached the top of the sky and was just starting to inch its way back down, Icheol set out from home. The alleyways reeked of the cooking oil everyone was using to prepare food for the annual harvest celebration of Chuseok. The streets were empty by midnight, as though everyone had fallen into a deep sleep for an early start the next day. Even the colonial police's hounds would have headed home early for their families' sake and have conked out by then. Icheol headed toward the Ghost Rock near Banghagot Ferry Landing. He'd been going there to bathe and swim ever since he was a boy, so he could probably find his way around it with his eyes closed. And he had a nearly-full moon to guide him. It was also one of the first rendezvous points he'd had with Yeowok.

From the top of the hill overlooking Ghost Rock, next to the swimming hole, Icheol watched the road. Soon, the faint outline of someone came into sight. As the man drew near, Icheol recognised Daegil from his gait. When Daegil came close enough, Icheol stepped out into the middle of the path. Without a word, he headed down toward the water, with Daegil following. They circled the pool and crossed a small stream to reach a thick patch of trees and silver grass. As soon as they had sat down among the silver grass, they gave each other a hug.

'You had it rough, didn't you?'

'Well, only in the beginning, but I managed to play dumb the whole time. It was okay in prison. They even sent me to work at a factory.'

Daegil asked Icheol about the main thing that had been worrying him. 'Where's Wuchang Hyeong? Wasn't he released before me?'

'He went underground after getting mixed up in the arrest of Mr Kim from the International Party.'

'He needs to take it easy. Where is he now?'

'Incheon. He's safe, so don't worry.'

Icheol told Daegil about all that had happened during his absence. They agreed that they had to get back in touch with the core as soon as possible. They decided on what signals they'd use to contact each other and how they would exchange messages.

As the saying goes, as soon as the crow flies away, a pear falls from the tree. And in other complete coincidences, someone happened to come looking for Daegil at the restaurant a couple of days later. Dressed like a peddler, the man walked in past lunchtime with an A-frame on his back loaded with two wooden crates of dried fish that he'd been selling. He took a look around and then set down the A-frame and took a seat in the maru. Instead of addressing Daegil, who'd been hovering nearby, he called out to Daegil's mother, who was taking a much-needed break after the lunch rush.

'Ajumeoni, can you bring me a bowl of gukbap soup and some makgeolli?'

Quick to catch on, Daegil brought him a spoon, chopsticks, and a small bowl of kimchi. The man double-checked to be sure no one else was within earshot and spoke quietly.

'I've come up from Incheon.'

Daegil stared at the man for a moment before finally managing to say, 'And?'

The man grinned. 'I don't suppose you'd be interested in some dried big-eyed herring. I've got some good stuff from Mr Bang's store in Incheon.'

Instead of giving an answer, Daegil just nodded and turned away. As he came back with a tray carrying a steaming bowl of gukbap cooked by his mother, he said, 'Eat first. Business can wait, don't you agree?'

'As a matter of fact, I do,' replied the man with a grin. Daegil stood in front of the kitchen and watched him eat. When he was finished, Daegil said, 'Why don't you come in? Let's take a look at that big-eyed herring.'

As soon as the two men took a seat on the kitchen floor, their demeanour changed.

'Who are you, and where did you come from?'

'I'm Kim Geunshik and I work at a factory in Incheon. Comrade Bang Wuchang is working at a rice mill and is keeping in touch with the organisation.'

Still wary, Daegil posed another question.

'Did he have anything else to say to me?'

'He asked how Dusoe is doing.'

Daegil finally relaxed, and nodded as he shook Geunshik's hand. They stuck to the essentials, as they had to keep their meeting to ten minutes or less.

Before leaving, Geunshik said, 'We've found a connection with Shanghai, so we'll be able to interact more actively with the International Party.'

Daegil had been following protocol, so he assumed that he wouldn't be able to meet Wuchang in person for a while. All he could say in response was, 'Dusoe will pay a visit soon.'

Yamashita's team was unaware of Geunshik's trip to Gyeongseong;

otherwise, they would have tailed him. Geunshik had set out from home at dawn. At the dock, Foreman Jo helped him dress like a peddler. With dried herring and anchovies on his back, Geunshik left Incheon on foot and walked to Bupyeong. From there, he took the train to Yeongdeungpo Station. Although it was still early in the morning when he arrived, the station was bustling with labourers and office workers. Geunshik spent the whole morning peddling the dried fish around residential areas in Yangpyeong-jeong and Dangsan-jeong. As a seasoned activist, he believed in the importance of truly playing the part, regardless of whether he was being tailed or not. That seemed to be the only way to avoid any looks of suspicion that even he might fail to notice. He didn't make it to the restaurant until late in the day, around two in the afternoon and well past the lunch rush. On his way back to Incheon, as well, he got off the train early at Bupyeong and walked the rest of the way, avoiding the main streets, still carrying his heavy A-frame. It was very late by the time he was able to reach the dock and change out of his disguise. By the time he made it back home, it was almost midnight and the alleys had long been deserted.

Icheol received word from Gwansu. Apparently still somewhere in Gyeongseong, Gwansu and Jaeyu were sorting things out even as they refrained from taking any action. To them, sorting things out meant minimising damage and advising others. Unexposed connections had to be pared down, and instructions were to be passed on only in writing. These brief, hand-copied messages were then to be memorised or hand-copied again for forwarding. Once he received word from Gwansu, Icheol headed to downtown Gyeongseong, to an emergency rendezvous point near the Dongmyo Shrine just outside Dongdaemun Gate. The narrow alley coursing through the shanties that had popped up around the Dongmyo Shrine was always bustling with merchants. Icheol was supposed to walk back and forth along a roughly 200-metre-long section between half past five and six in the afternoon. When he was making his third trip along the section, Gwansu came walking toward him. At first, Icheol failed to recognise Gwansu dressed like a farmer in a quilted coat and a fur hat drawn low over his eyes. Icheol was about to walk by when the man addressed him.

'Excuse me, could I ask you for some directions?'

Icheol recognised Gwansu's voice.

'Sure, ask away.'

'Can you tell me where Dongmyo is?'

Without hesitating, Icheol said, 'I'm on my way there right now. Follow me.'

Together, the two men turned into a side road through the shanties and headed toward the edge of the village. Once they were sure they weren't being followed, they stepped out to a field where the vegetables had already been harvested. An early winter dusk fell around them. They walked through the field as they talked. It turned out that the person going by the name of Gwon had previously been in contact with their arrested comrades Jeong and Professor Miyake; Icheol had been unable to meet this Gwon's request for a get-together. But to gain a better grasp of what was going on in the field, they needed some of the remaining organisation members to collaborate with International Party associates like Gwon. Publications would be issued in the name of the Joseon Communist Party Reconstruction Council, which could later serve as the title for the coalition of various organisations. Another comrade who had been in charge of the student activists would handle communication between the orgs left in Gyeongseong. Access to publications would be limited to a minimal number of orgs. Icheol gave Gwansu an update on the situation in Incheon.

'Do you know someone named Kim Geunshik?' he asked.

'Oh, he's an old friend of Jaeyu. They met in prison. He's one of us,' said Gwansu.

'According to him, they've developed a connection in Shanghai.'

'It's Incheon, so it's possible. But they know so little about the circumstances here in Joseon, we should avoid communicating directly with them.'

'Wuchang Hyeong was in contact with the International Party's Kim Hyeongseon while working with our group. I suppose you're aware of how he escaped to Incheon?'

'I am. Ask him to arrange a meeting for you with this Gwon person.'

Their business concluded, they skipped having dinner together and parted ways in a field in Wangsimni. Icheol went home to talk to his wife. She offered to visit Incheon on his behalf, but Icheol was against the idea. As Kim Hyeongseon's reppo, Yeowok had been at the centre of their network and thus risked exposing Wuchang if she went to meet him. Icheol thought that she shouldn't get involved in missions like that again. Besides, the baby was due any day now.

He decided to send Seonok. Dressed plainly in a knee-length skirt, jeogori blouse, and coat, Seonok headed to Incheon looking just like an office or factory worker on her day off. Being the experienced activist that he was, Geunshik had chosen an unusual place to meet. Seonok was to go to a chapel. She waited until the end of the service and stopped to talk to the reed-organ player on her way out. Seonok asked the woman whether she knew the dried-fish peddler. The woman said she had no idea what Seonok was talking about. Only when Seonok said she'd enjoyed the big-eyed herring the peddler had sold her did the look on the woman's face change. The woman, who worked at Dongyang Textiles, was Geunshik's reppo. That evening, Seonok and Geunshik rendezvoused at Manguk Park, where they agreed on a time and date for Icheol and Wuchang to meet.

12

At the start of the bitter cold in mid-December, Icheol boarded a train for Incheon. There, at precisely 6.00 pm, he waited at the darkened entrance to Eungbongsan Mountain.

Yamashita's surveillance team was watching Wuchang, waiting for the decisive moment. They'd split into pairs to take turns tailing him. Wuchang, who worked at the rice mill, kept to a regular schedule and hadn't deviated from it very much. The meet-ups at the pub had also grown less frequent; they'd either changed location or had changed their strategy so that they were no longer meeting in person. Yamashita was getting nervous. He knew that waiting too long could mean the difference between perfectly cooked rice and burnt rice. The book club they'd started as a front was going along nicely. They were able to keep track of Yun and Wuchang's movements without losing either of them. Yamashita was resting in their rented house when one of the surveillance-team members who'd been on stakeout came rushing in.

'He left his room!'

'What? Where'd he go?'

'We're tailing him now. I think you better come, too.'

Yamashita checked his watch. It was dinner time. Or maybe Wuchang just had a hankering for a drink. But it had been a very long time since Wuchang had gone anywhere after work. There was no harm in checking it out. If Wuchang were to meet with someone and Yamashita wasn't there, all of his hard work would go to waste. Yamashita laced up his shoes and hurried out. Unfazed by the looks they got, they ran to catch up with the surveillance-team member who was still tailing Wuchang. Once they confirmed that he was there, walking far ahead of them, the two assistants switched places: the one who'd come to get Yamashita stayed close to Wuchang, while the other dropped back and walked with Yamashita.

'He's definitely on his way to meet someone, sir.'

'What makes you so sure?'

'You see how he's heading away from the main street? That must mean he's not on his way to eat or grab a drink.'

As they followed Wuchang at a distance, it became more obvious that he was up to something. He was headed towards Eungbongsan. He took the walking path next to the Anglican Church in Manguk Park. In the dark, they could just make out Wuchang as he turned onto a smaller, secluded path.

'We'll hang back and watch from here,' Yamashita whispered. 'You go ahead and see who he's meeting.'

'Are we going to arrest him?'

'*Baka!*' Yamashita hissed. 'The whole point of waiting is so we can catch a chicken, not a chick. Just go see what he's up to.'

The assistant vanished into the dark and then returned.

'He's with someone.'

'*Yoshi!* That's our target. Wuchang will head back to his lodgings after this.'

Yamashita thought on his feet. This person must have come from outside of Incheon to meet Wuchang. Which meant he would have to go back. He would not be staying. Renting a room for the night would leave a trace. There were only two ways out of town: on foot or on the Gyeongin Line. It was too cold for walking, which meant he'd definitely take the train. He considered how close the final stop, Haincheon Station, was to the pier and made a quick decision. One of their surveillance team would tail the man from here, while another would wait at a midway point and tag in. Meanwhile, Yamashita, as team leader, would wait at the station.

When he got there, he checked the timetable. There was only one train left for the night. He bought a ticket for Yeongdeungpo. He would have to either tail the man or arrest him en route without any backup. After about thirty minutes, passengers began to trickle into the station. Yamashita sat in a corner to the right with a newspaper spread open. After a few more passengers, one of Yamashita's team members came in, spotted him, and headed straight over.

'It's the man in the khaki coat and fur hat.'

Yamashita followed his gaze to the ticketing booth, where the man stood with his back to them, presumably checking the schedule for the last train. Yamashita got up and slowly walked over. He wanted to get a look at the man's face. When he was only a few steps away, the man turned. Unfazed, Yamashita brushed past him with his head down and stopped near the timetables. Even while pretending to study the train schedules, his heart raced and the back of his head itched terribly. The moment he had seen the man's face, Yamashita felt like he'd been poked with a hot needle. The waiting room filled with noise and motion as boarding began. Passengers were lined up and heading through the gates. Instead of joining them, Yamashita stood where he was and watched as the man in the khaki coat vanished into the crowd. His team member, who'd been watching from a distance, rushed over to him.

'Aren't you going to follow him?'

Yamashita said simply, 'That's no longer necessary.'

He headed out of the station and put a cigarette in his mouth. His crew member took out a match and lit it for him. He took a deep drag and let out a long plume of smoke before speaking.

'I know that man.'

The next morning, Yamashita went to the Yeongdeungpo Police Station to report on his surveillance activities and discuss what to do about Bang Wuchang, the dock worker Foreman Jo, the person calling himself Yun who'd been showing up at their fake book club, and the contact who'd met Wuchang the night before. Their undercover investigation had revealed that Foreman Jo was part of the Pacific Labour Union in Wonsan before coming to Incheon, and it was surmised that both he and Wuchang were connected to the Comintern's Far Eastern Bureau. Thus, the assumption was that Wuchang had sought out Foreman Jo through his connections with the International Party in order to stay hidden.

'If we squeeze those two hard enough, they'll rat out every member of the International Party who's been hiding in Gyeongseong.'

'The person he met yesterday must be involved, too, right? Assuming he's a liaison?'

'There's no need to rush on that one. He could've just been asking Wuchang how to stay in contact with him.'

'No need to rush?' Chief Inspector Matsuda asked. 'What're you talking about?'

'He's someone I've been keeping tabs on. We might be able to use him as bait if we leave him be for now.'

'You don't think he's a ringleader?'

'Ringleaders don't meet face-to-face with wanted criminals.'

Yamashita sounded very sure of himself, and Sergeant Mori agreed. 'If he is a liaison, then he'll be part of a lower-level yacheyka.'

Chief Inspector Matsuda gave them a doubtful look and said, 'Let's send an undercover team to keep an eye on him anyway.'

They chose Tuesday night to put their plan into action. Sergeant Mori decided to take two Japanese detectives with him and head to Incheon to join Yamashita's surveillance team. Before they could leave, a police assistant who'd gone to scout out Icheol's tteok shop came rushing in and reported to Yamashita.

'The door to the tteok shop was locked. I took a look around, but no one was inside.'

Yamashita mulled this over, then told the assistant, 'I'll take care of it. Keep your mouth shut for now.'

They were planning to arrest Foreman Jo and Bang Wuchang in Incheon, and to hand over the intelligence they'd gathered to the Incheon Police Station: namely, a list of the names and workplaces of the Korean workers they'd snared with their fabricated book club, and a report of their findings regarding what appeared to be another book club run by Yun. But when Mori and Yamashita showed their report to the head of the Incheon's Special Higher Police, the Japanese inspector grew furious at only finding out about all of this now and threw the report at their feet.

'Who the fuck are you to trespass on someone else's territory and pull these pranks?'

'We were only following the orders of the Police Bureau,' Sergeant Mori said stiffly.

'So you thought you'd be the heroes by taking down the big guys, and order us to wipe up behind you?'

'I'm terribly sorry, but the Police Bureau has been handling this directly as a matter of public security.'

Everyone was quiet for a moment, and then the inspector turned to his subordinates, his anger unabated.

'Go round them up. This network is linked to Shanghai.'

After the inspector left, one of the Incheon officers smirked at Yamashita.

'Stay the fuck out of Incheon. If I ever see you again, I'll have you immediately arrested as a communist from Shanghai.'

At ten o'clock on Tuesday night, they arrested Wuchang and Foreman Jo and sent them to Yeongdeungpo. They knew how critical that first night was. If they wanted a bigger payoff, they'd have to get as much information out of them as possible before sunrise. From Foreman Jo, they uncovered a network of contacts with Wonsan, and through focused torture of Wuchang, they learned that he had already told Icheol how to contact Gwon, who was one of the core members of the International Party in Gyeongseong. Among the Yeongdeungpo factory network, several International Party orgs were also named. They further learned that Wuchang had been in contact with both the Communist Party reconstructionists and International Party members in Gyeongseong, and that there was movement towards uniting these two groups, just as the police had suspected. The brutal torture dragged on into the wee hours of the night. Wuchang passed out three times, and each time a doctor on stand-by came in and injected him with a stimulant.

As dawn broke, Wuchang broke, too, and confessed the location of Gwon's hideout near the Ikseon-jeong cigarette shop. The inspector who'd come in person from the Police Bureau placed an emergency call to dispatch a detective unit to Ikseon-jeong. Soon, news arrived that Gwon had been arrested. The Korean detectives, including Yamashita, who had personally tortured Wuchang under the orders of Sergeant Mori, went to each of the factories under their jurisdiction in Yeongdeungpo and began rounding up workers. That afternoon, Wuchang took his last breath. The doctor recorded it as a heart attack, but there was obvious lung damage from prolonged electrical and water torture.

*

How on earth was Icheol able to slip through the deadly net of this initial round-up? He was walking to Haincheon Station after having met with Wuchang when a funny feeling came over him. There, behind a telephone pole on the corner leading to the main street, stood a man smoking a cigarette. He paid close attention to the small, glowing ember despite the distance. As he passed the man, Icheol stole a glance at how he was dressed. He noted the rabbit-fur earmuffs and the fur-trimmed coat. He kept going until he reached a spot where he'd be nearly invisible in the dark and turned for another look. Two shadowy figures merged into one. He knew at once that he had a tail. All too late, Icheol realised that they'd been watching his rendezvous with Wuchang. Which meant that they'd first been tailing Wuchang. Which also meant that they were most likely hounds from the Incheon Police Station. He weighed his options. Should he slip away and escape through the darkened fields, or go to the station as planned and grab the next train out of there? He was already downtown. He did not look back again. He crossed the main street and quickly shook off his tail. He would stick with the plan.

When he entered the station, he spotted the man in the rabbit-fur earmuffs again, and watched as he sat down next to another man. Icheol kept his back to them as he stared at the train timetables. Then suddenly he turned. The man who'd been reading a newspaper was coming towards him. Their eyes met. The other man dropped his head and hurried past, but Icheol recognised him the instant they made eye contact. It was Choi Daryeong. He knew him well, Daryeong, the pig farmer who'd been friends with his older brother when they were growing up. His brother had told him that Daryeong was working for the police, and he'd spotted him sometimes, at a distance, lurking around in the market or out in front of the train station. Icheol waited for Daryeong to approach him, but to his surprise, Daryeong pretended not to know him. Icheol boarded his train, and Daryeong did not follow him onto it.

As soon as he got home, Icheol told his very pregnant wife what had happened.

'You have to contact your reppo right now and raise the alarm!' she said.

'I don't have a direct line of contact. We always use two different live drops.'

'But won't that take at least two days?'

'Yeah, and we don't have that kind of time. Daryeong knows who I am, too. We don't have time for this.'

Yeowok thought it over, then said, 'I'll go talk to Mageum Gomo. You better lie low.'

Icheol made no effort to meet Gwon's reppo. He'd never had reason before to rendezvous with him. In his opinion, it was far more important and urgent that he clean up the mess in Yeongdeungpo. He was considering severing the link between the International Party and the Communist Party reconstructionists in Gyeongseong. The Japanese Government-General's Police Bureau was busy tracking down the International Party; following Jaeyu's escape, hundreds of reconstructionists in Gyeongseong had already been rounded up. He met with Seonok first and informed her of the situation, and advised her to run, or if she did end up arrested, to testify to having been a mere errand runner, in order to lessen the danger to herself. Then he informed Daegil that he and Wuchang would be arrested soon, and spread word to Jo Yeongchun, who had ties with the International Party, and to Ji, to let them all know that they were each free to make their own choice.

However, he asked them to please protect Seonok.

Yeongchun reassured him that the members of his book club were just ordinary workers, so even if they were arrested, they knew so little that they couldn't inflict much damage. He added that he was planning to stall for time before handing over a list of their names. The fact of the matter was that, aside from Wuchang, he'd had no direct contact with any groups outside Yeongdeungpo.

Icheol knew that the moment the sun came up, detectives would be lurking outside his house. Neither he nor Yeowok could return home. The Willow Tree House was likewise out of the question, and so he asked Seonok to contact his sister-in-law.

For a long, long time after, Shin Geumi remembered every last detail of the fate that befell her husband's younger brother; his wife, Yeowok; and the baby in her belly, Jangsan. She would describe the way Seonok came to her, trembling, both hands in the air, to tell her of the emergency they were in. And when she spoke of dropping dinner preparations to rush out of the house, she never failed to mention how her mother-in-law, Juan-daek, appeared, as she always did when danger was afoot.

'We'd arranged to meet right outside the neighbourhood church's kindergarten. When I came out of the house, there was my mother-in-law, already walking a few steps ahead of me. I didn't say anything to her, but she knew exactly where to go. The church was surrounded by a brick wall, and through the bars of the gate I could see a slide and a swing set. When I stepped inside, my brother-in-law whispered to me from the shadows right next to the gate.'

Icheol briefly explained the situation and told her that his wife had gone to see Mageum Gomo and that they both had to make a run for it. Geumi asked where they were planning to go, and he said that he didn't know yet but either way they had to get out of Yeongdeungpo. The whole time, Juan-daek was standing next to them, stooped over, listening to their conversation. Normally, whenever she appeared to them, she would just sit or stand there or follow them around silently, but that day her husky voice sounded in Geumi's ears. *Hey, who was that one guy? You know, the guy, the teacher fella. You know who I mean. The nice one who spoke at your wedding. They should go there. He'll hide them.* Without thinking, Geumi blurted out what her mother-in-law was trying to tell her.

'Why don't you go see your old teacher Heo Sangwoo?'

Icheol nodded, and asked, 'You know where he lives, right?'

'Of course I do. I just saw him last Chuseok.'

Geumi took her brother-in-law to Dorim-jeong. Across the street from the primary school they had attended was a housing project for munitions workers. She felt awful about dropping in on Mr Heo's family right at dinner time. But Mr Heo's wife welcomed their unannounced visit. She knew the family well and regarded Geumi as a daughter-in-law. After enjoying the meal Mr Heo's wife offered them, Icheol explained the situation he was in.

'I'd heard here and there that you were involved in ideological struggle,' Mr Heo said. 'I was reminded of an old saying about avoiding the tip of the spear. You'd best lie low until things have died down.'

With that, he suggested that they stay the night and head out at dawn for his childhood home at the foot of Gwanaksan Mountain. His hometown was Nakkul in Siheung County, right on the border of Yeongdeungpo. It was a cozy place, surrounded by the foothills of Gwanaksan, which made it feel like more of a backwoods than it really was. The Yi boys had spent a couple of days there one summer.

When Juan-daek whispered to her to go see Mr Heo, Geumi knew at once that she was being guided in the right direction, because she believed Mageum Gomo's story about Juan-daek appearing during the floods to help. Later, when she told her husband, Ilcheol, about this, he nodded and said she'd done the right thing. He believed more firmly than Icheol that their mother was still looking out for them and had even experienced it himself.

The next day, Icheol left for Nakkul with Mr Heo. The country house was occupied by Mr Heo's younger brother, who had taken over the farm after their elderly parents passed. It had an extra building with two spacious rooms, so Icheol went ahead with imposing on them.

In Incheon, a handful of activists, including Geunshik, were able to lie low and keep their groups safe, but in Yeongdeungpo ordinary workers who'd participated in strikes over the past couple of years were all arrested and interrogated. Daegil, Yeongchun, Ji, Seonok, and others were caught in the first sweep. Around forty workers were arrested in Yeongdeungpo. Wuchang received the worst of the torture; after he died, the rest of the investigation focused on Daegil, who had been convicted and imprisoned before. The interrogations revealed that Icheol had been among the very first organisers, along with Wuchang, Daegil, and Ji, dating back to the time of the Yeongdeungpo Rail Works. It was also revealed that Icheol was the main liaison for the chief reconstructionists, and that his wife, Yeowok, had been the reppo for Kim Hyeongseon.

Yamashita came looking for Ilcheol at the Willow Tree House. Ilcheol took him to a tavern near the market. As he drank the makgeolli that Ilcheol poured for him, Yamashita didn't mince his words.

'If Icheol isn't captured, your family will be destroyed.'

Ilcheol chose his words carefully.

'Doesn't every family have its troublemaker? I am a law-abiding citizen of the empire. I graduated from the Government-General's railway academy and have been employed ever since by the Railway Bureau. As you well know, our father also devoted his life to working on trains and has a flawless record at the rail works as a technician. So please tell me how I can be of assistance.'

Daryeong gave him a hard look and said, 'Make your brother turn himself in. My loyalty to you was what kept me from arresting him when I first spotted him in Incheon. I deliberately let him go. But while interrogating those other guys, we learned all about Icheol's crimes, so I cannot continue to look the other way. Turns out even his wife is wrapped up in it. They could be arrested on the spot. Are the two of them together right now?'

Ilcheol felt panic set in.

'My sister-in-law is with child. She's due any day now. I'm sure she was only running errands that my brother put her up to. If you promise me one thing, I'll convince my brother to turn himself in to you.'

'Fine … as long as it's within reason!'

'Please don't arrest my pregnant sister-in-law. That is all I ask.'

Daryeong tapped his fingers on the table as he mulled over his answer.

'Very well. If Icheol is willing to convert, then I'll only bring his wife in for some informal questioning and then I'll let her go.'

'I'll do my best to convince him.'

'Don't take too long, though. Yi Jaeyu is on the run. If Icheol can tell us his whereabouts, I'll let him go as well, with only a warning.'

Ilcheol knew, having heard it from his wife, that his brother was hiding out at Mr Heo's childhood home in Nakkul. He went looking for him on his day off. Icheol was surprised to see his brother there in person. Ilcheol told him what he and Daryeong had discussed.

'How could you do this to me?' Icheol said. 'I know being a slave to the Japanese is how you survive, but …'

'That's right. Our father has spent his whole life carving away at metal and trying to raise us without our mother, and now it's my job to take care of our family for him. You can curse at me all you want, but this is how all people without a country live. Our father may not say anything, but he would understand you as well as I do. But what about your wife and your unborn child? You say you want to be an activist, but then you drag the womenfolk into it. You have a baby on the way, you should be protecting your family instead!'

Icheol began to cry. He didn't bother to wipe away the tears as he tilted his face up and let out a deep sigh.

'I didn't set out to do that. It just happened.'

'He promised to let your wife go with only a warning if you write a statement renouncing the cause.'

'I could never do that to my comrades. I'd sooner be tortured to death.'

Ilcheol pleaded with his younger brother, pouring his heart into his words.

'They're saying that Bang Wuchang died on the very first day of his interrogation. Can you imagine what they must have done to him? You have to find a way to stay alive. It's just a stupid piece of paper! Who cares? Your comrades will curse you for it, but you'll keep your health and live to fight again. It's not as if you're someone famous or one of the party leaders.'

The brothers were up all night together. The winter wind rattled the paper doors. Ilcheol tossed and turned and was just barely on the edge of sleep when his younger brother murmured in the dark, 'Hyeong, you awake?'

'Huh? Yeah.'

'Let's go to Yeongdeungpo tomorrow.'

'Are you sure?'

Icheol hesitated before answering.

'Just give me a chance to see Yeowok first, and then I'll turn myself in to Daryeong the day after.'

At Mageum Gomo's around lunchtime the following day, Yeowok was resting in the back room where she and Icheol had stayed before finding their own place, the very same room that Geumi had also lived in before getting married. She heard someone out in the courtyard and took a peek through the window, then ran out in surprise. Ilcheol was standing there with Icheol.

'I know you two have been through a lot,' Ilcheol said. 'Talk it over carefully before you decide.'

Mageum Gomo had run out, too, and was already overcome with tears from seeing how haggard Icheol had become.

'*Aego*, why can't you just run the tteok shop and drop all that other stuff?'

Ilcheol returned to the Willow Tree House, having promised to come get his brother the next morning.

That night, Icheol and Yeowok lay next to each other holding hands as they talked. There were a great many details they had to agree on in order to keep their written statements as simple and concise as possible. Everyone in Yeongdeungpo knew Icheol's story, but Yeowok's past would have to be erased entirely. They kept the part about where she grew up and about her going to Japan, but they left out everything that happened after she got married in Gunsan. Naturally, the details about her going to China or becoming an activist were also deleted. They decided to keep the part of her story where she came to Gyeongseong to work as a cafe girl after her first marriage ended, and happened to meet Icheol and agreed to run some errands for him.

Icheol worked on his story, too: He had met Bang Wuchang and Ahn Daegil, among others, during the strike at the rail works, and followed Wuchang's order to return to Gyeongseong and meet with a man named Yi Gwansu. It was regarding some sort of document; as far as Icheol could recall, something to do with strikes in Yeongdeungpo. After that, he acted as a reppo to meet with Yi Gwansu and someone from the International Party. Around that time, Han Yeowok was also acting as a go-between. He didn't know who Kim Hyeongseon or Yi Jaeyu were, only that he was meeting with a couple of bigwigs from the International Party and the Communist Party reconstructionists and that there would be an extra layer of security, which meant he would need an extra person as well. Thus, Han Yeowok had followed his orders and gone to the rendezvous point, completely clueless as to why, and returned having learned only the location of the next rendezvous point. Icheol had initially been drawn to the idea of workers' rights, but any deeper meaning or philosophy was too difficult for him to grasp. He liked the idea of independence from Japan. But that was too much for an individual to tackle on their own. Given the chance, he would abandon all of that nonsense and work hard as a faithful subject of the empire.

His written statement complete, husband and wife looked at each other and burst into tears.

'It's so humiliating,' Yeowok muttered between sobs. 'How am I supposed to live with this?'

Icheol choked up as he spoke. 'We have to reserve some of our forces. We need people who will stand up for the cause, but we also need those who can fight later. I'll do whatever it takes to get over this hurdle and come back to you. All you have to do is keep the tteok shop going while I'm gone.'

The next day, Ilcheol took his brother to the cafe nearest the police station, between the train station and the market. He telephoned 'Yamashita', who arrived at the cafe dressed in a natty suit with a black overcoat. Following close at his side was a police assistant. He addressed Icheol the moment he sat down across from him.

'Dusoe, it's been a long time. I take it you've come to a decision.'

Icheol said nothing and kept his head down while Ilcheol spoke.

'You'll leave my sister-in-law out of it, just like you promised?'

'Ah, well, that depends on what our Dusoe here does. Don't worry too much about it. I'll just get a statement from her before I release her.'

Yamashita turned to his assistant, who was watching from another table. The assistant came over and handcuffed Icheol. Ilcheol followed them as they led Icheol to the police station.

'Take good care of him,' Ilcheol said. 'I'll never forget your kindness.'

Yamashita smiled brightly and said, 'He'll have to do some time, as a crime has been committed. By the way, why are you still using a Korean name? Didn't you hear the announcement? Everyone will be falling into line now.'

Those words hit Ilcheol hard. Ah, he would need a Japanese name. If he wanted to stay on the Railway Bureau's payroll, he would have to do whatever the Government-General told him to do. Especially since he was one of the few Koreans they were allowing to become a locomotive engineer. He stopped at the entrance to the police station and watched his little brother being taken inside.

Icheol must have felt his older brother's gaze, but he never once looked back. When Icheol entered the interrogation room, the members of Yamashita's team were preparing for his rite of passage. Yamashita gave Icheol a push inside.

'Go easy on him,' he said to his team. 'He turned himself in.'

With that, he disappeared into the next room. One of the men punched Icheol in the face, sending him staggering to one side, where another man grabbed him by the collar and punched him on the other cheek. As Icheol stumbled forward, a third man pulled him up and kneed him in the stomach. Icheol fell backwards.

'Ho ho, you don't seem tough enough to be a communist! Where's the fight in you?'

Icheol's nose and mouth were already bleeding. His torturers, who were all Korean, took their time beating him. Then they stripped him out of his shirt and pants and sat him in front of the interrogation table in his underwear. Yamashita came back in to take his statement.

It was evening before they were finished, so they sent for Yeowok the following morning. Her interrogation was completed before noon, and she waited at the station until the end of day. Since their stories matched and Icheol had been cooperative, Yeowok was allowed to return home.

The prime suspects had already been interrogated, but even more than that, Gwon's network, the main line to the International Party, had been nearly all rounded up, which meant that resolving Icheol and his wife's roles as reppo was only a matter of matching up dates and times with the other's stories. Wuchang's death under interrogation ended up helping to protect all of the other workers in Yeongdeungpo from being systematically rounded up and tortured in turn. From the outset, the focus of the Government-General's Police Bureau's investigation had been on discouraging the International Party from trying to organise Korean workers, and so ordinary workers who expressed even a hint of remorse in their written statements were let go with a warning or had their charges suspended.

The exceptions included Daegil, Yeongchun, and Icheol, though Yeongchun and Icheol were still made to write statements, as dictated by Yamashita, swearing their allegiance to the Japanese Empire. Their punishments were also more severe, to match their more prominent ties to the movement. Daegil, a repeat offender, was sentenced to four years; Yeongchun, who'd run the book clubs, two years; and Icheol, the reppo, one year and six months. The prisons at the time were in such an awful state that a one-year sentence was as good as a death sentence: many grew ill during their imprisonment and suffered for a long time or even died after being released.

The International Party leaders, of course, received harsh sentences of three to four years or more. And after serving their prison sentences, they were remanded to detention centres to be kept under surveillance for public safety. A full year after the round-up, Jaeyu was arrested at last, but Gwansu escaped again and headed down into the provinces.

About a month after Icheol's arrest, while he was still undergoing his preliminary hearing, Yeowok gave birth. Geumi remembered it like it was yesterday. The Lunar New Year was only a few days away. Yeowok had planned to reopen their tteok shop, but Mageum and Geumi wouldn't let her and convinced her to move into the back room at Mageum's house instead. Someone had to be with her at all times since she could go into labour at any moment. Around 10.00 pm one evening, Geumi was asleep alone in her bedroom at home. Ilcheol had been promoted from assistant to the engineer of a freight train that ran between Gyeongseong and Sinuiju. As such, he was in charge of his own route. On that night, he was probably also asleep, far away, somewhere in the distant border city of Sinuiju. Geumi was awoken by someone shaking her.

'Huh … Who's there?'

'Yaeya, get up. Looks like my grandchild is coming now.'

Geumi opened her eyes and saw Juan-daek sitting next to her in the dark.

'Eomeoni, what're you doing here so late?'

As Geumi sat up, pulling her dishevelled hair back, Juan-daek gave her another shake.

'Hurry up already. Your sister-in-law's about to give birth.'

'Huh? Now?'

Geumi sprang up, pulled her clothes on, and stepped out into the maru, listening for sounds from her father-in-law Baekman's room. She heard him snoring. Deliberately, she let out a loud cough. Baekman's snoring stopped at once, and he asked in a sleepy-sounding voice, 'Is that you, Jisan Eomma?'

'Yes, I'm heading over to Mageum Gomo's house. I think my sister-in-law might be in labour.'

Baekman sat up and pushed the door open. Though he liked to

pretend otherwise, he was aware of his daughter-in-law's gift and couldn't help blurting out a question.

'So, uh, another boy this time?'

'Yes, Abeonim.'

'All right then. Hurry along. I'll keep an eye on Jisan.'

She went as fast as her feet would carry her to Mageum's house in Saetmal. Juan-daek had arrived first and was waiting for her. She knocked on the gate, waking Mageum. When Mageum saw the two of them, she knew why they were there.

'I take it the baby's coming soon. Shall I call the midwife?'

'Why bother? There's already three of us.'

'Three?' Mageum started to ask, then laughed. 'I guess you're right. It does feel reassuring to have her with us.'

Not even five minutes later, Yeowok's labour pains began, and the baby was soon born. Geumi and Mageum caught the baby, cut the cord, and bathed and swaddled him. Her ordeal over, Yeowok fell asleep while the sweat was still beaded on her forehead. The baby closed its eyes and fell asleep beside its mother.

Geumi and Mageum had known since before the birth that the baby's name would be Jangsan. Geumi was busy admiring Jisan's cousin when she suddenly saw a dark energy, like a black cloud, surround him, and the baby's face turned pitch-black. Then she saw the baby lying in a bamboo basket. A white cloth was coiled around the basket. This baby was going to die. Tears spilled down her face.

Mageum came back in with some seaweed soup for the mother and saw Geumi crying.

'Why the sudden tears?'

'Oh, it's nothing. Just, the baby is so beautiful.'

Mageum Gomo thought about Icheol, the boy she'd raised like her own, being in prison, and now this baby without his father, and started to cry, too.

'Things will get better someday!'

Twenty-one days later, when Yeowok had finished her lying-in, Geumi brought her and the baby to the Willow Tree House. Baekman had offered to sleep in his workshop, and asked Geumi several times to move Yeowok and Jangsan into his room. Mageum Gomo had insisted on looking after them herself, since her sons were both attending primary school during the day, but when Geumi conveyed Baekman's earnest wishes, she helped to pack their belongings.

'*Aigo*, that stubborn brother of mine,' she said. 'I guess I'm running the tteok shop on my own, then.'

Jisan was two years old by then, and the two boys reminded Baekman so much of his own sons when they were little that he felt like he had become a young man again. When Jangsan turned a hundred days old, Baekman decided to throw a small celebration. After all, they were no longer as poor as they used to be. Mageum Gomo explained in detail to Geumi how a baby's hundred-day celebration was held. First thing in the morning, they set a table in honour of Samshin Halmeoni with cooked white rice, seaweed soup, white tteok, tteok with red beans, sweets, and fruits. Uncooked white rice, white thread, and money were placed on a small tray covered with white paper. Yeowok sat facing the table with Jangsan on her lap and Mageum Gomo and Geumi on each side of her. Together, they bowed and prayed for the baby's long life. As the hundred-day celebration was meant to be led by women, Baekman stayed in his workshop until they were done. Then they all sat together in the main room. Other than Icheol being in jail, everything up to that point had been relatively calm and peaceful for Baekman's family, compared to the lives of other Koreans, at least.

It was late May or early June, after the azaleas had reached full bloom and were set to wither on their stalks. Jisan and Jangsan both caught colds. Jangsan's cold started first, with a runny nose that developed into a cough. Then Jisan followed his little cousin and showed the same symptoms. Geumi and Yeowok kept the boys confined in separate rooms and consulted with each other as they looked after them. They ran a fever for three days, and then red spots flowered on their faces and chests, which was when the women realised that this was no ordinary cold. Mageum Gomo rushed over to the house to check on them. Her face turned dark.

'That's not the sniffles, that's the measles. You can tell from that rash!'

The two women ran neck and neck, carrying Jisan and Jangsan, to a herbal-medicine clinic near the intersection. The doctor there confirmed that it was definitely measles. The measles had long been known as untreatable: medicines were useless, and surviving it was the will of heaven. Those who were to get better suffered a high fever for several days, and then a rash broke out over their whole bodies and made its way down to the tips of the toes, after which the fever let up on its own and the person was out of bed. But for those who were to die, the rash would linger on their bellies as their cough worsened, until finally they passed. At the time, the measles had been making its way through the neighbourhood, taking the lives of several of its children. Jisan's rash spread to his toes and went away, but Jangsan's didn't.

Though Geumi knew this would happen, she hadn't breathed a word of it to Mageum Gomo, let alone to Jangsan's mother. She also didn't tell them that she had seen it with her own eyes, the evil spirit that spread disease. This was before Jisan and Jangsan had fallen ill with coughs and fevers. It was near dusk, and the setting sun was shining right into the alley outside the Willow Tree House, casting some parts in deep shadow and dazzling her eyes where she stood. She had just stepped out of the gate to go to the market when she saw a little girl standing in front of the house. The girl wore a yellow blouse and a pretty red skirt, with her hair in two long braids, and she was hopping around on one foot like she was playing a game of hopscotch.

'Girl, what are you doing here,' Geumi muttered sharply, 'messing around in front of other people's houses?'

The girl stopped short, looking surprised.

'Ajumeoni, you can see me?'

'Of course I can see you. I can also see that you've got your eye on our house. You wanna find out what it's like to be cooked in a steamer?'

The girl stuck her tongue out and ran away, but not before saying, 'Ha! I've already been inside your house!'

Geumi's heart sank when she heard that. It seemed the evil spirit had slipped inside while she was napping. The girl was running to this house and that, flapping the hem of her skirt as she went, backlit against the setting sun. And yet Geumi, being a modern woman and not the type to seek out shamans or fortune tellers, had done nothing. The morning that Jangsan died, Geumi caught sight of something near the gate, and set to work filling a gourd bowl with cold water, stirring some ground chilli into it, and sprinkling it in front.

'Damn you, you evil thing! Get away from here!'

A man came from the bier house to prepare Jangsan. He dressed the little one in his newborn clothes, swaddled him in a clean cloth, and placed him inside a bamboo basket. He wrapped the basket round and round with a length of white cotton and carried the tiny coffin on his back with the help of two shoulder straps. Baekman and Mageum Gomo went with the man, while Geumi held onto the grief-stricken Yeowok to keep her at home. Later all they told her was that they'd put him to rest in the corner of a public graveyard.

After saying goodbye to Jangsan, Yeowok ailed for two weeks, and then suddenly it was summer. She went to visit Icheol in the faraway Daejeon Prison. She never told anyone about that visit, and Icheol as well kept his silence after being released and returning home, and so no one knew what had been said between the two of them. But Geumi assumed that Yeowok must have told her husband about Jangsan's birth and death and her reasons for leaving.

One day that autumn, Yeowok suggested to Ilcheol and Geumi that they all go out for dinner. Their curiosity was piqued when she said she'd reserved a table at the neighbourhood's biggest Chinese restaurant. After they were seated and the food had been served, Yeowok told them her plans.

'I'm so sorry for everything that's happened. I just wasn't meant to be an ordinary housewife. Jangsan Abeoji and I talked it over when I visited him. I'm leaving.'

Geumi had already guessed what she was going to say, and tried to stop her, despite feeling helpless to change anything.

'But why leave when you have so much to look forward to when your husband gets out?'

Yeowok gave her a weak, wry smile.

'I've come too far to leave this path, and I owe my comrades so, so much. I'm going back to Manchuria, to where I was before.' She sounded resolute as she added, 'Over there, there's a clear line between life and death. Because there, the battle is fought with guns, not politics.'

Ilcheol broke his silence.

'Do you have a place to stay in Manchuria?'

'I'm planning to head back to a village where I know some people.'

'Where is that?'

'Near Chientao.'

'The Japanese have tightened up security along the Dumangang River,' Ilcheol said. 'It's not like it used to be. You'll be safer if you head along the Amnokgang River and travel by train from Manchuria. But will the thought police let you leave?'

'I know it's shameless of me to ask, but I was hoping you might help me ...'

Geumi teared up when she heard that, and dabbing at her eyes with a handkerchief, she whispered to Ilcheol, 'Yeobo, we have to help her. I would have done the same.'

Ilcheol mulled it over.

'Give me a few days,' he said at last. 'I'll get things ready.'

After Ilcheol had driven the Gyeongui Line freight train back and forth a couple of times, Yeowok's departure date was set. Geumi got back the deposit for the tteok shop and gave it to Yeowok for her travel expenses. Of course, no one imagined at the time that Mageum Gomo would move to Manchuria, too, only a year later. Yeowok went to Yongsan Station, and following Ilcheol's directions, stowed away on his freight train. Ilcheol's assistant was a fellow Korean. This was possible because the intensified war effort in Manchuria and the expansion of the continental battlefield meant that Japanese rail workers were being conscripted into the Kwantung Army, leaving vacancies that were filled by Koreans, who were not yet permitted to join the army. Ilcheol put Yeowok in the very first carriage, right behind the locomotive. That carriage mostly held the Railway Bureau's own freight or items belonging to VIPs. Senior engineers had outfitted it with bedding, where they took turns sleeping during the long-distance sections of track. The presence of side doors in addition to the large sliding doors made it easy to move back and forth between there and the locomotive. Yeowok lay down in a corner covered up by boxes. The train raced through the night. While the locomotive was being replaced in Pyeongyang, Ilcheol stayed at his post rather than retire to the break room. When they reached Sinuiju, Ilcheol used his day off there to escort his sister-in-law to Guuiju. They waited until nightfall, then met the ferryman that Ilcheol had made arrangements with when he'd asked around a few days earlier. The river crossing that avoided the border guard posts was used by many merchants, labourers, smugglers, and anti-Japanese organisers, and was even easier to manage in the winter when the river was frozen over. Yeowok wore a Western-style outfit, which would be safest in Manchuria. Korean hanboks stood out too much, and Chinese clothes somehow didn't fit Koreans very well, but Western clothes could be worn by anyone. Before boarding the ferry, Yeowok bowed deeply to Ilcheol.

'I don't know when I will see you all again. The day Joseon gains its independence, I will go to your house in Yeongdeungpo. Please give my regards to Geumi Hyeongnim, too.'

Ilcheol returned her bow and said, 'We will wait for you, Jangsan Eomma. Please stay well until then!'

13

Jino awoke while it was still pitch-black out. Today was the 300th day of his sit-in. He had started preparing for the occasion a few days earlier. Leaders from the Metal Workers' Union and various civic groups had organised another ochetuji-style demonstration. The plan was to gather at the base of the chimney early in the morning, hold a brief rally, and then make their way together to the Blue House, prostrating themselves on the ground as they went.

Though it was now March, the air was chilly; it was still winter at the top of the chimney. A doctor was being sent up to check on Jino's health. They also had to upload a video to YouTube that the public-relations staff were working on, so that everyone could see what was happening. For safety reasons, no one aside from the doctor was allowed to climb the chimney. Which meant that Jino had to somehow film himself explaining why he'd climbed up there in the first place, what his demands were, and how his sit-in was going.

He wiggled his hands until he was able to slip an arm out and unzip the sleeping bag in one quick move. The cold cut him to the bone. He quickly layered on more clothes and pulled a pair of snow pants over his long underwear. He got out of the sleeping bag wearing wool socks and hurriedly pulled on his winter boots. At last he was ready. A look at his mobile phone told him it was 5.10 in the morning. Wasn't it too early? No worries — his colleagues had said they would be there at seven. The two hours would fly by. Jino knew he had a lot to get done before then.

His first task was to hang the banner his colleagues had sent up the previous day. He took care not to let the wind blow it away or tangle it up. He was planning to hang it all the way around the catwalk. The fabric had been punched with holes and threaded with rope, so all he had to do was tie the rope to the metal bars. Holding it tightly under one arm, he unfolded one end first and began securing it to the railing, tying off the knots as he went. Visible through the back of the banner, the bright-red text read:

STOP THE SELL-OFF, RESTART THE FACTORY!

Multi-talented Cha, the youngest of the five of them, had texted him a graphic that he'd made. Jino couldn't stop looking at it. It was a digital flyer announcing the events they had planned to mark the 300th day of the chimney sit-in.

DEFEND THE DEMOCRATIC LABOUR UNION!
RESTORE EMPLOYMENT!
STOP THE SELL-OFF!

HE GAVE HIS YOUTH TO THE FACTORY
THEY BLED HIM DRY AND SAID THEY DIDN'T NEED HIM

SO HE TOOK THEIR CHIMNEY!

COME SUPPORT YI JINO
ON THE 300TH DAY OF HIS CHIMNEY SIEGE

Superimposed over a picture of the chimney, the words looked like living, moving things. His throat suddenly closed up and his breath stopped. He let out a long sigh. Three years of cold indifference had passed while he'd fought the lay-offs on the ground, and the company's surprise shutdown of the factory had triggered a conflict of interests between permanent and casual workers and splintered the union branch's leadership. Then, the company-sponsored union had been born and the lay-offs rationalised. He gazed up at the still-dark sky. A hard wind swept over the chimney. The cold was clinging jealously and refusing to move on. That old line of poetry, 'spring has arrived but is nothing like spring', wasn't talking about the weather, but rather about the challenges that workers like him were facing.

As soon as Jino sat beneath his tarp canopy, all he wanted was to crawl back into his sleeping bag. Then he saw Yeongsuk's bottle leaning up against Geumi's. That's right. Yeongsuk Nuna had done this, too. She had endured over a year at the top of a shipyard container crane several years earlier. Everyone called her the woman of steel, but she herself said she only wanted to be a nuna — an older sister — to the younger men. As some factory worker-slash-poet had written, Yeongsuk was a beautiful person who'd transformed those enormous steel cranes into towering green trees, like some sort of earth goddess. During the time of year when the enormous steel tower grew hot in the blazing sun and burned Yeongsuk's frail flesh, she had written a letter to her colleagues about a dream she had one night in the metal room of the crane's cab, still hot and stifling from the day's heat: She felt a faint vibration creep its way up from below the crane. The heavy, square support pillars of the crane began to move, then turned into roots that squirmed and wiggled their way into the ground. They bore their way deep into the earth and spread, then sprouted leaves, and their dull yellow paint came back to life as a vibrant green. The metal turned into a living tree, while the leaves grew thick and abundant, casting a cooling shade as they grew taller and taller. Finally, all traces of the container crane were gone, transformed, into an enormous tree. The story of Yeongsuk's dream was more beautiful than anything Jino had ever read in a book. During her crane sit-in, a worker had jotted down the main points of her life story up until then. Jino still remembered it.

Ran away from home at fifteen.
Delivered newspapers, worked in a sweatshop, then as a bus attendant,
before becoming Taesan Heavy Industries & Construction's first female welder.

Fired at twenty-six, dragged into the interrogation room three times,
sent to prison twice, and on the run for five years,
now a fifty-three-year-old woman with greying hair.
Her scars tell the story of the suffering
of the workers and common folk throughout modern Korean history.
But even atop that crane of despair,
she remains brighter and livelier
and more full of humour than anyone else in this land.

When Yeongsuk Nuna was at the top of that container crane, Jino raced down south to the port city along with his co-workers and concerned citizens to support her protest. What strength had propelled that woman, who was no longer young and robust, up the ladder? Because of her years of unwavering activism, the union had given her the stiffly formal title of Advisory Councillor, but to her younger colleagues, it was nothing more than another name for their Big Sister. Later it became known that she had planned to die on top of the tower, so that more people would understand why the co-worker who'd been fired and protested alongside her had taken his own life. After enduring over a year up there, her body had grown as weak and thin as a fallen branch, but her eyes still sparkled. That was when the authorities arrested her and slapped her with a year and a half behind bars. As a wave of anger swept across the country in response, Yeongsuk was transferred to a hospital, and once things died down she returned to a quiet, everyday life free of rumours or commotion. She cut off all contact and went into seclusion, maybe because she was exhausted, or simply because she needed to get her life in order. Then, news came that she was ill, and soon she was gone, leaving only what she had stood for. Across the country, protesting workers began taking to high places instead of the streets. Demonstrating their ability to endure a long, drawn-out, and perilous struggle was the only way for poor, powerless, nameless people to share the injustice they'd suffered with the people of the world. It became apparent to them that the world was not on their side, and that change would only come one tiny and very, very slow step at a time. He called out her name. Yeongsuk Nuna.

She was standing on the railing, dressed in dark-blue work wear, her greying hair shaved into a crew cut. Jino forgot all about having already seen Little Clippers and Jingi and his grandmother, and muttered in surprise, 'Nuna! What are you doing here?'

'You survived 300 days, so of course I had to come see you, Union Branch Chief.'

'Nuna, you said that between Jeon Tae-il taking his life in the 1970s and Juik Hyeong taking his in 2003, Korea hasn't changed at all.'

'Wasn't I right?'

Jino asked her the same question he'd asked his grandmother.

'Then why do we have to keep fighting?'

Yeongsuk sat down next to him.

'It's okay to stop now, if it's too much.'

He hung his head for the longest time before answering.

'It's not really about me, it's about the three hard years that my colleagues down there went through. And it's not just us. They say there are ten million workers.'

'Where'd the company vanish to after laying everyone off? The Philippines. They went looking for a country with cheaper, more-docile workers with even less power than us, and moved their entire operation over there. They just started, and already dozens of Filipino workers have been injured or killed.'

'I've been a coward ever since I was little. Ever since hearing that my family was branded as three generations of commies.'

Yeongsuk responded without a trace of surprise, 'What does that mean?'

'It means that the men in my family have always been labourers, from the time Japan colonised us and even during the war.'

'In North Korea, the leaders claim to be the same as us — from the labouring class. But in the end, there's only one thing that needs to be said.'

Yeongsuk Nuna spoke of an autumn night many years ago, when

she was around fourteen years old. School was over for the day, and she was helping her mother at home. Her father had quit tenant farming and was travelling around to different construction sites for work, spending only a few days at home every couple of months. While working far away in another province, he injured his back and returned home in terrible shape. After that, he spent every penny he found on alcohol, then would wander the village alleyways, going near the houses of people he hated to scream at no one, only to return home to pass out. That night, Yeongsuk and her mother went to a sweet-potato field that had already been picked over and groped around, hurriedly turning over the soil with a hoe in the dark, until they managed to find one or two potatoes that had not yet been dug up. They worked that way deep into the night, making their way along the expanse of furrows, until they had collected a sack. That would be enough to keep them fed for the next two weeks. They were half-carrying, half-dragging the sack home together when someone came running after them. It was the grandmother of the family that owned the sweet-potato field. She ran after them so fast, she was panting for air, and grabbed the sack with both hands and dug her heels in.

'You took this from our field, didn't you? Who said you could take these without permission? We were going to harvest them tomorrow!'

Sounding crestfallen, Yeongsuk's mother said that, as a matter of fact, she was planning to visit them tomorrow to explain herself, and that the two of them would be happy to work for the potatoes.

The grandmother dug her heels in deeper and said, 'I don't care what happens tomorrow, you're not taking these tonight.'

With nothing to eat for supper, mother and daughter trudged home in low spirits. Yeongsuk's mother plopped down in front of the gate and burst into tears.

'Why can't you let us live, too, you bastards? Let us live …'

Jino understood that this was what Yeongsuk Nuna meant by the one thing that needed to be said.

He said, 'The fact that workers are staging sit-ins in these high places in order to spread the word to more people about the conditions we face and what our demands are is already a huge form of social change. My grandmother always used to say that the world moves forward one teeny tiny step at a time.'

Yeongsuk Nuna nodded.

'That's true,' she said. 'When I was a kid, forget about unionising, if you even discussed walking out or going on strike — or, heck, if you even whispered in a co-worker's ear about it, you'd get arrested. That's why we used to seek sanctuary in churches and cathedrals. To try to avoid being branded as commies. You violated the Assembly and Demonstration Act, right? That's why you went to prison ...'

'Yes, but I got out after one winter. Whereas they kept dragging you off to the interrogation room over nothing, and put you away twice. Then you had to go underground for five years. Meanwhile, we were pussyfooting around and only started fighting back after it was too late.'

A young university student lost his life while being tortured in the anti-communism interrogation room of the National Police Headquarters. Up until the entire facility was eventually shut down under the pressure of public sentiment, the organisers of labour disputes called it 'the torture factory'. When Yeongsuk was dragged there along with her male colleagues, she was separated from the rest of them as the only woman. The room had cement walls painted white, a single desk, two chairs, and a military-issue wooden cot. Attached to the room was a bathroom. Inside the large bathroom was a disproportionately large bathtub, making it look like some sort of VIP suite. But once that tub filled with water, it transformed into a place of death. According to Jino's older colleagues, the things they did in that room had all been passed down from the Japanese colonial occupation. Electrodes placed on your heels would send shockwaves up through your calves, rattle your intestines, shred the nerve endings clustered like spider webs in your spine, and explode inside your brain. Two men held Yeongsuk upside down and dunked her head into the bathtub. They sat her down and placed a handkerchief over her face and slowly dripped water from a teapot onto it until the fabric clung to her skin and suffocated her as the water trickled into her nose and throat. They stripped her naked and strapped her to a chilseongpan — the board drilled with seven holes, one for each star in the Big Dipper, to carry the deceased in their coffin — doused her with water and used the electrodes on her. Dislocated all her joints and left her to suffer, then popped them back into place one after the other. For those coming out of the interrogation room, the fear of torture was outweighed by the shame and humiliation. Weeping and begging on their knees, saying yes, yes, and writing down whatever confession they were ordered to write. Job loss, hunger, poverty, overtime, exhaustion, illness, and other silly, specific sufferings were reduced to mere personal circumstances, and reports were filled with nonsense words like revolution, struggle, Pyeongyang, Kim Il-sung, spies. The detectives knew damn well that the goals of the strikes and walkouts were slightly better pay and working conditions, but throwing around accusations of communism was a longstanding investigative technique. Hence, the name of the government-mandated 'Anti-communism Room'.

'Do you know what the hardest part of retreating from the world was?' Yeongsuk Nuna asked.

'The first thing that comes to mind is the day I was fired,' Jino said. 'I felt like I'd suddenly been cast out of the world. Thrown away because I was useless.'

'Yes, first I was disposed of, and then I was saddled with the social sin of being a wanted criminal. The hardest part was the loneliness.'

Jino knew all too well about the loneliness he was struggling with at the top of his chimney. Every time his colleagues appeared without fail to send up his meals and news of the world down there, he pulled himself together again, he got a hold of himself, but he would just as quickly find himself sinking back into the treachery of his daily routine. The question would grab him suddenly by the throat: what the hell was he thinking with this pointless stunt of his? On those bitterly cold winter nights when he would look down at the glowing windows of apartment and office buildings or the stream of headlights from cars racing swiftly, sleekly, and without end along the riverside highway, it sunk in all over again, that the world was forever indifferent. It wasn't that he'd been tossed aside or forgotten; he was simply of no more interest than a tree planted next to a road.

Yeongsuk Nuna half-whispered, 'Ages ago, when I was on the wanted list, I went back to my old hometown.'

'Yes, I think I might know this story.'

She was walking up ahead along a newly built road, and Jino was following her. The sun was setting behind them, and the road was unpaved.

'Nuna, why are we suddenly in your hometown?'

'My first stint in prison lasted a year and two months. I'd worked in factories for so many years without ever once catching a cold, but after only a year in prison I was in bad shape.'

A wanted criminal, Yeongsuk drifted from place to place, taking whatever work she could find, which meant frequently going hungry and working herself to the bone, until it all caught up to her and she came down with a bad case of the flu. After a long ordeal, she finally seemed to be on the mend except for a slight cough that refused to go away. With the help of colleagues from a local union branch, she was able to see a doctor, and found out she was in the early stages of tuberculosis. The doctor said that the disease had supposedly been all but eradicated from society, but could still be contracted by anyone whose immune system was weakened by poor nutrition and overwork. She began a course of medication, and was supposed to get lots of rest and eat well, but this was compromised by the anxiety of never knowing where or when she might get arrested, and by the poor air in her cramped, coal-heated tenement room.

She longed for her hometown in Chungcheong Province. There, her mother was still alive, and though her four siblings had all scattered in search of work, her second-eldest brother had stayed behind to look after the farm. She took an intercity bus to Cheongyang and walked from there along the new road for thirty kilometres or so, following the upper reaches of the Jicheon Stream to the village of Murangol. Many of the homes in the village had been abandoned; only the elderly remained. She had deliberately waited until evening to avoid being seen by any of the villagers, but there were still a few people out walking. She sat on the slope of the hill facing her old neighbourhood until it was good and dark, and waited for things to grow quiet. When she figured everyone would be sitting around their dinner tables, she went to her old house. Jino went, too, following her careful stride. An unfamiliar dog barked, and the door of one of the small houses swung open. She heard her older brother's voice.

'Who's out there?'

Yeongsuk approached the house.

'It's me, Yeongsuk!'

Her mother, who'd been sitting on the floor behind her brother, scooted over to the door and poked her head out.

'Who? Yeongsuk?'

Her sister-in-law came out of the kitchen at the far end of the house, then her two nephews who'd been eating dinner came running out, too, and stared as Yeongsuk and her mother hugged. Jino stood against the wall and watched as the family sat down around the dinner table. Under the pale fluorescent light, with her mother's food in front of her, Yeongsuk was becoming a child again. Her mother brought her a hot bowl of soup and a bowl of rice, and handed her a spoon and chopsticks. As Yeongsuk lifted a spoonful of rice to her mouth, her mother placed a bite of salted mackerel, Yeongsuk's favourite, on top of it.

'After all these years with only your letters that my grandson reads to me, I finally get to see you again — all grown up now.'

Yeongsuk's older brother introduced her to his wife and kids for the first time, as well as to Dolsoe, the yellow dog who'd barked at her in the yard. The scene changed: Yeongsuk was resting in the small room attached to the kitchen when she heard someone cough. Her brother entered. His eyes gleamed from a darkly suntanned face.

'What'd you do this time?' he asked.

'It was no big deal. They'll let me off soon enough.'

'I wish I could say that were true, but they came looking for you again just a few days ago.'

'Who?'

He answered, sounding annoyed, 'Who do you think? A detective from the intelligence unit in town.'

'They came all the way out here?'

'What do I know? They said something about you being a pinko and asked if we'd heard from you.'

Jino sat behind Yeongsuk and thought about how his family had been hearing this same thing their whole lives. Workers with opinions of their own were always branded as commies in this country. Whereas if you kept your head down, focused only on work, and accepted the few pennies they tossed your way, then they said you were one of the good ones. They never, ever said you were a slave.

Yeongsuk's brother said, 'I just don't get it. I was so jealous when you became a welder, I regretted staying behind and getting stuck on the farm. Why'd you have to go and get fired from that good job and do time and be called a commie? Why suffer like that?'

'It's such a long story that I wouldn't even know where to begin. Everyone is struggling to get by. But if you work hard, then you deserve to be treated well for it.'

'There've been so many times where I, too, had nothing to show for all the lettuce, peppers, and other vegetables we grow in the greenhouse. Some years we break even, and others the price drops so badly that I end up tossing it all back into the fields. But we just see it as the luck of the draw.'

'All of that is just doing hucksters a favour. The people we're fighting are even bigger hucksters. All they think about is money. They don't care about people. And those with power are all on the side of those with money.'

'But at least you're not starving. Isn't that a good thing?'

'Oppa, I'm not well. I came here so I could rest up for a few days, then be on my way.'

Her brother let out a sigh and gazed up at the ceiling.

'I'm the neighbourhood chief. I have to tell them you're here, by tomorrow or the day after tomorrow at the latest, just in case anyone saw you.'

Yeongsuk was not upset by this. Back in the old days, when female factory workers went on strike, the police would bring their families to the factory to drag them out. The cops would stand back and laugh at the sight of mothers screaming at their daughters, older brothers dragging their younger sisters out of the building. Yeongsuk stayed in her room the next day and avoided even stepping into the courtyard to give Dolsoe a pat on the head. After two nights of rest, she got up before the crack of dawn and left Murangol.

While on the run, her health worsened again, so she went looking for Jeongja Eonni, hoping to be able to stay with her. Five years older than Yeongsuk, Jeongja was also from Murangol but had moved up to Bucheon, which was where Yeongsuk went looking for her when she ran away from home at the age of fifteen. Jeongja used to say that if you wanted to move to the big city, you first needed a hill you could lean up against, meaning someone or something you could rely on. So Jeongja had started out at her taxi-driving older brother's house until she landed a job and moved into a jjokbang tenement. Hardworking and nimble-fingered, she moved quickly up through the ranks in the sweatshop, from fetching materials to assisting to manning her own sewing machine. When Yeongsuk came calling, Jeongja was reminded of herself when she first came up to the big city, and readily invited Yeongsuk to stay with her. Yeongsuk delivered newspapers in the morning, ran sundry errands at a small factory during the day, and got a job in a clothing sweatshop. Yeongsuk was able to become a labourer on the threshold of Seoul thanks to her Jeongja Eonni. She found another job as a bus attendant, calling out the stops and helping passengers on and off, but she soon realised the pay wasn't enough to survive on. At twenty-one, she took welding classes, gained practical experience, and passed the certification exam. It was a small success, six years in the making. She left Bucheon when she landed the job at Taesan Heavy Industries & Construction. At twenty-six, she joined the union and was fired, after which she went from job to job at various subcontracting factories. She was in her late thirties when she was put on the wanted list.

Yeongsuk contacted Jeongja and was amazed to learn that she was still working at the same Bucheon sweatshop, which by some miracle had not gone under. There were always small businesses to be found on the outskirts of the city that were keeping themselves afloat by taking subcontracting work. The factory owner-slash-manager-slash-crew chief, a kind-hearted man in his fifties who'd started out as a sewing-machine operator, said that skilled workers like Jeongja were as good as business partners to him.

Jeongja had married a worker the same age as her. Most female factory workers grew old doing the same work they'd always done without wanting more, whereas, unless they were engineers, the male labourers, including Jeongja's husband, grew bored of doing the same repetitive, menial tasks that were typical of the light industries. But if they quit the factories, the only business they could hope to start for themselves was making or selling food, which they had no training in, and if those businesses went under or didn't go well, the only work left for them was in construction. Nowadays there were many foreign workers, which made it harder to find manual labour jobs with good pay and working conditions. If they stood around and waited with the other day labourers on the corner at dawn and got selected, they'd make some money that day, but it didn't happen every day. Some left the city in search of work and never returned. That was what had happened with Jeongja's husband. When Jeongja finally got around to looking for him, he was living with another woman on an island somewhere in the south and working on a fish farm.

Meanwhile, she'd given birth to their daughter and had nothing left besides their fifty-square-metre rented apartment. Her daughter had just started secondary school and was already breaking her mother's heart. She often didn't come home, and Jeongja was tied to the factory and unable to keep track of her whereabouts. Yeongsuk offered to help ease Jeonga's worries, and went to the school in search of her daughter, only to find out that she had been skipping school for over a month. From a girl in the daughter's class, Yeongsuk found out which computer-game cafe the daughter frequented, and from the young man working part-time at the cafe, she found out which motel she could find her at. Male and female students who'd run away from home would bunk together at that motel.

Yeongsuk agonised over whether to tell her; when she did, Jeongja nearly blew her stack. Before working in the sweatshop, Jeongja, too, had worked as a bus attendant at the baby-faced age of twenty. Dealing with the rough-mannered drivers and stubborn passengers had given her a core of steel, which was now molten and bubbling over from the news of her daughter. Yeongsuk was no stranger to this inner steel; she believed she was filled with it, too.

'I'm gonna bash some heads in!' Jeongja shouted.

She searched around the apartment and pulled a baseball bat out from behind the rubbish bin next to the kitchen sink. She had joked that it was there to protect her and her daughter. Though Yeongsuk had only told her the name of the motel, Jeongja rushed out of the apartment and hurried through the maze of alleyways.

'Eonni, do you know where it is? The Mate Boutique Hotel?'

'Boutique hotel, my arse. It used to be called the Arirang Motel.'

Sure enough, it turned out to be an old, shabby, three-storey cement building with some sloppy tiling slapped on the front. Jeongja burst through the entrance and accosted the older-looking woman behind the desk.

'I hear you're allowing minors to shack up here? Where are they?'

'Wha-what? What're you talking about …'

Jeongja tapped the bat against the cement floor and shouted at the woman. 'Are you the owner? Tell me the room number right now, before I report you and have this shithole shut down!'

The woman stammered. She was probably just a desk clerk. 'I think they're on the top floor. The last room. I had nothing to do with it.'

Before the woman could even finish speaking, Jeongja was racing up the stairs, two at a time, breathing hard. She went to the room at the end of the darkened hallway, as instructed, and paused to press her ear to the door before knocking. Standing behind her, Yeongsuk could make out the sounds of multiple people inside, talking and laughing. She heard someone say, 'Who's there?' Jeongja knocked again without responding, and the door cracked open. She shoved the person back, flung the door open, and rushed inside, with Yeongsuk right behind her.

There were six teenagers: four boys and two girls. There were piles of blankets and bedding everywhere, beer and soju bottles discarded in the middle of the room, and crumbs littering the floor. Jeongja held the baseball bat out in front of her like she was aiming a rifle.

'Everyone, on your knees!' she shouted.

One of the two girls, of course, was her daughter.

A tall, gangly, long-haired boy said, 'You can't tell us what to do. You're not a cop.'

Jeongja went right up to him and jabbed him in the chest with her bat. The boy gasped and sat down, pretending that he couldn't breathe.

'You son of a bitch, I'm worse than the cops. I'm a mother!'

'Eommaaaa, I'll go home.'

Yeongsuk pulled Jeongja's daughter away by the hand and said, 'Let's go.'

'Go? Go where?' demanded Jeongja. 'We need to turn these little shits over to the police.'

Once Yeongsuk was able to calm Jeongja down and get her out of the room, Jeongja burst into tears and started smacking her daughter on the back. Yeongsuk struggled to keep them apart and to keep the daughter from running off. As soon as they got home, Jeongja seemed to let go completely, and broke into a loud and bitter wail.

'They say women who have bad luck with men also have bad luck with their children. Why did I work so hard to feed and school a slut like her?'

She searched for a pair of scissors and grabbed her daughter by the hair, roughly cutting the girl's hair off, striking her daughter randomly as the girl squirmed in her grip. Yeongsuk took Jeongja's daughter into the other room and covered her up with a blanket.

'What happened to you?' Yeongsuk asked, keeping her voice calm and quiet. 'You were doing so well before.'

'Quit acting like you're better than me!' Jeongja shouted. 'You got yourself a nice job in a big factory that kept you well fed, and now you go around talking about union this and movement that? I'm so sick of jerks like you. People like you make it harder for people like me, who didn't get to go to school, and have to work ourselves to the bone. You're a commie, aren't you? Don't try to fool me with all those lies about the world getting better. Just fuck off! I don't want to see you!'

Jeongja grabbed Yeongsuk's ugly, old bag from the corner of the kitchen and threw it at her feet, then pulled Yeongsuk's clothes from their hangers and threw them on top of the bag.

'Get the fuck out!'

Yeongsuk told Jino that if she could have, she would have gone out and bought a lot of soju and stayed up all night talking things out with Jeongja, but by then she was too tired from being on the run. 'I didn't cry. Not even after being kicked out in the middle of the night and wandering around for a place to sleep. Everyone eats and works and sleeps and lives their lives without thinking about how exhausted they are, just going around, like balloons but filled with anger instead of air, and all it takes is a single poke of a needle for that anger to explode.' Yeongsuk Nuna looked at Jino and said, 'What I don't understand is why they hate *us*.'

Jino pondered this. Why, indeed?

'Maybe because we're close to them? Maybe she's jealous that you have the strength left to fight?'

'What strength? I'm more worn out than she is. But, sure, I still have dreams.'

At the word 'dreams', Jino looked up. Yeongsuk Nuna was gone.

A thin band of light appeared far off in the eastern sky. Dawn would soon break. Today as well, he did three sets of thirty push-ups and nearly a hundred squats. The morning air striking his cheeks was still freezing, but unlike in the middle of winter his forehead and the back of his neck were wet with sweat. The sun rose at 6.33. He shaved his beard off with an electric razor, then took the plastic bottle of water that he'd used for warmth from his sleeping bag, poured the still-lukewarm water into a small plastic basin, and washed his face with it. He had guests coming. He couldn't let them see him looking shaggy and grubby. Normally, his colleague Jeong came by early in the morning with food before heading to his own job, but since the preparation for the day's events was scheduled for seven and the kick-off ceremony for eight, a female labourer from the shelter was bringing his food instead.

Jino heard murmuring voices somewhere nearby, but more importantly he also heard an engine approaching. The five conscripted police who'd been trading shifts at the guard post below came running and stood in formation. A bus came through the front gate and stopped at the base of the chimney, and dozens more conscripted police got off and lined up at their lieutenant's command. It looked like they were getting ready for the day's events as well. At 7.20, two women with backpacks appeared under the chimney. One of them was the female labourer who managed the shelter.

She cupped her hands and shouted up at him, 'Union Branch Chief Yi, it's us today.'

Jino shouted back, 'Yes, I heard!'

'We're sending up your food.'

He lowered the rope attached to the pulley. Below, they tied the rope to a backpack and tugged on it twice. He pulled out a thermos and an insulated lunch box. He packed up his empty dishes from the night before and sent them down.

The shelter manager yelled, 'It's a special meal in honour of your 300th day! Hang in there!'

Hot beef-and-radish soup, juicy grilled bulgogi, jeon fritters, greens, kimchi — it was like a birthday or a holiday meal. People were beginning to gather in the empty lot outside the fence, where the organisers had set up a marquee. No one was being allowed inside the factory gate; right at the base of the chimney, the police stood waiting, just as they did every time an event was held. But it didn't matter, as the empty lot offered a better view of the chimney and made it easier for them to communicate with Jino. The police never interfered with whatever happened outside the fence.

While the authorities took a neutral stance and didn't get involved in issues between labour and management, if they saw collective action or violence as disturbing the peace, they would go in and break up the protest. In previous years, when the police used ruthless military tactics to suppress auto workers striking on the roof of a company building, or declared all-out war on a mass protest of tenants and residents who'd been displaced by the demolition of their homes in Yongsan, innocent lives had been lost. Since then, they'd resorted to ignoring one-man protests and solo sit-ins by labourers, claiming the principles of non-intervention and non-responsibility.

Teams from the Metal Workers' Union and civic groups gathered one after another, until the crowd had swelled to over 500 supporters. At exactly 8.00 am, the ceremony to commemorate the 300th day of Jino's sit-in and to kick off the march to the Blue House began. The ochetuji marchers included over a hundred people from the civic groups and from each branch of the union. They wore white Korean-style shirts and pants that had been provided to them by the labour union's culture section, along with headbands printed with slogans. The other marchers carried picket signs and banners. At the MC's suggestion, they turned as one to face the chimney and shouted:

> We love you, Yi Jino! Keep the faith!
> Bring back the money they took, and cancel the lay-offs!
> Approve the union, and restart the factory!
> Fight, fight, fight!

A statement was read. An impassioned voice poured out of the portable speaker and reverberated all the way up to the top of the chimney, making Jino feel as if the person was standing right at his side.

> Today marks the 300th day of our comrade Yi Jino's chimney sit-in, which first began on May 27 of last year.
>
> A small number of workers fought for three years, unable to simply hand over the factory they'd grown from the blood and sweat of their youth, the factory they'd won back after a five-year-long struggle to oppose its closure, to the owner who'd rather take the money and run. Their desperate struggle to survive and overcome this showdown against an owner who refuses to budge has lasted for four seasons, and now spring has come again, and

> with it the 300th day of this fight.
>
> The owner, who has been waiting for the workers to tire and drop out of this battle, is now rushing to tear down the empty factory. Let's show that even capitalists, who hold nothing sacred if it means they can make money, have their limits.
>
> We cannot always stand side by side like this, but this moment calls for us to join forces. We must not miss this moment! Let's put out a call for solidarity, and spread the word about the Hanyang Heavy Industries chimney sit-in, so that this fight to protect the lives of workers will be less lonely, less isolated.

The ceremony continued. Representatives from each civic group read their statements, and individuals and social groups alike who'd joined the cause shared their thoughts. Afterwards, they would prostrate themselves on the ground in procession up to a preselected point, then proceed on foot to the front of City Hall, and from there continue prostrating all the way to the Blue House. Ochetuji had originated in Buddhism: it was a way for Buddhists to physically humble themselves and express their devotion to the dharma. It was also a form of nonviolent protest and a nonresistant acceptance of any violence coming from the authorities or one's opponents. Nowadays it was mainly performed at large temple events, and was a common form of prayer in Tibet. The person performing ochetuji would press their hands together in prayer and take a couple of steps forward, then bend forward and kneel at a signal from a drum. They would lie down and extend their arms forward and legs back, pressing the full length of their bodies into the ground. Finally, they would lower their heads and press their foreheads to the ground, as well. They say this was originally done so that those bowing to the Buddha could press their foreheads to his feet, but it also looks like becoming one with the earth. It's not ochetuji unless elbows, knees, and forehead are all touching the ground at the same time. The bow is completed by raising your palms to the level of your ears, to signify gently lifting the Buddha's feet to place your own head underneath them. When you rise, you press your palms down to lift your upper body and bring your feet in at the same time to return to a squat. Then you return your hands to prayer position and press your heels together, touch your hands to the ground again briefly, extend your head forward, and rise in one smooth motion. If you've ever watched a bird walk, it's not unlike the way they bob their heads, using it like a spring to move forward lightly. You empty your mind and heart and pray in earnest. A Buddhist monk from one of the civic groups gave a quick lesson, and the ochetuji marchers practised it several times before setting off. While they prostrated and rose and prostrated again, the rest of the protesters followed behind, a few of whom beat drums to keep rhythm.

They were no longer visible from the chimney, but the sound of their drums continued for a long time, growing gradually fainter. Ten or so people had stayed behind under the marquee to carry out various tasks. Prerecorded slogans and rally songs kept pouring out of the speaker. At exactly 9.00 am, Kim Changsu, who was the same age as Jino, came through the factory gate with a doctor and lawyer from one of the civic groups. They would have been patted down and questioned already by the guards at the front gate, but when they reached the base of the chimney, the police searched the backpack that Changsu was carrying as well. All five — the doctor, the lawyer, Changsu, and the two guards accompanying them — climbed the narrow, winding staircase.

Right below the catwalk was a metal ladder covered by an acrylic shield. Back when he first climbed the chimney, Jino had loosened the bottom screws and removed the top screws entirely, then tilted the ladder up against the plastic shield to prevent anyone else from climbing up. He couldn't trust the authorities; they could come charging up after him at any time depending on how things changed. Seeing as how nothing had really happened so far, they'd probably decided to just wait and see. But for the others to come up now, the passageway had to be restored. Jino put a spanner and the bolts he'd saved into a sack and tied it to the rope to lower it down.

Changsu grabbed the rope and retrieved the bag. The police sergeant who was escorting them up along with one of the conscripted police shouted in alarm.

'What do you think you're doing? What is that?'

Changsu held the sack open and shoved it in front of the sergeant.

'Look for yourself! Bolts and a spanner. Or do you want to try climbing that ladder as is?'

The sergeant backed down without another word.

Changsu shouted to Jino, 'Pull!'

Jino tugged the ladder away from where it rested against the plastic shield. It was stiff at first, but when he pulled harder the ladder swung back into place. Changsu began to climb, tightening the loose nuts and replacing the missing ones as he went. When he'd replaced the final bolt and threw a leg over the railing, Jino offered him a hand to help pull him over. They hugged, each suddenly overwhelmed with emotion.

'You're doing a hell of a job up here!' Changsu said, wiping his eyes. Jino should have been the one crying, but he was calm.

'Eh, this is nothing … The real work is being done on the ground.'

Changsu called down to the others waiting just below. 'Come up slowly!'

The doctor came up first, followed by the lawyer, climbing one at a time for safety. The two cops waited at the bottom of the ladder. The visit was limited to thirty minutes. The doctor removed a blood-pressure cuff, a stethoscope, a syringe, and other equipment from his backpack. First, he checked Jino's blood pressure, then he listened to his chest and back with the stethoscope. Next, he drew a small amount of blood with the syringe. Finally, he examined Jino's eyes and had him open his mouth to check his tongue. Jino's blood pressure was lower than usual, but aside from a few signs of frostbite, nothing else appeared to be physically amiss. The doctor said that the results of the blood test would take a few days. He asked Jino to do a few exercises while he watched.

'You've got weaker. It's to be expected: you're not young anymore, and you've been sleeping outdoors for nearly a year now.'

'But I've been working out. Look,' Jino said, and flexed his arm to show off his bicep.

As Changsu laughed, the other two, who'd been looking tense, laughed, too.

'Yes, it's a good sign that you haven't lost that muscle.'

The lawyer was recording everything with a small camcorder. With his eye to the viewfinder, he told Jino, 'Please show us where you've been living.'

'Sure, we are at the top of a chimney belonging to a combined heat-and-power plant. The chimney is forty-five metres high and six metres in diameter. The catwalk is one metre wide and about fifteen short steps long. This blue tarp on the outside helps to block the wind. It's secured to the railing with this rope. Back here I have a one-person mountaineering tent with a sleeping bag and a blanket.'

Jino began to talk about why he was occupying the chimney and the statement they were trying to make, when Changsu interrupted.

'We don't have much time, so maybe save that part for later, when you're filming yourself.'

The lawyer lowered the camcorder and said, 'We'll leave this here for you to use, and we'll upload the video for you later.'

'And who knows?' Changsu added. 'Maybe Jo Taejun himself will see the video. And come negotiate with us in person.'

The lawyer attached the camcorder to a small tripod and explained to Jino how to adjust the focus and start and stop the recording.

'These are much simpler to use nowadays. It's pretty much the same as recording on a mobile phone.'

They'd been on the chimney for over forty minutes already. The police called up to them.

'You've been up there too long. Time to come down.'

'Okay,' Changsu called back to them. 'We're heading down now.'

He handed the camcorder and tripod to Jino and said, 'After we send your breakfast up tomorrow, send this down in the same bag.'

The doctor and lawyer each shook Jino's hand.

'Keep up the exercise and don't skip any meals.'

'We'll keep pushing for the company to come to the table and negotiate.'

The three men headed down the ladder. Jino stood at the railing and watched until they were all on the ground, then he waved. The marchers had just reached the Blue House — photos were arriving on his mobile phone. Jino looked into the camcorder and thought about what to say.

'The factory where we worked for ten to twenty years was sold in 2006. We fought for five years to keep our employment, labour union, and collective agreement in place under the new ownership. This was what we called the "three conditions". But the new company president, Jo Taejun, who bought the factory for practically nothing, decided to fire everyone instead and hire casual workers, to make up for his so-called loss. Then they created a company-sponsored union filled with workers who would do the company's bidding. Once they advise you to resign or you voluntarily retire, you can no longer maintain your union membership. The people who accepted the condition of casual employment were each given consolation money and severance pay, and were admitted into a branch of the company-sponsored union, which forfeited the three conditions that our union had insisted upon. The new board of directors' goal from the outset was to destroy the union, change to a casualised workforce, and liquidate the factory, then sell it all off for double the purchase price. You can tell this from the fact that they're trying to liquidate the factory after it's only been back in operation for a year and a half. We workers were like one happy family, until those who control the capital turned us against each other. They sow distrust, and are pressuring us by applying for an injunction against our legitimate claims. We've had to pay hundreds of millions of won in damages for protesters and for anyone who has used the slogans on this banner.'

Jino got a lump in his throat and had to stop. The whole world was against him. It wasn't just the capitalists and the politicians, but even the banks and courts and government officials, everyone, they were all in cahoots and holding the hands of those with power. He felt suddenly ashamed and couldn't bring himself to keep speaking. Changsu's joke about Jo Taejun seeing the video and joining them at the negotiation table had got to him. He was fighting a just fight, he told himself. He was not hurting anyone. He wasn't even imposing.

He pulled himself together and added a greeting to his family, and segued to talking about his colleagues who'd been laid off. Having gone years now without pay, their lives were slowly becoming as parched and shrivelled as trees in a drought, illness spreading from leaves to branches and all the way down to the roots. Instead of much-needed rain, they'd made it through these last few years on brief, sporadic splashes from a watering can.

In the evening, the ochetuji marchers and people from the civic groups returned to the empty lot behind the factory and wrapped up the events celebrating the 300th day of Jino's sit-in. They shouted slogans to encourage Jino one last time, and Jino responded with a short speech. Darkness fell before he could finish eating the dinner they sent up. The air was cold, but at least it was spring; the harsh winter chill that had sliced right through him was gone. He walked back and forth a hundred times, thirty steps each round trip. Since he'd stopped doing his full-body exercises during the winter, this seemed like a good time to restart his routine. When he thought about all that he'd accomplished today, he felt overcome with fatigue.

14

Jino climbed into his sleeping bag and rolled onto his side without zipping it up.

'You did good today.'

Shin Geumi Halmeoni was there, sitting next to him.

'Halmeoni, tell me about back then.'

'When back then?'

'When you lived in the rail workers' housing? Around the time my dad started going to school?'

'No, hang on, we moved into the rail housing when your father was five.'

Geumi remembered the year clearly. Because that was the year they sold the Willow Tree House and moved into the rail workers' housing, after Ilcheol was appointed locomotive engineer on the continental line connecting Busan to Hsinking. Meanwhile, the Railway Bureau had been working to improve the railway tracks and locomotive carriages for the sake of better transportation facilities and capacity. On the Gyeongin Line, a super-express train was added that could go from Gyeongseong to Incheon in forty minutes, making it possible to complete thirteen round trips a day. The Railway Bureau also did test runs to try to shorten travel times, ultimately succeeding at reducing the ten-hour-plus Gyeongseong–Busan leg to eight hours and the twelve-hour Gyeongseong–Sinuiju leg to eight hours, fifty-four minutes. When the Sino-Japanese War broke out, the ultimate goal of linking Joseon to Manchuria was to complete the Busan–Antung leg in sixteen hours and get from Tokyo to Hsinking in seventy-two hours. When Ilcheol was driving a freight train as Hayashi's assistant, the *Hikari*, a direct-express train between Busan and Hsinking, debuted, followed by the *Nozomi*, between Busan and Fengtian, shortening the travel time from Tokyo to Hsinking by twelve hours. Towards the Dumangang River in Hamgyeong Province, a direct passenger train ran from Gyeongseong to Unggi and a direct freight train ran between Gyeongseong and Cheongjin. The *Akatsuki*, which travelled between Busan and Gyeongseong in six hours and forty-five minutes, was also put into service at this time. After the war broke out, a new direct-express train could get from Busan to Beijing in thirty-eight hours and forty-five minutes. The Railway Bureau's goal in speeding up the trains was to more firmly assimilate Joseon and China into Japan by shrinking the temporal distance between Japan, Joseon, Manchuria, and China as much as possible.

Ilcheol's new assignment was the *Hikari*. Both engineers and locomotives were changed three times a day, and there were three men for each segment — the Gyeongbu, Gyeongui, and Antung Lines. Two shifts meant a total of eighteen engineers driving the route. Before, barely two of them were Korean. But with the start of the Sino-Japanese War, those numbers changed to ten Japanese and eight Koreans, and by the end of the Japanese Empire, more than half of the rail workers were Korean. Also, more freight trains carrying urgent war supplies were put into service than passenger trains. As more Japanese rail workers were drafted as commissioned and non-commissioned officers, many more Korean assistants found themselves promoted to engineers.

At the end of the following year, after Icheol had been sentenced to a year and a half in prison and Yeowok had left for Manchuria, Mageum decided to leave her old home in Saetmal. Early one morning, she came in search of Geumi.

'Jisan Eomma, let me in!'

Geumi had been having anxious thoughts about Mageum Gomo ever since waking up that day. She rushed to open the gate, scuffing her shoes as she went, and saw Mageum standing there in a fur-collared coat that she'd never seen before and carrying a cloth bundle. Wide-eyed at the fur, niece-in-law Geumi couldn't help remembering the fortune teller who'd said that Mageum was destined to live in a strange land far from home.

'Are you going to Manchuria or something?' Geumi asked.

Mageum flopped down dramatically on the maru floor.

'*Aegomeoni!* That gift of yours is terrifying! The Uncanny Shin Geumi, indeed. Why you don't go into business as a fortune teller is beyond me.'

Geumi hadn't meant to say anything. She decided not to press her surprised aunt-in-law with any more questions and waited for her to tell her what was going on instead.

'Carpenter Kang returned from his business trip to Manchuria yesterday.'

Mageum explained that new houses were being built in Manchuria for Japanese and Korean migrants. The company that her husband worked for had previously subcontracted the build of houses for factory workers — following that success, Hong, the owner of the company, had accompanied an executive from their headquarters in Japan, along with Mageum's husband, to Manchuria to sign a construction contract there. And so, the family was moving to Manchuria, Mageum said breathlessly.

'I see. Do you know which city?'

'Where do you think? The capital, of course.'

'*Omona!* A strange land far from home …'

'Yes, well, they do say it's quite the sprawling city. And what was the other thing they said? Something about how Gyeongseong is a country town in comparison.'

Mageum Gomo paused to unwrap her bundle. Inside was a piece of deer antler, a mushroom the size of her hand, and some black manna lichen, among other items.

'This was a gift from the trip. They say that area is known for these — what's it called? Specialty items? There were two antlers, but I nabbed this one. Your father-in-law has that lingering cough from being around so much metal dust. They say there's nothing better than powdered deer antler for treating a nagging cough.'

'If the whole family is going, does that mean you're leaving for good?'

Mageum Gomo leapt up and shook her head hard.

'Goodness, no! The construction contract is only for three years. We'll come back to Yeongdeungpo after that. That's why we're only renting out our house in Saetmal instead of selling it.'

Several years before instigating the Sino-Japanese War, the Government-General had been promoting and actively encouraging Korean peasant farmers to emigrate to Manchuria. There, they said, landless farmers could acquire arable land of their own and farm it, and so tens of thousands of farmers left for Manchuria with their families. Not only Koreans but Japanese nationals as well were flocking to Manchuria. Educated, middle-class Koreans went to the newly flourishing metropolises of Fengtian, Hsinking, and Harbin in search of work and business opportunities. Of course, among the emigrants were young people looking to join the freedom fighters in Manchuria who were engaged in armed struggle against Japan.

Baekman took the news of his sister's leaving in stride. Ilcheol's days were filled with driving the *Hikari*: it took four days to cover the Gyeongui Line, rest, change shifts, take the Antung–Hsinking Line, and come back. Once home, he would rest for two days, then repeat it all over again. He didn't hear the news from his wife until a few days after Mageum had dropped by. Father and son talked about the family in Baekman's workshop over makgeolli.

'You know your gomo's family moved to Manchuria?' Baekman said.

'Yes, it seems my gomo's husband has many talents.'

'He and the owner work well together, and construction in Yangpyeong-jeong is a success, so the Japanese head office is trusting them with the project. Apparently, they're renting out the Saetmal House while they're gone. It's a nice house, very sturdily built, and with a big yard ...'

Ilcheol understood what his father was hinting at, and shifted uncomfortably where he sat.

'I'm on the waiting list for the rail workers' housing. I think I'll be assigned a place in another two months or so. Since I'm driving an express train now, I have to do whatever the Railway Bureau tells me to do. If they think they can't trust me because of Icheol, I could lose my job.'

The winter that marked Icheol's first year in prison, Yi Jaeyu was arrested. He had been hiding out in Yangju, Gyeonggi Province. News of his arrest made the headlines of several papers, which described it as 'Evil Korean Communist Party Rooted Out At Last'. To Koreans, he had been the last hope for the domestic socialist independence movement. Taken to commemorate his capture, a photo of him — still disguised as a farmer, handcuffed, tied to a horse, and surrounded by the twenty-seven detectives who'd gone undercover, who were still in their own disguises as members of various social classes and occupations — adorned the front page of the papers. All of Joseon was in an uproar over it. After serving seven years in Gongju Prison following his arrest on 25 December 1936, Jaeyu was remanded to Cheongju Prison in accordance with the Public Safety Act. And then, sadly, he died on 26 October 1944, a mere ten months before Liberation.

It was in the summer of 1938, when Jaeyu's trial was in full swing, that Icheol was released from prison and returned to the Willow Tree House in Yeongdeungpo. His father, who was normally so gruff, personally went to the market to purchase dog meat for a medicinal soup to help his son recover from prison life. The hunk of meat with its singed fur was a new challenge for Geumi. But after talking to the lady next door and jotting down notes, she soaked the meat in cold water to draw out the blood and parboiled it with doenjang paste, ginger, soju, onions, and perilla leaves to tame the gaminess. From there, she used the prepped meat to make several dishes, including boshintang soup, slices of tender suyuk, and a spicy, braised duruchigi. In the years that followed, she would use her newfound skill at cooking boshintang to feed and nurture back to health men from each living generation of the

Yi family, from her father-in-law, Baekman, her husband, Ilcheol, and his brother, Icheol, to her son, Jisan, who would narrowly survive the hell of war, and even her grandson Jino.

'What is Icheol doing with himself now?' Baekman asked.

Ilcheol was quiet at first, and regretted having mentioned his younger brother's name. After being released, Icheol had stayed at home, convalescing, for exactly 100 days, before disappearing without any warning when Ilcheol was away at work. As if he'd been planning to do just that all along.

'I have no idea,' Ilcheol said at last.

'He didn't say anything to Jisan Eomma?'

'No, he just left home without telling anyone and hasn't returned.'

'Is it possible he's still in Gyeongseong, somewhere within the four gates?'

Ilcheol answered quickly, 'He wouldn't have gone that way.'

Baekman kept drinking and didn't ask any further questions.

Ilcheol assumed that Icheol must have confided in Geumi, and remembered that she had dropped some hints, too.

'It takes less than an hour to get to Incheon by train,' she had said, 'same as going to Jongno.'

'Huh? Why'd you suddenly bring up Incheon?'

Geumi tried to take it back. 'Oh, no reason, I was just remembering that someone told me if you buy a crate of yellow corvina and dry it yourself, you can save a lot of money on food for the whole season.'

'You're going to Incheon to buy fish?'

'No, no, I was just thinking about Jangsan Eomma. She really liked dried corvina from Yeonpyeong.'

'What? So you haven't heard anything?'

Geumi clammed up after that, but it had finally occurred to Ilcheol that his younger brother might be hiding out somewhere in Incheon. Much like her comrade Bak Seonok, Geumi tended to see Icheol as a fellow activist first and a brother-in-law second. She couldn't help feeling a little sorry and regretful to have married his older brother, Ilcheol, and to be enjoying a comfortable life during such turbulent times. Though it hadn't been long, the experience of getting to know Yeowok, helping to deliver Jangsan, seeing Icheol go to prison and his baby pass away, and then standing by while Yeowok left the country forever, she couldn't help feeling responsible for the younger brother and caring for him in his older brother's place. Icheol had, of course, shared his thoughts with her the day he left the Willow Tree House. He would have assumed that she would pass his words along to his older brother.

After being released from prison, Icheol had come straight home and stayed there, never once going out. On designated days, he was required to voluntarily report to his parole officer at the Yeongdeungpo Police Station — none other than Yamashita. Yamashita had become chief detective of the Special Higher Police. He had more or less inherited the position when Sergeant Mori was reassigned to another department. The first time, when Icheol explained the purpose of his visit to the guard posted at the front gate of the police station, the guard made a call to someone, and after a moment a police assistant came out and escorted Icheol to the Special Higher Police office on the second floor. Most of the staff were out on field duty; Yamashita was still there, along with one other detective. He was taking a phone call at his desk. When he saw Icheol enter with the police assistant, he pointed at an empty seat with his fountain pen and gestured for him to sit, all the while chattering away in fluent Japanese. Icheol sat, while the police assistant stood obediently behind him. Yamashita hung up the phone and directed his attention to Icheol.

'Hey, Dusoe, did some hard time, huh? Your parole is the same length as your sentence, so you'll be reporting to us for the next year and a half.'

'I know,' Icheol responded curtly.

Yamashita stared at him for a moment before saying, 'Why do you have to go around stirring up trouble anyway? Your baby died as soon as he was born and your wife ran off. Now your family is falling apart, isn't it? And your father and brother are such good, hardworking men ... What are you planning to do with yourself now?'

'Haven't really thought about it yet.'

What Icheol really wanted to do was to wring Yamashita's throat, but he just sat there instead, tensing his jaw and gritting his teeth. Yamashita tapped his fountain pen against the desk out of habit and muttered in a low, threatening voice.

'Haven't thought about it? We still have your statement of conversion on file. We all know it's full of lies. If you don't prove to everyone that you've turned your life around, then we can lock you away again at any time. Write an affidavit right now, in your own hand, explaining what you'll be doing with yourself.'

He pushed a pen, ink bottle, and double-sided lined paper across the desk to Icheol.

'Write it here. Your thoughts on your imprisonment, and your life plan going forward.'

Yamashita stepped away for a moment, leaving the police assistant at Icheol's side. Icheol stared down at the sheet of paper with its black lines. He'd been ordered to record his life within those lines. He glared at Yamashita's chair with no intention whatsoever of picking up the pen. Thirty minutes later, Yamashita returned, and exploded with anger when he saw the untouched paper.

'Are you fucking with me? I told you to write an affidavit!'

'I don't know how to write one.'

'That so? Then start with this: name, date of birth, address.'

Icheol scribbled down his answers while Yamashita continued.

'Now write: I made the stupid mistake of becoming involved with a group of unruly Koreans, for which I was arrested and imprisoned, and after completing my one-and-a-half-year-long sentence, I was released on July 21. I sincerely regret my mistakes and pledge to be a loyal subject of the Great Japanese Empire and work hard and devote myself to ...'

Yamashita glanced down at the paper mid-sentence and burst into anger again, smacking Icheol on the head with his palm and shouting, '*Baka!* You son of a bitch! Who told you to write in Korean? Use the national language, you arsehole.'

'I forgot how to write in Japanese.'

Yamashita's anger reached full boil.

'You finished primary school *and* technical secondary school but don't know the national language? I see there's no reasoning with you. Maybe we should take you back downstairs to the interrogation room?'

The police assistant had reached the limit of his patience, too. He slapped Icheol across the face and shoved him out of his chair.

'On your knees!'

He took Icheol's place on the chair and began writing down what Yamashita had dictated in eloquent Japanese. After a moment, he paused and directed a question to the back of Icheol's head.

'What's your plan for the future?'

'I haven't given it much thought, so why don't you just tell me what to do with my life.'

Yamashita bellowed out before the police assistant could respond, 'You have to earn a living, don't you? You need a job!'

'I promise to work hard.'

'Doing what?'

'I'll reapply at a factory —'

'That won't work,' Yamashita interrupted. 'No factory will take you in now that your name is out there.'

'How should I survive then?'

'Work as a porter, or a peddler, or open a store. I don't know. Figure it out.'

'I'll be a porter, then.'

Yamashita looked displeased.

'Go talk to your older brother first. In the meantime, we'll write down "*labourer*".'

The police assistant composed a few sentences about Icheol's future plans, and read them out loud. As expected, it also said he would obey the laws as a subject of the Great Japanese Empire and endeavour to rehabilitate himself through work.

'Stamp it here.'

Icheol wrote his name at the bottom of the affidavit, pressed his thumb hard into the red ink pad, and stamped the paper with his thumbprint.

Yamashita looked it over, then said, 'Why haven't your father and older brother changed their names yet? They both work for the Government-General.'

Icheol didn't respond. Yamashita continued his browbeating.

'We are at war. Right now it's only recommended, but soon Japanese names will become the national policy. Koreans must become Japanese to the bone if we're to survive. That is the only way to be reborn as first-class citizens. Anyway, report back here at the same time next month.'

Icheol turned and was on his way out when Yamashita added, 'Give my regards to your brother!'

The police assistant escorted him back out to the front gate.

'The rules prohibit you from leaving the Gyeongseong area,' the police assistant warned. 'If you must travel for some reason, then report to us first and get permission. Leaving the area without permission will result in your re-arrest. Got it?'

Icheol bowed in lieu of an answer and turned to leave. His experience at the police station had left him feeling so mortified and angry that his back was covered in sweat. He said nothing of this to his family, though, and simply ate the food his sister-in-law had cooked for him. The curative powers of the dog meat seemed to do the trick, because three months and ten days later, the colour had returned to his face and he was full of energy once more. A few days after the Chuseok holiday, Geumi was sitting in the courtyard, warmed by the autumn sun, arranging wicker trays of sliced squash, radish, and radish greens to dry and store for the winter. Jisan was playing with a toy train his grandfather had made for him. Icheol, who'd been cooped up inside his room, came out quietly and sat down on the maru floor.

'Hyeongsu, I'm leaving home tomorrow.'

'What? Where are you going?'

'Anywhere. I have to get out of Yeongdeungpo.'

Geumi had seen the look of torment on her brother-in-law's face each time he'd had to self-report to the police station as a security risk.

'Hyeongsu, I know you know this already, but I have to keep fighting.'

'Who would dream of stopping you?' Geumi said, smiling flatly. There would have been a note of bitterness and sorrow in her words.

'Please ask Comrade Bak Seonok to come see me.'

'Seonok got in a lot of trouble back then. She quit the factory and is focused on the tteok shop now.'

'I'm not trying to drag her into anything. I was just thinking that the two of us could take a romantic rendezvous to Incheon. That's all.'

Geumi knew what he meant by 'romantic rendezvous'. It was code among activists for making contact or arranging meetings with each other. She laughed out loud.

'The widower wants to seduce a virgin? Ha! She could be meeting her future husband any day now.'

Oblivious to how his sister-in-law was trying to lighten the mood, Icheol brought up the heavy subject of his wife's whereabouts.

'Is there any way of finding out what happened to Jangsan Eomma?'

He'd heard the details from Geumi as soon as he was out of prison: how she and his aunt had helped deliver Jangsan, how Jisan and Jangsan had both caught the measles and fought for their lives but poor Jangsan had lost the struggle, and how Yeowok had decided to leave for Manchuria.

'She probably joined the anti-Japanese resistance,' Geumi said. 'That's what she was doing before returning to Joseon. If she's staying in one place, then maybe you could track her down. But otherwise, there's no way to stay in touch with someone who's roughing it in the mountains with a rifle.'

'I wanted to go with her, but our collective goal right now is to rebuild the party from within Joseon. We have to try again.'

Geumi nodded.

'Someone's got to do it,' she said. 'Shall I call Seonok over?'

'Yes, please, Hyeongsunim. I'll sound her out myself about going to Incheon with me.'

It was about a ten-minute walk from the Willow Tree House to the tteok shop that Seonok's grandparents had owned. Geumi washed her hands at the tap and got ready to leave.

'I'll be right back. Could you keep an eye on Jisan until then?'

Geumi found Seonok working hard in the kitchen of the tteok shop. Seonok rushed out to welcome her, both hands still coated in powder.

'How long has it been?' she exclaimed. 'I feel like I haven't seen you in years!'

'We had cold noodles together just last summer at the market.' Geumi said, then lowered her voice to a whisper. 'My brother-in-law wants to see you. He needs to talk to you about something.'

'Ah, I'd heard he was out, but I wasn't sure if I should come over, especially since he hadn't contacted me yet. How is he? Is he all better?'

'Yes, he's much healthier now.'

Geumi brought Seonok to the house, where Icheol was waiting for her in his room. They spoke so quietly in there that Geumi couldn't hear what they were saying. She made no attempt to eavesdrop, but she had the feeling they were planning to meet someone in Incheon. The next day, around ten o'clock, when Baekman was at the factory and Ilcheol was still driving a train somewhere far away, Icheol came out of his room with a small trunk. He spoke to Geumi before leaving.

'Please don't say anything to my father or brother. Only you can know that I've gone to Incheon. I might be able to send word after things have settled.'

'Seobangnim, I have to tell you something before you leave.'

When he saw the serious look on her face, Icheol sat down.

'Did you know? Your mother has been keeping watch over you every night since you got out of prison.'

Icheol did not laugh at this or make jokes like he normally would, but just sat quietly and listened.

'She sometimes brings Jangsan with her.'

Icheol choked up at this and lowered his head. Fat teardrops plunked onto the floor. Geumi couldn't hold back her tears anymore, either.

'There isn't much difference between life and death. So do what you have to do.'

Icheol left in a hurry and never saw the Willow Tree House again.

Partly this was because of the misfortune that later befell him, but more than that, Ilcheol moved his family into the rail workers' housing early the very next year. They stayed there for three years. Jino heard all about their lives in the rail workers' housing from his grandmother and father.

Identical, box-like houses stood along a street large enough for cars to come and go. Seven steps across a yard brought you to the front door. Behind the house was a small backyard about three or four paces long, and behind that was the identically sized backyard of another house. The lucky ones were assigned the south-facing houses, while others got stuck with the west- or north-facing houses. The sliding front door had glass windows in a lattice frame. A pulley was installed at the bottom of the door, and a wire was set into the threshold: with a push, it would rattle open automatically. When you stepped up into the house from the front door, you would find yourself in a wood-floored hallway, to the right of which was a washroom with a toilet, then a small bedroom. The hallway led to a kitchen. To the left was a latticed paper door that slid open to reveal a living room floored with six tatami mats, where the family could gather to eat, talk about their day, and entertain guests. Inside and to the right was the main bedroom, which had another tiny door, so low that you had to stoop to go through it, which connected to the kitchen. To the left of the main bedroom was a third bedroom. The front wall of the living room had floor-to-ceiling latticed paper windows that slid open to reveal a long wood-floored verandah, on the other side of which were floor-to-ceiling windows made of glass.

The glass windows were usually left wide open during the summer and shut tight again in winter, the cracks sealed with paper weather stripping to keep out draughts. On mild winter days, the inner paper doors could be left open to let the sunlight shine through the glass and warm the tatami. But that was partly the luck of getting a house with southern exposure. Only a handful of Koreans had been offered any house at all; most of the rail workers' housing was occupied by Japanese employees. Since the houses were the property of the Government-General, they were essentially rentals, which meant that no one could make any renovations or modifications; even repairs required approval and were carried out by a government maintenance man. But for most Koreans, tatami flooring was unfamiliar and ill-suited to the climate, and so they would take it upon themselves to redo the floor in at least the main bedroom so that it could be heated from underneath. Without official permission, of course. They tried at first to do as the Japanese did and ward off the cold by filling a tin bottle with hot water and placing it beneath their bedding. But it never failed to go cold by the wee hours of the morning, leaving the elderly especially to suffer. Also, tatami rooms were usually warmed by charcoal braziers; if the room wasn't frequently ventilated, those inside could suffocate. Baekman built a small cast-iron stove and placed it in the middle of the living room. When they burned lignite in it, the whole house turned warm and cozy.

As war took hold on the continent, daily life began to change. Ilcheol was made an express-train engineer: his salary went up, and he enrolled in the Rail Workers' Mutual Aid Association, which meant he could apply for emergency loans and turn a small deposit into a considerable chunk of cash. Daily necessities, like food and clothing, were rationed, but the consumer team of the Rail Workers' Social Club purchased such items in bulk for rail workers and their families, enabling them to get those items right away and for cheaper than market price. But as Baekman and his family moved in and found themselves living among the Japanese, they had no choice but to conduct themselves as loyal subjects of the Japanese Empire by following rules that in the outside world, which is to say Korean society, had been promulgated but were not yet enforced. Companies had been gently pushing their employees to change to Japanese names, and it would be another two years before Koreans countrywide were forced to do so, but no sooner had the family moved in than the Korean housing chief was telling them to volunteer. And so Yi Ilcheol became Inoue Ichitetsu. Yi Baekman became Inoue Hyakuman, and Jisan was changed to Ikeyama. Shin Geumi took her husband's family name and chose Kinu for her given name, which meant the same thing but was a little easier to pronounce.

A year and several months later, the Government-General issued a name-change-enforcement ordinance; when only a very small number of Koreans voluntarily complied, they allowed for a six-month grace period, after which everyone was forced to change their full names. Children from families that had not changed their names were not allowed to start school, and even those who were already attending were suspended or expelled. Private schools that didn't comply with the regulations were forced to close. Parents who didn't change their children's names were likewise compelled to when their children pleaded with them, complaining of unexplained reprimands and beatings at school. Adult men and women who hadn't changed their names were unable to find work in either public or private industries, and those currently employed were laid off but could get their jobs back if they made the switch. Government offices refused to handle civil requests from Koreans with Korean names, and even went so far as to treat them as traitors or 'unruly Koreans', submitting their names to police ledgers so they would be subject to investigations. They were first to be targeted for conscripted labour and excluded from rations of food and other necessities. The railroad refused to deliver freight or other items labelled with Korean names and would immediately return them. Koreans with Korean names could not travel to Japan. And in the case of children born after the decree had been enacted, any attempt to report their births under a non-Japanese name were rejected, essentially forcing the parents to change their names.

'Naisen ittai' — Joseon and Japan are one — was the slogan that every workplace and household was made to display. It was painted in large Chinese characters on the front window of the rail workers' community centre. At the monthly patriotic neighbourhood meeting, pledges of allegiance to Japan were recited in chorus. Everyone was supposed to bow every morning in the direction of the imperial palace in Tokyo, but none of the Korean families voluntarily observed this. Instead, the community leader chose the occasional Japanese holiday or national holiday to gather everyone in the community centre or neighbourhood plaza and lead them through a round of bows to the far-off palace. Even Baekman, who was normally so taciturn, complained to his son Ilcheol after a month of living there.

'Why does it feel like we've come to a worse place than that prison Dusoe went to?'

Ilcheol didn't respond.

'We're lucky we haven't had to deal with any shortages here,' Geumi said. 'Out there, white-rice rations are unheard of, and even black-market goods are three to four times more expensive. Eating rice on your birthday sounds like an old proverb now.'

Around that time, Ilcheol had stopped discussing current affairs altogether with either of them. Jisan was five and was attending the childcare inside the housing complex. Geumi had begun working at the community centre. The community centre was a wooden building that held a small auditorium, several small offices, a storehouse, shops, and so on. Japanese and Korean housewives were divided into sewing, knitting, and mending teams and would gather in groups of ten or so to contribute their services and make a little money. Geumi joined the knitting group and learned how to knit. She used bamboo needles and crochet hooks to knit wool and make lace. Gloves, socks, and jumpers in many different patterns were delivered to the Rail Workers' Social Club. The leader of the knitting team was a Japanese woman in her forties whose husband was an engineer at the rail works.

One afternoon, Geumi was hard at work knitting when a Korean messenger from the community centre told her that someone was looking for her. When she went to the entrance, Bak Seonok was waiting there and looking around nervously. Geumi's heart sank as she wondered what bad thing had happened this time.

'What are you doing here?' she asked.

'Are you able to take a break?' Seonok asked simply.

Geumi told her to wait and went right away to the team leader to explain that something had come up at home. Seonok kept her silence until they reached Geumi's house. Once they were inside, she appeared to relax and explained what had brought her.

'Icheol says he's hoping to see you …'

'Where is he now?'

'Incheon, of course.'

Geumi let out a sigh. 'With things the way they are, he really should think about taking it easy.'

'Will you meet him?'

'I guess he wouldn't come looking for me unless it was really important.'

Seonok took that as a yes. 'Take a trip to Wolmido Island with me tomorrow.'

'Tomorrow? So soon?'

'Are you worried about Jisan? You can leave him at our house and take the train.'

As soon as her father-in-law left for work, Geumi took Jisan to Seonok's family's tteok shop and headed for the station to catch a train to Incheon. It was a forty-minute ride from Yeongdeungpo, so the two women arrived at Haincheon Station just after ten in the morning. Seonok had been working as a reppo for years at that point and was very skilled at it. They left downtown, walked to the top of Manguk Park, and sat on a boulder from which they could see in all directions. This was so they could be sure that no one was following them. After a two-hour-long picnic, when they were certain they had no tail, Seonok took Geumi to the local Chinatown. Checking the restaurant names carefully, Seonok led her to a private room on the upper floor of a restaurant where they could feel a cool breeze blowing in from the sea. The two women sat drinking tea and were about to order food when Icheol suddenly pushed open the door and strode right in. Dressed in khaki work clothes with a cap pressed down low on his head, he looked like any other factory worker.

'Hyeongsu!' Icheol quietly exclaimed, as Geumi rose awkwardly from her seat.

'I'll get going so you two can talk,' Seonok said.

'Oh no, stay and eat lunch first,' Geumi said.

But Seonok had already vanished without a word out the same door that Icheol had come in. Geumi and Icheol ordered udon and sat there quietly. Neither of them said anything until after the waitress had brought their food.

'I thought you were safe and sound,' Geumi said finally. 'Has something happened?'

'I have to leave town for a while.'

'To where?'

Icheol hesitated before answering.

'To the frontier. Do you think he could get me to Sinuiju?'

Geumi thought about her husband and shook her head hard.

'The authorities know that you and your wife are both organisers. And aren't you basically a wanted criminal? Yamashita is still sending detectives to our home once a month to ask where you are. And now you want Jisan Abeoji to help you leave?'

'I know how much trouble I've caused you and my brother, and all the rest of our family. Everyone who knows me knows it, too. They also know what Ilcheol does for work and that I'm his younger brother. This is a once-in-a-lifetime request,' Icheol pleaded.

'What is it exactly?'

'I need to bring someone back safely from Sinuiju.'

Geumi's eyes immediately filled with tears.

'You can't use Jisan Abeoji for something so dangerous!'

Icheol jumped out of his chair, dropped to his knees, and clasped his hands together.

'Please, Hyeongsu, I beg of you. Please help me.'

'Sit back down, please,' Geumi said in shock. 'I'll find out what Jisan Abeoji thinks, first.'

Nationwide connections were beginning to form among the prime movers who'd done time in prison, groups in contact with the International Party, and those left behind after Yi Jaeyu and most of the Communist Party reconstructionists had been arrested. The idea was to bring in someone with political influence from Manchuria and have them sit down with a local comrade who would then take over local leadership. Icheol conveyed the gist of it without going into every detail.

'That's all I can say,' he added. 'If you don't trust me as family, then I can't tell you anything more. If you and my brother don't help me, then we'll consider this conversation as having never happened.'

Geumi gazed down at her now-cold udon and murmured, 'I'll go home and talk it over with him. But you have to tell me first when and how you plan to meet him.'

Icheol explained that he would board the train on a scheduled date, but it would be somewhere in Gaeseong, not Gyeongseong. Likewise, on his way back from Sinuiju, he would jump off somewhere between the two cities. All future contact would be through Seonok, so Geumi would not have to go to any further trouble.

Their business concluded, Geumi handed her brother-in-law a rolled-up fifty-won note.

'I wish I could have given you more when you left home last time.'

Icheol took the money without a word.

*

On the surface, the movement had collapsed, but there were still remaining yacheykas, made up of workers in separate factories who had not yet been exposed. Icheol felt it was the survivors' responsibility to bring these scattered cells together and unify them nationally. Certain that he had to escape his parole and get out of Yeongdeungpo and Gyeongseong entirely, he had made contact with Kim Geunshik through Seonok and gone to Incheon to meet him.

In keeping with his many years of experience, Geunshik was tough and ballsy but knew what he was doing. Book clubs and social gatherings were bustling at every factory in Incheon. But they were all refraining from any sort of direct action that would bring them into conflict with the authorities or the company owners. Literature was distributed, read, and then promptly burned on a daily basis. Every worksite — whether Eastern Mill, Incheon Ironworks, Ninomiya Ironworks, Arima Rice Refinery, Kato Rice Refinery, Gyeongin Hosiery, the Incheon Pier, or another — had from three to eight orgs. They stuck to their factory cells and deliberately avoided each other's book clubs and any joint meetings; if problems arose, they met one on one.

Icheol remembered what Foreman Jo, of the Incheon Pier, and Yun, who'd tried to connect the scattered reading clubs, had confessed to and what they'd managed to keep secret. Those who were arrested not only managed to protect Geunshik but also all of the embedded organisers who were connected to him in Incheon for the duration of their investigations. They named a few people who'd circulated literature at work, and insisted that they were only trying to understand the world better. Meanwhile, Geunshik and the orgs ceased all activity and stayed in contact via pamphlets and other literature.

The day after Icheol left Yeongdeungpo, he met Geunshik for the first time, on the Munhaksan Mountain trail. They spent the time swapping stories and sizing one another up. After an afternoon of strolling and chatting, Geunshik came to a decision.

'Comrade Yi, it looks like you'll have to get a job here.'

'I learned how to operate a lathe. I'll be proficient at it after a few days.'

'Let's find a spot for you at Incheon Ironworks. Go there next Monday and look for Comrade Bak Yonggil. I'll let him know you're coming.'

Offering to find Icheol a job meant that Geunshik was accepting him into the local circle of labour organisers.

Before parting ways, Geunshik asked him, 'Do you have someone you can stay with?'

'There should be plenty of boarding houses around here, right?'

Geunshik shook his head.

'Those are full of spies for the police. You can do better than that. For now, I'll see if it's possible for you to just bunk inside the factory.' He mentally ticked off the dates. 'Today's Friday, so that's three nights you'll need somewhere to sleep before Monday. There are plenty of cheap inns in the alleys close to the pier. Sailors like to stay there, so they're used to strangers. All right then, assuming nothing goes wrong, we'll be seeing one another again soon.'

Icheol took his advice and found a room in an inn in the back alleys of the Incheon waterfront. Right across the street were bars and restaurants crowded with sailors until late into the night. He knew that his uncles Cheonman and Shipman lived nearby, and where their homes were. His older uncle, Cheonman, who'd worked as chief engineer on a cargo ship, was now captain of a mid-sized ship that sailed back and forth to China, while his younger uncle, Shipman, had done accounting for rice-market speculators and a rice mill and was now a rice wholesaler. He was the most successful of the three brothers. But with the start of the war, rice was requisitioned for rationing, making it impossible for the private sector to see a large profit outside of black-market deals. He became the director of a public distribution company while still overseeing grain production. He and Cheonman worked together to bring soybeans, corn, millet, and other grains from Dalian and Yantai in China to supplement the Japanese military's rations.

Icheol avoided his uncles' houses at first. Though they had not grown up together, he did know his cousins' names and faces, as they had seen each other once or twice every few years, whenever an event brought the whole family together. The Yeongdeungpo police would also have looked into Icheol's family register, but would have confirmed that there'd been virtually zero visits among the relatives back when everything had transpired a few years ago. Icheol figured that the authorities probably wouldn't be overly concerned about parole breakers unless something happened, but he thought he should keep his distance from his relatives anyway, just in case.

Icheol met the man named Bak Yonggil at Incheon Ironworks and got a job. Yonggil introduced him to the head of the lathe team, who in turn asked him a few professional questions and understood at once that he was an experienced technician. Incheon Ironworks employed around a hundred workers, most of whom were Korean. Only the owner, engineers, and administrators were Japanese. Behind the factory were six small houses: the Japanese engineers, managers, and administrators occupied five of them; the sixth was for the workers. It had three rooms, plus a kitchen, a toilet, and a washroom. Two of the rooms were for the factory's security guards, while the third was reserved for workers doing overnight shifts. It was an ordinary room with tatami flooring. A native of Incheon, Yonggil was a lathe technician in his early forties who'd been working at the factory since it first opened. He was a quiet man who would smile without saying anything. Neither he nor Icheol uttered a single word about organising or about Geunshik. Icheol found himself trusting Geunshik's style of leadership.

One day, when he'd ended his shift and was heading to the night-duty room to sleep, Yonggil slipped him some papers and said, 'In case you need something to wipe with.' This meant he should read them privately on the toilet and dispose of them there. They consisted of a few brief dispatches on recent trends and happenings in Incheon, as well as a transcribed excerpt from *Red Flag*, which he had not had access to since his arrest. Though the excerpted issue was three years old, the mission felt no less urgent. It was also a sad vestige of Jaeyu's attempts to restore the organisation right up until he'd been arrested. The excerpt was from *Red Flag*'s mission statement after the announcement of its inaugural publication.

> The Korean communist movement, which has been facing political challenges both at home and abroad and is tasked with nothing less than revolution, has been theoretically, practically, organisationally, and technologically scattered. As a result, otherwise upstanding communists have been limiting their activities and narrowing their perspectives much to the impediment of their political training and proficiency and thus hurting the movement. Because this is no different from the bygone days of *Iskra* in Russia, if we are to eliminate these errors and shortcomings and turn these local shards of a movement into a focused, unified national movement, then it is our urgent mission that we progress from newsletters produced at separate factories to a single, collective, nationwide political publication that will be a propagandist, an instigator, an organiser, a leader. As we are lacking a political party, which is to say, so long as the reconstruction of the Joseon Communist Party is incomplete, we are also lacking a political mouthpiece. We lack

> even the power needed to build a soapbox from which we might voice our politics before the masses. However, this does not mean that we are opposed to launching a local political publication within Gyeongseong, so as to fulfill our mission. Hence, to meet the earnest demands of our dear comrades in every camp and the wishes of freedom fighters everywhere, we introduce the inaugural issue of *Red Flag*, a transitional, political mouthpiece that strives to become a propagandist, an instigator, an organiser, and a leader for all of Gyeongseong and for the nation.

Two months of bunking in the factory's night-duty room passed before Icheol learned of two other orgs aside from Yonggil: namely, Kim Sunam and Yu Changbok. He took their advice and rented a room in the house next to Yonggil's. It was a Japanese-style, two-storey wooden house common in Incheon at the time. He rented the room at the top of the stairs, which offered him the advantage of being able to see down both ends of the alley. The other side of the alley was on the down slope, so his window looked onto the roof of the house across from him. Beyond that were the pier and the sea. He was happy with his new residence. Another three months passed before Yonggil spoke to him again, on the way home from work one night.

'If you're not doing anything, let's go get some makgeolli.'

This caught Icheol off guard, as it was the first time Yonggil had invited him out for a drink since he'd started working at the factory.

'I was under the impression that you don't drink.'

'Yeah, well, no, I don't, of course,' Yonggil said, and then added as Icheol stared at him bewildered, 'I'll just walk you to the bar.'

Where the road divided in Jemulpo — with one fork heading downtown and the other narrowing into the alley of bars filled with sailors and the inn where Icheol had stayed when he first arrived all those weeks ago — Yonggil chose the alley. This put Icheol at ease, as the place felt familiar. The tavern they chose was a classic Jemulpo establishment, where the floor was always wet and the air redolent of salt and low tide. Boisterous sailors, still dressed in waterproof coats smeared with fish scales, sat close together, talking and laughing loudly. Just inside the latticed glass door, right next to the wide-open display window, sat Geunshik, enveloped in the thick smoke of grilling fish. He raised his hand slightly in greeting. Meanwhile, Yonggil had already slipped away without saying goodbye. Icheol sat down across from Geunshik. A plate of sashimi and a pot of soup were on the table. Geunshik handed his own cup to Icheol and poured him some makgeolli.

'I figured you must be all settled in by now and ready to meet.'

Icheol downed his first cup before even taking the chance to say hello. A fresh cup and set of cutlery were brought out to him. Geunshik, who'd arrived first, had gone ahead and started drinking — only one cup, so far, judging by the weight of the large nickel kettle. Icheol handed Geunshik's cup back to him and refilled it.

'The comrades at the factory are treating me well,' Icheol said. 'I feel right at home.'

'Incheon is far enough from Gyeongseong that it should be a big change from Yeongdeungpo.'

'It seems like each area handles things on their own. But aren't we just across the sea from the rest of the continent?'

Geunshik nodded.

'Yes, which is why the sea border is heavily guarded.'

The two men drank quietly for a moment.

Geunshik lowered his voice to ask, 'So I hear your older brother drives an express train?'

'That's right. Our father has been working for the Yeongdeungpo Rail Works ever since it first opened. He's a technician for them now. My brother graduated from the railway academy in Yongsan and drives the *Hikari*.' Worried he might be inadvertently bragging, Icheol hurried to add, 'They're the unconscious, colonised petit bourgeois, focused only on survival.'

Geunshik didn't agree.

'They could be potential comrades. After all, they are, first and foremost, industrial workers. And haven't you, Comrade Yi, been able to do as much organising as you have because you've had their support?'

'I suppose you're right.'

Geunshik glanced around the tavern. The place had filled to capacity and become deafeningly loud. He took one more look and poured the last of the makgeolli into their cups.

'Let's finish this up and go.'

They left the tavern, crossed the main street, and headed down to the pier. When they reached a quiet spot near the beach, Geunshik got to the point.

'Despite what the Japanese claim, we have not been completely wiped out. There are still many orgs left in Incheon and Gyeongseong, and outside of the capital there are groups working to organise not only labourers but also farmers. The problem is that there's no alliance, only individual lines of contact. That's why the Comintern proposed the formation of a Popular Front, albeit too late. It's a call for revolution tailored to the situation and circumstances of each specific area. To do that, you have to form a unified front rather than focus only on class struggle. We've already been heading in that direction due to the nature of this region. It is critical that we create a nationwide unified front. One of our key leaders, an older comrade, was recently released from prison. It's practically a miracle that they let him go at all. He managed to fool the colonisers by passing himself off as insane the entire time he was in prison. He's gone underground, so the thought police are probably going crazy trying to find him. Rumours are flying that he really did lose his mind and is either living in the streets or is receiving treatment somewhere. Up in Manchuria, the armed struggle against the Japanese with China has slowed down because of the Japanese imperialists' continued suppression tactics. Small battles keep breaking out, though. A Korean member of the International Party is being sent from the continent to meet with local activists here.'

Icheol chose his words carefully. 'Won't this go badly, like what happened with Kim Hyeongseon?'

Geunshik nodded.

'You're right. I wasn't expecting Comrades Kim Hyeongseon and Gwon, who was our domestic liaison for the International Party at the time, to resort to agitprop, with the public statements and leaflets and everything. Accusing Comrade Yi Jaeyu of sectarianism and Comrade Kim Hyeongseon of petit-intelligentsia adventurism wasn't exactly fair of us, but looking at them critically, there is some truth to both points.'

'I was taught that the Communist Party reconstruction movement must be organised from below, through the struggle of the poorest workers,' Icheol said.

Geunshik nodded.

'Up until the start of the Sino-Japanese War, we were going the right way in principle. However, things have come to an impasse. Japanese fascist oppression, which started the war, is growing worse. Judging by the situation in Europe, war will continue to spread until it engulfs the entire world. Right now, the Western imperialist powers are forming a strategic alliance with the Soviets and the rest of the socialist block in order to build a united anti-fascist front in response to Nazi Germany. In this world war, if fascism falls, then Japan falls, too. Which means that Joseon will have a golden opportunity to rise up. Activists must not act blindly and squander this moment. We must seize the moment of revolution by quietly winning new converts and preserving our capabilities. With the way things have changed, we need avant-garde leadership and someone at the head of that leadership. To preserve our revolutionary capacities, there must be continuous development of class consciousness via an official mouthpiece for political unity and solidarity among activists. The avant-garde leadership's task at this current stage is to publish this mouthpiece and distribute it via our orgs.'

Before parting ways, Geunshik said to Icheol, 'By the way, Comrade Yi Gwansu has returned to Gyeongseong from where he's been hiding in the countryside. He contacted me. Shall I set you up with him?'

Icheol's heart raced. He thought about his meetings with Gwansu at his comrade's hillside agit in Changsin-jeong, and of Gwansu's efforts to protect Yi Jaeyu. The last time he'd seen Gwansu was when Gwansu had confirmed Geunshik's identity and dedication to the movement.

Icheol followed Geunshik's instructions to meet Gwansu's younger sister, who had just been released from prison for being part of the same group of organisers. They had all been in the group since it first started. She was going around to rubber factories and silk mills and other places in Dongdaemun to check up on old orgs. She took Icheol to Gwansu's agit hideout. He was renting a small hanok near Donam-jeong. He was as healthy and full of energy as ever, but his clothing style had changed. Instead of the shabby labourer's outfits or working uniform he'd worn before, he was dressed in a natty suit, just like an urbane white-collar employee, complete with a perfectly knotted necktie. When he saw Icheol stepping into the courtyard, he jumped down from the maru to welcome him.

'How've you been holding up?'

'Me? You know … Same as everyone else.'

'I was happy to hear about you from Geunshik.'

Gwansu had been lying low in Yangju with Jaeyu up until Jaeyu was arrested. After that, he'd escaped to the countryside, where he disguised himself as a beggar and made it all the way on foot to Daegu, where he opened a small banchan shop. He didn't just stay put, though. After forming several study groups to organise textile workers in Daegu, he returned to Gyeongseong. Among the early members who'd been released from prison, fewer than ten men and women were still active in the movement, but they were all dedicated activists with an ironclad faith in their objectives. They began publishing an underground monthly using Kim Hyeongseon's old publication's name, *The Communist*. They'd agreed to overcome their failures and start over. Around the same time, Gwansu was in contact with senior activists who'd participated in the founding of the Joseon Communist Party, and was expanding their reach by sending reppos to the Pacific Labour Union in Hamheung and Wonsan, among other places. They called themselves the Gyeongseong Communist Group, or Gyeongseong Com for short. In some ways, they were realising Jaeyu's plan of forming a vanguard from those who'd proven themselves through on-the-ground struggles.

Gwansu seemed to have grown calmer and more open-minded than before. He invited Icheol to stay the night before making the long trip back to Incheon. They had finished dinner and were settling in for the night when Gwansu finally broached the subject.

'Something important is coming up, and I was sort of hoping you might be able to take care of it.'

Icheol already had an idea of what it might be. Geunshik hadn't said anything specific, but Icheol had figured this was why he had sent him to Gwansu. He waited for Gwansu to continue.

'I heard that your brother drives an express train.'

'Yes, he drives the *Hikari* on the Gyeongui Line.'

'We need to get someone from Sinuiju to Gyeongseong. The group has concluded that you're the right man for the job.'

His suspicions confirmed, Icheol said, 'I'll do it.'

'Then I will send word to Incheon later regarding the date and method of contact.'

A few days later, Icheol received notice from Geunshik. That was when he had summoned Geumi from Incheon.

As soon as Geumi returned from meeting with her brother-in-law, she told her husband everything that had happened to his brother and about his request. Ilcheol sat quietly, deep in thought, a dark look shrouding his face.

'I'm sorry to put this upon you so suddenly. But your brother sounds like he could really use your help …'

'What've you got to be sorry for? He's my brother. He's always been the black sheep of the family, but it's not like he's robbing people. How can we look the other way when he's out there risking his neck to fight for our independence? If the date he has to go on doesn't line up with my schedule, I can just change my schedule by a day or two. It won't be a problem.'

15

The date set, Icheol memorised what time the *Hikari* would arrive at Gaeseong Station and worked out a plan for getting himself there. Naturally, his reason for going all the way to Gaeseong to board the express was to avoid the police. Government offices and public transportation were the riskiest places for convicted thought criminals like him. At Gyeongseong Station, to say nothing of Yeongdeungpo, the thought police and military police were keeping a sharp lookout and checking every passenger. To make matters worse, surveillance of the Gyeongui Line was even more thorough than of the Gyeongbu Line, since the former crossed the border. There was no relaxing once on board, either, as the transit detectives and military police were known to make frequent sweeps of the passenger carriages alongside the conductors. But Icheol trusted that, with his brother's help, he would find a way to board at Gaeseong Station. People had been travelling by boat around Ganghwado Island, into the mouth of the Hangang River, and all the way up to Mapo since the Joseon Dynasty; there were now even ferries that made the trip regularly. His plan was to charter a fishing boat and cross from Ganghwado to Gaepung County. Then all he'd have to do is spend the night in Gaeseong before catching the train.

With the help of organisers embedded at Incheon Pier, he was able to board a fishing boat going out to Yeonpyeongdo Island. As planned, he reached the shore opposite Ganghwado, the mud overgrown with reeds and bulrushes, Songaksan Mountain visible to the north-east. Icheol walked the two hours to Gaeseong and holed up in a tavern on the outskirts of the city until evening. When the sun was setting and the *Hikari* from Gyeongseong was scheduled to arrive, Icheol approached the back of a package depot a short distance from the station. He pushed open the low metal gate, walked right up to the building, and waited in front, as if he were any other shipper there to deliver some cargo. None of the workers pulling carts paid any attention to him. A long whistle blew, he assumed to announce the arrival of the express, and a pair of lights appeared at the far end of the tracks and came towards him at great speed. He knew there was a break room for station employees in a single-storey building at the end of the row of warehouses. Icheol was walking slowly towards it when someone said his name.

'Dusoe, is that you?'

'Hyeong …'

Dressed in the uniform of a train engineer, Ilcheol came over to him and clasped his hands. No one else was around. Ilcheol took him to the break room and handed him something wrapped in fabric.

'Go inside and change into this,' he said. 'Hurry.'

The bundle contained a rail worker's uniform and cap. Icheol pulled on the khaki uniform, strapped the gaiters onto his legs, and put the cap on his head. When he came back out, Ilcheol looked him over closely from head to toe and led the way. They crossed the tracks to where the express train was parked at the platform, and climbed into the engine cab.

After seeing the outside of the locomotive and the dashboard, Icheol asked his brother, 'Is this a Teou?'

'Yeah, it's the largest of the Baltics. The Japanese call it a Tehoi. It can haul twenty tonnes.'

'Why not a Mater?'

'Those are the most common, but they're mostly used to pull freight. And they're well-suited to mountainous terrain, so most of the northern lines use them. They say Mikados aren't much use in the mountains.' Ilcheol gave his younger brother a long look. 'I heard they've started building Teou engines in Yongsan and Yeongdeungpo now, after Kawasaki. If you'd kept your nose down and worked hard, you could've been one of their best technicians by now.'

He gave his brother a warning before the assistant driver arrived: 'All large tank locomotives are equipped with mechanical stokers. Not that you need to concern yourself with it, of course, but just keep it in mind.' He went on, 'Luckily my assistant today is Korean. I told him about you already, so he shouldn't get suspicious. You drive a freight train. I told him you're going up to Sinuiju to catch your train there. Your wife's family lives in Gaeseong. You got your start as a stoker, not from the training school. Just remember those things, and don't talk too much.'

The assistant came running and grabbed the metal rail on the outside of the engine. He was carrying a large thermal flask. Icheol automatically took the flask and held out his other hand to pull the assistant into the cab.

'Ah! I heard all about you.' The assistant, who looked to be in his mid-twenties, took the flask back from Icheol. 'They'd just boiled a whole jug of ginseng tea when I stopped by the office, so I brought plenty back for us.'

He took two porcelain cups out of his locker, offered them to Ilcheol and Icheol, and carefully poured them some tea. It was customary in the winter for locomotive engineers arriving at Gaeseong Station to drink tea made from the root hairs of a ginseng plant. A whistle sounded, and the block signal went up. A station employee on the platform held up a dark-red flag. The departure announcement followed. Ilcheol pulled a cord above his head to blow the train whistle. That meant the train was about to leave. He pulled the regulator, and with a loud thudding noise, the pistons began to move. As they pulled further away from the station, the locomotive picked up more speed until it was puffing away at a steady rate of sixty to seventy kilometres per hour. The assistant kept an eye on the equipment and controlled the furnace by making adjustments to the mechanical stoker. Soon, the train was racing across the plains of Hwanghae Province.

'I'm only three years out of rail school,' the assistant said. 'In the past, it would've been unimaginable for someone like me to be assigned to an express so soon. That's a lucky break for a Korean.'

Ilcheol simply smiled in response, and Icheol as well did his best to avoid saying too much.

'Everyone who started before me had to work for over a decade before they got assigned to a passenger train, and the express is considered the crowning glory of the rail. Anyway, I hear you drive a freight train?'

'Huh? Ah, yes.'

'What line were you on before?'

'Gyeongin, and also Gyeongwon.'

'Did you go through the training school?'

Having been warned by his brother, Icheol was careful with his answers.

'I was even luckier than you. Tataki agari.'

The assistant recognised the Japanese expression, which meant he'd risen from the bottom.

'Ah! So you started out as a labourer?'

'Yes, as a stoker.'

He launched into the rest of his back story without prompting. He lived in Gyeongseong, but his wife's family was in Gaeseong. She'd been talking for a long time now about wanting to visit her family, but everyone knew how hard it was for railmen to get any sort of down time. So he'd used his shift change to take her to Gaeseong and was planning to pick her up again on his way back.

The train arrived in Pyeongyang late at night and departed again, crossing the Cheongcheongang River bridge at dawn and entering Sinuiju in the morning. Instead of sleeping in the dorms, Ilcheol accompanied his brother downtown and grabbed a room at an inn. The person Icheol was meeting was most likely an activist, which meant he would obviously not be entering the country via the immigration office in Antung. Icheol double-checked the address in Uiju and started walking. It was a four-kilometre walk to Uiju, where the old government offices of the Joseon Dynasty had been located — Sinuiju, or New Uiju, had only recently sprung into being with the laying of railways and steel bridges.

Icheol went to a herbal-medicine clinic at the corner of the pre-colonial government compound. The clinic itself was in the outer wing of a tiled-roof house that faced the street; a long verandah wrapped around the front. Patients and guests used this building, while the rear wing was for the family. Icheol peered inside and saw an older, bespectacled man in the back room and a younger man up-front, kneeling off to one side, chopping medicinal herbs with a jakdu straw cutter. The younger man greeted Icheol.

'How can we help you?'

'Is the doctor in? I have a question.'

'What seems to be ailing you?'

'I'm not feeling too well, so I thought I should have my pulse checked.'

The man in glasses overheard them and coughed to get their attention.

'Just send him on in.'

Icheol stepped into the room and sat down.

'Sit closer,' the doctor said. 'Roll up your sleeve and show me your arm.'

Icheol did as instructed and rested his bare forearm on the desk. The doctor placed his index and middle fingers on Icheol's wrist to time his pulse.

'Where are you from?' the doctor asked.

'I just arrived from Gyeongseong.'

'That's a long trip.'

'Well, I'm on my way to visit my uncle.'

The doctor grinned and said, 'I'm guessing your name is Dusoe?'

'That's correct.'

Dr Jang stood.

'You missed breakfast, so you must be starving. Let's go inside.'

Icheol understood that the formalities were over, and he followed Dr Jang into the private wing of the house. The rear wing had its own men-only quarters: the sliding door opened to reveal a middle-aged man in a Western-style suit. His hawk-like gaze moved past the doctor and fixed on Icheol's face. The doctor told them to talk among themselves and turned to leave.

While waiting for Icheol to make himself comfortable, the man in the suit said, 'You must be Comrade Yi Icheol.'

'Yes, but my family calls me Dusoe.'

The man laughed.

'Then your brother must be a Hansoe.'

'That's right. He drives the express. We were asked to escort a Mr Kim to Gyeongseong.'

Mr Kim said, 'I apologise for putting you through the trouble of such a long journey.'

He explained that he'd crossed the river on foot while it was still frozen over about a month earlier. Word had been sent back and forth by his contact in Sinuiju.

'When can I go?' he asked.

'The express bound for the capital leaves this evening. We have to be at the station two hours before departure.'

'Well, then that means we've got plenty of time.'

He asked Icheol about the state of the movement in Gyeongseong and who was involved, and about the literature and other material they'd acquired from abroad and what the orgs were using to get the word out. Icheol told him everything he knew and explained that most people were lying low after the recent roundups.

'There's no such thing as a good or bad time for us,' Mr Kim said. 'We can only keep fighting for revolution until the day of our liberation.'

Icheol took Mr Kim to Sinuiju, to the inn where his brother waited. Ilcheol briefly explained his plan to them.

'The express always has a transit detective and a transit MP on board. They, in turn, each have an assistant, which means four people, working in pairs. They're authorised to stop the train at any station in an emergency and to call for back-up at any of the stations. So I do not recommend that you risk riding in the passenger carriages. You can ride in the mail carriage instead. It's right behind the engine. It's the size of a regular freight carriage but split into two compartments: a cargo room where mailbags and boxes are stowed, and a mailroom where workers sort the items. The two of you will have to hide in the cargo room behind the boxes. It's a long trip, so it won't be easy.'

'But at least it's an overnight train. We can sleep the whole way,' Icheol said.

Mr Kim asked Ilcheol, 'Will we be able to move back and forth between the mail carriage and the cab?'

'No, the back of the locomotive is blocked by the tender, which carries coal and water. There's an emergency passageway next to the chimney, but it's not safe to use when the train is moving.'

'We'll be like rats in a trap,' Mr Kim murmured. 'But at least it should be safe enough while the train's in motion.'

When evening began to fall, they left the inn. Ilcheol handed his brother a small backpack. It contained an army-issue canteen, two bags of army crackers, and two empty hot water bottles to use as urinals. He had purchased all of it while Icheol was in Uiju.

'I'm guessing there will be two or three people in the mailroom: a foreman in charge, a clerk who keeps the ledger, and a worker who hauls the mail up and down at each stop. Not much cargo means only two people, but when there's a lot, there could be up to four postal employees on board. Since there are no holidays right now and the seasons are changing, I'm thinking there won't be much cargo.'

They went to the express platform and boarded the mail carriage. Ilcheol led them through the darkened mailroom and into the cargo room via a small door. Packages were stacked inside, and the walls were lined with mailbags. Further inside, smaller items were sorted neatly in wooden crates. They pushed the crates away from the wall to create enough room for the two men to hide. Mr Kim and Icheol sat down with their backs against the wall, while Ilcheol restacked the cargo. The packages furthest inside were destined for Gyeongseong, of course, while the rest were arranged in order of each city they would stop at.

'We probably won't reach Gyeongseong until morning,' Ilcheol said.

'The train slows down after Susaek Station. I'll leave it to you to decide where to jump.'

Thirty minutes before departure, two employees entered the mailroom. They went into the cargo room and pushed open the hanging door to receive any late arrivals. A cart loaded with mailbags and packages was brought over, and the employees sorted and stacked everything inside. The express was departing Sinuiju and making stops in Pyeongyang and Gaeseong before arriving in Gyeongseong, while skipping the whistlestops in between. When they arrived at Pyeongyang Station, Ilcheol jumped down from the cab and paced around on the platform, pretending to get some air, while surreptitiously scanning the mail carriage. The two mail employees were swapping out old cargo for new. The sliding doors left the mailroom and cargo room open to view on both sides. Fortunately, it was a quiet night, and the moment passed without incident.

The two stowaways dozed and woke, dozed and woke, in their cramped positions behind the wooden crates. The roar of the train crossing a steel bridge woke them, and the smooth rhythm of the rails as they crossed the plains lulled them back to sleep. Icheol figured that with Pyeongyang behind them only Gaeseong was left. The mailroom was quiet; the postal workers seemed to take a break whenever the train was in motion. He could predict that they would enter the cargo area again before arriving at Gaeseong Station, just as they had before arriving at Pyeongyang Station. The two men ate a midnight snack of army crackers and relieved themselves using the tin bottles. Now that they could relax, they stretched their legs out between the crates and leaned back against the wall to get more shut-eye. When they heard the train whistle and the rattling of another steel bridge, the mailroom door opened and the postal workers came in and turned on a light. A thirty-watt globe hung from the ceiling. They shuffled parcels to one side, swapping opinions as they went. The train was almost at Gaeseong Station: it belched out steam and slowed. As before, a parcel worker at the station loaded a handcart with incoming mail and handed up the outgoing mail. The postal workers stretched and yawned as the train left again. They would change shifts with the Gyeongbu Line workers at Gyeongseong Station along with the engineers.

Icheol and Mr Kim were fully awake now and getting ready to jump. They heard the rattle of another steel bridge and figured that they were crossing the Imjingang River. The lack of any sound from the mailroom suggested that the postal workers were fast asleep, now that they were nearing the end of the line and could relax. The men unlatched the side door and cracked it open. Cold air rushed in mercilessly. The train was crossing darkened fields. The faint glow of the whistlestops they passed indicated that they were almost to Susaek. Sure enough, the train let out another belch of steam and a long whistle, then began to slow.

'Let's jump out here,' Icheol whispered to Mr Kim.

Icheol tossed the backpack into the darkness first and then jumped. He rolled down a slope overgrown with weeds and came to a stop in the dry mud at the edge of a paddy. He could just make out in the dark Mr Kim rolling down the hill a moment after him. They clambered back up to the tracks. Icheol walked over to Mr Kim.

'Are you hurt?' he asked.

'I'm fine. Where do we go now?'

Icheol started walking without bothering to search for the backpack.

'Gyeongseong's not far.'

They arrived at the top of Aeogae Hill just as the sky was beginning to brighten. The city was waking up. Peddlers shouldering A-frames loaded with tofu, fish, cooked food, and other items rang bells or shouted at the tops of their lungs for others to get your tofu here, or fresh herring, herring for sale! As the streets crowded with people heading off to work, the two men boarded a tram and took it to the last station in Donam-jeong.

Yi Gwansu's house was in a hillside alley. When Icheol knocked, the gate swung open immediately as if someone had been waiting for them. Sure enough, Gwansu was hovering just inside. The three of them followed him into the house without a word.

'I figured you might arrive right about now, so I was waiting,' Gwansu said.

'Thank you,' said Mr Kim.

Gwansu turned to Icheol as well.

'Your help was invaluable.'

Icheol lingered in the doorway instead of sitting down.

'I'd better get going,' he said. He knew that this was where a reppo's job ended.

Gwansu nodded.

'Understood. It's a long way back to Incheon. Take care.'

Icheol went back the way they'd come, riding the same tram to Mapo, and then a ferry to Incheon. He could only assume that this Mr Kim of the International Party and Mr Pak, leader of the Gyeongseong Com, were successfully brought together. Mr Pak, or Pak Hon-yong, was the old comrade of Kim Hyeongseon and Kim Danya. Together they had founded the Joseon Communist Party in 1925. He had been arrested but was released after fooling the guards into believing he'd lost his mind by eating his own excrement while in prison, and immediately went underground with the help of his comrades. Years later, he was contacted by the Joseon Communist Party's reconstructionist faction. Then, following Yi Jaeyu's imprisonment, the Gyeongseong Com made contact with the remaining reconstructionists, as well as members of other factions, and centred the organisation on Pak Hon-yong. Every activist knew his name. Whereas the Gyeongseong Com had cells in various worksites, Pak Hon-yong had been working abroad for a long time and lacked a popular base within the country from which to work due to his past arrests and imprisonment. But recruiting him held great symbolic meaning to the activists. He was a clear successor from the International Party, and could give an objective account of the Gyeongseong Com. Their plan was to create and distribute a publication as their first step towards uniting the badly divided socialist movement.

Geumi was the only person who knew the full story of how Icheol had been arrested. Seonok gave her bits of information now and then about what Icheol was up to, which she'd never done before. She had begun serving as a key reppo connecting Yeongdeungpo, Gyeongseong, and Incheon. She also believed that, despite the fact that Geumi's husband was a hardworking engineer for the Government-General's Railway Bureau and therefore a tool of the empire, his help with spiriting Mr Kim from Sinuiju to Gyeongseong must have earned their family some recognition from International Red Aid.

*

The following spring, Seonok received instructions to go to Incheon. Having already dropped by Icheol's house several times to make contact, she went for a walk in Manguk Park before heading over to his place again in the evening. Row after row of small houses packed the hillside, and there were narrow alleys and stairways everywhere. The house, which Yonggil had found for him, had a small knitting factory on the ground floor that was run by the landlady and six female workers. The landlady's husband had an office job at the wharf. The two rooms on the upper floor were rented out to workers employed at nearby factories; Icheol lived in one of those rooms. When Seonok came knocking, Icheol slid open the door in his singlet.

'What's going on?'

'I'm starving.'

'What? Who says they're starving the moment they see you? Couldn't find a dinner date in Yeongdeungpo?'

Seonok slid the door open wider and glanced back down the narrow hallway and stairwell.

'Is the other room empty?'

'It is. For about ten days now. They moved.'

Having confirmed that they were the only two people on the floor, Seonok got to the point.

'I received word that someone's coming at 7.00 pm tomorrow.'

'Who … ?'

'I have no idea. Tell me where you want to meet them, and I'll pass it along.'

Icheol thought it over.

'The walking path near the Anglican Church in Manguk Park is good.'

After hearing from Seonok, Icheol went to visit Geunshik. Geunshik smiled brightly at what Icheol told him, as if he'd already known what was up.

'If it's word from Gyeongseong, Comrade Yi Gwansu must've sent it, which means it's an important mission.'

Sure enough, waiting for him the next day on the walking path near the Anglican Church in Manguk Park was Gwansu's sister, Yi Geumsun. He'd met her once, right before Bang Wuchang and the others were arrested, so they recognised each other immediately. She was a diehard activist who had refused to quit organising in factories despite two or more stints in prison. She came up behind Icheol, who was strolling near the church, and naturally fell into step with him.

'The forsythia are in bloom, but the weather is still quite cold. Let's walk for a bit.'

They spoke as they walked.

'I need a safehouse,' she said. 'Monthly rent is fine, or jeonse rent is okay, too.'

'How soon do you need it?'

'The sooner, the better. Talk it over with Kim Geunshik, and once it's decided, please come to Gyeongseong yourself, Comrade Yi. You'll be bringing someone important back with you.'

'Understood. I'll head to Donam-jeong as soon as I can.'

Their business concluded, she stopped and indicated that she was leaving.

'Don't head home just yet,' she said. 'Walk a little further.'

As Icheol bowed goodbye and resumed walking, he heard her cheerful voice ring out behind him.

'You did a great job last time!'

'Ah … thanks,' he said.

Icheol walked a short way then looked back; she had already vanished into the shade of the trees.

He contacted Geunshik right away, and they came to the conclusion that the safehouse would need to be kept separate from where they worked. Icheol's boarding house was near Soebbul Hill, whereas Geunshik's neighbourhood, just past the Baedari Intersection, was filled with factories. They decided to use Icheol's place to work on their publication and rented out the entire second storey. Icheol also decided to quit his job at the ironworks so he could focus entirely on his role as Pak Hon-yong's reppo. They looked for a place for their guest from Gyeongseong to stay in Yulmok-jeong, which took its name from the older Chestnut Tree Village it had replaced. Yulmok-jeong was a 'new village', where merchants who'd made a fortune off the port had built fancy tile-roofed houses for themselves. If the area around Manguk Park was known as a wealthy Japanese neighbourhood, then the wealthy Korean neighbourhood was Yulmok-jeong. Most of the merchants' money had come from rice refineries and breweries. Geunshik enlisted a member who worked at a refinery to find a safehouse and learned about a banchan shop near the entrance to the neighbourhood. It was owned by a widow who lived there with her daughter; they had a two-room guesthouse. The refinery's electrician had boarded there for over a year. Geunshik had his man sign a lease immediately. Once preparations were complete, Icheol went to Gwansu's place in Gyeongseong. He spent the night there and discussed several important matters.

'We invited all the old members of the Tuesday Society and the Shanghai faction to meet up again. They're the ones who formed the Joseon Communist Party early on and survived all kinds of ordeals without betraying the cause. Pak Hon-yong was among them. You know he studied in Moscow and lived in exile in Shanghai, then survived the hell of prison by the skin of his teeth. Bringing him in will give our movement a centre and unify all the different factions. We must be ready to give our own lives to support him and keep him safe.'

Gwansu added that they'd decided to use the safehouse to put together the publication in order to reassure Hon-yong.

The following night, Icheol rode the tram to its final stop in Mapo. The riverside embankment and the streets were all covered in cobblestones, making it look more like some foreign country than Joseon. Freight ships and passenger ships of all sizes were moored along the river. Yi Geumsun waited just until Icheol got off the tram and spotted her before turning and making her way down to the wharf. There, she boarded a wooden boat with a round awning. Icheol followed her aboard. Sitting beneath the awning was Hon-yong in a western business suit. Two oarsmen rowed until they reached the middle of the river and then raised the twin sails. Having timed the tides just right, the boat swiftly headed downstream. Hon-yong appeared to be studying the river in the dark; Geumsun sat quietly beside him. Icheol chose a seat further away, facing away from them. The three of them dozed off in the swaying boat, waking every now and then and gazing out at the distant passing lights of riverside villages. At dawn they passed Daemyeong Port of Ganghwado Island and reached the waters of Yeongjongdo Island. The coast was crowded with boats coming and going, as the fishing boats that had left the night before were now returning home. Icheol led the two of them to his boarding house on the slope of Soebbul Hill. It wasn't until they were inside his second-storey room that Hon-yong finally acknowledged Icheol and spoke to him.

'Thank you for your troubles, comrade.'

Hon-yong's eyes were cold and expressionless as they gazed at Icheol over his horn-rimmed glasses. The three of them rested in the morning and had a bite to eat at one of the pubs that lined the top of the hill before heading out to the banchan shop in Yulmok-jeong. At the corner where the alley split off in three different directions stood the shop, its latticed glass door facing directly onto the street. Next to it was a smaller door made from sheet metal. Inside, towering stacks of wooden and bronze bowls of all sizes were filled to the brim with mouth-watering banchan. A kindly, middle-aged woman in baggy pants with a white apron tied around her waist invited them in.

'We spoke to you a while ago about renting your guesthouse,' Icheol said politely.

'Oh, of course. As a matter of fact, I was told you'd be arriving today.'

She gave the three of them a quick once-over and smiled.

'This way, please.'

She led them through the store and out the back door, into an inner courtyard where there was a well, a water pump, and several trees. There was a jangdokdae for storing preserves, and on the far side of the courtyard where a shed must have once stood was the guesthouse. The single-room house had a narrow verandah on the outside, a kitchen with an agungi stove that warmed the house from below, and a sliding door that divided the living space. It had been newly wallpapered, making the place look bright and inviting. Under the window was a pole for hanging clothes, and the bedding was folded up and covered with a white cloth, since there was no cupboard or attic for storage. Hon-yong looked around at the room without a word and gazed out the window. Geumsun paid the owner. Hon-yong became a clerk who'd just been transferred to Incheon without his family, Icheol became one of his junior staff members, and Geumsun became his younger sister.

The owner, delighted at receiving several months' worth of rent in advance, cheerfully said to Geumsun, 'I'll feel much safer having him here. The guesthouse has been empty for a while, and it was getting a little scary.'

Being the type of pure intellectual who'd never so much as set foot near a factory, Hon-yong was not a naturally charismatic leader. But he was a revolutionary to the core in both principle and practice, and his struggle history and political writings were widely known among socialist activists. Several critics would later attest that the Gyeongseong Com was the first and last true association of labour activists to come together in the Gyeongseong area under Japanese colonial rule. During this time, a hundred or so activists joined for the first time or became associate members. Under the Gyeongseong Com's leadership, all domestic socialists who'd remained committed to agitating for revolution were included. It became proof positive of the reconstruction faction's victory in eradicating the factionalism caused by the International line under Gwon.

Geumsun moved in with Geunshik and they became an 'agit couple'. They enlisted male and female activists from Gyeongseong with strong writing skills to work on the publication with them. Local news items were gathered from all over the country and forwarded to Gyeongseong, where they could then be broadcast to other activists via the publication, to break through the dark and gloomy fog of war. There was news of a strike by factory workers in Pyeongyang, and investigations by the Police Bureau into a steadily increasing number of labour disputes, including walkouts and slowdowns, following the strengthening of the controlled economy, with at least one case occurring every single day nationwide. The publication also carried stories of female workers going on strike at the Pyeongyang Dongwoo Rubber Factory and the Gyeonggi Rubber Factory, as well as that of young men in Daegu, in the south-east corner of the peninsula, arming themselves and hiding out on Palgongsan Mountain to avoid conscription. Despite circulating a limited number of transcribed or mimeographed copies via point groups under tight security, they found themselves caught red-handed by the Japanese authorities.

The police began tracking down everyone who had been convicted of thought crimes. A special unit was formed to zero in on suspects who had not yet been arrested and convicts who'd absconded from parole. They shadowed and monitored the daily lives of those who'd been involved in past incidents. By secretly investigating both liberal intellectuals and relatively moderate student activist groups that had been involved with the Popular Front, the Japanese caught on to Yi Gwansu's existence and activities. The thought police's Yi Gwansu task force shadowed a Choongang Secondary School student who worked as Gwansu's reppo and managed to arrest Gwansu at the Hyehwa-jeong roundabout intersection. He was there to hand off copies of a publication that had just arrived from Incheon. With his coat collar popped and a rolled-up newspaper in his hand, Gwansu was walking from the direction of Dongsung-jeong, and slipped the newspaper into the reppo's hand as they passed each other, before strolling off leisurely towards Hyehwa-jeong. The copies were hidden inside the newspaper. While one detective searched the student, the other ran after Gwansu. Realising that he was being followed, Gwansu began to run, but another team of detectives was already lying in wait in front of the Hyehwa-jeong roundabout.

Trapped, he darted across the main street, which was streaming with cars and trams. The detectives blew hard on their whistles as they ran after him. A pedestrian walking by saw this and instinctively stuck his leg out to trip Gwansu, who took a fantastic spill on the ground. His leg seemingly sprained in the fall, he stood and limped a few more steps before falling back down and getting captured. The Police Bureau ordered all Special Higher Police divisions in the Gyeongseong area to round up thought criminals with any connection to Gwansu.

Meanwhile, Yamashita had been promoted from chief detective to deputy chief inspector of the Yeongdeungpo Special Higher Police. But it continued to weigh on him that Icheol had skipped parole and could not be found. He decided to summon Ilcheol, to see what he could learn. Ilcheol's entire family was living in the rail workers' housing while he faithfully carried out his duties as a *Hikari* engineer on the Gyeongui Line and Antung–Hsinking Line. His credentials as a loyal subject and employee of the Railway Bureau were unimpeachable.

'Where the hell is that younger brother of yours and what is he doing?'

No sooner was Yamashita's question out than Ilcheol heaved a deep sigh and threw the question right back at him.

'I'm as frustrated as you are. Isn't there anything you can tell me?'

'He violated his parole and will be sent right back to prison the moment he's arrested.'

Ilcheol sipped his tea before muttering under his breath, 'Is it possible he left the city, or the country entirely?'

Yamashita's eyes widened.

'You stowed him away on the train and took him over the border, didn't you?'

'I wish I'd thought of that. What a great way to rid the family of troublemakers!' He made sure to add, 'It would never work, though. We've had to tighten security on the express trains because of the war.'

'Ah … of course … uh, anyway, you must contact me immediately if you hear from him. The higher-ups have been putting pressure on me about it.'

'I'm counting the days until he's arrested and put away. Then maybe I'll sleep easy at night.'

After that, Yamashita assigned an undercover team to follow everyone related to the old case, and received daily reports from them. One day, a member of the team came to see him.

'Bak Seonok just came back from Incheon.'

'Huh? Bak Seonok? Who's that again?'

'A female factory worker who was rounded up last time. She's been living with relatives who own a tteok shop.'

'A tteok shop, huh? Wasn't she in that book club that Icheol was running … ?' Yamashita tapped his fountain pen against his desk while deep in thought. 'You say she went to Incheon? Starting tomorrow, let's focus on her and see what we find out.'

He assigned a task force of one detective and three assistants to follow Seonok. The plan was to not only keep an eye on her but track her every move and investigate every single person she met with.

'Yes, Incheon,' Yamashita murmured. 'Something's afoot in Incheon.'

Roughly two weeks later, Yamashita received a call. Seonok had boarded a train for Incheon. He took two detectives with him and caught the next train headed the same way. They went to a cafe downtown and waited for the undercover team to contact them. Two hours passed before the detective who had been tailing her arrived. His face was flushed.

'Chief Yamashita, you better brace yourself for this! Guess who Bak Seonok just met.'

Yamashita leapt out of his seat.

'Who? Who was it?'

'Yi Icheol.'

He rapped the top of the table and fell back in his chair.

'*Yoshi!* You found out where he's staying, right?'

The detective filled him in on the details. Seonok had passed the Baedari Intersection and headed for the walking path behind the Methodist church in Changyeong-jeong. Unable to get too close, the tail had observed her from a distance. Half an hour later, a man appeared. The tail didn't recognise him at first. Seonok and the man walked for about thirty minutes and then sat for a while at the top of the hill. Then they came back down and parted ways at Soebbul Hill. Since Seonok's next moves were already apparent, the tail decided to focus on the man. He followed him to a boarding house in an alley on top of a hill in Changyeong-jeong and watched him go upstairs. The tail, who was Korean, then raced back and delivered the stunning news to the detective: the man had looked both ways, carefully studying the street, before entering the house; even at a glance, it was unmistakably Yi Icheol.

'Shall we bring him in now?' the Japanese detective asked.

Yamashita mulled it over. There were four detectives, including him, and at least two experienced police assistants. That was more than enough to arrest Icheol, regardless of what unexpected situation might arise. He thought about it long and hard before making a decision.

'First, a stakeout. No arrests for the next twenty-four hours. Let's see who he meets before we bring him in.'

They booked a room in an inn near Icheol's boarding house and took shifts. They kept a close watch until late at night, when the windows of the house finally went dark, and resumed at first light. Though there was no need for disguises at night, they couldn't very well get caught loitering around in broad daylight, so they borrowed a roast sweet-potato cart and stationed it at the north-west entrance to the alley. Another agent dressed in rags to disguise himself as a vagrant sat at the south-east entrance to the alley.

Icheol had received a telegram that Seonok was coming to Incheon. Naturally, the telegram was delivered via Geunshik's other reppo. Two weeks had passed since he'd picked up copies of the new publication, and he'd been sensing that something unexpected had happened. Sure enough, Seonok's news was that Gwansu had been arrested. This did not bode well. Gwansu had direct connections to the core. Icheol sent Seonok on her way and returned home, his nerves on edge the whole way there. He'd stolen a glance at a man who'd passed them as they were coming down the otherwise deserted walking path, a man a little too nicely dressed for hiking up a dirt path by himself. If he wasn't a local, then he would've had to be on his way to visit someone, but there were no houses in the direction he was going. After saying goodbye to Seonok, Icheol deliberately took the main street through Changyeong-jeong and was walking up a hill when someone rushed by right behind him. It did not look like the same man from the path. Icheol paused in front of his house and looked around carefully. A man in a hunting cap walked by with his head down, but Icheol could feel the man's eyes on him. It had to be a spy, one of the hounds for the police! He was sure of it. As soon as he got upstairs, Icheol rushed to the window and peeked out the curtain to study the alley below. Just as he thought, the man had turned around and was walking past the house again. He gazed up at Icheol's window as he passed. Icheol went ahead and turned on his lamp. Having a tail meant they already knew who and where he was. He lay down on the tatami mat without bothering to change clothes and thought things over. Then he leapt up, pulled his coat back on, rushed outside, and broke into a sprint. There was no sign of the tail, but he ran anyway. His quick thinking worked: he managed to slip through their fingers. Now that they'd confirmed his location, they would alert each other and cordon off the area. He ran to Geunshik and Geumsun's safehouse. His neck was slick with sweat despite the winter cold. He banged on their front door. Geumsun asked who was there, and opened the door the moment she heard Icheol's voice. He told them the news.

'I just found out today. Comrade Yi Gwansu has been arrested.'

Geumsun brought her hand to her mouth and murmured, 'Ah, not my brother.'

'We need to get out of here,' Geunshik muttered.

'There's no time to waste,' Icheol said. 'My reppo just came from Yeungdeungpo and clearly had a tail.'

He gave them a quick rundown of everything that had happened. As longtime activists, Geunshik and Geumsun trusted Icheol's expertise.

'We can't waste a single second making up our minds. You take Pak to a second location. Comrade Yi and I will clean up here.'

Geumsun did not argue. She stuffed clothes into a bag, pulled on an overcoat, covered her head with a scarf, and was halfway out the door when she paused and tried to hand a few banknotes to Geunshik.

Geunshik pushed her hand away and said, 'You'll need that more than us, considering where we're headed next.'

Geumsun didn't bother to wipe the tears that were already wetting her face. She gave him a brief hug and hurried out the gate. She was headed for the banchan shop in Yulmok-jeong, where she would help Pak Hon-yong escape.

As soon as she was gone, Icheol told Geunshik, 'Please save yourself, too. I'll stay and take the blame for everything.'

'Fine by me. And anyway, if we're to create a diversion, it'll help if I disappear for a while before they catch me. But they will be ruthless with you.'

'I just have to hold out for twenty-four hours.'

Geunshik nodded. They had already matched up their alibis. The publications were delivered from Gyeongseong, and Icheol received them and made copies, which Geunshik distributed. That meant they were in charge of copies and distribution for all of Incheon.

'I can't leave Incheon,' Geunshik said. 'I'll just keep my nose dry for a few days while I tie up loose ends in the group, and then I'll let them catch me.'

'I better go home.'

Geunshik's plan, as well, was to get his house in order and quickly alert the nearest yacheykas. Icheol returned to his lodgings on Soebbul Hill. He'd been gone for no more than thirty minutes and had left his light on while he was gone. It looked like the undercover agents had not yet returned. He collected all of his mimeographs and other literature and burned them at the tap in the backyard. After washing the last of the ashes down the drain, he returned to his room and lay down, but sleep did not come.

The following day as well he got up and ate breakfast at a restaurant nearby and returned to his room, the same as he always did. A vendor in a wool cap was selling roasted sweet potatoes from a cart at the entrance to the alley. Icheol knew at once that it was an agent.

Late in the afternoon, Icheol put on an overcoat and headed out, to make it look like he was going to meet someone. Once he was sure he had a tail, he made sure not to cross streets or detour down any alleyways but simply headed straight for the Sinpo-jeong main street, packed with banks and shops and inns, and went into a Japanese grill restaurant. Though it was still early for dinner, he was thinking of ordering one of the newfangled Western-style meals served in courses, starting with soup. He had just picked up his knife when someone suddenly plopped down in the seat across from him.

'Hey there, Dusoe. Long time no see.'

It was Yamashita. Icheol wasn't exactly surprised.

It was while tailing them that Yamashita had realised his mistake. In delaying their arrest, he'd inadvertently bought them time. The moment Icheol casually walked into Sinpo-jeong by himself and sat down to dinner, Yamashita understood that his target had known he was being tailed from the outset.

Icheol smiled and said, 'The food here is great. Shall I order something for you, too?'

Before the waiter could hand him a menu, Yamashita ordered a hamburger steak and said, 'Why not? Seeing as how this is our last meal together …' He lit a cigarette to calm his anger. 'This must be a lot for you to handle on your own. If there's something I should know, I'd appreciate it if you would just tell me now.'

'Let's eat first.'

The food came out. They ate in a congenial silence punctuated only by the clattering of their silverware. The rest of Yamashita's team watched from their posts at the entrance and seats nearby.

'Shouldn't you alert the Incheon Police Station?' Icheol asked.

Yamashita smiled and slowly stirred a cube of brown sugar into the cup of coffee that came with their meal.

'That's not your concern. The only thing you should be worried about is your family. How you conduct yourself right now will determine whether your brother loses his job or goes to jail.'

Icheol laughed out loud.

'So collaborators are now in charge of catching collaborators. What a great role model for assimilation.'

'Laugh while you can. If I take you in this time, you won't be coming back out. Cooperate, and we'll both get through this with less of a headache.'

Their meals complete, the two men walked out of the restaurant like old friends. A different detective handcuffed Icheol. Yamashita had sent word to the Incheon Police Station before they ate.

Following Icheol's interrogation, local activists were arrested and basic investigations were completed as quickly as possible so they could be transferred to the Jongno Police Station, in the capital, since ideological cases fell under the purview of the Government-General. What became known as the Gyeongseong Com Incident, beginning with Yi Gwansu's arrest in December 1940, ended the following spring with the arrest of over a hundred members. Icheol remained at the Incheon Police Station, where his interrogation and torture at the hands of the thought police began. He obediently confessed to having received copies of the publication in Gyeongseong and having made more copies for Geunshik to distribute. Workers who'd been caught up in the book-club scam were brought in and began confessing everything they knew, which led to the quick discovery of Geunshik's dockside hideout. Of course, this had all been planned out in advance, so when the police arrived on the scene, Geunshik was sleeping peacefully and was arrested while still in his underwear. Likewise, as planned, Geunshik pretended to give in to his torture and named several people who'd distributed literature; they in turn were arrested and named several others during their torture. Twenty or so labourers from the Incheon area were rounded up on charges of having received and read prohibited literature. That was more than enough for Yamashita to save face at the Incheon Police Station, but inwardly he knew that the mission was a complete failure. He did not let it show, though. Ultimately, Icheol and Geunshik were confirmed to be leaders of the movement in Incheon and were able to keep Pak Hon-yong's existence concealed to the very end. They and everyone else involved in the Gyeongseong Com Incident were separated and sent to the Dongdaemun and Jongno Police Stations.

After sneaking out of Incheon, Geumsun escorted Hon-yong out of the city and hid him in the countryside of North Chungcheong Province until the Gyeongseong Com Incident had died down. That took about a year, after which they went further south to Gwangju. Hon-yong went underground as a worker in a brick factory and went by the name Kim Seongsam until Liberation, with Geumsun as his sole contact with the outside. This was the final gasp of the socialist movement in Joseon during the Japanese occupation. From the collapse of the Gyeongseong Com in 1941 to Liberation, both the movement within Joseon and the armed struggle against Japan by Koreans overseas entered a period of decline.

Japan expanded its aggression from war against China to war in the Pacific and against the US with its attack on Pearl Harbor. Activists saw this as a sign that the collapse of Japanese fascism was drawing near, and began minimising contact with each other and focusing on their individual survival. Koreans were officially forced to change to Japanese names, and basic commodities of all variety were subject to rationing or were requisitioned for the war effort. Koreans, too, were subject to conscription: for battle, for labour, and for sexual slavery. Korean-language newspapers and magazines were shut down, and even private secondary schools and private professional schools were put under the direct supervision of the Government-General.

Very late one night, Geumi awoke. Someone had shaken her awake. Juan-daek was sitting there in the dark with her legs sprawled out.

'What brings you here again?' Geumi asked.

Juan-daek sputtered and sobbed.

'*Aego*, my baby! My little boy, Dusoe, is dead!'

'Wait, what? When?'

'Just now ...'

Geumi pushed the blanket away and sat up. Juan-daek had faded back and was standing near the door. Beside her was Icheol, dressed in a prison uniform. Together, they opened the door and were about to leave when Geumi shouted, waving her hands at them to stop.

'Hold on! Where are you going?'

Ilcheol, who'd been asleep at her side, woke and pulled at her sleeve.

'What's wrong?'

The two had vanished. Geumi turned to Ilcheol in tears, her face a question mark, and murmured, 'Dusoe Seobangnim ...'

'Huh? What about him?'

Geumi wept, and Ilcheol, long familiar with his wife's ways, pulled her close and stroked her back.

'Seobangnim died in prison.'

'How do you ... ? Did my mother come?'

Unable to say anything more, Geumi simply nodded.

A few months had passed since Icheol had been transferred to Jeonju Prison to serve a four-year sentence; the trial itself had taken nearly a year. While awaiting transfer at Seodaemun Prison, he spent most of his days unable to eat or suffering from bloody diarrhoea brought on by the effects of his torture. Each time Geumi visited him, it pained her to see her brother-in-law reduced to skin and bones. He was overcome with remorse at the fact that Seonok and Jo Yeongchun had been sentenced to a year and a half because of him. He pleaded with Geumi to give any food or commissary money meant for him to them instead. Each time she reassured him that Seonok had a family of her own and so he didn't have to worry, and that she would help support Yeongchun since he was on his own and far from home, Icheol would plead again for her to help them both equally.

Two days after Geumi's visit from Juan-daek, a telegram arrived from the prison, informing them of Icheol's passing and ordering them to collect his body. Ilcheol was unable to change his work schedule, so Icheol's father, Baekman, and sister-in-law Geumi took the Honam Line south to Jeonju to bring him home. Inmates of Jeonju Prison were only given cheap coffins clumsily thrown together from wooden boards, and yet transporting them to Gyeongseong was an enormous undertaking that few could afford in those days. Near the prison was a public cemetery and crematorium. Baekman couldn't bear the thought of burying his son so far away from home, where he would forever be separated from family; instead, he decided to have him cremated. The tiny fragments of bone culled from his son's ashes were placed in a small jar and wrapped in white cloth; Icheol's father brought him home clutched to his chest. In a public cemetery on the outskirts of Yeongdeungpo, Icheol's family interred his ashes and put up a small tombstone.

As soon as the funeral was over, Baekman turned to Ilcheol and said firmly, 'We're moving.'

Baekman had long hated living in the rail workers' housing with all of its rules and restrictions. He insisted that they move into his sister Mageum's Saetmal House, which she had been renting out ever since she'd left for Manchuria. After they left the rail workers' housing, Baekman retired from the Yeongdeungpo Rail Works and built himself a workshop in the courtyard, just as he had at the Willow Tree House. Following the loss of his second-born, he locked himself away in his workshop and drowned his sorrows in metalwork.

Jisan was ten years old when they moved to Saetmal, but was only in his third year of school, as the public primary school kept changing, from sohakgyo to botonghakgyo back to sohakgyo, and now to gukminhakgyo, open only to imperial citizens. He had always been proud of having a father who drove a locomotive. At school, the children of factory workers who lived in company housing all envied him, and even his Japanese teachers kept asking him if it was really true that his father drove an express. At some point, Jisan made up his mind that he, too, would grow up to be a train driver. His grandfather Baekman crafted a toy train from tin and gave it to him. As a train repairman who knew more than anyone else how locomotives were put together, Baekman made his grandson an almost perfect replica, complete with wheels and smokestack and a tiny driver's compartment. He painted it black and attached a passenger carriage. But even more unforgettable for Jisan was the trip he took with his mother, Geumi, to Manchuria to celebrate his graduation from primary school. As family members of a Railway Bureau employee and engineer, mother and son were given first-class seats on the express. Their plan was to visit Mageum and her family in Hsinking.

The *Hikari* crossed the Amnokgang River and stopped at Antung Station. Jisan and Geumi headed to the dining carriage. Their table was reserved. Jisan's father joined them, having changed out of his uniform and into a Western-style suit. They ordered drinks and ate sushi. The trip from Gyeongseong to Sinuiju had been long, but they had an even longer ride still left ahead of them. Before they could depart again, the locomotive had to be replaced with one fully stocked with coal and water.

After dinner, Ilcheol asked his son, 'Didn't you say you've always wanted to ride in the locomotive ?'

'Yes, Abeoji! May I?'

Geumi asked, 'Are we allowed to come and go like that?'

'Usually, no.'

Geumi turned to Jisan and said, 'If you ride in the locomotive with your father, you won't be able to come back to the first-class carriage.'

'Is that true?' Jisan asked worriedly.

'Have you been to the observation car yet? It's through here, past two first-class carriages.'

'Yes, sir. There were no other Koreans. And it was boring.'

'Yes, well, on the other side of the observation carriage is the mail carriage. Right next to where they store the mail is a tiny door that the engineers use to get into the locomotive. As long as an employee is with you, you can use that door, too.'

Jisan looked back and forth from his mother to his father and then told his mother, 'If I get bored riding in the cab with Abeoji, I'll come back and join you!'

Geumi knew that Jisan had been crazy about trains for a long time and couldn't bring herself to say no. And besides, he had just recently entered his teens and would soon be starting secondary school. Ilcheol accompanied them back to the first-class compartment, where Geumi took her seat, and father and son continued on past the observation carriage and into the mail carriage.

After Ilcheol had changed clothes in the break room provided inside the mail carriage, the Railway Bureau postal employee looked at Jisan and asked, 'Inoue-san, is that your son?'

'Yes, I brought him back here because he says he's always wanted to see the inside of a locomotive cab.'

'Oh-ho, that must mean you want to be an engineer like your dad! What's your name?'

Clever Jisan answered in Japanese, '*Hai!* Inoue Ikeyama desu!'

'That's a smart kid you got there.'

Ilcheol opened the small door next to the parcel compartment and led his son along the narrow walkway that surrounded the coal bin and into the driver's compartment. The assistant, a fellow Korean, greeted Jisan.

'Come on in! You must be Jisan?'

'Yes, I am. How do you do, sir?'

Ilcheol explained every part of the instrument panel to his son, from the gearbox control lever for putting the train in forward or reverse to the brake handle right next to it, the lever that controlled the water, the automatic stoker, and the regulator-valve handle, as well as the gauges for measuring speed and pressure and more, and he further explained the principles behind how the firebox heated the boiler to boil the water inside and turn it into compressed steam, which, when released, powered the pistons that turned the wheels and made the train move. After receiving the go-ahead from the signalman, Ilcheol blew the whistle, pulled the control lever, and put the train in motion. The assistant next to him hung the pass handed off to him at the station on the back wall of the cab. The train picked up speed as it headed north. Open fields spread out before them all the way to Fengtian, with low hills off in the distance. The endless wilderness was broken only by the occasional field of corn or sorghum. The soil in those vast fields devoid of crops looked dark and rich, so different from the ochre soil of Joseon. The great plains seemed to go on for hours. The assistant regaled Jisan with stories of his first winter in Manchuria.

'You've come at a good time. It'll be cold soon. The snow comes early here. It starts out like coal dust, it's this fine, barely-there powder scooting all around, but after a while the air is filled with it, just packed tight with flakes. Then the snowflakes get bigger and start to clump together until they're the size of a child's head! And you can hear them hitting the ground, *boosh boosh!* They fill all that empty space out there. And that's nothing! If you were to cross the Heilong River in Harbin and keep going to Siberia, the streams and waterfalls would already be frozen solid.'

'Train drivers are so lucky,' Jisan said, his eyes sparkling as he sat perched on the driver's seat. 'They can go to any faraway country and meet strange people and see foreign cities.'

The assistant driver decided to spice up his story.

'Yeah, but there is also no other job as difficult and dangerous as driving a train.' He snuck a glance at Ilcheol and added, 'Bandits have been known to bury explosives next to the tracks and set them off to derail a train. A few years ago, when I was driving freight, there were times when we'd have an armed train, driven by the Japanese Kwantung Army, going ahead of us to keep watch.'

Ilcheol cleared his throat to get the assistant's attention and said, 'Watch your gauges. It could use some water.'

The assistant took the hint and made a show of returning to his work.

'Where do the bandits come from?' Jisan asked his father.

'There aren't really any bandits. This is Kwantung Army–occupied territory. It's safe.'

Realising how much time had passed, Ilcheol patted Jisan's shoulder. 'Time to head back to your mother.'

He left his assistant in charge of driving the train, which was maintaining a steady pace through the plains, and led Jisan back around the coal bin.

After opening the small door to the mail carriage, he told Jisan, 'I'll see you at the last stop, in Hsinking.'

Jisan returned to his mother in the first-class carriage. At Fengtian Station, they stepped onto the platform to buy hot tea and mandu dumplings from the Chinese. He also tried a sugar-coated bingtang-hulu skewer, which reminded him of the taste of hotteok pancakes back home, but it was so overwhelmingly sweet that he couldn't finish the whole thing.

In the half-light of dusk, the red evening sun, looking about the same size as a washbasin, was slowly sinking below the far end of a sprawling green field of sorghum. Corn leaves swayed in the wind, crashing over and over like waves, the parts that caught the setting sun shimmering with light. A large bird diligently flapped its wings as it flew over the vast green toward the darkening edge of the sky. A briefly opened window somewhere let in the coal smoke as it washed over the roof of the train, filling the inside of the carriage with the acridity of sulphur, which lingered for a moment before vanishing. Geumi lay Jisan down on the seat with his head resting on her leg and started to doze off herself. Why was it that, back then, every time someone you knew disappeared, they all turned out to have gone to Manchuria?

By the time they got off the train at Hsinking Station, it was already night. The platform was filled with people who'd come to meet the passengers; in the station entrance, some held up signs with names written on them. Geumi and Jisan were standing in line for inspection when they heard a familiar voice.

'Jisan Eomma, over here!'

As expected, it was Mageum Gomo, dressed in an unfamiliar outfit and waving at them from the crowds on the other side of the checkpoint. Their tickets went to a station employee and their papers to a police officer, who asked them a few questions, and then they were inside and Mageum Gomo had her arms wrapped around Geumi, her nephew's wife, in a tight embrace. Then she bent over and patted Jisan on the head.

'You must be hungry and tired from the long journey. Hansoe hasn't come out yet?'

Without waiting for an answer, Mageum went to the entrance to try to look for Ilcheol.

'He told us to wait inside the station. He said he has to check in at the rail office, which takes about half an hour.'

'Ah, okay. I guess I should know that since I just saw him last month.'

Geumi took a good look at Mageum as she walked back to them. She was dressed in stylish Western clothing. The two-piece suit had a skirt that clung to her body and a jacket with big, padded shoulders. On top, she'd draped a light autumn coat left unbuttoned, and even her brown hat was ornamented. Mageum seemed to feel Geumi's eyes on her, because she gave herself a once-over and giggled.

'So? What d'you think … ?'

'You're a New Woman,' Geumi said.

Mageum couldn't resist commenting on Geumi's outfit, which was a one-piece dress and a short coat.

'Big deal. You're in Western clothing, too. Did Hansoe warn you?'

'About what?'

'That you have to dress Western when you come to Hsinking.'

They went into the station waiting room and found a seat in a cafe near the entrance, just as Ilcheol had instructed. When the waiter came, Mageum ordered in Japanese: two kohi for them and an aisu kurimu for Jisan.

'It's impossible to get any service here unless you speak Japanese. You can use Chinese at the market, but hotels, cafes, and teahouses will treat you badly unless you speak Japanese.'

'What about our own language?'

'If you try to take a taxi or a horse-drawn carriage while wearing Joseon clothes or speaking Korean, the cabbie will pretend not to understand you or will tell you to get out and walk. The Manchus and Hans all speak badly of us. They say we're slaves with no nation.'

Geumi covered her mouth as she laughed.

'I mean, that sounds about right.'

'That's how it is around here. The Japanese are first-class, Koreans are second-class, and the Manchu, Han, and Mongols are third-class.'

'Even though the Hans and Manchus are no different from us?'

Geumi broke off mid-sentence, her eyes filling with tears, as she suddenly thought of her brother-in-law.

'What is it? What's wrong?'

Geumi murmured, 'I couldn't help thinking about Icheol.'

Mageum Gomo's eyes reddened, too, and she took out a handkerchief to blow her nose before continuing.

'What's the use of dwelling on the past? Ah, but that poor boy … I raised him since he was a baby.'

'When will it be Japan's turn to fall and our country's to be free?'

'Shh! Watch what you say. You never know who's listening.'

'But they say Japan will lose the war any day now. That they're bound to fall.'

Mageum lowered her voice and said, 'So you know. Are you still seeing ghosts?'

'Don't you see them, too, Gomonim?'

'Yes, but never my sister-in-law since coming here. Maybe it's too far?'

After Ilcheol finished checking in, he changed into a suit and headed to the station cafe. Mageum hurried ahead as she led them out to the station square. Black taxis were lined up, and across the street were two-horse carriages.

Mageum turned to Ilcheol's family and said, 'Let's take a carriage so you can enjoy the scenery.'

In later years, Geumi would always say that the Yis were known for their brains, but she was really talking about Mageum. Despite not finishing primary school, she'd mastered the ability to go back and forth between Japanese and Chinese not long after coming to Hsinking. Compared to Hsinking, Yeongdeungpo was nothing more than a tiny factory district in a little corner of the city, and she herself had been a poor girl from a country village. Now she read all kinds of Japanese magazines and other printed matter that was pouring into Hsinking, but what she was really drawn to was the theatre: both the new types of plays from all over the world and the movies, from America, Europe, Japan, and China, that could be seen in theatres and cinemas downtown.

Geumi used to laugh and say of their Mageum Gomo of Manchuria, 'She soaked up all that new civilisation.'

Mageum's husband, Carpenter Kang, was now a field engineer for the Japanese civil engineering company that had advanced through Joseon and into Manchuria by building housing for factory workers. Despite his lack of any particular education, his experience was untouchable. He had built many hundreds of buildings, including Japanese-style nagaya rowhouses, company houses, and three-to-four-storey wooden buildings, among others.

Datong Avenue led straight from the train station south to Datong Square at the centre of the city; on each side of the street were hotels, department stores, cinemas, theatres, and government offices. Running to the east and west of Datong Square was Xingren Avenue. If you took a right from Datong Avenue and passed the government buildings and crossed the park, you would come upon a residential neighbourhood lined with homes made of brick, a material that was new to Joseon and Japan but had been in use there for a long time. Mageum Gomo's home was only one storey, but the ceilings were high and it had a pechka, a Russian-style stove that also heated the house.

Though the weather wasn't that cold yet, a few sticks of firewood were burning and the house was pleasantly warm when Ilcheol's family arrived. A Korean servant girl had set the table and was waiting for them; as the drawing room grew noisy, Mageum Gomo's husband, their gomobu, came out of his room to join them. Trailing awkwardly behind him was Mageum's younger son, who they said had graduated from a technical secondary school and was beginning an apprenticeship. Their elder son had found a job up north in Fengtian and came home to visit every few months. Mageum's determination to return to Joseon after three years had clearly gone awry.

Every time Geumi missed Mageum Gomo, she would say, 'It seems to me that bad times always follow the good. They were up there living the high life, and then Liberation came and they were stuck. Maybe since fate knew what was in store for them, they were allowed to enjoy themselves first?'

According to those who'd returned home from Manchuria, as soon as the Japanese Kwantung Army was defeated, the Manchus stole the property of not only Japanese but also Koreans, killed thousands of people, and cut off all means of transportation. Geumi's best guess was that Mageum's husband had been the first in their family to die, or that something bad had happened to their boys. Or, possibly, husband and wife both survived but waited so long for their elder son that they missed their chance to come home.

16

Bak Seonok heard the news from Jo Yeongchun at just past three in the afternoon. She had been running a fish shop out of her maternal grandparents' former tteok shop ever since getting out of prison. She'd returned home after her year-and-a-half-long prison sentence only to find that her grandfather had passed away and her grandmother was in declining health and unable to do much. Rice and other grains were being heavily rationed by then, and places that processed grain, like alcohol or soy-sauce breweries, not to mention tteok makers, had long since been driven out of business. But Seonok, with her strong will to survive, remained undaunted and had been managing to make ends meet for the past few years. She had converted the front of the house, which had conveniently been swallowed up by the rest of the marketplace long ago, into a fish stall, where she sold dried fish and jeotgal salted seafoods that she travelled back and forth to Incheon to get. It was time to prepare for the evening rush, so she got to work, refilling the display stands with dried fish, sprinkling salt over it, and hanging flypaper from the eaves and diligently chasing the flies away. Customers had not yet begun to arrive to shop for their dinner, leaving the alleyway completely empty from one end to the other, which made it easy to see the person running towards her from the market street. She took a closer look and saw that it was Yeongchun. Her heart sank. She was scared that something big and terrible had happened again, and that this time the flames had spread to her activist group at the factory where she used to work. Yeongchun saw Seonok out in front of her house and slowed to a walk while gasping for breath. Seonok didn't dare ask what was wrong but just waited, her eyes like saucers. When their gazes met, Yeongchun suddenly looked away and started laughing.

'Look how big your eyes are right now! But you have good reason — something shocking has happened that would make heaven and earth change places!'

Yeongchun kept laughing and pointing at her eyes, which were still wide with alarm. Seonok was suddenly convinced that he'd lost his mind, and felt even more afraid.

'We're free! Joseon is free!'

'Shh! Let's go inside first.'

Seonok pulled at his sleeve, but he shook her off and kept laughing.

'Japan surrendered! The announcement went out in all the factories. Everyone stopped working and went home.'

The news of Joseon's Liberation was so unexpected and dreamlike that no one believed it at first. Those who heard the broadcast themselves could not understand the Japanese spoken by Emperor Hirohito, whose quiet voice was nearly lost in the radio static. It was the solemn tones of 'Kimigayo', the imperial anthem, and the sorrow in the news announcer's voice that hinted that something big had happened. That, and all the Japanese people dropping to their knees and weeping. It was clear that something hopeless for Japan, but hopeful for Joseon, had taken place. The Japanese bosses explained it in simple terms to the Korean engineers and supervisors at the factory.

'The war is over. Take the rest of the day off and go home.'

The Koreans whispered to each other about what the end of the war meant and why the Japanese were sad. It was a self-evident fact that since Japan had lost the war against the Allied forces, the Japanese would have to go home and Joseon would be its own country again. As the realisation sank in, one of the workers turned off their machine and shouted hooray: '*Manse!*'

'Long live an independent Joseon!'

Those who'd been standing around confused began to shout '*Manse!*' one after the other until everyone was up on their feet and walking out and the entire factory rang with the sounds of their voices. The street outside began to fill with men and women from other factories. More spontaneous shouts of '*Manse!*' rang out near and far, rolling through the crowd like a wave. Yeongchun had heard the same news from several of his fellow activists who'd come running to find him, and then walked the factory streets of Yangpyeong-jeong and Dangsan-jeong, experiencing firsthand the triumphant shouts of workers, growing more and more excited as he went. That was when he'd hurried off to find Seonok, his comrade org, who'd suffered through the hard, early days of organising alongside him.

Seonok put away the dried fish she'd set out, and told Yeongchun, 'There's somewhere I need to be.'

As she was heading out, he said, 'I should get going, too. I have a lot of other stops to make. We're meeting at the sawmill this evening. You should join us.'

'What time?'

'Six o'clock.'

Seonok nodded and hurried away towards the new road that led north-west away from the market. She was going to Geumi's house in Saetmal. If Baekman were still working at the rail works like he used to, or if the family had still been living in the rail workers' housing, they would have been the first to hear this world-shaking news. Instead, Geumi had just finished cooking lunch for her father-in-law over a portable stove, sweating in the summer heat. She washed her face and sat in the shade, fanning herself as she rested. That was when Seonok knocked on the front gate and called out to her.

'Geumi Eonni! Eonni-ya, open up!'

Geumi was startled by the shouting. Instead of responding right away, she tiptoed to the gate and waited with her hands over her heart.

'Eonni, I have good news!'

When Geumi cracked open the gate, Seonok pushed it wide open and rushed inside.

'Japan has surrendered!' she shouted.

Geumi just stared at her blankly and said, 'What are you talking about?'

'Japan lost to the Allied forces, which means we've got our country back. Joseon is free.'

Geumi was tongue-tied, still not quite believing what she'd heard, but when Seonok started describing how all the factory workers had left their posts when they heard the announcement and flooded out into the streets, she burst into tears. Baekman, who'd left his workshop to hear what she had to say, threw on a shirt and rushed out. Late that night, after the storm waves of emotion and excitement finally subsided, Ilcheol returned home from a long round-trip shift with details of what had happened.

Ilcheol had actually been hearing rumours buzzing about it in Hsinking for the past ten days, though he hadn't mentioned any of it to his family. The professionals and intellectuals of many different nationalities living in Hsinking were more inclined to listen to radio broadcasts from China, England, the Soviet Union, and the US, rather than Japan, and therefore had access to more accurate news around the clock. In March, there'd been news of Japan's many lost battles in the Pacific War, as well as news of hundreds of US planes carpet bombing Tokyo and killing and injuring hundreds of thousands of people. The latest rumours, based on the radio broadcasts, were that, on the morning of 6 August, a squadron of American B-29 bombers had dropped an atomic bomb on Hiroshima. Tales of the carnage and ensuing horrors had begun finding their way abroad the next day. The city of Hiroshima and its thousands upon thousands of civilians were reduced to ash in the blink of an eye. Then, three days later, another B-29 dropped a second atomic bomb on Nagasaki. Ilcheol knew nothing of this until he reached Hsinking, where it was all people were talking about. On 9 August, the day after Nagasaki, the Soviet Union declared war on Japan; hundreds of planes, 5,000 tanks, 26,000 cannons, and 1.6 million Red Army soldiers advanced on three different fronts in Manchuria and northern Joseon. The Soviet offensive was faster and more powerful even than their capture of Berlin, and the Japanese Kwantung Army was annihilated. Japan's surrender was practically a fait accompli. Between the US atomic bombing and the Soviet's blitzkrieg tactics, Japan had no choice but to put the emperor's voice on the radio as saying, 'Our Empire accepts the provisions of the Potsdam Declaration,' which had called for Japan to surrender.

On 16 August, the day after Japan's surrender, political prisoners were released from Seodaemun Prison, and a parade of supporters, complete with a brass band, poured into the streets to welcome them. The text of Emperor Hirohito's broadcast was translated into Korean and spread throughout the capital and, over the course of several days, to the rest of the country.

TO OUR GOOD AND LOYAL SUBJECTS,

After pondering deeply the general trends of the world and the actual conditions obtaining in Our Empire today, We have decided to effect a settlement of the present situation by resorting to an extraordinary measure.

We have ordered Our government to communicate to the governments of the United States, Great Britain, China, and the Soviet Union that Our Empire accepts the provisions of their Joint Declaration.

To strive for the common prosperity and happiness of all nations as well as the security and wellbeing of Our subjects is the solemn obligation which has been handed down by Our Imperial Ancestors and which lies close to Our heart. Indeed, We declared war on America and Britain out of Our sincere desire to ensure Japan's self-preservation and the stabilisation of East Asia, it being far from Our thought either to infringe upon the sovereignty of other nations or to embark upon territorial aggrandisement. But now the war has lasted for nearly four years. Despite the best that has been done by everyone — the gallant fighting of the military and naval forces, the diligence and assiduity of Our servants of the state, and the devoted service of Our 100 million people — the war situation has developed not necessarily to Japan's advantage, while the general trends of the world have all turned against her interest.

Moreover, the enemy has begun to employ a new and most cruel bomb, the power of which to do damage is, indeed, incalculable, taking the toll of many innocent lives. Should We continue to fight, not only would it result in an ultimate collapse and obliteration of the Japanese nation, but also it would lead to the total extinction of human civilisation. Such being the case, how are We to save the millions of Our subjects, or to atone Ourselves before the hallowed spirits of Our Imperial Ancestors? This is the reason why We have ordered the acceptance of the provisions of the Joint Declaration of the Powers.

We cannot but express the deepest sense of regret to Our allied nations of East Asia, who have consistently cooperated with the Empire towards the emancipation of East Asia. The thought of those officers and men as well as others who have fallen in the fields of battle, those who died at their posts of duty, or those who met with untimely death and all their bereaved families, pains Our heart night and day. The welfare of the wounded and the war-sufferers, and of those who have lost their homes and livelihood, are the objects of Our profound solicitude. The hardships and sufferings to which Our nation is to be subjected hereafter will be certainly great. We are keenly aware of the inmost feelings of all of you, Our subjects. However, it is according to the dictates of time and fate that We have resolved to pave the way for a grand peace for all the generations to come by enduring the unendurable and suffering what is insufferable.

Having been able to safeguard and maintain the Imperial State, We are always with you, Our good and loyal subjects, relying upon your sincerity and integrity. Beware most strictly of any outbursts of emotion which may engender needless complications, or any fraternal contention and strife which may create confusion, lead you astray and cause you to lose the confidence of the world. Let the entire nation continue as one family from generation to generation, ever firm in its faith in the imperishability of its sacred land, and mindful of its heavy burden of responsibility, and of

> the long road before it. Unite your total strength, to be devoted to construction for the future. Cultivate the ways of rectitude, foster nobility of spirit, and work with resolution, so that you may enhance the innate glory of the Imperial State and keep pace with the progress of the world.
>
> We trust that Our subjects will bear in mind and respect Our wishes.

Emperor Hirohito's public broadcast reflected on the choice to invade other countries but included not a single mention of surrender or defeat. Worse was the long-winded sophistry about how colonisation was necessary to stabilise East Asia against the US, Britain, and other Western powers, and that aggression and attacks on other countries' sovereignty were supposedly never their intention. They even managed to remain vague on the subject of accepting the terms of the Potsdam Declaration.

One of the post-Liberation freed political prisoners later recalled in a column:

'In Joseon, freedom lasted all of one day: 16 August 1945.'

At noon on 15 August, Hirohito's voice recording of the 'Statement Regarding the Conclusion of the Greater East Asia War' was broadcast, but it was clearly not a surrender but rather a cessation of hostilities. It was not an objective fact that the Japanese Empire surrendered unconditionally on 15 August. That did not happen until 9.00 am on 2 September 1945, aboard the USS *Missouri* anchored in Tokyo Bay, when they signed the Instrument of Surrender. Why did Japan hold out? Because they were waiting for the Americans to land in Japan so that they could surrender to the US.

The official story behind the division of the peninsula along the 38th parallel is that the line was drawn in haste on 11 August by American strategists as an emergency countermeasure to block the southward advance of Soviet troops, who'd declared war against Japan on 9 August and had already made their way through Manchuria and entered Joseon. But there was no truth to this claim that the division was led spontaneously by the US and that the Soviets agreed to it with no knowledge or understanding. In fact, this had been decided upon by the US much, much earlier. US strategists had identified three key ports and decided that two of them — Busan and Incheon — had to remain on their side, which meant the line would have to be drawn to the north of Seoul — of Gyeongseong. That was how the 38th parallel was chosen as the best option. The US president and secretary of state had submitted the division of the Korean peninsula as an unofficial agenda item at the Potsdam Conference.

Starting in August, patriots like Lyuh Woon-hyung established the Committee for the Preparation of Korean Independence, organised a peacekeeping force overseen by the committee, and created 145 branches across the country. On 6 September, they drew up a set of basic laws and conditions, formed the new government of the People's Republic of Korea, and elected committee members. They also decided to create a Provisional Government Welcome and Preparation Committee as well as a US Army Welcome Committee.

On 8 September, the liberating forces of the US Army landed at Incheon. Key members of the Committee for the Preparation of Korean Independence and the peacekeeping forces who'd been fighting for independence under Japanese colonialism gathered citizens and workers from the factories and docks to welcome the American occupiers. Standing at the front of this welcome party, Kwon, a member of the Incheon Central Committee of the Joseon Workers Union, was shot in the chest and stomach, along with a young member of the Incheon peacekeeping force, who was shot in the back and waist. More than a dozen others were shot, too. The Japanese police officer who fired the gun would later testify in a US-led court that the victims had crossed the police line. The US ruled that the shooting was justified. Over the next few days, more than forty people were killed across the country in clashes with Japanese police. This catastrophe had practically been foretold.

On 7 September, one day before the US troops landed, MacArthur issued a statement to the Korean people, which was leafleted over Gyeongseong by military aircraft.

Proclamation No. 1 by General of the Army Douglas MacArthur
Yokohama, September 7, 1945

To the People of Korea:
As Commander-in-chief, United States Army Forces, Pacific, I do hereby proclaim as follows:

By the terms of the Instrument of Surrender, signed by command and in behalf of the Emperor of Japan and the Japanese Government and by command and in behalf of the Japanese Imperial General Headquarters, the victorious military forces of my command will today occupy the territory of Korea south of 38 degrees north latitude.

Having in mind the long enslavement of the people of Korea and the determination that in due course Korea shall become free and independent, the Korean people are assured that the purpose of the occupation is to enforce the Instrument of Surrender and to protect them in their personal and religious rights. In giving effect to these purposes, your active aid and compliance are required.

By virtue of the authority vested in me as Commander-in-Chief, United States Army Forces, Pacific, I hereby establish military control over Korea south of 38 degrees north latitude and the inhabitants thereof, and announce the following conditions of the occupation:

Article I
All powers of Government over the territory of Korea south of 38 degrees north latitude and the people thereof will be for the present exercised under my authority.

Article II
Until further orders, all governmental, public and honorary functionaries and employees, as well as all officials and employees, paid or voluntary, of all public utilities and services, including public welfare and public health, and all other persons engaged in

essential services, shall continue to perform their usual functions and duties, and shall preserve and safeguard all records and property.

Article III

All persons will obey promptly all my orders and orders issued under my authority. Acts of resistance to the occupying forces or any acts which may disturb public peace and safety will be punished severely.

Article IV

Your property rights will be respected. You will pursue your normal occupations, except as I shall otherwise order.

Article V

For all purposes during the military control, English will be the official language. In event of any ambiguity or diversity of interpretation or definition between any English and Korean or Japanese text, the English text shall prevail.

Article VI

Further proclamations, ordinances, regulations, notices, directives and enactments will be issued by me or under my authority, and will specify what is required of you.

Given under my hand at Yokohama
this seventh day of September 1945

Douglas MacArthur

Commander-in-Chief, United States
Army Forces, Pacific

*

Proclamation No. 2

CRIMES AND OFFENSES

TO THE PEOPLE OF KOREA: In order to make provisions for the security of the armed forces under my command and for the maintenance of public peace, order and safety in the occupied area, as Commander-in-Chief, United States Army Forces, Pacific, I do hereby proclaim as follows:

ANY PERSON WHO:
violates the Instrument of Surrender, or any proclamation, order, or directive given under the authority of the Commander-in-Chief, United States Army Forces, Pacific, or does any act to the prejudice of good order or the life, safety, or security of the persons or property of the United States or its Allies, or does any act calculated to disturb public peace and order, or prevent the administration of justice, or willfully does any act hostile to the Allied Forces, shall, upon conviction by a Military Occupation Court, suffer death or such other punishment as the Court may determine.

Given under my hand at YOKOHAMA
THIS SEVENTH DAY OF SEPTEMBER 1945

DOUGLAS MACARTHUR
General of the Army of the United States
Commander-in-Chief, United States Army Forces, Pacific

At 3.45 pm 9 September 1945, a victorious US and defeated Japan came together to confront their common enemy, the Soviet Union, and to block Korean unification and independence. Though it was called the signing of the Instrument of Surrender, it was really a handover of colonial rule. The Japanese governor-general and the commander of the US occupation forces of South Korea signed their names right next to each other's on the handover-of-sovereignty document. The switch complete, the two countries held a flag exchange ceremony at 4.35 pm of the same day in front of the Japanese Government-General building. No Koreans were invited.

For the people of Gyeongseong, the full meaning of Liberation wasn't understood until later. And despite the hoisting of the US flag over the capital, the Japanese flag continued to fly in the provinces until well into October. John Hodge, commander of the US occupying forces, dismissed officials from the Japanese Government-General, including the governor-general, on 14 September without taking any legal action against them; then, on 17 October, he dismissed the rest of the Japanese officials out in the provinces. On 19 September, the governor-general of Joseon and officials who had handed over colonial rule to the American occupation forces returned to Japan in military aircraft provided by the US military.

*

On the evening of Liberation Day, a group of twenty labourers, including Jo Yeongchun and Bak Seonok, gathered at a sawmill across the street from the Yeongdeungpo Market. They updated each other on everything they knew about what was happening inside the factories and talked about establishing the Committee for the Preparation of Korean Independence and a peacekeeping force. In less than a week, they'd formed the Yeongdeungpo branch, while the Incheon, Suwon, and other Gyeonggi Province branches also came together almost simultaneously. This was possible because of the groundwork that had already been laid by the farmers' and workers' movements, which had been conducted nationwide and in coordination with each other throughout the Japanese colonial era. In any case, a mere three weeks after Japan officially ceased its hostilities, the Committee for the Preparation of Korean Independence had 145 branches across the country, complete with a peacekeeping force. With this new government apparatus in place, they proclaimed the establishment of the People's Republic of Korea.

Despite being an engineer on the *Hikari*, Yi Ilcheol was no longer able to travel to Manchuria. Most factories had paused production, while workers formed self-governance committees in order to take over operations from the Japanese. Aside from colonial officials and police, ordinary Japanese civilians all over the country were in a hurry to leave, and a great many companies were signing over ownership and handing over their facilities to the Korean workers' self-governance committees.

One day, in August of that year, Ilcheol happened to meet Yeongchun and Seonok. Yeongchun told him that he'd put together a Committee for the Preparation of Korean Independence peacekeeping force, most of whom were factory workers and friends of Icheol.

'We need to find that traitor Choi Daryeong — or Yamashita, as he likes to call himself,' Yeongchun said. 'He's not a true Korean, he's a Japanese bastard. He clawed his way up to inspector while sucking the marrow from the bones of our people. He must pay for what he did to Icheol.'

'You do know he's from Moraetmal, don't you?'

'We're working on taking control of the police station,' Seonok said in response to Ilcheol's question. 'The Korean cops and assistants all fled along with the Japanese officers. We went to Daryeong's house already, but no one was there. Even his wife and children were gone.'

'In my opinion,' Ilcheol said, 'our priority should be establishing an independent government. Then, that government can put the pro-Japanese collaborators on trial and punish them legally.'

Regardless, there was no news of Choi Daryeong until mid-October. In late August, Seonok brought Kim Geunshik to see Ilcheol at the Saetmal House. Geunshik had spent four years in prison and was only free thanks to Liberation. He was convinced that Icheol's older brother, despite being more politically moderate, could yet prove himself to be an activist, and a more proactive one at that than International Red Aid, which was restricted to a supporting role. As the one responsible for Communist Party reconstruction in Gyeongseong and Incheon, Geunshik had his eye on Ilcheol.

'I came to see you because there's something I'd like to discuss. It stands to reason that rail workers should play the most central role among the industrial unions. You drive a locomotive, right?'

'Yes, when I was first assigned to drive a train, only twenty out of every hundred engineers were Korean. By the end of the war, sixty per cent of all rail workers and about half of the drivers were Korean. Right now, Japanese engineers and rail workers have abandoned their posts, so most of the train lines are no longer operational. Even the major routes — the Gyeongbu Line, Honam Line, Gyeongui Line, and Gyeongwon Line — are barely running once every few days. Local lines are pretty much dead. I was in charge of the Gyeongui Line and the Antung–Hsinking Line, but the continent is off-limits now. Because I live in Gyeongseong, I can only go as far as Gaeseong, since it's right over the border. Everything to the north is run by the Soviet Army.'

Geunshik made a careful suggestion.

'Look, anyone can drive a train or repair railroad tracks or run a train station. What we really need are organisers, activists who can lead people. I'm hoping that you'll join the Yongsan Rail Bureau's labour union and help run it. Or would you consider the Yeongdeungpo Rail Works?'

Ilcheol mulled it over before answering.

'The Yongsan Rail Bureau was mostly run by Japanese, who never entrusted any important management positions to Koreans. And they treated train drivers like we were all foreigners. I mean, the pay was good, but we were never seen as anything more than technicians. If your plan is to start a union in Yongsan, then you'll need seasoned party activists to go in and do it themselves.'

Geunshik smiled.

'And Comrade Ilcheol is not a seasoned activist?'

'I prefer to stay in Yeongdeungpo. This is where I was born and where my father worked his whole life. I practically know everyone who lives here. I'd rather do union work here.'

Geunshik smiled brightly.

'That's what I was hoping you'd say! I'd love it if you would lead the industrial workers' union in Yeongdeungpo.'

Shin Geumi remembered how quickly her husband changed after Liberation. He remained outwardly moderate and unassuming, but his hatred of his enemies grew and grew. She felt like he was drifting away from the family. His brother's death was like a nail hammered dead into his chest. He came home drunk once and confessed all of his feelings to her. How he blamed himself for having served as a loyal tool of the Japanese Empire by working on their railroads for them, and for patting himself on the back for having passively pretended to aid his younger brother's anti-Japanese activism. He seemed determined to live his life differently than before in their now-liberated country. Perhaps he thought he could finally help bring into existence the world his brother had only dreamed of.

By 16 August, workers for the Party Reconstruction Faction had hung posters all over Gyeongseong that said, 'Pak Hon-yong, the great leader of the working masses of Joseon, come guide us!' Hon-yong had been living in seclusion in Gwangju as 'Kim Seongsam' and getting by first as a manure scavenger then as a brick-factory worker and again as a day labourer, but on 19 August he ended his retirement and returned to Gyeongseong. The first thing he did was instruct his followers to join the Committee for the Preparation of Korean Independence and become core members of the peacekeeping force. He joined them in proclaiming the new republic, and on 11 September — after the US occupation authorities had declared military rule — he announced the Committee for Reconstruction of the Korean Communist Party and reorganised the nationwide network of activist cells to centre on the Committee. The goal was to relaunch the movement by firmly basing it on the workers, farmers, and masses who'd fought for independence on the ground within Joseon right up until the final moments.

Ilcheol received orders from the central office of the Yongsan Railway Bureau to report to work at the Yeongdeungpo Rail Works. Most of the workers, engineers, and managers at the works, where only Koreans were left, had known his father, who'd worked there for decades. They also knew that his brother had died in prison for resisting the Japanese. Nationwide, the labour union came together quickly, with the most close-knit industries — metalwork, rail, and publishing, for example — forming the vanguard. Ilcheol was elected head of the Yeongdeungpo Rail Works Union. As a Korean train engineer who'd driven an intercontinental express, his kind of experience was hard to come by, so he immediately attracted the attention of the union members. They made him chairman of the Yeongdeungpo branch of the National Council of Labour Unions.

The clouds gathered, and a bleak grey sky hung heavy and low over Namsan Mountain for the two straight days of 5 and 6 November when the National Council was formed at the Jungang Theatre, to represent the voices of the 200,000 members of sixteen different trade unions. In accordance with the emergency proposal, four resolutions were adopted: a message of thanks to Comrade Pak Hon-yong, patriot and leader of the working class; a message of gratitude to the workers of the Allied nations; a resolution to eradicate the troublemaker Ri Yong's faction; and absolute support for Comrade Pak Hon-yong's line.

*

On the day the emperor's broadcast aired, Yamashita Choi Daryeong urged his wife to go to her hometown of Anyang and lie low for a while. Then he packed himself a small bag and left. He went to the Japanese neighbourhood near Yeongdeungpo Station and called Chief Inspector Matsuda.

'Sir? This is Yamashita.'

'Yeah, where are you?'

'I'm near your house, sir.'

Matsuda didn't sound like his usual self.

'What? Why didn't you just come straight over? Let's meet.'

Yamashita Choi Daryeong had been to Chief Inspector Matsuda's house several times before. This time, when he knocked on the front door, Matusda greeted him in a haori jacket. They sat down in the drawing room, and Matsuda's wife brought in two bottles of beer and two glasses on a tray. Matsuda opened one of the bottles and poured him a tall, frothy glass.

'We stored the beer in the pump water, but it's still not very cold. It's impossible now to find ice, or anything else, for that matter.'

'What did His Imperial Majesty's broadcast today mean?'

'Mean? Just what he said, that Japan would accept the decision of the Allied nations and end the war.'

'So the Japanese will all be going home?'

'Of course. Now it's up to people like you to step forward and develop a Korean police force.'

'An independent Korea means that people like me will be punished.'

Matsuda laughed quietly.

'I doubt it. We lost, but Korea did not win. When the US military arrives, they'll take over the security administration without changing any of it.' Matsuda pointed up. 'The communists are coming in from the other end. And the capitalist Americans will come in on this end. The US military will want people with your talents. You've been good to us, and they'll naturally look for people who'll be good to them, too. And besides, you're an expert at taking down communists.'

Understanding hit Choi Daryeong like a lightning bolt.

'You're not the only one who's worried,' Matsuda continued. 'I noticed this afternoon the Korean cops and assistants sneaking away. We'll all be put on leave, as well, but I bet it won't last more than ten days. When the Americans arrive, order will be restored.'

'In that case, I'd better take some time off, too. I'll return after the US occupation forces are here.'

'Of course, of course. Report back to work when that happens. And in the meantime, keep your guns on you.'

The lightning bolt that had hit Daryeong left him feeling energised, so he took the all-stop train on the Gyeongbu Line to his wife's family home in Anyang.

Young men from the Committee for the Preparation of Korean Independence's peacekeeping force and the Student Soldiers Union seized police stations all over Gyeongseong and clashed with Japanese police. Dozens of Korean police officers were killed or assaulted over past grievances, but those cases soon subsided. In contrast, North Korea under Soviet occupation investigated all prosecutors and judges, as well as Japanese civilian and military police, established a court to hear the testimony of Korean victims, and sentenced offenders accordingly. Because of this, a great many police and government officials of Korean birth fled to the south. As expected, by the beginning of September, the fears of unrest had vanished from every police station in Gyeongseong. The Japanese army began to guard downtown Gyeongseong, while the Japanese police chiefs officially handed over control to Korean police chiefs.

Daryeong passed the time hiding out in his wife's family home in Anyang. Though he maintained an outward appearance of calm indifference, inwardly he was on tenterhooks. He knew that the rank he'd earned of inspector, within the hierarchy of the imperial Japanese police force, was an exceedingly rare one among the many possible jobs an ethnic Korean could hold. After the US landing at Incheon, Daryeong cautiously returned to work at the Yeongdeungpo Police Station. According to MacArthur's proclamation, all workers were to return to their posts and perform their usual duties. It only stood to reason that the police should be the first to do so. As soon as Daryeong stepped into the office, Chief Inspector Matsuda called out, *'Oi!'* and waved him over.

'I was waiting for you to get here,' Matsuda said warmly. 'We Japanese officers have all been fired. They're going to appoint a Korean police chief instead. You're being reassigned to Yongsan.' He handed Daryeong the transfer papers. 'I know Yeongdeungpo is your home turf, but you must have a lot of connections elsewhere, too. Seems like the US military authorities have taken that into account.'

The ten police chiefs in Gyeongseong and twenty-one police chiefs in Gyeonggi Province appointed by the US Army Military Government in Korea, or USAMGIK, were all former police or government employees of imperial Japan. Daryeong reported to Yongsan Station. The newly appointed chief was likewise a Korean who'd worked for the Japanese police; he had officially passed the police exam and acquired a leadership position. Though, of course, the only way into the upper ranks of the police was by arresting and imprisoning large numbers of Korean independence activists. The new chief skimmed Daryeong's resume and nodded.

'Your immediate supervisor, Chief Inspector Matsuda, was my colleague. The country needs talented professionals like you right now. I'll promote you and put you in charge of investigations.'

'*Hai!* I shall put the emperor's needs before my own!'

The chief grinned. 'This isn't imperial Japan anymore.'

Daryeong was promoted from inspector to senior inspector. His new rank put him in charge of the division — one that only months earlier was the Special Higher Police of Japan. A mere month after Liberation, in mid-September, the USAMGIK police department held its first recruitment exam at the colonial-era police academy. This was not a pencil-and-paper exam, though, but rather an interview. Daryeong asked around and contacted former associates, including a Korean detective and two previous informants, and got them to sit for the exam; he conducted their interviews personally. Former township officials and prison guards, clerks and labourers, and others who'd fed at the hand of the colonial Japanese government all passed the exam unconditionally. As long as they could write down their own names and thus prove they weren't illiterate, they passed. Among those hurriedly pressed into service by the military authorities, the ones whose political views differed — all from non-police backgrounds — stepped down, leaving eight police stations in downtown Gyeongseong without any chiefs to lead them. The Yongsan police chief moved to a different government position and was replaced by Choi Daryeong. This was mid-January 1946, a mere five months after Liberation. He changed his name, too. To Choi Yong.

*

Ilcheol was working on expanding the Yeongdeungpo branch of the trade unions, centred on the Yeongdeungpo Rail Works, Gyeongseong

Electric, and Joseon Textiles, among others. It was a darker and more dismal time than even the last days of empire, with only the ardent desire to build a new homeland keeping hope alive. Eighty per cent of manufacturing, capital, technology, and labour had been controlled by Japan; with their defeat, all of that capital and technology was pulled out of the country, and the majority of factories were shut down. Making matters worse, with agriculture concentrated south of the 38th parallel and industry concentrated to the north, the farmlands in the south were left without supplies of manufactured products — including farm chemicals, fertilisers, and electric power. As the country entered the early winter of 1945, wholesale prices jumped to nearly thirty times that of 15 August. Even with a freeze on the government purchase price of rice, the cost of rice went through the roof, making it impossible for ordinary people to buy any. With the USAMGIK's issuance of Bank of Joseon currency, the cash supply increased to three or four times. Prices soared like there was no end to how high they could go. The USAMGIK printed money left and right so they could scrape together the funds needed to run the country. By the end of the year, prices were seventy times higher than they'd been in August.

That same year, the US military authorities issued an official denial of the People's Republic of Korea established by Lyuh Woon-hyung; Rhee Syngman, as well, had returned to Korea and refused to participate in the PRK. As a result, the political alliance led by Pak Hon-yong, the Korean Communist Party's People's United Front, was broken up.

Whenever Shin Geumi spoke of those days, she would mention her parents, who were middle-class farmers living in a village in Gimpo, and would recall how she'd sought their help several times.

'The thing is, the US military had the police and youth leagues going door to door to collect rice. They said they did it to crack down on hoarding, which was driving the price of rice up, and so they were redistributing it instead. But there's no way to keep things fair by doing it that way. It just messes the market up even more, because then you get people in the middle pocketing rice for themselves.'

At the time, Ilcheol was mostly away from home, either sleeping in the factory's tiny night-duty room or travelling around to other factories. He was no longer the responsible and reliable family man.

'I was mostly worried about Jisan. He was a growing boy — fourteen years old and a secondary-school student. I knew my father-in-law was struggling, too. He'd all but stopped speaking. I would offer him two meals of sweet potatoes every day, and each time I'd find the bowls empty, so I figured he must be forcing himself to eat no matter how hard a time he was having. But then, one day, I went into his workshop to look for a bowl for some mul kimchi. My father-in-law was in there napping. I crept in and started clearing the dishes when I found three or four sweet potatoes lying underneath the table. He'd been skipping lunch. Or maybe he'd left them there to eat later when he was really hungry.'

For Geumi, the year that passed from Liberation to the following autumn felt more like decades. It felt like something from an ancient time, far older than the now-hazy, mythical-sounding stories of the big floods and her mother-in-law fishing pigs from the water to feed the other flood survivors and building a raft to rescue stranded rail workers or appearing as a ghost to rescue her two boys and the rest of the family from the tree they'd named their house after, stories that Geumi had only heard from others. Unlike those stories, the first year of Liberation was a terrible and terrifying story, a time when far too many people died or were split apart, north and south, never to meet again.

From Liberation to the following autumn to the year after that, when her husband Ilcheol vanished, felt like one long, long dream to Geumi.

'They say Korea has been through so many twists and turns that one year here is a decade in another country. And ten years here is equal to a century. Which means we're all hundreds of years old.'

In Yeongdeungpo, the streets, the people, and everything that happened there were reduced to a dream. It turned it into a hazy, semitransparent world, like the inside of a soap bubble. An enormous cover, a film, a fog, draped itself over the whole of Yeongdeungpo from the thin air above. People who died screaming, bloody, beaten, fighting to the death, did not disappear after their funerals but became grey phantoms that flickered and wandered inside that thin film. In every single house, ghosts lived with their families, as visible to them and easy to talk to as Juan-daek was. And so, Yeongdeungpo was sunk into a long sleep, or maybe it suffered insomnia. Maybe it had always been prone to sleepwalking, or maybe it was awake but passed each day in a half-conscious daze.

Around that time, not only the people of Yeongdeungpo but everyone in all of South Korea was on a daily hunt for rice. The fields had been rippling and golden, filled with ripening heads of rice, in autumn. But even before winter came, it all vanished. Geumi wasn't the only one who took to folding up empty rice sacks and strapping them to the waist of her pants before leaving the house. The Bank of Joseon banknotes that the big-nose Americans had hurriedly printed were becoming worthless among individuals. No one dared dream of meat or fish. Grain, potatoes, sweet potatoes, and all kinds of vegetables had to be bartered for. The exception was rice, for which they had to get a ration ticket from the neighbourhood office then go to the distribution centre to receive their daily share. But after just a few days, the distribution centre would close its doors, saying they'd run out.

One evening, Geumi was walking past a distribution centre she hadn't seen before when she noticed a long line of smoke-like ghosts waiting with all manner of bowls, baskets, and basins in their hands. She found herself drifting to the back of the line, where she joined them. Back in those days, if you saw a line, you just stood in it without question. The living would have greeted each other warmly and swapped gossip while waiting, but the ghostly figures were as limp as laundry on a line, silent and sullen. Finally, Geumi couldn't take it anymore and addressed the woman in line in front of her.

'How long has this distribution centre been here?'

The woman was dressed in plain, cotton clothes, but everything else about her was a smoky grey, even her face. Geumi, alone, was in full colour. The woman looked at her in shock.

'You can see me?'

'Why wouldn't I see you? I can also see that halmeoni who was just at the front of the line walking away with her rice.'

This created a stir all along the line, and she could hear their whispers.

'That woman can see us.'

'What, so she's dead, too?'

'No, she's alive and well.'

'But I thought we were only visible to family.'

'It's different with each family. Without the gift, even your own children can't see you.'

Undaunted, Geumi stood tall and waited her turn.

'How long has this been here?' she asked again.

The grey apparition standing in front of her said, 'This location just opened today. They say it moves around every day.'

'How much do they give per family?'

'They fill up whatever you bring.'

Geumi didn't look behind her until she was at the very front of the line. When she did, she saw that no one had got in line behind her. No one else was waiting. The long line of greys had collected their rations and melted away into thin air. When Geumi gazed into the dark portal before her, an indistinct figure approached and held out its hand. Geumi looked closer and saw that Juan-daek was running the distribution centre.

'Eomeoni!' Geumi said, startled.

Juan-daek smiled brightly, still holding out a hand as large as a cauldron lid.

'Give me that sack.'

Still half in shock, Geumi plucked the empty rice sack from her waist and handed it to her mother-in-law, who filled it to bursting with rice, tied off the top, and handed it back. When Geumi took the bag, the sudden heavy weight of it caught her off guard and she dropped it on the ground. She bent over to pick it up, and when she stood up straight again, the distribution centre was gone.

She looked all around and called out, 'Eomeoni! Eomeoni!'

She was standing in an empty field on the outskirts of Saetmal.

She later remembered receiving rice rations from Juan-daek in a hazy, dreamy sort of way, but she did not remember actually bringing the overstuffed bag of rice home. It was a miracle: for the first time in months, the entire family was able to eat their fill for several days.

Wages fell so far behind the rate of inflation that they dropped to less than a third of the starvation wage of the mid-1930s, during colonial Japan's war economy. Workers had to toil for over a hundred hours a week for monthly pay that was equivalent to the cost of a sack of rice. It wasn't until the spring of 1946 that a dispute broke out between the management and workers of a factory, which had been reorganised either under the direct management of, or after being sold off by, the USAMGIK after several months of being run by the workers after the Japanese owner had left. By then, the National Council had already formed trade unions all over the country. A representative for the textile-factory workers spoke without exaggeration to their trade-union colleagues who came to support the strike.

'The issue this time between the company and us workers is not so much a dispute as a plea. I came to work here last December, lured in by their fraudulent offer of two and a half yards of cloth and a hundred won per day. But by March all I had received was twenty yards of cloth in total, and was given only sorghum to eat. How is anyone supposed to survive on that?'

Then, one day, the Maruboshi Factory near the train tracks burned down. It happened in the middle of the night. Geumi felt someone shaking her awake.

'Get up. You need to feed your family.'

As always, it was Juan-daek, and as always Geumi knew who she was from her silhouette alone — so tall and broad-shouldered compared to other women.

'What? Where should I go?'

Geumi, still half-asleep, sat up in bed, but Juan-daek hauled her daughter-in-law to her feet by her armpits.

'Everyone is running over to the Maruboshi Factory.'

As Geumi rushed to leave the house, Juan-daek handed her two empty rice sacks.

'Fill these up, all the way!'

Outside on the streets, she saw grey people everywhere, and in the distance, to the south-east, dark-red flames. From where she stood, the fire had to be burning near Yeongdeungpo Station. People were pouring into the dark and calling out in search of each other; mixed in among them were the grey shadows of those who'd died after living hard lives. Juan-daek was one of them. As Geumi passed Yeongdeungpo Market, the crowd swelled to hundreds of people. On the other side of the station, across the tangle of tracks, right before her eyes, people were swarming through the wide-open front gate of the Maruboshi Factory. All of the warehouse doors were open and packed with people. The factory building itself was on fire; the smell of burning oil and machinery was foul. The factory was a brewery that made sake and beer, and even with production halted, the warehouse was still stacked to the ceiling with sacks of rice and flour and other provisions. Geumi carried two sacks of flour out on her shoulders. Then she went back inside and groped around in the dark until she found something that felt like rice and filled her sacks with it. But the sacks were so heavy that she had to drag them out across the ground. She couldn't imagine how she was going to transport everything to the Saetmal House. She barely made it across the tracks and out to the station plaza by dragging one sack at a time, backtracking over and over to retrieve the others. Her husband hadn't been home in days, and she regretted not having woken up Baekman or Jisan to come with her. Just then, Juan-daek reappeared from wherever she'd disappeared to, hoisted the two sacks of flour onto her back and strolled off like it was nothing. Geumi hurried after her ghost-in-law with a sack of grain balanced on each shoulder. By the time they reached the house, Geumi was drenched in sweat. She put the sacks in the kitchen and looked for her son.

'Jisan! Jisan! Get out here, quick!'

Startled awake, he rushed outside along with a dishevelled-looking Baekman, who'd been asleep in Jisan's room.

'What's all the fuss at this hour?'

'Abeonim, I have no time to explain. The Maruboshi is on fire, and people are mobbing it to grab food. We need to hurry back.'

Geumi handed Jisan a small wooden tub and wrapped a thin blanket around her own shoulders. On the way out of the house, she called out to her father-in-law.

'Abeonim, your bike! Please bring your bicycle with you.'

All the way to the market, they passed people headed in the opposite direction with sacks of rice on their backs or on A-frame carriers, and a few lucky people pulled handcarts loaded up with hessian sacks of flour, the sight of which made Geumi more anxious to get there. As she suspected, when they reached the train tracks behind the station, the road was filled with people. They were swept into the factory gate by the crowds, where they saw through the wide-open warehouse doors that the piles of flour sacks and mountains of grain were noticeably smaller. Just then, a shot rang out, and truck headlights cut through the darkness. Hurriedly grabbing whatever they could, Geumi and her family loaded flour sacks onto Baekman's bicycle cargo rack, filled the wooden tub and blanket with grain, which Geumi carried on her head, and hoisted two more sacks of rice onto Jisan's back. Police officers and American soldiers leapt out of the truck and raced to the front of the warehouse, where they started firing blanks to try to scare people off. Geumi and her family just managed to slip out the gate and cross the train tracks. As soon as they were across from the station, they headed into the back alleys instead of taking the main street. The factory would be off-limits now. They realised they had got away by the skin of their teeth.

When they got home and counted up their haul, they found that they'd managed to gather at least four sacks of rice and five sacks of flour. Later still, they realised the rice was all broken rice, not whole grains, and flavourless. But when boiled into a porridge with vegetables, it was good enough. The flour, they made into dough for hand-torn sujebi noodles and rolled out thin for knife-cut kalguksu noodles. Spring that year was a lucky one, as Baekman and his family did not have to go hungry for a while.

17

Ilcheol joined the central committee of the National Council of Labour Unions and was elected deputy chief of the Yeongdeungpo branch, while his brother's friend Ahn Daegil was elected chief. All of the leadership roles in Gyeongseong were filled by former members of the reconstructionists and the Gyeongseong Com. This was the fruition of the anti-Japanese struggle, which had been going strong since the latter half of the 1930s. Though they hadn't been at it long — what with the people's committees, the National Council, and the Nationwide Federation of Farmers' Unions all forming in the six short months after Liberation — the Korean people had taken a huge leap toward building the independent nation and democratic society of their hopes and desires. Having those hopes crushed by the US military occupation so immediately after Liberation gave the people a bitter education in history and the laws of social development. And despite the increasing pressure and oppression from pro-Japanese forces intent on seizing political and governmental power with the blessings of the USAMGIK, the people were not afraid.

Right-wing politicians couldn't have cared less about organising workers and farmers, but the Moscow Conference of Foreign Ministers ignited a debate between pro- and anti-trusteeship while driving home the importance of labourers' and farmers' unions. The right-wing hurriedly organised a youth group called the National Youth Association for the Rapid Realisation of Korean Independence to be run under their umbrella, and created other right-wing youth groups, such as the North-West Youth League, by gathering jobless people and young defectors from the north. They even formed their own labour union for the sole purpose of trying to crush the National Council unions, using the anti-communist logic of right-wing politics. Naturally, their union was not by or for labourers at all, despite their claims of supporting labourers. They grew by letting violent, right-wing youth groups forcibly disband the National Council unions and then replacing them with their own. The right-wing labour groups were backed by factory owners and other business owners, and their funding mainly came from Rhee Syngman's political party, business owners, and USAMGIK officials.

In mid-April 1946, the National Council of Labour Unions met in the Railway Bureau's welfare hall in preparation for the first May Day since Liberation. There were around 200 people in attendance — all of whom were crew chiefs or technicians or held key positions within their unions. At the podium, someone read a missive addressed to Kim Il-sung and Kim Tu-bong, chairman and vice-chairman respectively of the Provisional People's Committee of North Korea, and to Lyuh Woon-hyung, Ho Hon, Pak Hon-yong, and others of the left-wing National Front for Democracy in South Korea. At the same time, with only a few days separating the events, Rhee Syngman and Kim Gu were appointed president and vice-president of the National Association for the Rapid Realisation of Korean Independence. The reading was met with thunderous applause from all in attendance, when an even louder commotion was heard and young men began pouring in through the front and back doors of the conference hall, having smashed their way in through the glass panes and lattice frames. They wore strips of white cloth tied around their foreheads, and they were armed with bats and clubs; some even carried sharpened sickles.

At the head of the mob were two men Ilcheol recognised. One of them, who went by his family name of Hong, had been dispatched by the Railway Bureau to manage workers at the Yeongdeungpo Rail Works back when Joseon was still under Japanese rule. He had claimed to have been a labour activist in Wonsan. The first thing he did when he started at the rail works was to hire several people he knew and form a clique with them. They started what was essentially a yellow union operating on behalf of the company.

Hong started yelling at the assembled National Council members.

'You sons of slave bitches! What gives you the right to keep May Day for yourselves? You think you commie bastards can just take ownership of this factory?'

'Please keep it down,' someone called back. 'We're in the middle of a meeting. And anyone who isn't a union member needs to leave right now.'

'You first! This is an unlawful assembly.' Hong raised one arm high and waved his followers forward, shouting, 'Drive them out!'

They came in swinging and began attacking anyone and everyone at random. The union members, who were having their heads cracked open and shoulders and backs beaten where they sat, rose up, hoisted their chairs, and fought back. But the union leaders, including Ilcheol, thought better of it and jumped out of the window and into the flowerbed below and escaped. Later, they learned that the same thing was happening in meeting halls everywhere, not just in Yeongdeungpo. In some cases, both sides already knew each other, but most of the violence was carried out by strangers and outsiders. Even the way the intruders dressed varied. Some wore dyed US military uniforms; others, school uniforms; and still others, sharp suits as befitting organised criminals. They were led by older-looking men in police or military uniform jackets.

On 1 May, International Workers' Day, the right-wing Federation of Labour Unions for the Promotion of Korean Independence and the left-wing National Council of Labour Unions both held events at Seoul Stadium, the former bringing together 3,000 people in the track-and-field stadium; and the latter, over 50,000 in the baseball stadium. The differences went beyond numbers, though. The Federation straightaway made it clear in their statement of resolution that they were not a labour union: 'This is not a time for revolution, nor even for class struggle, but rather for looking after the nation.' In their celebratory address, they stressed that workers 'must work more than eight hours a day to rebuild the country' and that 'workers should be working sixteen hours, and even twenty-four a day when necessary'. The Korean spokesman of the USAMGIK's labour department, which was secretly funding the group, was the same person who'd managed conscripted labour for the Japanese Government-General's labour ministry. In other words, the USAMGIK's and the conservatives' ideology was always one of collaboration and 'pursuing amity between labour and capital', and their one and only political goal was anti-communism and the overthrow of the National Council.

After May Day, the right-wing youth groups began a campaign of terror against individual labour activists, prompting the National Council to form a self-defence corps. Ilcheol had young workers stand guard in the union office and had two bodyguards accompany him every time he went out. In early summer, the US military authorities fabricated a counterfeiting scheme and tried to pin the blame for the out-of-control inflation on the Korean Communist Party. At the same time, Rhee Syngman was campaigning in Jeongeup for the establishment of a separate South Korean government. Above the 38th parallel, the Workers' Party of North Korea was formed, headed by Kim Il-sung and Kim Tu-bong. The USAMGIK ordered the arrest of Korean Communist Party leader Pak Hon-yong and others, after which all socialist organisations in South Korea went completely underground. Several legendary anti-Japanese activists and socialists were arrested.

September brought with it the National Council's general strike and the Autumn Uprising. In the bloody aftermath, the Workers' Party of South Korea was born, and Ho Hon and Pak Hon-yong were elected to lead.

Ilcheol was attending the meeting to decide on whether to hold a general strike. It was being held at the National Council's meeting hall, and he was there as a central-committee member representing the Yeongdeungpo Rail Works. Yongsan police chief Choi Yong, aka Yamashita, aka Choi Daryeong, had deployed not only investigators and detectives but an entire squad of uniformed police around the perimeter of the building. He'd received orders from the USAMGIK's police department and reconfirmed them before sending in his men. The plan was to have the right-wing youth group and Federation members attack first. The police would have the area surrounded until after both sides had clashed, and then they would arrest the labour-union leaders.

Daryeong knew in detail what Ilcheol had been up to in Yeongdeungpo. He had even gone to see him in person right after the events of May Day. That was when left-wing leaders and politicians were being rounded up and civic groups were being watched and investigated. He had no idea how the situation would unfold, and was frankly dying with curiosity to find out more about the activities of Ilcheol and his acquaintances. He dispatched a detective to Ilcheol's Yeongdeungpo office in Dangsan-jeong. The detective had worked with Daryeong for a long time as an assistant. When he arrived at Ilcheol's office, he was stopped by a brawny young man at the bottom of the stairs leading up to the second-floor office.

'I'm here to see the Deputy Chief Yi Ilcheol.'

The man looked the detective up and down.

'Who're you and what d'you want?'

The detective grinned and showed him his badge.

'We have some things to discuss.'

The man called to someone upstairs, and the other person came running down. They whispered to each other. The second person ran back up again; after a moment, he stuck his head out the door and shouted.

'You can come up now!'

When the detective entered the office, he was greeted by hard stares from the men sitting with Ilcheol.

'What is this about?' Ilcheol asked.

'You know Choi Daryeong, right?'

'You mean Yamashita? What's he up to these days?'

Ilcheol leaned forward in his chair like he was ready to charge forward, but the detective was unalarmed. He knew the whole story in and out.

'He's a police chief now. He asked me to deliver a message.'

Jo Yeongchun interrupted, raising his voice to say, 'What could that bastard traitor have to say to us …'

The detective kept smiling and answered calmly.

'Haven't we all done our share of things in the past? He said that he and Mr Yi used to be good friends and that he hopes to meet with him in person again.'

'How about you tell us where he is, and we'll go deal with him,' Yeongchun said.

Ilcheol scribbled something down on a piece of paper and handed it to the detective.

'Give him this. It's where and when he can find me.'

After the detective left with the note, Yeongchun said, 'This is not just a personal matter. Yamashita is a traitor who we must punish.'

Ilcheol let out a long sigh and stood.

'First we need a proper government in place, and then we can punish him according to the law. But right now, the USAMGIK is no different from the Japanese Government-General. They hold all the power and responsibility for public safety. The only reason I agreed to meet with him is so I can get a sense of what they're up to.'

'At least discuss it first with the branch chief.'

'Of course I will.'

Ilcheol met with Ahn Daegil in secret that night. As he was wanted by the police, he wasn't able to make any public appearances. Daegil's mother still ran the same restaurant, while Daegil was hiding out on the second storey of an ironworks near Saok-jeong where many small factories were clustered. When Ilcheol told him about Daryeong, Daegil couldn't hold back his anger.

'How will our dead comrades ever rest in peace if we can't punish traitors like him?'

Ilcheol was struck by the thought that Daegil and Yeongchun were bigger victims of Choi Daryeong than he was, being only the older brother of someone who'd died in prison.

Daegil said, 'The USAMGIK has forced us to vacate our meeting hall and has issued arrest warrants for all the leaders of our party, including

Pak Hon-yong. They'll see this as the perfect opportunity to crush the life out of us. We need to go on the offensive.'

'I understand that, but let's hold off on making any decisions until after I meet with him.'

'We need to assemble a special task force to punish people like him.'

Ilcheol could feel in his bones that an all-out battle was imminent.

Three days later, Ilcheol went to the same izakaya near the station where he'd met with Daryeong before. The Japanese had all left, and the businesses in the neighbourhood had changed ownership multiple times, but the izakaya was still run by the same Korean chef, who'd taken it over from the owner. When Ilcheol was being shown to his seat, Daryeong stood up awkwardly from behind the partition. He looked better than before: he wore a sharp suit and his hair, slicked back with pomade, gleamed in the light.

'*Oi!* Long time no see!'

The welcoming look on Daryeong's face made Ilcheol so uncomfortable that he met Daryeong's two outstretched hands with a limp, single-handed shake of his own.

'You seem to be doing as well as ever, Mr Yamashita …' Ilcheol murmured.

Daryeong let out a hearty laugh and handed him a business card.

'Ah, that was my Japanese name, now, wasn't it? And you were Mr Inoue.'

Ilcheol looked down at the card. It read, 'Choi Yong, Senior Superintendent, Chief of Yongsan Police Station.'

'Choi Yong? That's new.'

'Yes, now that we're liberated, I figured it was time to wash off the past and become a new person. I want to do my part to build a new country. You should, too.'

Ilcheol drank half of the large cup of sake Daryeong had poured for him.

'This from the man who arrested and killed my brother?'

'Come now, there was a lot more to it than that, wasn't there? Just as you drove a train for a living, I did police work — for a living. If Dusoe had only changed his ways and lived a quiet life, pursued a proper career like you, nothing would have happened.'

A great wave of sadness washed over Ilcheol at once, but he struggled to hide what he was feeling and instead asked, 'Why did you want to see me anyway?'

Daryeong lowered his voice.

'I came to warn you that arrest warrants are about to drop all over the country. The whole world knows that you guys are backed by the Korean Communist Party. We can't just look the other way on that. To put it another way, you should think of your family and quit the Council. I plan to put in a word with my superiors and recommend you for a management position at the Railway Bureau.'

'No need to worry about me. But do you think Icheol's old comrades are willing to forget Yamashita and let it all go?'

Daryeong responded calmly.

'Listen, other than the damn Japanese leaving, nothing else has changed. The real problem now is commies. Do you know what they call people like me? Experts. Just like you're an expert at trains, I'm an expert at catching commies. The US needs experts like us, Koreans with power need us.'

Ilcheol threw what was left of his sake in Daryeong's face and shouted, 'Oh yeah? Well, good luck with that, you traitor!'

Ilcheol stood to leave.

Daryeong wiped his face with a handkerchief and quietly said, 'Don't be stupid. You will regret this later.'

In the end, the only thing Ilcheol regretted was letting his feelings get the better of him.

While the police were taking their positions around the National Council's meeting hall, military trucks pulled up. Riding in the backs were hundreds of young men brazenly armed with wooden clubs and metal pipes. They fancied themselves members of the Federation, but most belonged to the North-West Youth League and other conservative political parties' youth corps, and their leaders were men who'd terrorised people in Gyeongseong in the name of the Japanese

Government-General. The workers standing guard at the front door and in the halls and staircases were quickly subdued by the thugs at the head of the pack, some of whom were even armed with guns. The sound of gunfire was deafening. Dozens were killed or injured. The police followed, entering the blood-spattered meeting hall and arresting 140 ordinary workers and union leaders.

Ilcheol and his colleagues made their way to Seoul Station, where they waited until nightfall to stow away on a freight train and retreat to Yeongdeungpo. There, they barricaded themselves inside the Yeongdeungpo Rail Works and began a sit-in protest.

Geumi was woken in the middle of the night by the sound of the front gate rattling. She tiptoed over and whispered, 'Who … who's there?'

'It's me. Let me in.'

At the familiar sound of her husband's voice, she undid the latch, and he slid inside. Half of his face was bandaged, and his arm was in a splint. She didn't see the blood seeping through the bandages until they were inside, in the lamplight.

'What happened?' she asked, in shock. 'Are you okay?'

'Could you bring me some water? And do we have anything to eat?'

For a long time after, Geumi was haunted by the image of Ilcheol grabbing the brass bowl brimming with water from her hands and gulping it all down at once, then letting the empty bowl fall to the floor and opening his mouth to the sky to draw in a long breath. It filled her with the kind of pity and heartbreak she might have felt at seeing a runaway dog return home, dragging its limbs, covered in unexplained wounds, and hiding under the maru, panting as it slurped from its water bowl. The barley rice left on the stove had gone soggy, and all they had to eat with it was some old radish-greens kimchi and salty braised mackerel. But he filled a rice bowl with water and shovelled huge spoonfuls of rice into his mouth, punctuated by more spoonfuls of fish and kimchi, until his cheeks were stuffed with food. It was plain to see how wracked with hunger he was. His late-night meal complete, he asked his wife for a fresh set of underwear and changed into them, then packed a bag with more socks and underwear and stood to leave.

'Where on earth are you going?' Geumi asked.

Ilcheol hugged her and patted her on the back and said, 'Is Jisan asleep? And my father … ?'

'Of course, they're both asleep. You should get some rest, too. Leave in the morning.'

'I have to go now. They're all waiting for me.'

Geumi couldn't bring herself to stop him. She could see the faces of the men waiting for him; she knew something important was happening. When Ilcheol looked back at her, his face swollen beneath the bandages, she took one look at his tear-filled eyes and had to turn away.

'I'll meet you at the factory tomorrow,' she said.

Ilcheol vanished out the front gate without responding. He would never return home again.

The next day, armed thugs descended upon the Yeongdeungpo Rail Works. This time, the workers occupying the site were ready. They'd barricaded the entrance with whatever they could find, built fortifications, collected piles of stones for throwing, and even prepped Molotov cocktails. Three thousand police officers had the main streets and buildings near the factory surrounded. The non-police thugs were the first to go in, charging the barricaded entrance, and when the rocks came flying, they returned fire with carbine rifles. It was later speculated that they'd used heavy machine guns, but in actuality they were firing automatic bursts from M2 rifles. It was also reported that the thugs who jumped the wall and breached the factory yard responded to the workers' Molotov cocktails with hand grenades.

There were so many casualties that the battle didn't last long. The workers were overwhelmed by the ferocity of the attack, having never experienced such overt bloodshed even at the hands of the Japanese. They retreated a block at a time from their desperately held positions, collecting their wounded as they went. When Ilcheol, already wounded, arrived on the scene, the younger workers begged him to leave.

'Deputy Chief, please, you shouldn't be here.'

'Don't be ridiculous. I'm staying with you all until the end.'

'We've received word from outside. They need you to keep the group together.'

As they were arguing back and forth, Jo Yeongchun came running.

'What're you doing? Get out of here! I'll handle things here. Daegil has already been arrested.'

Even before he could decide for himself, two young men were dragging him to an out-of-the-way spot at the back of the factory. He saw an open manhole cover and a small metal ladder leading down. One of the men went first, followed by Ilcheol, who groped his way down in the dark. The other man, who'd been keeping guard from behind, came down, too, and closed the manhole behind him. They crept, bent over, through the old sewage tunnels beneath the factories, wastewater up to their ankles. When they emerged from another manhole in the darkness of the factory district, they could see crimson flames rising from the rail works in the distance.

The sit-in ended with dozens of workers killed and truckfuls of workers arrested. And yet, the nationwide general strike survived, and grew and expanded from economic struggle to political struggle. The striking workers' slogans had started out as calls for increased rice rations, guarantee of workers' rights to free association, enactment of democratic labour laws, and release of political prisoners, but were now a revolutionary demand of 'POWER TO THE PEOPLE'S COMMITTEES'. As the strike continued, students all over the country joined the fight by boycotting classes, and the majority of newspapers were sympathetic in their reporting.

Seventeen hundred rail workers in Yongsan and Yeongdeungpo were arrested. But the violent crackdown in Seoul did not extinguish the flames of uprising; in Daegu, another fire was lit, a fire that would spread across the entire country. The first to strike were the electrical, postal, and textile workers' unions; by 30 September, nearly all of the factories in Daegu had gone on strike. The workers went on a hunger march through downtown Daegu, demanding 'More rice!' Students taught the crowds of protesters the lyrics to a song they'd written, called 'Let's Go Steal Some Rice', which they'd set to the Italian folk song 'Santa Lucia', which they'd learned in music class.

Warehouses piled high with rice, sticky rice, short-grain rice
You're not the only hungry one, I'm hungry too
Grab your sack and let's go steal some rice
Grab your sack and let's go steal some rice

In addition to the USAMGIK's prohibitions on collecting or transporting rice, a curfew had been instituted in Daegu in order to stop an outbreak of cholera, but this made it impossible for residents to acquire food from outside the city. The people of Daegu were starving. The situation had grown so dire that the workers at the Monopoly Bureau's tobacco factory had taken to eating the paste used to roll cigarettes. The US Army and the local police gathered up people who were bedridden from hunger and forced them into quarantine facilities by claiming they had contracted cholera. When female hunger marchers burst into the mayor's office to confront him, he lashed out at them by saying that foul-mouthed women like them needed soap more than rice and that their lack of rice was their own fault for being bad at housekeeping. Word of this only stoked public outrage.

On 1 October, workers from 400 factories in Daegu lent their support to the strike, along with students and the general populace. Numbering in the tens of thousands, the protesters poured into the streets, shouting, 'US troops out of Korea!' A coal-briquette-factory worker was killed by a police officer's warning shot. Fifteen thousand or more enraged Daegu citizens protested late into the night and assembled in front of the Daegu Police Station at 10.00 am for a rally. One young man stood before the crowd boiling over with anger and excitement and spoke with passion, declaring that there was no better time than now to avenge their fallen comrade's death, when he was suddenly felled by a police officer's bullet. Five more speakers took the stage to try to continue the fight only to spill their blood in turn at the hands of police sharpshooters. The angry crowd threw stones, and the police returned their volley with rifle fire, killing seventeen. The citizens of Daegu braved the bullets to charge into the police station and occupy it; some of the young men even managed to arm themselves by seizing weapons. In groups of hundreds, they attacked all of the police boxes in the city and took control of Daegu. From midnight to daybreak, the officers who'd been the objects of resentment ever since colonisation were murdered by citizens. The residences of the mayor, the governor, and the head of the Monopoly Bureau were also attacked; citizens brought the rice and cotton they'd seized to Dalseong Park and redistributed it in an orderly fashion. In every neighbourhood, young men wore armbands and helped direct traffic, and the owner of a shoe store even started giving shoes away for free to demonstrators. By afternoon, the South Chungcheong Province police began to arrive, and martial law was declared in all of Daegu. US troops, armed with tanks and machine guns, poured into downtown Daegu, while the Korean police launched a massive counterattack. Curfew was declared starting at 7.00 pm, and protesters and organisers were rounded up and arrested, but rallies had started in neighbouring towns — from Yeongcheon to Euiseong, Gunwi, Waegwan, Seonsan, Pohang, and Yeongil — and quickly turned into uprisings that spread with more violence and ferocity through the countryside. The struggle in farm villages grew much more violent because nothing had changed under the military occupation, let alone any sort of land reform. The police were just as tyrannical as they'd ever been under Japanese rule, leaving farmers frustrated at the fact that Liberation was, in fact, no liberation at all.

The farmers sang a rewritten version of the 'Rice Planting Song':

After opening all the sluice gates, where did your boss go?
He went to visit his concubine with an armful of octopus and abalone.
Sun's setting, it's growing dark, smoke rises from every house.
Where did our parents go? Don't they know our houses are burning?
A foul smell, a rotten stench, the black dog reeks of blood.
Our brother walks away, leashed like a dog in prisoner's ropes.
Say no to forced rice collections even if the military government presses charges.

The farmers' demands were straightforward: 'Abolish the rice collections, implement land reform, and hand power to the people's committees!'

The flames of rebellion engulfed Gyeongsang Province and spread to the rest of the country, to Gwangju, Hwasun, Mokpo, and beyond. The US military mobilised the police, the newly established National Defense Force, and right-wing youth groups and gangs to suppress the riots. The only thing different from the past was that they thought nothing of inflicting civilian casualties. In Masan, they fired indiscriminately on 6,000 protesters. Nationwide, 28,000 people were killed and 15,000 were arrested and detained. Their homes were looted and destroyed by the police and their thugs, and they were dragged away to police stations to be brutally tortured. With jails and prisons at capacity due to these mass arrests, temporary prison camps were installed to lock away demonstrators and strikers. This strife lasted for three months.

On 3 October, Jisan was on his way to school despite boycotting classes in solidarity. He'd received word from some senior students who were members of the left-wing Mincheong youth association. At the time, fifth-year students were the graduating class, which left Jisan and his fellow third-year students stuck in the middle, and infamous at every school for being troublemakers. Jisan had not yet joined the Mincheong, but he was well-versed enough in theory to be able to debate current events with the fifth-years. This was undoubtedly due to the influence of his father and his late uncle. Around 300 students assembled at the school; by the time they reached the USAMGIK command centre, housed in the former Japanese Government-General building, their numbers had swelled to the thousands. They were joined by workers and people from all walks of life, forming a crowd of over 20,000. They passed through Gwanghwamun Gate and gathered in front of the USAMGIK building.

'Give us rice! Down with colonial education! Release our imprisoned patriots! Denounce terrorism!'

The riot police arrived, their guns loaded with live ammunition, and were followed by mounted police wielding the same batons used during the Japanese occupation. They approached the USAMGIK building in two flanks, with another squad marching over from Namdaemun Gate. They surrounded the protesters gathered in the plaza in front of the building and began firing into the air. The crowd was squeezed into the centre of the plaza. The mounted police drove right into the middle of them and began bashing at people with their long clubs. Twenty were killed in the melee. Jisan bandaged his wounded head with strips of cloth from his undershirt and stumbled the whole way home, barely making it back to Yeongdeungpo. It was already after dark by the time he got there.

Geumi had come out to the entrance of the alleyway and was pacing back and forth with her heart in her mouth; the moment she saw her son staggering towards her, she ran to him and threw her arms around him.

'*Aigu*, what happened to you? Let me see …'

She later said that Jisan, who was as tall as her by then, sobbed like a baby in her arms. Of course, Jisan later insisted that he'd done no such thing, and Baekman took his grandson's side.

'Sobbing, what sobbing? The boy was just panting! With fury!'

When Jino was in primary school, he'd asked Geumi Halmeoni about it.

'I get why it was like that under the Japanese, but why does our family only ever side with the losers and never the winners?'

'What, you don't like siding with the weaker folk?'

'Of course not. All we do is get hurt!'

The wrinkles around his grandmother's eyes had grown even deeper as she smiled widely and said, 'It always looks like you're losing at first, but in the end, the weak are destined to win. It's just frustrating that it takes so long, is all.' Then she added, 'If you live long enough, you figure this all out. Everyone else knows it, too. They just don't like to show it.'

After the rail workers' sit-in was broken up by right-wing thugs, Ilcheol and the other National Council leaders went on the run. Though they remained in communication with each other, they had to keep it to a minimum, and it was in this state of affairs that the group split between the working activists who called for intensifying the struggle and those who insisted on taking a break from direct action while they focused on strengthening the organisation instead. Those who'd taken over leadership of the Worker's Party of South Korea after Pak Hon-yong went underground met with the USAMGIK to seek a compromise while the fervour over the general strike cooled down. But the party had no actual power at the time to control or lead the strike on a national scale. In the countryside, police violence was growing worse, and arrests and summary executions were becoming an everyday event; the hunted fled into the mountains where they banded together, armed with whatever meagre weapons they could find. The will to fight also returned to Seoul, as Gyeongseong was now officially and increasingly called, where resistance had been weakening, and groups began forming among students and younger workers who insisted on continuing the struggle and were willing to step into battle themselves. Their main targets were those known for collaborating with the Japanese and who had regained power with the support of the USAMGIK. More to the point, they were mostly hunting those who'd worked for the Special Higher Police under the Japanese regime.

From underground, the central secretariat of the Gyeongseong Com put together and distributed a list of names and workplaces. Number one on the list of collaborators who deserved punishment was Choi Daryeong. Jo Yeongchun assigned Bak Seonok and Sohn Yeongsun to follow Daryeong and report on his movements, and teamed up with four other men for the stakeout and mission. They used a house on a hillside near Noryangjin as their base; the house had been abandoned after its Japanese owner left the country. They gave themselves ten days. Any longer and they would start to attract attention. They posed as two families who'd left North Korea, pretending that they were part of the influx of sampal ddaraji, or '38th-parallel wretches', who had been flocking to the outskirts of Seoul. Seonok and Yeongsun pretended to work at a factory across the Hangang River; their 'husbands' posed as peddlers, and their 'younger brothers' as teenage apprentices. Yeongchun was a 'relative' who made the occasional visit. They all returned home at around the same time in the evening and ate together. They began their meeting at the dinner table.

'We need to know his movements first,' Yeongchun said.

'We went to his house in Cheongpa-dong,' Seonok said. 'There were seven people there: a guard on rotation, a maid, Daryeong, his wife, and their son and daughter, who are in school. And their driver, of course.'

The rest reported on their assigned tasks.

'If they have a car, it must be an army jeep, right? Does he take the car every day?'

'To and from work.'

'He also walks the dog at a nearby park before breakfast.'

'Same time every day?'

'He goes out early in the morning, but not every day.'

'Does anyone go with him?'

'I observed him three times, and he was alone each time.'

'I heard he raised pigs for a living when he was a kid,' Yeongchun said. 'And that he liked animals so much he was able to talk with the pigs.'

'Wow, from swineherd to police chief. He really made his way up in the world. Who told you about that anyway?'

'Deputy Chief Comrade Yi. He said they went to primary school together.'

After tracking Daryeong's movements for five days, they chose Hyochang Park for carrying out their mission. One day, as he was gazing out at the western sky, Yeongchun told the others, 'Weather's looking good. Let's do it tomorrow!'

The next day, Yeongchun and the other four men left the house at five in the morning. Sure enough, Yeongchun seemed to have an eye for predicting the weather, because it was a beautiful autumn day without a cloud in the sky. He later told Seonok that the best way to divine the next day's weather was by examining the sunset the day before. They crossed a footbridge over the Hangang and arrived near Daryeong's house around 5.40 am. Yeongchun and two of the men took their positions in a grove of pine trees near the entrance to Hyochang Park, while the other two men waited in separate spots near Daryeong's house. They were nervous, worried that luck would be against them and Daryeong would not come out for a walk or would have someone with him.

At exactly six o'clock, things started to happen. Behind the wall surrounding the formerly Japanese-owned house and its many spindle trees and junipers pruned into circles, they heard a dog bark. At twenty past six, the iron gate opened; the dog came out first, followed by a man holding its leash. It was a German shepherd, and a big one at that, but it had a certain spindliness to its legs and a puppyish look that suggested it was only about six months old. Daryeong was dressed in clothes suitable for jogging. He chided the dog as it tried to speed ahead, its leash pulled taut, and set out on their walk.

The young 'apprentice' purposefully crossed his path and informed the older 'peddler' who was coming up from behind, 'That's him.'

They kept a good distance from each other as they went ahead of Daryeong along his usual walking route. Then, their part of the mission complete, the apprentice headed off toward Namdaemun-ro, the peddler trailing slowly behind him. When the peddler could see the pine grove across from the minari field, he figured that the others had spotted Daryeong, too, and he ducked down a side path.

Meanwhile, as this was his usual walk, Daryeong had let his guard down and was giving the dog time to finish his business. He broke into a jog now and then, to keep up with the dog, but he would scold it and they would drop back to an easy pace. When Daryeong was at the base of the hill that led up from the park entrance, two men with towels slung around their necks came jogging down. He examined them with the eagle-eyed gaze of a longtime police officer. But they were ordinary young men out for some morning exercise. He relaxed his guard and continued walking when another man, dressed in the standard-issue jacket of the era, came towards him holding a rolled-up newspaper. Struck by how familiar he looked, Daryeong kept thinking, 'Where've I seen this guy before?' Just then, the two joggers who'd passed him rushed up from behind and grabbed him by the arms and shoulders. Daryeong let go of his dog's leash; he didn't even have time to scream. The man in front of him had already thrust the knife wrapped in the newspaper into his stomach. The two men behind each held him in place with one arm, and they used their other arms to pull out their own knives and stab him over and over in the sides. Blood spilled from him like water from a broken levee, and he collapsed on the spot. As he lay on the ground and stared up into the sky, the man who'd stabbed him first grinned at him.

'Yamashita! I'm Jo Yeongchun. Our patriotic martyrs Bang Wuchang and Yi Icheol will be waiting for you on the other side.'

Daryeong tried to say something in response, but his head flopped over and he died. They dragged him by his legs and tossed him into the pine grove. Then they took a good look around. The puppy had smelled something in the minari field and was romping and nosing around in there. No one else was out. They examined each other. The front of Yeongchun's jacket was soaked with blood, while the other men were stained on their right and left sides respectively. They took off their jackets, discarded them under some bushes, and fled the scene in their undershirts.

The next day, the investigative units at the Yongsan and Yeongdeungpo Police Stations were turned inside out as they went on the hunt for suspects. Between the two stations, there were about sixty detectives combined. Leading the hunt were Daryeong's old spy-team members who were now running their own sections. After examining the background reports and interrogation files on former activists, whom the police still spoke of in the present tense, they concluded that the members of the Yeongdeungpo Gyeongseong Com had to be involved in Daryeong's murder. Their long experience also told them that the suspects were all active members of the National Council.

The police had already ransacked the National Council's empty office, of course, as well as the homes of all the union representatives and members of the central committee and secretariat, and of all the rank-and-file members who were on the police's list. A hundred people were brought in for questioning, and all of the factories in Yeongdeungpo had to pause operations.

The very day that Daryeong was murdered, Seonok went to see Geumi at the Saetmal House in the evening. She was carrying a backpack and looked like she was going somewhere far away. The two women sat in the courtyard and whispered to each other.

'The black dogs will go on a rampage,' Seonok said.

'Black dogs' was the term people used back then to refer to the police who'd inherited their positions under the USAMGIK after having worked as informants for the Japanese colonial government.

'We finally took care of Yamashita.'

'Ahh …'

The way Geumi described it, her blood went cold when she heard that. Because she was more concerned with the safety of her husband, who was already on the run, than with thoughts of avenging her brother-in-law. A crushing sense of despair that she would never see her husband again came over her.

'Yes, it'll be chaos tomorrow. We can't stay here. Eonni, you have to get your family somewhere safe.'

Geumi stilled her racing heart and thought it over carefully. Her husband would never be safe in Yeongdeungpo again, let alone at home. She realised that the only way she'd be able to make contact with him while he was underground was for her to leave home, too. And the only person capable of getting her in touch with Ilcheol was Seonok. Geumi assumed that Jisan was fast asleep, as there were no sounds coming from his room, but the light was on in her father-in-law's workshop on the other side of the courtyard. She went to his door and whispered, 'Abeonim.'

'What is it?' he asked.

He took off his magnifying glasses and set them on his workbench. He'd been in the middle of grinding and smoothing a piece of buffalo horn.

'Abeonim, the union organisers executed Yamashita today.'

'No, no, all hell will break out now.'

'They've already been hunting everywhere for Jisan Abeoji. They'll probably come at daybreak to arrest us, and you know what that means.'

Baekman had always been a man of few words, no matter whether things were good or bad, but that didn't mean that he did not understand the urgency they were facing. He had watched his son Dusoe fight for years for independence from the Japanese, and he'd suffered the agony of personally retrieving his son's body from prison. Then, in the year since Liberation, his own hopes and dreams had been snatched away, while his eldest son, Hansoe, had become the hunted.

'The detectives will be here soon. We have to go into hiding for at least a month — or no, just two weeks, at least.'

Baekman was silent in response to this for the longest time, but then he finally said, 'This is my home. Where on earth do you suggest we go?'

'Jisan is practically all grown up now, too, and knows what's going on in the world. They won't just leave him alone.'

'I said, where do you suggest we go?'

'I'm thinking of taking you to my family's home in Gimpo until things calm down.'

Baekman fell silent again.

'Please, we have to go,' Geumi said, panic rising in her.

'But the thing is … don't you think someone needs to stay behind, to give them a piece of our mind?'

'If you do that, you'll be tortured. Besides, what would you tell them when they ask where we've all gone?'

'I don't know. I guess I would just say that you all ran off while I was out running an errand.'

'They'll be looking the hardest for Jisan Abeoji.'

'Jisan Abeoji is dead to me now,' Baekman said flatly.

Geumi immediately understood what he meant by this. Each time Daryeong and his team had come looking for Icheol, Baekman had told them the same thing. That since commies had no love for their parents or their wives and kids, he'd long since stopped thinking of Icheol as his child. And that he hated his commie son even more than the cops did.

'I'll do what I did under the Japanese,' Baekman muttered.

Geumi later said that hearing those words broke her heart. After the October filled with strikes and uprising passed, 537 people were put on trial, and sixteen were sentenced to death. It was also a time of untold summary executions by firing squads all throughout the countryside.

'When the police come,' she said, 'tell them we went to Chungcheong Province. Say that I went back to my friend's village near the factory where I used to work. And say that we haven't heard anything from Jisan Abeoji and have no idea whether he's alive or dead.'

Geumi talked it over with Seonok and decided they should catch what little sleep they could and leave before dawn. The two women lay next to each other in the main bedroom.

'I think we might have to cross the 38th parallel,' Geumi said.

'I can't do that,' Seonok murmured. 'There are three million party members. How could I save only myself and run away? And the core members are still active underground. We're only supposed to cross the border if it's absolutely unavoidable.'

'There've been more and more people coming south.'

'That's because they enacted land reform and nationalised the means of production right away. There must be a lot of people struggling to adapt to revolution.'

'Sure. If Ilcheol crossed over, would he be able to find us eventually?'

Seonok was brimming with confidence when she answered this.

'It wouldn't take him long. We Koreans aren't so easily overcome. Once the Yankees leave, the North and South Korean people's committees will merge, and we'll be reunified.'

'Yes, the big noses will leave!'

That was how they spoke of their uncertain future. Geumi was on the verge of a deep sleep when Seonok mumbled, 'Eonni, are you awake?'

'Huh? I am now. What is it?'

'I was in love with Icheol. It wasn't easy.'

Geumi woke fully at this.

'You were? When?'

'I thought you were only pretending not to know. I fell for him when we first started those book clubs.'

Geumi suddenly remembered that time when she was a newlywed, when her brother-in-law had come by the house after being in hiding. She had seen two women hovering behind him as he sat at the head of the table and had unintentionally muttered something about it. Her husband had scolded her, and Icheol had dropped his spoon and left. From Icheol's arrest, Jangsan's death, and Yeowok's leaving home to Icheol's sentencing and death in prison, Geumi had wondered more than once about the identities of those two women who'd haunted her brother-in-law. But it had never occurred to her to consider Seonok, despite how close they were. She must have been terribly heartbroken.

'But … that means you were in love with him from the day you met.'

'Yes, from the moment Icheol Oppa answered one of my questions. You were there, too.'

'I don't remember …'

'I asked him what the word "proletariat" meant. Icheol Oppa explained that it means people who have nothing, like us, and my heart skipped a beat.'

Geumi sat up in bed.

'You should have told him. Weren't you his reppo right up until the end?'

'Jangsan Eomma was my comrade. We were activists together in the same group. I could never bring myself to say anything.'

They both lay back down. And cried quietly.

'What awful times we've been through!' Geumi murmured between sniffles.

Seonok woke at first light. Jisan was groggy and only half-awake, so Geumi had to help him up while also juggling all their belongings. When the three of them left the house, Baekman was waiting in the courtyard.

'Abeonim, please don't forget to eat, and if anything at all comes up, ask for help from the people at the rail works.'

'Sure, get going, and don't worry about me.'

Seonok and Geumi left at dawn with Jisan in tow. Their plan was to cross the Omokgyo Bridge to Yeomchang Dock, where they would catch a boat heading for the harbour on the ebb tide. Seonok said she would stay at Geumi's family home in Gimpo for a few days before heading to Incheon. Geumi's father had passed away a few years before Liberation, and her older brothers were running the farm and looking after their mother. Ilcheol's work had been preventing him from visiting his wife's family lately, but Geumi had taken Jisan for a visit just the year before. As a community leader, her eldest brother had to bite his tongue, but the younger brother's anger was through the roof at having to turn over their rice harvest to the USAMGIK. He'd had enough of low-ranking village bureaucrats and former colonial police taking over all the government offices and police stations and going around with an US Army escort to forcibly collect everyone's grain. And so he'd joined the Nationwide Federation of Farmers' Unions. The moment Geumi and the others stepped into the courtyard, her brother, who was in the maru, called out to the rest of the family.

'Geumi's here. Eomeoni, Geumi's here. Jisan, too!'

Her eldest brother and her sisters-in-law came running out of the house. After they'd all greeted each other, they asked how Ilcheol was doing.

'I guess that son-in-law of mine is too busy driving trains,' Geumi's mother said, sounding disappointed.

'Eh, why are you asking about him when you've got Jisan here?' Geumi's brother said, trying to change the subject.

He had read all about what the National Council had been up to, and he also knew what danger they were in. He moved his children into the main house and had Geumi, Jisan, and Seonok use the extra, two-room building in back. After a few days, Seonok left for Incheon. She said she would let Ilcheol know where they were if she was able to send word to him, and promised to come back in person if he sent word back.

As expected, the morning they left, four detectives from the

Yeongdeungpo Police Station came to the Saetmal House. They knocked on the door without announcing themselves, and the moment Baekman opened it, they stormed in and immediately began turning every room in the house upside down, including Baekman's workshop, without even the courtesy of removing their shoes. They ransacked every chest and cabinet until the rooms were littered with clothes and miscellaneous objects.

'Has Yi Ilcheol contacted you?' asked the detective who appeared to be in charge.

'Didn't you already search our house the last time you came looking for him?' Baekman snapped. 'It's been over three months since that boy left. Like I told you then, I've seen neither hide nor hair of him since he left to go to that union meeting hall.'

'But what about his wife ... ? Your daughter-in-law?' another detective asked. 'Where is she?'

'She said she was going to see an old friend down in Chungcheong Province. She took my grandson with her.'

The detectives sat side-by-side on the edge of the maru floor and fired questions at Baekman, who stood below them in the yard and answered each one politely, as if host and guest had changed places.

'Is it possible that Ilcheol took his family north, over the 38th parallel?'

Baekman exploded with anger at this question.

'Those commie sons of bitches! They all deserve to die for not caring about their families. I disowned him ages ago, as did my daughter-in-law. She no longer considers him her husband. So please don't even suggest that she'd go with him. The very idea makes me want to retch!'

Having worked on Yamashita's spy team, the detective was well aware of Ilcheol's case and of the fact that Baekman, unlike his two sons, had worked for the Railway Bureau his entire life and was known as a faithful citizen of the empire back when he lived in the rail workers' housing, and so his words rang with a certain degree of sincerity. The 'ideological tendencies' report he'd reviewed contained similar information. People had been massacred in the provinces, and though the violence had worsened during the war, the city had not yet been subjected to such outright violence. The detectives left empty-handed, as they'd more or less expected they would. Before exiting the front gate, the lead detective paused and turned back.

'We know that Ilcheol had nothing to do with Choi Yong's death,' he said slyly to Baekman. 'But someone has to take the blame for it. Whoever it is can't live here anymore. They'll be better off on the other side.'

Baekman later relayed the story to Geumi, who took to saying, 'It is and isn't true what they say about cops and their informants, that they aren't all good or bad. We may decide what roles we're going to play, but sometimes you just have to do things as insurance. Because, back then, the tables could turn overnight.'

18

Ilcheol was lying low at Heo Sangwoo's childhood home in Nakkul at the foot of Gwanaksan Mountain. Just as they had under the Japanese occupation, a reppo from the National Council of Labour Unions kept a line of communication open for him.

Mr Heo had also stayed in touch with the Yi family. After Icheol turned himself in, Mr Heo visited his former student in prison. He went on to serve as principal at his school, until his retirement, upon which he left the principal's residence in Dorim-dong to return to his hometown of Nakkul. His son followed in his footsteps and became a teacher, and his younger brother, who'd been taking care of the house in Nakkul, moved to central Seoul. After Liberation, a national foundation preparation committee was formed in each district. Mr Heo became chairman of the committee for Siheung County, all because former students who knew his character had recommended him. He remembered his students well. When Ilcheol came to Nakkul after the protest at the Yeongdeungpo Rail Works was thwarted, Mr Heo welcomed him. Choi Daryeong was another student he remembered. One day, when the murder of a 'Senior Superintendent Choi' was splashed across the headlines, Mr Heo ran to Ilcheol's room with a newspaper in hand.

'Big news! Choi Daryeong was murdered. This is the same person who called himself Yamashita, right? It says he changed his name to Choi Yong.'

Ilcheol took the newspaper Mr Heo handed him and let out a long sigh after skimming through the article.

'I'm relieved … but sorry, too.'

'Well, I guess he had it coming.'

'It's the work of leftist adventurism. He practically gave them an excuse.'

'Really?'

'We should be the ones taking the blows instead, to get people outraged.'

'The Soviets seem to think they have the upper hand, considering the living conditions in Joseon, and the Americans keep pushing for a separate South Korean government. That's probably why Rhee Syngman went to the United States.'

'The war began the day the Soviet troops landed in Najin and the American troops landed in Incheon. Japan knew exactly what was going to happen, even before its defeat.'

Ilcheol spent the winter at Mr Heo's place in Nakkul, staying until early March of the following year. His reppo in Yeongdeungpo sent word that more than half of the secretariat members had been arrested and that Ilcheol and Yeongchun were at the top of the wanted list. Seonok, who was hiding in Incheon, informed Ilcheol that his wife had gone to stay with her parents in Gimpo. He also heard the news that the progressives were preparing a nationwide commemoration of the March 1st Independence Movement.

On 1 March, the leftists held an event at Namsan Mountain, while the rightists held an event at Seoul Stadium. Afterwards, leftist groups came down toward Namdaemun Gate, while rightist groups marched along Euljiro Avenue and passed the Mitsukoshi department store and the Bank of Joseon before turning onto Namdaemun-ro. With students and labourers leading the way, the leftist procession had passed Namdaemun Gate and was heading toward City Hall when it was suddenly cut in half by hundreds of right-wing youth armed with clubs at the forefront of the rightist procession. Armed officers had been standing by in anticipation of such a clash and opened fire on the leftists. Dozens were killed or wounded. Others were arrested for violating MacArthur's Proclamation No. 1. Another sweep of arrests was made, and the pursuit of leading regional members of the National Council and the Workers' Party of South Korea became routine.

That day, Ilcheol was playing baduk with Mr Heo in his study. The study was in the inner wing of the house and had a lofted maru that looked out onto the backyard. Mr Heo's house sat to the left of the newly built main road on the east end of town. Though, it barely qualified as a town: apart from Mr Heo's and a couple of other tiled-roof houses, there were maybe another ten or so lookalike thatched-roof houses, and everyone knew each other's business, down to what they had for dinner each night. When all the neighbourhood dogs started barking, Mr Heo dropped the baduk stone he'd been playing and strained his ears.

'Do you hear someone coming?'

That's when they heard multiple footsteps outside the straw fence. Ilcheol, who'd been living in a constant state of tension, sprung up and cracked open the sliding door to the backyard. The paper covering the door made it difficult to see anything, but he could hear people approaching. Just then, the doors on the other side of the room were flung open, and men charged in: two from the foyer and one from the courtyard, with an army of armed policemen behind him. The detectives in front had their guns aimed at Ilcheol and Mr Heo.

'Freeze!'

The moment the doors opened, Ilcheol leapt into the backyard. The policeman closest was the first to shoot. The bullet hit Mr Heo in the chest. Another policeman, who was still in the foyer, turned and tried to shove open a door that faced north, but it had been tightly latched from the outside over the winter. Ilcheol had already rehearsed his escape routes. He raced across the backyard and disappeared into the hill to the north.

'Which way did he go?'

The detectives and officers missed their best chance at capturing Ilcheol as they scrambled across the courtyard and through the study to reach the backyard.

'There — that way, sir!'

They caught a glimpse of a man through the trees and then nothing.

'What are you waiting for? Go after him!'

Fifteen policemen and five detectives were there that day. The chief inspector in charge stood in Mr Heo's study, disappointed. A few steps away, Mr Heo was bleeding to death on the floor. He hadn't breathed his last just yet. A detective rolled him over with his foot and bent over to yell in his face.

'When did Yi Ilcheol come here? Where is he headed?'

Mr Heo let out a slight cough, blood poured from his mouth, and he stopped moving.

'Looks like he's dead,' said another detective standing just outside.

'That's the price you pay for getting in the way. Didn't he serve as chairman of Siheung County's preparation committee?'

Their raid on Mr Heo's place was the result of spending days combing through the Special Higher Police records and reports from before Liberation, which were still kept at the Yeongdeungpo Police Station. They had learned that Mr Heo had taught both Yi brothers and officiated at Ilcheol's wedding. When they scouted the neighbourhood that morning, they found out that a guest had been staying at Mr Heo's house for quite some time. They were convinced that the guest was Ilcheol and had called for backup to arrest him.

The only other people likely to be at home were Mr Heo's wife and a neighbour who helped with household chores, but the two women had gone to a nearby field to pick shepherd's purse and were luckily not there when the police arrived.

Ilcheol climbed up the north side of Gwanaksan Mountain and took a detour to head south-west. He waited on the mountain until darkness fell before descending toward Gwangmyeong. With no time to put on shoes as he fled from the house, his socks were now covered in dirt and holes. At the entrance to Gwangmyeong-ri, he ran into a young man who was willing to hand over his shoes in exchange for some cash. With shoes on his feet and money he'd stashed in the inside pocket of his work jacket for emergencies, Ilcheol felt as though he was out of the woods. He made up his mind to go to Incheon, and had dinner on the way in Sosa. He knew who he was supposed to reach out to in an emergency. The woman had been a longtime reppo of Kim Geunshik. Ilcheol met her at a church and was able to contact Seonok through her. He found a safe place to stay in Baedari. The activists in Incheon turned out to be calmer and more secure than those in other areas, probably because they stuck to their own course instead of complying with the National Council's decision to go on a nationwide strike. The Incheon activists were preoccupied with broadening and reinforcing their network across multiple factories.

Geunshik cried when he met Ilcheol.

'It seems like only yesterday that I last parted ways with your brother, Comrade Yi Icheol.'

Ilcheol was touched to see someone weep over the memory of his brother. It made him wonder how many times Icheol had been driven into the same corner he was in now.

'I didn't understand how deep my brother's involvement with the movement was until after Liberation. Everyone's been telling me that things now are no different from what they were under the Japanese.'

Geunshik shook his head.

'That's not necessarily true. We now have millions of comrades around us. No one knows how long this chaos will last, but a new society is bound to emerge someday, even if we ourselves are long gone by then.'

Geunshik kept coughing lightly. Ilcheol would later learn that he had died right before the war, while still working underground, from the tuberculosis that had been ailing him for years.

'Still,' Geunshik said with a smile, 'there's one thing I've often found kind of strange. Doesn't it seem like life is always falling short or turning into something other than what we hope for? And it's usually only after a very long time has passed that anything changes. Compared to the passage of time, we're no more than specks of dust.'

He then got to the point of their meeting.

'Leading members of the organisation who can no longer work here are supposed to head north, above the 38th parallel. The party's centre is now in Haeju.'

'Does that mean we won't be able to come back?'

'Ah, of course it's just a temporary measure.'

Ilcheol couldn't bring himself to ask about his family. He knew that no matter where they were, activists could barely afford to look after themselves, let alone their family. Geunshik caught Ilcheol's hesitation.

'I'm sure you'll be able to return to your family after things improve, don't you think?'

'Then when and how will I cross over?'

Geunshik chuckled as he answered, 'I believe you know him well … a certain Mr Yi Shipman.'

'I haven't seen him in years.'

'He'll be able to help in more ways than one.'

Geunshik took out a piece of paper, scribbled a few words, and handed it to Ilcheol.

'This is his address. It's a stone's throw from here. Before you go, I'll give him a call. I've already talked it over with him, so there's nothing to worry about.'

Ilcheol went to the address in Yulmok-dong. It turned out to be a hanok built on a high embankment rather than behind a stone wall; at the top of the stairs was a thick hedge. When he rang the bell, an older man appeared. He led Ilcheol past a garden to a modernised daecheong maru complete with glass windows, where the familiar outline of his uncle Shipman stood watching him. Shipman introduced his nephew to his wife and showed him into the parlour.

As soon as all three of them were seated, Shipman blurted out, 'What in the world is the matter with you and your brother? And your father seems to be as bad as the both of you. Before Dusoe passed, I'd heard he was somewhere in Incheon, but he never came to see me.'

'I'm sorry I didn't make more of an effort to visit you after seeing you at my wedding. Please forgive me.'

Ilcheol rose, pressed his hands together, and knelt, bowing all the way to the floor in a proper show of respect to his aunt and uncle. Shipman nodded and paused before he went on.

'Even after surviving the Japanese occupation, I'm still walking on a tightrope. I traded mostly in grains back then and still do, except now I'm smuggling them to the north.'

Though his brother had heard about their uncle's wealth, Ilcheol assumed that he'd kept his distance while in Incheon not out of class consciousness but to protect everyone he cared about. But in just a few years' time, the war would wipe out all trace of such things as centuries-long village bonds and brotherly love. For now, though, the 38th parallel wasn't guarded too strictly, since separate governments were yet to be established, and the American and Soviet troops only controlled roads and railroads.

'I do business between north and south, although I'm not sure how long I'll be able to keep it up. Manufactured goods come south, and grain goes north. Your people have asked me to take you to Haeju, but can't you just stay put, keep your head down, and take care of your family?'

'A lot of my beliefs have changed since Dusoe passed. And we've been liberated.'

'You know full well that the world hasn't changed. Oh, and for the record, I'm not taking sides. If you weren't family, there's no way I'd agree to do something like this.'

The grain cargo ship was scheduled to leave early the following week. Geumi received word from Seonok and rushed over to Incheon to meet her husband the day before his departure. She wasn't quite sure what to expect, so she brought Jisan with her. Shipman let Ilcheol, Geumi, and Jisan spend the night. When Ilcheol left at daybreak to head to the pier, Geumi said her farewells to him in front of the house. Shipman and the sailor who came to pick Ilcheol up were waiting there as well. Even after saying goodbye, Geumi trailed after her husband down the stairs.

'When will you be back? How can I reach you?'

Geumi always regretted that her last words to her husband were such foolish ones. Their last goodbye was so precious and so fleeting, and that was the best she could come up with? But then, all partings are fleeting. And like a wisp of wind, they leave nothing behind but a faint glimpse of the look on the other's face.

'I won't be long.'

Geumi stood at the bottom of the stairs and watched her husband turn and walk away.

Shipman walked ahead a few more steps and said, 'I'm thinking of going to Japan. Cheonman's there. The political situation here makes me nervous. Take care of yourself and … this is just based on my experience, try not to stand out too much.'

When Ilcheol reached Haeju, he went to the central party's office. Pak Hon-yong was waiting for him there. Hon-yong remembered Icheol and the fact that he'd died in prison before Liberation, and briefly related a few memories from when Icheol had served as his reppo. But not being the sort of leader accustomed to charming the public, Hon-yong's face remained cool and expressionless as he spoke. Their meeting lasted a mere ten minutes, after which Ilcheol received instructions from a different party executive. In accordance with his work experience, Ilcheol was told to go to Pyeongyang, where he'd be needed in the transportation sector. At the time, there were only six proper locomotive engineers and less than twenty locomotive technicians left in North Korea. Ilcheol was assigned to the Transportation Bureau under the Provisional People's Committee and appointed as director of the Rail Workers' Training School. He was probably chosen for the position thanks to the wealth of experience he had on the Gyeongbu and Gyeongui Lines as well as on the continental route up to Antung and Hsinking, not to mention the fact that he used to drive the *Hikari*, the crowning glory of the continental rails. But his background must have been the biggest consideration: he'd been born into a family of poor farmers, his father had joined the working class at the very start of colonial industrialisation, and his younger brother had been an anti-Japanese revolutionary through and through.

The rail lines that had originated south of the 38th parallel — with the exception of the main north–south lines that connected with the rest of the continent: namely, the Gyeongbu, Gyeongui, Gyeongwon, and Hamgyeong Lines — were branch lines that had been built and operated by private railway companies, albeit to standard specifications. Unique exceptions were narrow-gauge railroads that served coalmines and coastal routes, but there weren't many of those. As the Provisional People's Committee was replaced by a formal government, North Korea's emergency transportation plan was to have the Transportation Bureau improve and connect these railroads under a unified administrative system. When the Japanese pulled out, the country had been left with a dire shortage of rail technicians. The North Korean Transportation Bureau's primary goal was thus to improve the railroads and train technicians who could be put to work as soon as possible. Despite having been a leading member of the National Council of Labour Unions, Ilcheol became a mere technician, uninvolved with the political doings of the Workers' Party of South Korea, which may have proved lucky for him later in life.

After Ilcheol went north, Geumi was left to take care of Baekman and Jisan. Baekman buried himself in making metal handicrafts in his workshop, and Geumi invested all the money she'd saved to open a small shop at Yeongdeungpo Market. Before she could do that, of course, she was taken into police custody and interrogated for days about her husband's whereabouts. For years after they released her, detectives would randomly turn up and ransack the family's Saetmal House until they eventually lost interest. Meanwhile, people who couldn't adapt to the revolutionary policies and living conditions in the north kept streaming across the 38th parallel to stay at refugee camps or form communities of their own in Gaeseong or other areas near Seoul. South Koreans were no less dissatisfied, as they continued to express their frustration and resist the American military occupation.

Jisan wanted to transfer to the Railroad Transportation Academy. The academy's name had changed since the days when Ilcheol attended the Government-General's training school for rail workers, but the curriculum was practically the same. Jisan had grown up hearing about his grandfather and father's work, and the memory of racing through the Manchurian plains on an express driven by his father had made a lasting impression on him. He'd dreamed of working for the Railway Bureau as an engineer like his father, but the political changes after Liberation gave him reason to suspect that he might have been hoping for the impossible. That suspicion proved to be true when his application was rejected after a background check revealed that his father was wanted for his leading role on the National Council.

A few months after Ilcheol crossed over to the north, Lyuh Woon-hyung, a centre-left politician who'd been pushing for a coalition of right and left, and who had dodged one assassination attempt after another, was finally shot and killed. The far-right nationalist Kim Gu, who called for and led South–North negotiations, was assassinated a few years later. On Jeju Island, an accidental clash on the same day as a commemoration of the March 1st Independence Movement sparked demonstrations and a general strike that resulted in more bloodshed. The following year, when Jeju Islanders who'd been driven to the brink rose up in April, suppression forces made up of the National Defense Force, the police, and the North-West Youth League, under the command of the USAMGIK, slaughtered innocent civilians. Leftists were arrested in droves, and more people were massacred.

Against this backdrop, at the urging of the Big Four, including the United States, the 'Korea problem' was added to the agenda of the United Nations General Assembly not long after its founding. In November 1947, the United States called a small United Nations assembly to approve a resolution that would allow separate elections to be held in South Korea. This triggered strong opposition, even from US allies, fearing that such elections could lead to a permanent division of the Korean peninsula and ultimately threaten world peace. Only four out of the nine nations that made up the United Nations Temporary Commission on Korea consented to it. Using the United Nations to gain approval for this was a serious digression from the original purpose of the organisation. Enraged at the possibility that their land and people could be permanently divided, Koreans all over the country revolted. Leftists came to refer to this as the 'February 7 Struggle for National Salvation'. Tensions continued to mount.

Elections were held in South Korea in May 1948, and Rhee Syngman declared the establishment of the Republic of Korea as its inaugural president. Four months later, the Supreme People's Assembly was formed in North Korea, and, as premier, Kim Il-sung declared the establishment of the Democratic People's Republic of Korea. North and South Korea's provisional security forces became both standing armies and mutual enemies on a divided peninsula. Some of the South Korean troops who had been dispatched to assist counter-guerilla efforts on Jeju Island mutinied in Yeosu and Suncheon, sparking a conflict between left and right that led to another massacre of civilians in those areas. Guerilla bases were set up in nearly all mountainous areas in the south including Hallasan and Jirisan, and along the 38th parallel. Clashes between the South and North Korean armies became routine.

Since January 1948, Jisan had been communicating with his comrades at the Korean Democratic Youth Alliance. He was a member of the Gyeongseong Student Council and involved in organising the Youth Alliance's Yeongdeungpo division. Student activists were aware that the National Council was about to launch a nationwide strike. Along with several other schools in Seoul, they joined the strike, distributed the National Council's propaganda flyers and posters, and planned a street demonstration for the first day of the strike. The strike lit the fuse of resistance, just like the strike that had led to the Autumn Uprising of 1946. Railroad and telegraph workers walked off their jobs, paralysing the American military administration. In the capital, factories of all sizes were shut down. Workers at major factories in Yeongdeungpo also joined the strike, including those of the Gyeongseong Spinning and Weaving Company, Jongyeon Textiles, Daehan Textiles, Joseon Leather, Gyeongseong Electric, and the Yeongdeungpo Rail Works. Labourers and students held dozens of protests in Yeongdeungpo and downtown Seoul, opposing the United Nations Temporary Commission's visit to Korea and the establishment of a separate South Korean government, and demanding the simultaneous withdrawal of all foreign forces from Korea. As office workers and ordinary citizens joined the protests alongside labourers on strike and students boycotting classes, their numbers swelled to two million nationwide. Outside large cities, more violent clashes took place.

Jisan was at the head of the procession on Namdaemun-ro near Yongsan. When clashes with suppression units came to a lull in the afternoon, he crossed the Hangang Bridge with a couple of other students. They'd heard word that the situation was escalating in Yeongdeungpo. The streets in front of Yeongdeungpo Station and the marketplace intersection were flooded with people. Although the sun had set, the crowd continued to besiege public offices, including the police station, tax office, and district office. The trapped police units that had been sent to guard the buildings fired warning shots. Hundreds of people were killed all over the country that day. A sweep of arrests followed over the next ten days. The police and the Korean Patriotic Youth League members were out to capture hundreds on the wanted list, including members of the National Council who led the strike, as well as secondary-school, professional-school, and university students who were members or executives of the Korean Democratic Youth Alliance. Nearly 9,000 people, including labourers and students, were arrested and sentenced to prison. Meanwhile, Jisan was on the run, moving around to the homes of different classmates in Yeongdeungpo; after a secondary-school comrade who'd housed him for several days was taken away by the police, he made up his mind to go search for his father. He hid in a church not far from Saetmal and waited for the curfew to begin. Late at night, after the streets had emptied and the lights had gone out in all the houses, he set out for home. To avoid alerting the neighbours, he climbed over the wall instead of knocking on the gate and calling out to his mother. He had just dropped into the courtyard and was about to tiptoe towards the house when he heard Geumi open her bedroom door and whisper.

'Jisan, is that you? Hurry up and get inside.'

As soon as he set foot in the room, Jisan flopped down and burst into tears. His mother scooted close and caressed her son's hands. Then she reached over and uncovered the tray of food she'd prepared for him, as if she had known he'd be coming home that very night.

'I bet you're hungry. Dig in. Or no, wait, I'll heat up the soup for you first.'

As she made her way to the kitchen, Geumi heard Baekman cough in his workshop. He'd been woken by the voices coming from her bedroom. Although she didn't say anything at the time, Geumi later revealed that Juan-daek had woken her earlier in the evening. Geumi knew that, just like her husband, her son was about to leave her as well.

After wolfing down the food without a word, Jisan turned to his mother who had been watching him eat.

'I've decided to … go look for Abeoji.'

Geumi sat there speechless for a moment, then tears began to well and fell onto her knees as she dropped her head.

'I see. You miss him, don't you?'

'Yes, and if I stay here, I'll be expelled and arrested.'

Geumi went across the room, opened the wardrobe, and packed up some of her son's clothes and underwear. Then she went to the kitchen to retrieve a bag of misugaru — a mixture of rice and beans that she had roasted and ground to a fine powder — and placed it on top of Jisan's clothing. Jisan sat quietly with a grave look on his face.

'Go to Incheon,' she told him. 'Seonok Imo will help you. Find your father … and then hurry back …'

As Geumi covered her mouth and struggled not to cry, the bedroom door opened. Baekman had been listening outside the door. With no more reason to muffle herself, Geumi burst into tears.

'What's going on? Where do you think you're going?' Baekman yelled as he pounded his grandson's chest with both hands. '*Aigu*, not you, too! I can't lose you, too!'

But with his heart set on leaving, the boy had few words left for his mother and grandfather. Jisan knelt down to offer them each a full bow. When he was heading out the front gate, Baekman stood absently off to one side, but his mother stopped him to say, 'Don't forget your halmeoni …'

Jisan understood what she meant. Normally, he'd say, 'Oh, come on,' and run away with a playful smile, but this time he straightened himself and knelt down to offer a full bow toward the wall beside the gate. Then, as Jisan rose again to leave, Geumi stepped up and whispered in his ear, 'Promise you'll come back to me soon!'

Jisan later said that those words would keep ringing in his ears like a spell.

When Jisan arrived in Pyeongyang after a brief stop in Haeju, his father was at the station to greet him. Ilcheol was wearing work clothes and an unfamiliar-looking Lenin cap. On the tram to the Rail Workers' Training School, his face revealed as little as the few words he spoke. Jisan had a late supper with his father at the school's cafeteria and afterwards filled him in on all that had happened to him and the family over a cup of barley tea in the director's office. When he mentioned that his mother had opened a shop at Yeongdeungpo Market, his father thrust his head back and stared at the ceiling for a moment.

Finally, as if he'd made up his mind about something, Ilcheol asked, 'So, you definitely want to be a rail worker?'

'Yes, I've never stopped thinking about becoming an engineer.'

'All the rail lines have been severed. And there's no one left to look after your mother ...' He took a long pause before adding, 'Focus on your training, I guess. Rail transportation is the most pressing task our country is facing right now.'

Their conversation ended when a staff member came to take Jisan to the dormitory.

During his six months of intensive training to become an engineer, Jisan saw his father four times: three times over shared meals, and once for an overnight stay at the director's residence.

Jisan was assigned to the freight division of the Pyeongwon Line that stretched from Jinnampo to Wonsan. During his probationary period, he served as an engineer's assistant on freight trains running between Jinnampo and Pyeongyang, and after his probation ended he worked as an assistant on freight trains running between Pyeongyang and Wonsan. The Gyeongui Line was mostly flat, but the line had been cut off at Uiju to the north and Pyeongsan to the south. The days of racing over the vast Manchurian plains like his father would never come again. The Transportation Bureau encouraged round-the-clock shifts so that freight transport could catch up to pre-Liberation levels, and local farmers joined in the efforts to repair and reconnect tracks. The slogan 'Charge Toward Production!' was splashed in red paint across all locomotives and along the tracks. But the days dragged on along the Pyeongwon Line as trains struggled to climb uphill and meandered through the slow, winding mountain routes.

The day the war began would always be fresh in Jisan's memory. He woke one morning in the dormitory only to be ordered to assemble in the yard with all the other rail workers. A party cadre came to the podium and announced that the 'Fatherland Liberation War' had begun. The 'invincible Korean People's Army' had swept past the 38th parallel and was advancing toward Seoul. Now all rail workers had to become revolutionary warriors and deliver supplies to the front. Jisan was only eighteen at the time, so he continued to work as a freight-train engineer's assistant on the Pyeongwon Line at the beginning of the war, but by late July he was promoted to engineer and ordered to stand by in Daejeon — in South Korea.

By then, Ilcheol had left his position at the Rail Workers' Training School and was helping to run the Transportation Bureau. Jisan went to visit his father at the old rail workers' housing complex near the Pyeongyang switching-yard workshop, which had been bombed to rubble. Half of the house had collapsed, and in the only room left standing, Ilcheol was cooking rice and pork tofu stew over a kerosene stove. A jumbo bottle of soju stood under the table.

'Congratulations, I hear you've been promoted to engineer.'

Jisan said yes, but his voice was emotionless.

Ilcheol glanced down at the meal he'd prepared. There were two steaming bowls of freshly cooked rice, a bowl of kimchi, and the large pot of stew. The empty metal bowls next to their rice bowls were for the alcohol. Ilcheol poured his son a drink and then held out his own bowl. Jisan poured his father a drink in return. When their eyes met, they downed the soju in one go.

'Remind me how old you are?'

'Eighteen.'

'Ah, that sounds right. I can't believe you've become an engineer and now you're off to war. Is time going by too fast or is there something wrong with the world?'

'They say unification will follow as soon as we can break through the Nakdonggang River front,' Jisan muttered.

Ilcheol used the handle of his spoon to scratch at his son's cheek.

'Look at that, your beard is coming in. You're starting to look like your Uncle Icheol.'

After sharing a couple of more shots, Ilcheol gazed at his child and said, 'This is not our home. We can't die here, no matter what.'

Father and son got completely drunk that night. In a low voice, Ilcheol sung songs like 'Moonlight Night of Shilla' and 'Flowers on the Hill'. Having enjoyed his first — and copious — taste of liquor, Jisan slumped over and fell asleep. When he woke at dawn, his throat parched, his father was asleep beside him. Although it wasn't cold, he pulled up the blanket that had slipped down to his feet and covered his father.

Later, when they parted ways, Ilcheol patted his son on the shoulder and said, 'Go back to your mother ...'

*

In a half-dream, Yi Jino saw two women standing side by side and looking down at him: a tall woman with broad, angular shoulders, and a slight, slender woman with narrow, sloped shoulders.

'Huh? Who's there?' he mumbled.

The smaller woman reached down and patted him on the chest.

'Keep sleeping. Long way still before the sun comes up.'

It was Shin Geumi Halmeoni.

'You'll be hearing some good news.'

Geumi Halmeoni looked and sounded exactly as she had in life, and was wearing the same white shirt and comfortable, baggy pants that she always wore to work at the market. The other woman had to be Juan-daek, Jino's great-grandmother — she had probably been by his side his whole life without him realising it. She wore a sashless white jeogori blouse and a black skirt. Compared to her daughter-in-law Geumi, who'd become a shrunken old woman with stark white hair, Juan-daek looked like she was still in the prime of her life, black hair shining with health. They both smiled at Jino and then turned and walked away into thin air.

'Halmeoni, where are you going? Wait for me!'

Jino tried to sit up but couldn't move his limbs. He was trapped in his sleeping bag. He unzipped it and lay there for a moment, gazing up at the edge of the tent. The pleasant chill of an early summer night grazed his shoulder.

Great-Grandfather Baekman had passed away the year Jino graduated from primary school. He was seventy-eight years old, meaning he'd lived a very long life for the time. Jino wasn't able to be at his side when he passed, but he heard about it from his grandmother. She told him that his great-grandfather had become short of breath and said sorry to her, and then called out his eldest son's childhood name twice — Hansoe! Hansoe! — before drawing his final breath. Jino thought about how his father, Jisan, had followed Jino's grandfather Ilcheol to the North only to return home battered and bruised and with one leg missing, and how his father and his great-grandfather — Jisan and Baekman — were inseparable after that, spending every minute together in Great-Grandfather Baekman's metal workshop. Jino had learned all about his grandfather Ilcheol and great-uncle Icheol by listening in as they whispered over their work. He also paid attention to the talk that passed quietly between his grandmother and his father each time his father, being the adoring and devoted son that he was, massaged Geumi's back and shoulders when she came home from working at the market. There was one particular story that Jisan had told to Geumi many times over.

Daejeon Station had been destroyed by multiple airstrikes from US bombers, so they were using temporary tracks on the north-eastern outskirts of the city. By day, the tracks were kept camouflaged with piles of branches and grass, but the moment the sun set and darkness fell, they were put into operation. The first section of tracks went from Daejeon to Okcheon, while the second section went from Okcheon to Chupungnyeong Pass, passing through the Hwanggan Tunnel along the way. The route, which carried military supplies, was nothing less than a lifeline, and any damaged tracks or bridges were repaired under cover of night by local farmers and People's Army engineers. By day, when the tracks were idle and concealed from view, supplies and reinforcements headed to the front lines were transported on foot, on paths that followed the tracks, on neighbouring mountain ridges, and on the backs of porters instead. Supplies were brought from cut-off routes by use of wheelbarrows, A-frames, and even yokes, and loaded into trucks hidden in the undergrowth. Jisan had spent the afternoon dozing on a large rock in the shade of a tree up the slope from the railroad tracks. He'd been awake all night, driving the locomotive to Yeongdong, making countless round trips to ferry supplies. Woken by the sound of an army song, he looked down to see a passing group of volunteer soldiers in new uniforms with grass covering their helmets and backpacks. They were nearly all of them new recruits, young men from the South who'd enlisted in the army of the North. Fully awake now, Jisan took a swig of water from his canteen and watched, only half paying attention, as they walked by, when he suddenly leapt up and ran down the hill.

'Seonok Imo!'

Bak Seonok was dressed in a brand-new uniform that still smelled of fresh cotton; the epaulets on her shoulders bore three small stars to signify her high rank. She took off her sweat-soaked cap and clasped Jisan's hands.

'Oh-ho, if it isn't my nephew Jisan!'

She wore the insignia of a political commissar over her heart. The two sat in the shade, bringing each other up to date with everything they knew. Jisan told her what his father was doing in Pyeongyang, and she talked about his mother and Yeongdeungpo. Seonok herself was on her way to the Nakdonggang River front. They used their brief time together to speak of the living and the dead. When she told him about Jo Yeongchun, her eyes suddenly turned red, and tears spilled, dampening both of her cheeks. Jisan remembered the 'uncle from Yangpyeong-dong' who used to visit them at the rail workers' housing and the Saetmal House. A few months before the war began, he'd been arrested and held at Daejeon Prison before being executed by firing squad. Jisan told her about Ahn Daegil, who had bumped into his father one day in Pyeongyang. He was one of a handful of leftist organisers who had survived Seodaemun Prison when the People's Army's vanguard unit and their tanks blitzed all of the prisons in Gaeseong and Seoul.

With her bobbed hair and deeply tanned face, Seonok looked into Jisan's eyes and said, 'Let's win this and go home.'

'Yes, please stay safe.'

As Seonok started to walk away, she glanced back at him, pulled a hairpin from beside her ear, and handed it to him.

'If you see Geumi Eonni … please give this to her.'

Jisan did his best to keep that hairpin safe in his shirt pocket over his heart, but several near-death experiences later, it was gone. The majority of the new volunteer army recruits sent to the Nakdonggang River front in its final days never returned.

Up until the US landing at Incheon broke the front and forced the North to retreat, the rail convoy was focused on its supply runs to Chupungnyeong Pass, which took it along a long, narrow valley between Yeongdong and Hwanggan. Later, they restricted their runs to a much shorter section from the Hwanggan Tunnel, past Chupungnyeong Pass, to the start of another narrow valley that led south-east to Gimcheon. That was how tense the war had grown. One day, after they'd been working until dawn and the train had just exited Hwanggan Tunnel and was making its way to the end of the section, a squadron of jets approached and launched a ground attack. Jisan watched as bombs detonated up ahead and hurriedly pulled the brake handle. Metal wheels screeched over metal rails, while directly in front of the locomotive everything vanished in an enormous cloud of black smoke, and a terrific boom shook the air — the engine bucked and tumbled over sideways as it left the tracks. When Jisan came to, it was the next day, and he was inside the tent of an American field hospital. His bandaged right leg was still attached to the rest of him then. But once he was moved to the rear, the leg, which had missed its window for treatment, was mercilessly lopped off. For a long time after, he would continue to reach down to scratch his missing big toe.

In the POW camp, Jisan was classified as a patient, exempted from all work details, and detained with other injured prisoners. When ceasefire negotiations got underway, the camp authorities screened each of them. A Korean interrogator seated next to an American officer asked Jisan questions.

'Your address is listed as Yeongdeungpo, Seoul. If you are released, where will you go?'

Jisan answered simply.

'I'll go home.'

Two months passed after Jisan's return to the Saetmal House. Though there was no way of knowing whether it was true or not, South Korean radio and newspapers were crowing about an announcement broadcast in Pyeongyang saying that Pak Hon-yong and the leaders of Namrodang, the Workers' Party of South Korea, had been arrested. The next day, Baekman asked Jisan to go out and buy a jumbo bottle of makgeolli, and grandfather and grandson drank together for the first time over a plate of tofu and stir-fried kimchi. Baekman drank his rice brew without speaking. When they'd nearly polished off the bottle, Baekman finally broke the silence.

'I wonder how Hansoe …'

After the man whom Jino had called Big Grandfather left this world, Jisan carried on in the workshop alone. Then, as the cottage industry of metal crafts went into decline, Jisan took to joining Bokrye, his wife, Jino's mother, at her clothing stall in the market, and Geumi Halmeoni spent more days at home. Jisan made it past sixty and almost all the way to seventy, all while getting around on crutches, while Geumi, who sent her son off into eternity first, lived even longer and took her leave when she was well into her nineties. Which meant that a mere five years had passed since Jino said his farewell to her. To think that all of this had happened in this family's lifetime. The years had been as rough as whirlpools, like water surging through a deep, winding ravine.

Another event had been held the previous week in the empty lot outside the wall of the power plant to commemorate the 400th day of Jino's chimney sit-in, and four days later the company, which had shown no response, either good or bad, for the entire year that he'd been occupying their chimney, finally made contact to request a meeting. It obviously wasn't so they could discuss demands or agenda items, since those had been repeated countless times over the course of the labour-management dispute that had dragged on now for years. More likely, seeing as how this year was the 70th anniversary of 8.15, or Liberation Day, the current administration wanted to put on a show of responding to the unions' and civic groups' demands and put to rest the problem of protracted labour protests before things started heating up again in July. Because it was highly *un*likely that the company had a sudden change of heart and decided to come to the table. Their side sent its chairman and executive director; Jino's side sent the negotiating-committee chairman for the Secretariat of the Metal Workers' Union and representative for the dismissed workers Kim Changsu. At the meeting, the company graciously offered to create a subsidiary factory where the laid-off workers would be reemployed and their unions fully recognised, and further assured that they would settle on a collective agreement by early next year. And in exchange for ending their siege of the chimney and promising to stop trying to turn everyone against the company, the protesters would be released from the civil and criminal charges that had been brought against them.

They drafted an agreement and informed the press of the terms of the settlement. Changsu was the first to inform Jino of all this, by mobile phone. On the 410th day of Jino's sit-in, the police were notified that he would be officially ending it. The union announced that they would hold a welcoming rally at the base of the chimney, but the police said that Jino would first have to be arrested for disturbing the peace and disrupting business, and that any such events could only be held in the empty lot as usual. To this, the union declared that the strike would continue, but now they would be protesting the unjust use of government power. The day before he was set to come down, Jino gave back-to-back phone interviews to the press. The labour union issued a public statement saying that threatening to arrest and imprison a laid-off worker who had just endured the world's longest aerial sit-in under the worst possible living conditions for one year and forty-five days straight would send a clear message to the world of just how inhumanely the Korean government treated its people. And that was what was afoot when Jino's last day up on the chimney began.

As soon as he was awake, Jino untied the ropes from the catwalk railing, folded the tarp, and took down his tent. He rolled up his bedding and lashed it all together with rope. He had acquired all sorts of things during his time on the chimney, and there was a lot to pack. He had not just one but two of those little double-decker bookshelves that a student might have on their desk, and each shelf was packed with books. There were also the plastic bottles that he'd cut open to plant flowers and lettuce and whatnot — he had at least ten of those. Then there were his tools: knife, spanner, hammer, pliers, screwdriver, and so on. There were winter clothes that he hadn't yet sent back down even after the seasons had changed. All packed up, it looked like he was a student moving house. He looked down at the row of empty plastic bottles lashed side by side to the railing, the ones he talked to often. He spoke each of their names aloud.

'Hey, Little Clippers. Jingi, you arsehole. Yeongsuk Nuna. Ghost Halmeoni Juan-daek. And the Uncanny Shin Geumi Halmeoni.'

None of them appeared this time. They must have known that he was returning to the realm of those who lived on the ground. He couldn't bring himself to throw them away with the garbage. He plopped down, took out his pocketknife, and carved their names from the bottles. He collected each piece with great reverence and placed them in his pocket.

The sun was slow to rise, but finally it was morning. After the long, bitter winter had passed and spring returned, Jino had resumed his exercise routine. He pushed himself up from a prone position, tucked his legs into a squat, and leapt straight into the air. Then he squatted again, kicked his legs back, and dropped into another push-up. When spring had returned, he was barely able to do even ten of these. Now he could easily do twenty; on a good day, he could add another two or three, and on really good days, an extra five. Today, he only managed twenty and stopped. He muttered to himself as he rose, 'Gettin' soft, are you?'

He reorganised his belongings and set aside things to be thrown away. He placed the things he planned to keep in cardboard boxes that had been sent up to him the day before and took a seat on top of the boxes. At 8.00 am, Changsu and Cha arrived with the breakfast prepared for him at the shelter. As usual, he leaned over the railing and watched as they passed through the main gate and headed for the chimney. They waved when they saw him, and he waved back with both arms. The guard on duty took a cursory look at what they had brought. Jino lowered the rope hanging from the pulley and hoisted up his breakfast.

Cha cupped his hands around his mouth and shouted, 'If we can come to an agreement with the police before noon, we'll have you down from there by two pm.'

Changsu shouted, too, 'We'll call you!'

They went back the way they came. After a moment, Jino's mobile phone buzzed. It was Changsu again.

'I know you're tired, but hold on just a little longer.'

'I made it 410 days, why not go for an even 500?'

Jino laughed, but the truth was that the moment he saw his two colleagues, the desire to hurry up and get down from there had crept over him, from belly to chest, as impossible to ignore as the urge to urinate.

'The police were refusing to budge until yesterday. After we get you down, there will be a welcoming rally at three o'clock and you'll get to see everyone.'

'No big deal if they arrest me. I'll just think of it as a vacation.'

Changsu's voice changed.

'What kind of bullshit is that? We won an important victory given the situation. And it's not just our union members who've been paying attention. You've got ten million workers watching your next move. Think of the other places that have been struggling with management for a long time. This is not our fight alone.'

'Thanks, man. But where's your sense of humour?'

Jino tried to make light of it, but his eyes stung with tears.

He ate every bite of his breakfast. It would be a long wait until lunchtime. Changsu had told him to think about the other places that had been bogged down in dispute, but no one knew more about that than Jino. Heavy industries, electronics, automobile factories — there were so many places that simply disregarded the agreements drawn up between labour and management. Even when a settlement had been reached, you never knew if the owners would simply shred it and do whatever they wanted. They could create company unions to weaken and destroy democratic unions, or hire thugs or mobilise state power to physically destroy the unions. There was even a joke that settlements were made to be broken. So, had Jino's side really won?

At lunchtime, the two laid-off workers who did the cooking at the shelter came with rice and banchan.

'Long time no see!' Jino shouted from his perch. 'Where did everyone else go?'

One of the women cupped her hands around her mouth and shouted back, 'A few are at the police station, and the rest are preparing for this afternoon's event.'

Jino's food basket went down and up. It was hard for him to believe that this was his last meal. He poured his soup over his rice. That was the only way he'd be able to swallow any of it today. Also, he was conscious of the fact that the two women were down there, waiting around just for him to finish his meal. The food basket went down again, and they waved goodbye and left.

At 1.00 pm, a commotion arose outside the wall, and a line of police buses began to arrive. There seemed to be a dozen of them, with every single window covered in chicken wire. They lined up all along the wall. The gate opened, a command was given, and the police conscripts who'd poured out of the buses got into formation and marched through the gate. Every single one of them was clad head to toe in riot gear. They wore helmets with metal grilles and thickly padded armour, and carried clubs in one hand and shields in the other. They marched over to the chimney and flanked it, while one team stood blocking the road that led in from the gate. Another stood right in front of the gate and erected barricades made from thick steel pipes. Another group, made up of plainclothes police with walkie-talkies and riot police wearing only helmets and light gear that was easier to move around in, stood waiting behind the guard shack. With a loud roar, an enormous crane trundled towards the power plant. The riot police in light gear moved the barricade and opened the gate as wide as it would go. The crane slowly and carefully passed through the gate and parked in the empty lot close to the chimney. Finally, a minivan that looked like some sort of police field-command vehicle appeared, and several uniformed cops who looked like they might be police inspectors got out. They all went into the guard shack.

From far off came the sound of a megaphone, then the strong, strident notes of a union song, followed by a parade of workers. They headed straight for the heavily armoured police conscripts blocking the gate. The police conscripts raised their shields to form a phalanx; the marchers stopped right in front of their shields and began chanting slogans. The police shouted at them through a megaphone. 'Ah, ah, please maintain order and assemble in the permitted location only! Any further disturbance will result in punishment in accordance with the law!'

Changsu moved to the left of the phalanx and said something to someone dressed in work wear who looked like he might be in charge, then followed the man through the gate and into the guard shack. There appeared to be some sort of agreement taking place. Changsu came back out and waved at someone: Jeong, Bak, Cha, and others who'd been involved in the sit-in, along with Jino's mother and his wife, broke through the crowd of demonstrators and came through the gate. They reached the base of the chimney and waved up at Jino from among the police conscripts. His mother shouted, 'Well done, son! You can come on down now!' His wife raised both hands and waved them around like crazy. Then both women hugged each other and burst into tears. In the vacant lot, the civic groups' solidarity event was getting started. Jino's mobile phone rang.

'Don't come down until they call off your arrest,' Changsu said. 'They say the higher-ups are reviewing it right now.'

'Understood. At least the weather's nice.'

It took another three hours before the crane was put into use. On board the crane basket were Changsu, Jeong, and two detectives. When the basket reached the railing, Changsu got out first, while Jeong held the detectives back.

'Give us a minute to talk first,' he told them.

The detectives didn't look too keen on climbing onto the narrow catwalk anyway, as they clung to the metal railing of the basket and said, 'Whatever, just get it over with.'

Changsu whispered to Jino, 'They're swinging their dicks around and insisting that your arrest warrant has already been issued so they can't take it back. We have to stall for time and try to get the word out. They won't be able to hold you for long, because public opinion is against them. What should we do? Your family's down there waiting for you, but the cops aren't going to let you spend any time with them ...'

'I told them to stay home. What the hell is my mother doing here?'

'Never mind that right now. You understand what you have to do? When they try to take you by force, just lie down on the ground. Stall and resist as much as possible. We'll fight, too.'

They placed the items he'd packed into the crane basket, and then they helped him over. As the basket began to slowly descend, Jeong handed Jino a wireless mini microphone. One of the detectives tried to snatch it back.

'What the — no! That's not what we agreed to!'

'If you fuck around up here, we'll all die,' Changsu growled, and the detective backed off.

Jino turned to face the citizens gathered outside the wall. Using the microphone, he spoke of his reasons for occupying the chimney and of the happiest and saddest moments of his sit-in, and he called out the names of every worker who had died over the course of their struggle. With each name, the crowd shouted along, calling the names of the dead in chorus.

'I spent hundreds of days in the air and met so many precious stars.' Jino pointed up at the fading sky. '*They* are all stars now, looking down at us from up there.'

As the crane dropped lower, the wall blocked out his view.

*

Yi Jino was released from jail a month later after many more twists and turns. Now it was the workers' turn, as the eleven who'd resisted their lay-offs to the bitter end were having their jobs reinstated. They gathered in Seoul and took an express bus to the new factory in the provinces. At the factory, they found a few rusted-out machines and no other workers. Their company housing turned out to be a long-abandoned tenement with black mould climbing the walls and faded and curling linoleum on uneven floors. Furious, they called the head office only to be told they could not speak directly to anyone in power. The rank-and-file employee on the phone could only tell them over and over that new employees would soon be hired and sent to join them and that they should just hold on until then. They let out hollow laughs, they argued with each other. Most left, a few stayed. They left the ruins and shared a round of soju before going their separate ways in front of the bus station. The final three avoided each other's gaze by looking only at their shot glasses.

Changsu, who'd had his head down, looked up at Jino.

'Let's go up again,' he said quietly. 'I'll do it this time.'

Cha spoke, too.

'Me, too. Kim Seonbae, I'll go up, too.'

Their voices broke off there, and nothing more was said.

Afterword

From the 2020 Korean edition published by Changbi Publishers

This novel was born from a conversation I had with an old man in Pyeongyang during my visit to North Korea in 1989. At the Pyeongyang Department Store, a destination recommended by the authorities, I exchanged greetings with the general manager and was introduced to the assistant manager who would be giving me a tour. Rumour had it that the general manager had played a major role in supplying daily necessities to a certain area during the Korean War, so I suspected that the reason the assistant manager had held his position until well into his old age was that he had also proven his abilities somehow in distribution or transportation.

I noticed that the man spoke in Seoul dialect. On top of which, the cadence of his speech and the words he used were old-fashioned. I couldn't help but ask where he was born, and when he said Seoul, I had to ask where in Seoul, to which he said Yeongdeungpo. Yeongdeungpo District was where I'd grown up. My family had settled there after leaving Pyeongyang and crossing the 38th parallel in 1947. Instead of admiring the goods on display as we roamed about the department store, we spent most of our time talking about what Yeongdeungpo used to be like. We bonded over our memories of the district. We had shared the same space and time: I, a boy who had just started primary school; he, a train engineer who belonged to the National Council of Labour Unions. One time, a colonial-era school building located somewhere between his old neighbourhood and mine caught fire. The wooden building burned all the way down to the toilets, leaving behind a stench that filled the air in both of our neighborhoods for days. We remembered it like it was yesterday and delighted over the shared memory.

A few days later, after pleading to my guides, I was allowed to meet him again; we shared soju at a fish market along the Daedonggang River. He told me all about how his father had worked at the Yeongdeungpo Rail Works, how he got accepted into the training school for rail workers, and all the things he saw while driving trains along the continental route. The scenes he described from memory were lyrical and moving: the red sun as big as a washbasin going down over the endless black fields of Manchuria; seas of sorghum rippling in the wind; snowflakes the size of a child's head filling the sky and cascading down to the ground; the beautiful mountains, rivers, and valleys of Joseon; rural train stations standing in empty fields. After Liberation, when the US Army Military Government in Korea cracked down on the National Council of Labour Unions, my guide fled to the North with his own son. With the outbreak of the Korean War, his teenage son, who had just completed an intensive course for train engineers, was put to work transporting war supplies to the Nakdonggang River front, from which he never returned. Thirty years now have passed since I met that old man and listened to his stories, thirty years during which I kept trying to write this book only to give up or put it off for later. Judging from how old he was when I met him, he must have passed away by now.

*

In reading Korean literature widely over the years, I couldn't help but notice what was missing. Namely, in both quality and quantity, short fiction has tended to outperform long fiction, very little of which in turn depicts the lives of modern industrial workers. Even the few works left behind by the colonial-era Korean Proletarian Artists' Federation were mostly short fiction focused on the urban poor, day labourers, or the 'lumpenproletariat', so it's not an exaggeration to say that there were no full-length novels that featured industrial workers as the main characters. Even among recent novels, most in this vein have centred on farmers.

Over the course of my research, it occurred to me that it seemed only natural that socialism would become the ideological root of the labour movement under Japanese colonialism and beyond. After Liberation and national division, workers who fought for their right to live were denounced as communists. Then after the Korean War and the onset of the global Cold War, all labour movements were seen as seditious during the decades of developmental dictatorship that followed. While undergoing our long period of division, it has never been easy to argue for North Korea's national legitimacy; meanwhile, the people of South Korea gained their legitimacy through the blood, sweat, and tears they shed in the process of becoming the subjects of modernisation, achieving industrialisation, and establishing a democratic system. But insofar as our system is still far from perfect, it may be best to refrain from debating legitimacy until the day the two Koreas become one again. If South Korea can overcome and make up for its shortcomings and equip itself with the capability to embrace North Korea and elicit change, that would probably be the right step toward a peaceful unification.

*

The railroad that once ran from the Korean peninsula to the rest of the Asian continent was a symbol of colonial modernity and imperialism. Global modernity itself practically began with the first railroad. In writing this book, I wanted to explore how the dreams of Korean labourers — who lived during a century or more of colonialism, division, and capitalist globalisation — were transformed and distorted. Labourers lost or hid their class consciousness, but their living conditions didn't really change. My idea was to depict the lives of people as if in a dream. I wanted to create a 'mindam'-style world centred on Yeongdeungpo with a plot built from personal, everyday anecdotes, rather than solely historical facts. Of course, historical facts still butted in now and then, but I approached the stories of anti-Japanese labour activists like tales from long ago. At times the book grows more serious, but in the end those tales of old have a way of gently wrapping their arms around the glaring light of facts, like a faded photograph or an antique. By bringing to the fore industrial workers who have been neglected from Korean literature, I sought to trace the journey they took over the past century and reveal the root of their lives today. My hope was to add another stone to the pillar of Korean literature that has weathered history's stormy twists and turns. Some say today's chaotic neoliberal world is in the middle of transitioning to a different order as the capitalist world-system heads toward collapse. Whether this period of suffering will be short or long is entirely up to the efforts of those of us living in the present. The traces of our lives and the time we lived in may be no more than a few specks of dust compared to the life of the vast universe. And though change happens slowly — very, very slowly — I don't want to abandon my hope that it changes for the better.

I received a great deal of support to write this story. I wish to thank the Korea Railroad Corporation (KORAIL) and the Yeongdeungpo District Office for providing me with sources, including *A Hundred Years of the Korean Railroad* (Korean National Railroad, 1999) and *Records of Yeongdeungpo-gu* (Yeongdeungpo-gu, 1999). Professor Kim Kyung-il's work, *The History of Labour Movements Under Japanese Colonial Rule* (Changjakgwa bipyeongsa, 1992) and *A Study on Yi Jaeyu* (Changjakgwa bipyeongsa, 1993), proved to be invaluable in learning details about the lives and struggles of labourers under Japanese occupation. *Gyeongseong Troika* (Sahoe pyeongnon, 2004) and other works by Ahn Jae-seong were also quite helpful. There are many other sources, including *A Historical Study of the Lives of the Poor Under Japanese Occupation* (Changjakgwa bipyeongsa, 1995), that aided me along the way, but I'm afraid there's not enough space here to list them all.

I would also like to express my gratitude to Cha Gwang-ho, a former branch chief of the Metal Workers' Union whom I met through the poet Song Kyung-dong. Mr Cha had staged a chimney sit-in for 408 days and was kind enough to share the details of his experience with me, even showing me how he did his burpees. I'm also grateful to the Korea Train Express (KTX) engineer Son Min-du. He allowed me to join him in the driver's cab, giving me an engineer's-eye view of several different rail lines. He also introduced me to Kang Hye-jin, an elderly, retired train engineer from the time of steam locomotives, who kindly taught me all about the components of a steam locomotive and the techniques involved in driving one. Mr Kang even gave me several demonstrations at a locomotive exhibit and described in detail the working life of an engineer.

Last but not least, I'd like to express my gratitude to my friends in Iksan who helped me in more ways than one while I was working on this novel and the Won Buddhist cleric Seo Jong-myeong for taking such good care of me during my stay. I also send my appreciation to the editors at Changbi who supported my research for this project and cheered me on from the very beginning.

*

While writing the novel, I went for many strolls around the neighbourhood in Yeongdeungpo where I grew up. It's the same with a lot of places on the edges of Seoul, but I would stumble upon these old alleyways and old buildings, and just have to stop and stand there for a while, studying the faces of people walking by, hoping to catch a familiar-looking one. Nearly forgotten memories came back to me then, and I saw my mother, sisters, younger brother, and even my father, who died young, in the alleys, the market, the spot where our house used to be, looking the same way they did back when we lived there.

Instead of the famous faces of Korean history that already star in countless texts, I modelled the characters in this book after the many workers who have been reduced to historical specks of dust. The activists who appear in these pages represent all the nameless workers who gave body and soul to the small parts they played. They were drawn from my imagination, but they can also be thought of as a composite of the numberless common folk whose names alone survive in police reports, court records, and other archives.

This novel is both a story of my hometown, replete with childhood memories, and a story of the labourers who lived there. I dedicate this novel to them, with hope that it will go towards filling the gap in Korean literature where their stories should be.

May 2020
At the foot of Mireuksan Mountain
Hwang Sok-yong